MEMORY LAWS, MEMORY WARS

Laws against Holocaust denial are perhaps the best-known manifestation of the present-day politics of historical memory. In *Memory Laws, Memory Wars*, Nikolay Koposov examines the phenomenon of memory laws in Western and Eastern Europe, Ukraine, and Russia and exposes their very different purposes in the East and West. In Western Europe, he shows how memory laws were designed to create a common European memory centered on the memory of the Holocaust as a means of integrating Europe, combating racism, and averting national and ethnic conflicts. In Russia and Eastern Europe, by contrast, legislation on the issues of the past is often used to give the force of law to narratives that serve the narrower interests of nation-states and protect the memory of perpetrators rather than victims. This will be essential reading for all those interested in ongoing conflicts over the legacy of World War II, Nazism, and communism.

NIKOLAY KOPOSOV is a Russian historian currently teaching at Emory University, having previously worked at the École des Hautes Études en Sciences Sociales and Johns Hopkins University. He was Founding Dean of Russia's first and only (to date) liberal arts college, Smolny College of Liberal Arts and Sciences, a joint venture of Saint Petersburg State University and Bard College (New York). His research deals with various aspects of modern historiography and historical memory, from Early Modern France to post-Soviet Russia. His book *How Historians Think* (2001) was translated into French by Éditions de l'École des Hautes Études en Sciences Sociales as *De l'imagination historique* (Paris, 2009). A vocal critic of Vladimir Putin's history politics, Professor Koposov left Russia in 2009.

NEW STUDIES IN EUROPEAN HISTORY

Edited by

PETER BALDWIN, University of California, Los Angeles
CHRISTOPHER CLARK, University of Cambridge
JAMES B. COLLINS, Georgetown University
MIA RODRÍGUEZ-SALGADO, London School of Economics and Political Science
LYNDAL ROPER, University of Oxford
TIMOTHY SNYDER, Yale University

The aim of this series in early modern and modern European history is to publish outstanding works of research, addressed to important themes across a wide geographical range, from southern and central Europe, to Scandinavia and Russia, from the time of the Renaissance to the present. As it develops the series will comprise focused works of wide contextual range and intellectual ambition.

A full list of titles published in the series can be found at:
www.cambridge.org/newstudiesineuropeanhistory

MEMORY LAWS,
MEMORY WARS

The Politics of the Past in Europe and Russia

NIKOLAY KOPOSOV

Emory University

CAMBRIDGE
UNIVERSITY PRESS

CAMBRIDGE
UNIVERSITY PRESS

University Printing House, Cambridge CB2 8BS, United Kingdom

One Liberty Plaza, 20th Floor, New York, NY 10006, USA

477 Williamstown Road, Port Melbourne, VIC 3207, Australia

4843/24, 2nd Floor, Ansari Road, Daryaganj, Delhi – 110002, India

79 Anson Road, #06–04/06, Singapore 079906

Cambridge University Press is part of the University of Cambridge.

It furthers the University's mission by disseminating knowledge in the pursuit of education, learning, and research at the highest international levels of excellence.

www.cambridge.org
Information on this title: http://www.cambridge.org/9781108419727
DOI: 10.1017/9781108304047

First published 2018

Printed in the United Kingdom by Clays, St Ives plc

A catalogue record for this publication is available from the British Library.

ISBN 978-1-108-41972-7 Hardback
ISBN 978-1-108-41016-8 Paperback

To the memory of
Yuriy Markovich Shmidt and
Leonid Mikhailovich Batkin

Contents

Preface and Acknowledgments

I first heard of the Gayssot Act, which criminalized Holocaust denial in France, shortly after it was passed in 1990, and I remember the typically Parisian debates (I was then an invited professor at the École des Hautes Études en Sciences Sociales) on whether it is acceptable to penalize speech in a democratic society. At that time, most French historians were supportive of this legislation, and I also thought then that it would not be a bad thing to prohibit, in the same way, the denial of Stalin's repressions in Russia. Unsurprisingly, many Russian democrats were reasoning along similar lines, and I discuss in Chapter 5 their attempts to ban the denial of both fascist and communist crimes.

But as time passed and legal interventions in historical memory began expanding both thematically and geographically, historians became increasingly critical of those laws. I observed, on my occasional visits to France in the 2000s, Pierre Nora's persistent efforts to have this legislation repealed. My own turn to intervene in similar debates in Russia came in 2009, when United Russia, the party in power, decided to use criminal law to protect the Stalinist interpretation of World War II. I am grateful to my Russian colleagues and friends who co-signed one of the many petitions against the proposed legislation, and especially to Rafail Ganelin, Yakov Gordin, Aleksandr Daniel, Dmitriy Dubrovskiy, Boris Firsov, Lev Kleyn, Boris Pustyntsev, Yuriy Shmidt, and Boris Vishnevskiy.[1]

Since then, I have researched the history of memory laws in Russia and Europe, as I felt that a historical perspective on them could help in assessing their legitimacy. I soon became convinced that the study of those laws provides an interesting entry into the problem of the present-day historical consciousness, which has always been central to my work. Indeed, while memory laws are a relatively new topic for me, my interest in modern historiography and historical memory harkens back to the late

---

[1] Boris Vishnevskiy, "Nasledniki Benkendorfa" [Benkendorf's Heirs], *Novaya Gazeta*, June 1, 2009.

1980s. In May 1990, Dina Khapaeva and I co-directed one of the first sociological surveys of collective representations of the past in Russia. Trained as a French historian but always interested in Soviet history, I could not but envisage post-Soviet historical memory in a broad comparative context.

All this largely explains my project in this book: to consider memory laws as a historical phenomenon, to discuss both their political functions and cultural meaning, and to compare their use in Russia and other European countries. Russia is too often viewed as a sui generis case, and integrating its history into that of Europe remains a largely unresolved problem.

It is a pleasure to acknowledge here my debt to those individuals and institutions on whose support I relied while working on this book. My understanding of the rise of memory and of the current history politics has been decisively influenced by the work of, and discussions with, Pierre Nora and Gabrielle M. Spiegel. In 2009, they both expressed, in the name of Liberté pour l'Histoire and the American Historical Association, respectively, full support for the aforementioned petition against the Russian memory law, and I remember with deep gratitude this manifestation of international solidarity among historians. Gabrielle M. Spiegel's comments on the first (much shorter) version of this book have, I hope, allowed me to find the right balance of various factors that have influenced the fin-de-siècle memory boom. Over several decades, personal friendship and professional dialogue with François Hartog and Laurent Thévenot have been crucial for my work, and they will find many confirmations of that on the pages that follow.

I owe a lot to the encouragement and invaluable advice of Korine Amacher, Wladimir Berelowitch, Alain Blum, Sophie Coeuré, Marc Ferro, Boris Gasparov, Claudio Sergio Ingerflom, Catriona Kelly, Tamara Kondratieva, Kevin F.M. Platt, William G. Rosenberg, and Ronald Grigor Suny. My particular thanks go to Timothy Snyder, both for his encouragement of this project and for his stimulating reflections on the Eastern European politics of memory. And I cannot thank enough my esteemed colleague and dear friend Jeffrey Brooks, whose advise has been most helpful on all stages of my work on this book (and on many other projects).

After I left Russia, several distinguished institutions – Helsinki Collegium, Johns Hopkins University, Georgia Institute of Technology, and Emory University – supported my work. I want to thank most cordially my friends and colleagues from Emory's Russian and Eastern European

Studies program, Juliette Stapanian-Apkarian, Mikhail Epstein, Vera Proskurina, Oleg Proskurin, Matthew J. Payne, Thomas F. Remington, Hubert Tworzecki, James Steffen and, most especially, Elena Glazov-Corrigan, whose wisdom and friendship have been crucial for me in more ways than one. I may never be able to fully repay my debt to her and to Kevin Corrigan. At Emory, I have been also fortunate to benefit from friendship of, and exciting exchanges with, Walter L. Adamson, Kathryn E. Amdur, Matthew H. Berstein, Cynthia Blakeley, Julia Bullock, Rkia and Vince Cornell, Clifton Crais, Joseph Crespino, Astrid M. Eckert, Robyn Fivush, Sander L. Gilman, Eric Goldstein, Ruby Lal, Deborah E. Lipstadt, Julia Lopez Fuentes, James V.H. Melton, Robert A. Paul, Gyanendra Pandey, Pamela Scully, Allan E. Tullos, and other colleagues.

I often recollect invigorating discussions with my friends and colleagues from Georgia Tech, especially Kenneth J. Knoespel and John E. Kriege. At Hopkins, I learned a lot from Peter Jelavich, Michael Kwass, John Marshall, Philip Morgan, Anne and Kenneth B. Moss, and Todd Shepard, whose suggestions, including their comments on my paper on memory laws presented at the History Department's famous Seminar in May 2013, were of utmost importance to the development of my book project. I am also grateful to Hopkins' President Ronald Daniel, Michael Cohen, and Emily Rose and her family for their support and inspiring conversations, which made my year at Hopkins both possible and very pleasant. I am grateful to Martin Kagel and Alexander Spektor (University of Georgia in Athens), Elizabeth A. Papazian (University of Maryland), Anton Weiss-Wendt (Holocaust Studies Center, Oslo), Uladzislau Belavusau (University of Amsterdam), Aleksandra Gliszczyńska-Grabias (Polish Academy of Sciences), Alexey Vasilyev (Institute of Central and Eastern Europe, Lublin), Irina Varskaya ("Gefter," Moscow), Sabina Loriga (EHESS), Sophie Coeuré (École Normale Supérieure), Olivier Salvatori (Éditions Gallimard), and Vododimir Sklokin and the entire team of the Ukrainian Catholic University at Lviv for the hospitality extended to my lectures, papers, and articles on memory laws and related matters: their comments on my work have been most helpful.

My thanks, as always, go to my dear friends in America, France, and Russia, Olga Bessmertnaya, Nathalie Heinich, Christian Jouhaud, Ilya Kalinin, Judith Lyon-Caen, Christophe Prochasson, Marianna Taymanova, and especially Irina Prokhorova, whose always interesting ideas and the attention to my work have been a condition sine qua non of this book and my previous publications. Working with Liv Bliss on my manuscript was both extremely useful and enjoyable. And I am most grateful to

Michael Watson and his colleagues from Cambridge University Press, as well as to the anonymous reviewers whose comments on my manuscript have helped me improve it.

My family's benevolent support has been invaluable during my work on this book, as it has always been in the past. For many years, my wife Dina Khapaeva has been my fairest and toughest critic. Many (perhaps most) of the ideas that I develop in this book were born of our long and (typically) amicable conversations. During the years I have been working on this book, our daughter Katia has grown from a thoughtful teenager into a rising Rubens scholar and has become a full-fledged member of our "home academy," whose judgments in intellectual (and other) matters are rapidly becoming priceless to her parents. I cannot sufficiently acknowledge my debt to both of them.

I dedicate the book to the memory of my late friends Yuriy Markovich Shmidt (1937–2013) and Leonid Mikhailovich Batkin (1932–2016). Yuriy Markovich was a distinguished lawyer and one of the leading defenders of human rights in Russia from Soviet times into the Putin period. Leonid Mikhailovich was an outstanding historian of the Italian Renaissance and one of the most brilliant members of my teachers' generation. But he was also an important figure in the Russian democratic movement and a founder (in 1988) of the Moscow Tribune, a political club whose role in the democratization of Soviet society is hard to overestimate. The wisdom, honesty, and courage of people like Yu. M. Shmidt and L. M. Batkin have forever made the memory of the democratic reforms of the 1990s the main source of hope for Russia's future.

Chronological Table

1915, May	France, England, and Russia condemn the massacre of the Armenians in Turkey as a crime against humanity
1939, April	French *Loi Marchandeau* prohibits hate speech
1945, August	Definition of crimes against humanity in the Charter of the Nuremberg Tribunal
1945, May	Austrian *Verbotsgesetz* (Prohibition Law, amended in February 1947) prohibits fascist party and ideology
1946, January	Article 86a of the West German Penal Code bans the use of Nazi symbols
1948, December	Convention on the Prevention and Punishment of the Crime of Genocide
1948, December	Universal Declaration of Human Rights
1950, August	Nazis and Nazi Collaborators (Punishment) Law in Israel
1952, June	*Legge Scelba* in Italy prohibiting the *apologia del fascismo*
1960, April	Austrian Insignia Act forbids Nazi uniforms and symbols
1960, May	Article 130 of the West German Penal Code bans incitement to hatred
1961, April–December	Eichmann trial in Jerusalem
1965, December	International Convention on the Elimination of All Forms of Racial Discrimination
1968, November	Convention on the Non-Applicability of Statutory Limitations to War Crimes and Crimes against Humanity

1970, December	West German Chancellor Willy Brandt's *Kniefall* before the monument to the Warsaw Ghetto Uprising
1972, July	French *Loi Pleven* bans hate speech
1977, October	Amnesty law in Spain
1978, December	*Affaire Faurisson* begins in France
1978, April	Television miniseries *Holocaust* broadcast in the United States (and in January 1979 in Germany)
1978, October	Portugal prohibits fascist organizations
1979, September	German Federal Court rules that Holocaust denial is punishable as an insult to the honor of German Jews
1980	France, the United Kingdom, and Brazil declare 1980 the Year of Heritage
1985, June	German memory law
1986, July	Israeli memory law
1986–1987	*Historikerstreit* in Germany
1987, June	Recognition of the Armenian genocide by the European Union
1990, July	French *Loi Gayssot*
1991, October	Czechoslovak Lustration Act
1991, December	Stasi Records Act in Germany
1992, February	Austrian memory law
1993, April	Hungary bans the use of fascist and communist symbols
1993, June	Swiss memory law (enacted in 1995)
1993, June	Mancino law criminalized the wearing of fascist symbols in Italy
1993, July	Czech Act on the Illegality of the Communist Regime
1994, October	Article 130 of the German Penal Code amended to ban Holocaust denial
1995, March	Belgian memory law
1995, May	The first (failed) attempt to pass a memory law in Russia
1995, September	Albanian law on communist crimes against humanity
1995, November	Spanish memory law (invalidated in part in 2007)
1996, July	European Council Joint Action/96/443/JHA

1997, February	A Holocaust Denial Act introduced in the British parliament
1997, July	Luxembourgian memory law (amended in 2011 and 2012)
1997, November	The Supreme Court of the Netherlands rules that Holocaust denial is punishable as a form of hate speech
1998, December	Polish memory law
1999, December	Liechtenstein's memory law
2000, January	Stockholm International Forum on the Holocaust
2000, May	Bulgarian law on the criminal nature of the communist regime
2000, October	Czech memory law (amended in 2009)
2001, January	France recognized the 1915 Armenian genocide
2001, May	*Loi Taubira* recognizing slavery and the slave trade as a crime against humanity
2001, November	Slovak memory law (amended in 2005)
2002, March	Romanian memory law (amended in 2006 and 2015)
2002, August	Slovak Nation's Memory Act
2003, January	Additional Protocol to the Convention on Cybercrime
2004, March	Macedonian memory law
2004, June	Slovenian memory law (amended in 2008)
2005, February	Andorra's memory law
2005, February	French *Loi Mekachera* on the memory of the Algerian war (repealed in part in 2006)
2005, June	Turkey criminalizes insults to the Turkish state
2005, December	Creation of the Liberté pour l'histoire association
2006, March	Cyprus ratifies the Additional Protocol
2006, October	A law criminalizing the denial of the Armenian genocide adopted by the lower house of the French parliament
2006, November	Ukrainian parliament recognizes the Holodomor as a genocide
2007, September	Portuguese memory law
2007, December	*Ley de la Memoria Histórica* in Spain
2008, June	Prague Declaration on European Conscience and Communism

2008, October	*Appel de Blois* against memory laws
2008, November	Accoyer Commission recommends the French parliament refrain from adopting new memory laws
2008, November	Albanian memory law
2008, November	European Council Framework Decision 2008/913/JHA
2009, May	Latvian memory law (amended in 2014)
2009, July	Maltese memory law
2010, January	Hungarian memory law (amended in June)
2010, April	Montenegrin memory law
2010, June	Lithuanian memory law
2011, April	Bulgarian memory law
2011, October	Cypriot memory law
2011, December	French law penalizing the denial of the Armenian genocide (declared unconstitutional in February 2012)
2012, May	Community of Independent States' model law against the rehabilitation of Nazism
2014, January	"Dictatorship laws" in Ukraine
2014, May	Russian memory law (the "Yarovaya Act")
2014, May	Second version of the Latvian memory law
2014, September	Greek memory law
2015, April	De-communization laws in Ukraine
2015, April	Cyprus criminalizes the denial of the Armenian genocide
2015, April	Spain reintroduces a memory law
2016, June	Italian memory law
2017, January	New French memory law

Introduction

The Meaning of "Memory Laws"

The term "memory laws" (*lois mémorielles*) was coined in France in the 2000s to refer to legislation that penalizes Holocaust negationism or recognizes certain events as crimes against humanity while not prohibiting their denial. The invention of a new term shows that memory laws were widely perceived as a novelty that could not be adequately described within existing categories. Laws such as these are indeed a relatively recent phenomenon, which dates back to the 1980s. Initially, the concept was colored by a strong ironic overtone and was used mostly by opponents of the new legislation, such as the eminent historians René Rémond and Pierre Nora and the novelist Françoise Chandernagor, who invoked its bizarre nature to repudiate it.[1] The *lois mémorielles* were deemed to be part of the *phénomène mémoriel*, or the rise of memory in the late twentieth century, which their adversaries typically considered a manifestation of the fragmentation and crisis of the French national identity.[2] But quite soon the term became more commonplace due to its remarkable success in the media, and transformed into a relatively neutral marker. An ad hoc polemical tool had thus grown into a historical concept, which is a typical trajectory for many notions in the historian's lexicon. Unsurprisingly, though, using it for purposes of classification creates problems, because this is not what the concept was coined for.

Precisely which laws does the term refer to? There seems to be a contradiction between its literal sense and its conventional use, the first

---

[1] Françoise Chandernagor, "L'enfer des bonnes intentions," *Le Monde*, December 16, 2005; René Rémond, "L'histoire et la loi," *Études* 404/6 (2006), pp. 763–773; Rémond, *Quand l'État se mêle de l'histoire: Entretiens avec François Azouvi* (Paris: Stock, 2006); Pierre Nora and Françoise Chandernagor, *Liberté pour l'histoire* (Paris: CNRS Editions, 2008); and Nora, *Historien public* (Paris: Gallimard, 2011).
[2] Rémond, *Quand l'État se mêle de l'histoire*, pp. 82–83.

being far broader than the second. In addition, the term's meaning in different languages is not exactly the same, the English concept of memory laws being more inclusive than the original French notion of *lois mémorielles*. Taken literally, "memory laws" in English would mean laws regulating historical memory or simply laws on memory. In contrast to the French notion, there is here no appreciable lexical relationship with the current memory boom. In other languages, the meaning of the term vacillates between the French and the English models.[3] Those nuances notwithstanding, however, in most languages the notion can be used both in a broad sense encompassing all laws that regulate collective representations of the past and in the narrow sense of prohibitions on Holocaust denial and other similar legislation. As a matter of fact, it is most often, although not always, used in the latter sense.

The tension between the two meanings can occasionally become politically charged. While many critics of memory laws in France stressed their "absolute novelty,"[4] the partisans of this legislation invoked precedents dating back to the period of the French revolution.[5] In this context, the demonstration of an established tradition of memory laws was intended to

[3] The expression *lois mémorielles* is translated into Italian as "laws on memory" (*leggi sulla memoria*). In Germany, which was the first country to pass a special Holocaust denial bill, in 1985, its original unofficial name was "the law against the Auschwitz-lie" (*Gesetz gegen die Auschwitz-Lüge*). Although the German term "*Erinnerungsgesetze*" came into being as a translation of *lois mémorielles*, its meaning seems closer to the English notion of memory laws. It is lexically connected to such concepts as *Erinnerungskultur* (the culture of memory), which contains a reference to the present-day obsession with the past, but its prevailing interpretation holds that the culture of memory is a universal phenomenon equally typical of ancient societies and our own epoch. See Jan Assmann, "Collective Memory and Cultural Identity," *New German Critique* 65 (1995), pp. 125–133; Aleida Assmann, *Cultural Memory and Western Civilization: Functions, Media, Archives* (New York: Cambridge University Press, 2011). The Spanish expression *leyes de la memoria histórica*, which is normally used in the singular and refers to the 2007 Historical Memory Act, evokes primarily the memory of the Civil War and the Franco regime, which this act regulates, and this brings the Spanish notion closer to the French. But the Spanish term can be also used in the plural, especially since the government of Andalusia proposed a regional bill titled "Law on Historical and Democratic Memory" (Ley 2/2017, de 28 de marzo, de Memoria Histórica y Democrática de Andalucía). In the Slavic languages, the terms for memory laws are usually calques of the French concept (e.g., *memorial'nyie zakony* in Russian, *memorial'ni zakony* in Ukrainian, *ustawy memorialne* in Polish). They refer to the French memory laws and hence, indirectly, to the memory boom. All these expressions are recent and have yet to become firmly established in their respective languages.
[4] Rémond, *Quand l'État se mêle de l'histoire*, p. 9.
[5] Arno Klarsfeld, "L'histoire n'appartient pas aux historiens," *Le Monde*, January 27, 2006. Similar arguments can be put forward without any ideological implications. See Serge Barcellini, "L'État républicain, acteur de la mémoire: des morts pour la France aux morts à cause de la France," in *Les guerres de mémoire*, eds. Pascal Blanchard and Isabelle Veyrat-Masson (Paris: La Découverte, 2008), p. 209; Timothy Garton Ash, "Trials, Purges and History Lessons: Treating a Difficult Past in Post-Communist Europe," in *Memory and Power in Post-War Europe: Studies in the Presence of the Past*, ed. Jan-Werner Müller (Cambridge: Cambridge University Press, 2002), p. 267.

serve as a gauge of their legitimacy. In 2008, a special commission of the French Parliament (the Accoyer Commission,[6] which had been created to investigate the legitimacy of the memory laws), reached the following conclusion regarding their uniqueness:

> The concept of *lois mémorielles* is very recent: the expression appears only in 2005 to retrospectively designate a group of texts the first of which dates back only to 1990. But the laws that this concept refers to belong to a long-standing commemorative tradition whose legacy they have both developed and problematized.[7]

This is, I believe, a reasonable conclusion, characterizing as it does the complex relationship between the "new generation" of memory laws (the term used in the Accoyer Report) and their historical predecessors. The tension between the broad and the narrow meanings of the term may, however, be heuristically productive, in drawing attention to both the novelty of the present-day memory laws and their multiple connections with previous legislation.

The group of texts mentioned in the quote above includes first of all the 1990 Gayssot Act that penalizes Holocaust negationism and three "declarative" laws – the "Armenian" Law of 2001 that recognizes the 1915 massacre of Armenians in the Ottoman Empire as a genocide; the Taubira Act, also of 2001, that proclaims slavery and the slave trade a crime against humanity; and the 2005 Mekachera Act that "acknowledges the sufferings and sacrifices" of the "civil and military victims" of the Algerian war on the French side. These statutes are usually viewed as canonical memory laws.[8]

However, there is no consensus in France on whether these four laws can even be seen as members of the same category,[9] and not only because

---

[6] The commission was chaired by Bernard Accoyer, President of the National Assembly.

[7] *Assemblée Nationale: Rapport d'information no 1262: Rassembler la Nation autour d'une mémoire partagée* (Paris: Assemblée Nationale, 2008), p. 11.

[8] Marc Olivier Baruch, *Des lois indignes? Les Historiens, la politique et le droit* (Paris: Tallandier, 2013).

[9] *Ibid.*, p. 111. Some French legal scholars use the term "purely memory laws" ("lois purement mémorielles" or "lois strictement mémorielles") to refer to declarative laws that establish "the truth of the past" but have no normative component. See Marc Frangi, "'Les lois mémorielles': De l'expression de la volonté générale au législateur historien," *Revue du droit public* 1 (2005), p. 243, and Nathalie Droin, "L'avenir des lois mémorielles à la lumière de la décision du Conseil constitutionnel du 28 février 2012 relative à la loi visant à réprimer la contestation de l'existence des génocides reconnus par la loi," *Revue française de droit constitutionnel* 3/95 (2013), pp. 589-610. From this vantage point, the Gayssot Act is but a "partially memory law" ("loi partiellement mémorielle"). See also Patrick Fraisseix, "Le droit mémoriel," *Revue française de droit constitutionnel* 67/3 (2006), pp. 483–508 ; Anne-Chloé Foirry, "Lois mémorielles, normativité et liberté d'expression dans la jurisprudence du Conseil constitutionnel: Un équilibre complexe et des

one of them criminalizes certain statements about the past while others do not. It is sometimes argued that the laws of 2001 and 2005 are declarations rather than real laws because they have created no new norms.[10] More significantly, these three laws are often viewed as products of electoral manipulation and a competition of victims, such criticism being rarely voiced with regard to the Gayssot Act.

Nonetheless, the term "memory laws" was coined to refer to all these acts. The Accoyer Report states that what they have in common is their goal of fulfilling the "duty of memory" (*le devoir de mémoire*),[11] which since the early 1990s has become a central theme of public debates in France.[12] This is, of course, just another way of saying that memory laws are legislation having to do with the *phénomène mémoriel*, and there are several other laws that fall under this definition,[13] not all of which are mentioned in the Accoyer Report. For instance, the report does not count as a memory law the enactment passed on October 8, 1987, that created *mort en déportation* (died during deportation) as an official status attributable to a deceased person. That could, of course, be a simple omission, for this piece of legislation was obviously in line with the duty of memory agenda. But are there good reasons not to designate as memory laws similar acts that had been passed long before the duty of memory became a fashionable idea? The law of 1987 was modeled after a law of July 2, 1915, that had introduced the concept ("*mention*") of *mort pour la France* (died for France) in the context of legislation aimed at commemorating fallen soldiers and granting privileges to their families.[14] If the former legislation belongs to this category, why should the latter not also be called a memory law? The only possible answer is that 1915 is distant from us in

---

évolutions possibles," *Pouvoirs* 4/143 (2012), pp. 141-156; and Thomas Hochmann, "Le problème des lois dites 'mémorielles' sera-t-il résolu par les résolutions ? La référence à l'article 34-1 de la Constitution dans le discours contemporain sur les relations entre le Parlement et l'histoire," *Droit et cultures* 66 (2013), pp. 57-69. This use of the concept is justified insofar as the problem of normativity of law is essential to legal theory. However, it obscures the novelty of laws that criminalize certain statements about the past.

[10] Until the reform of 2008, the constitution of the Fifth Republic did not give the parliament the right to adopt declarations; legislators had to pass a law should they want to express their official position on a given issue. See Baruch, *Des lois indignes?*, p. 110, and *Assemblée Nationale: Rapport d'information no 1262*, p. 23.

[11] *Assemblée Nationale: Rapport d'information no 1262*, p. 25.

[12] Olivier Lalieu, "L'invention du 'devoir de mémoire,'" *Vingtième siècle: Revue d'histoire* 69 (2001), pp. 83–94; Sébastien Ledoux, *Le devoir de mémoire: Une formule et son histoire* (Paris: CNRS Éditions, 2016); Myriam Bienenstock, ed., *Devoir de mémoire? Les lois mémorielles et l'histoire* (Paris: Éditions de l'éclat, 2014).

[13] *Assemblée Nationale: Rapport d'information no 1262*, pp. 25–33.

[14] Barcellini, "L'État républicain," pp. 209–219.

time, while memory laws are a recent fact. Similar arguments have been adduced in other debates on memory laws.[15]

As with most historical concepts, the category of memory laws should probably be conceived in terms of the prototype theory of classification. The prototype theory states that, contrary to Aristotelian logic, human categories, or the concepts that our minds naturally form, do not follow the principle of necessary and sufficient conditions but are formed around prototypes or good examples, to which less good examples and borderline cases are associated by means of a vague family resemblance. Definitions or general concepts, it is maintained, are of little use in the actual categorization process, which is guided by a holistic perception of objects, not by a trait analysis. Empirically formed categories tend to have a hard core and a complexly structured periphery. An object can belong to this or that extent to a prototypical class ("some dogs are more doggy than others"), which is impossible with regard to an Aristotelian class, whose members are all equal so long as they satisfy the required conditions for category membership. In response, critics of the prototype theory argue that humans form different kinds of concepts. In many cases, prototypical effects do indeed occur but this does not prove that a concept does not have a meaning that we spontaneously interpret analytically, in terms of necessary and sufficient conditions.[16] In a moderated version that emphasizes the plurality of forms of classification and the complexity of the semantic structures of our concepts, the prototype theory can arguably be a useful tool of historical research.[17]

Historical concepts (like many words of our everyday language) tend to have a general meaning and refer to concrete historical occurrences that can be seen as good examples of a particular category. In other words, they have aspects of both Aristotelian and prototypical categories. Given that these occurrences are unique historical phenomena, limited in space and time (or, to borrow from the language of the German historicists,

---

[15] Pierre Nora, "Malaise dans l'identité historique," in Nora and Chandernagor, *Liberté pour l'histoire*, p. 14; Rémond, *Quand l'État se mêle de l'histoire*, p. 40.

[16] George Lakoff, *Women, Fire, and Dangerous Things: What Categories Reveal about the Mind* (Chicago, Ill.: The University of Chicago Press, 1987); Eric Margolis and Stephen Laurence, eds., *Concepts: Core Readings* (Cambridge, Mass.: MIT Press, 1999); Gregory L. Murphy, *The Big Book of Concepts* (Cambridge, Mass.: MIT Press, 2004). I formulated my understanding of the prototype theory and its relevance to the study of historical concepts in my *De l'imagination historique* (Paris: Editions de l'Ecole des hautes études en sciences sociales, 2009), pp. 73–105.

[17] In one interpretation, Max Weber attributed a prototypical structure to his ideal types. See Jean-Claude Passeron, *Le raisonnement sociologique: L'espace non-popperien du raisonnement naturel* (Paris: Nathan, 1991), pp. 60–61.

"historical individuals," which includes collective individuals),[18] it may be said that historical concepts combine elements of a common and a proper name. We will return to this theory later, since it can help us understand an important aspect of the present-day historical consciousness. For now, however, I will limit myself to the following suggestion.

I believe that the hard core of the broadly understood category of memory laws consists of legislation penalizing statements about the past (or memory laws per se), while its periphery includes several other kinds of laws: declarative memory laws giving an official assessment of historical events, including those that recognize certain events as crimes against humanity; laws on state symbols, holidays, remembrance days, and commemorative ceremonies; acts renaming cities, streets, and public institutions to commemorate historical figures or events; laws on the creation of museums, erection of monuments, and organization of archives; laws on education that regulate the teaching of history; legislation on veterans and on the memory of fallen soldiers; laws granting amnesty to the participants in certain historical events (such as the Paris Commune and the Spanish Civil War) or rehabilitating victims of repressions and providing compensations for past injustices; lustration acts that aim at purifying public institutions from collaborators of a former regime; and laws prohibiting certain symbols, parties, and ideologies (which involves a historical assessment). This list is by no means complete.[19] In many cases, such legislation has practical political and social goals that extend far beyond the regulation of historical memory (for instance, combating the danger from the far right or defining veterans' rights). The more obvious the "memorial component" of a given act is, the closer it is to the center of the category of memory laws. Characteristically, most types of peripheral memory laws existed long before this concept was coined subsequent to the emergence of the category's hard core, as described here.[20]

My focus in the book is on that hard core of the category of memory laws, or legislation criminalizing statements about the past that I believe typifies the present-day historical consciousness. However, I also consider

[18] On the notion of historical individuals, see Heinrich Rickert, *The Limits of Concept Formation in Natural Science: A Logical Introduction to the Historical Sciences* [1896/1902], ed. Guy Oakes (Cambridge: Cambridge University Press, 1986); Ernst Troeltsch, *Der Historismus und seine Probleme, Erstes Buch: Das Logische Problem der Geschichtsphilosophie* (Tübingen: J.C.B. Mohr, 1922).

[19] For other kinds of memory laws see Chapter 3.

[20] Cf. Milosz Matuschek, *Erinnerungsstrafrecht: Eine Neubegründung des Verbots der Holocaustleugnung auf rechtsvergleichender und sozialphilosophischer Grundlage* (Berlin: Duncker & Humblot, 2012), pp. 43–44.

them in the context of other laws regulating collective representations of history. From among all kinds of memory laws in the broad sense of the word, anti-fascist legislation has been particularly important to the genesis of memory laws per se, and I consider it in Chapter 2. In Eastern Europe, memory laws have also continued another legislative tradition, namely that of de-communization, which I discuss in Chapter 3.

But even in the narrowest possible sense of enactments criminalizing statements about the past, memory laws are a complexly structured category that includes several subtypes and various borderline cases, and it is not always easy to decide whether a given law belongs to that category. One of this book's main goals is to propose a typology of those laws. Here, however, I will restrict myself to just one more brief comment on the changing meaning of this concept.

Typically, memory laws ban factual (or, more exactly, counter-factual) statements about history rather than assessments of the past. Initially (in the 1980s), they came into being to prevent Holocaust negationism, and one of the arguments in their favor was that they ban lies (the Auschwitz-lie) rather than opinions. That, in fact, is why those laws were called Holocaust *denial* laws. Indeed, occurrences of statements such as "Hitler was right to exterminate the Jews" could be more easily prosecuted on the basis of enactments prohibiting fascist propaganda and hate speech, while claims that "there had been no gas chambers" were, according to the deniers, an academic position that could not be outlawed. The goal of the new legislation was to identify that "position" as a lie and an expression of racism.

As time passed, however, the original notion began to change. Its scope expanded to include the denial of certain other crimes against humanity, so that the original target of the Auschwitz-lie had to be replaced with a broader formula. The expression "memory laws" no longer refers, therefore, only to denial, and many such laws (especially recent ones) penalize both denial and justification of those crimes. Criminalizing negationism remains crucial to the notion of memory laws because of their genealogy, but in some cases, which I would consider peripheral to the category, denial is not banned whereas justification is.[21] Moreover, prohibitions of utterances that contain certain assessments of past events seem to antedate the emergence of the legislation that bans factual statements about history. Thus, some postwar anti-fascist laws, both in Western and Eastern

---

[21] Thus, between 2007 and 2015, Spain banned only the justification but not the denial of crimes against humanity.

Europe, contained formulas that can be interpreted as bans on the positive historical evaluation of fascism.[22] But they were just remote predecessors, or early peripheral cases, of the category of memory laws, as it has emerged since the 1980s when the task of criminalizing untrue statements became urgent in the context of the growing Holocaust denial movement.

Memory Laws as a Pan-European Phenomenon

Pierre Nora once called memory laws "a distinctively French legislative sport."[23] He is right insofar as nowhere else have public debates on these laws been as passionate as in France, not to mention that the Gayssot Act of 1990 is a prototypical memory law that has provided a model for several other national enactments and international agreements. Yet the first Holocaust denial laws were adopted in Germany (1985) and Israel (1986). Since the 1990s, this legislation has become a pan-European phenomenon; to this point, some thirty European countries have laws criminalizing statements about the past on their books.[24] In some countries, "the French sport" has become at least as popular as in France. For instance, over the past twenty-five years, Ukrainian lawmakers have proposed more than ninety bills dealing with different aspects of historical memory. Given the variety of historical memory regimes in Europe, a comparative approach to memory laws is crucial to their understanding. My intention here is to consider this legislation in the various forms that it has taken at the mature stage of its development, rather than to fall under the spell of "the idol of origins" (Marc Bloch), which sometimes prompts us to explain a social phenomenon by the circumstances of its genesis.

---

[22] E.g., the 1952 Italian Scelba Law, which prohibited "publicly exalting proponents, principles, deeds, and methods of fascism," and the 1968 East German Penal Code, which criminalized "the glorification of fascism or militarism." Both formulas obviously implied a ban on certain claims about the past.

[23] Pierre Nora, "Lois mémorielles: pour en finir avec ce sport législatif purement français," *Le Monde*, December 27, 2011; Françoise Chandernagor ("L'histoire sous le coup de la loi," in Nora and Chandernagor, *Liberté pour l'histoire*, p. 37) calls memory laws a "French virus."

[24] To the best of my knowledge, there are almost no laws outside Europe that expressly criminalize statements about the past, which does not, however, mean that there is no censorship of historical thought there. See Antoon De Baets, *Censorship of Historical Thought: A World Guide, 1945–2000* (Westport, Conn.: Greenwood Press, 2002). The exceptions that I am aware of include the Israeli 1986 law and a series of Rwandan laws, including the Constitution of 2003 (Article 13) and Law No. 33*bis*/2003 on Repressing the Crime of Genocide, Crimes against Humanity and War Crimes, which has introduced a penalty of up to twenty years' imprisonment for the denial, crass minimization, or justification of genocide. See Yakaré-Oulé (Nani) Jansen, "Denying Genocide or Denying Free Speech? A Case Study of the Application of Rwanda's Genocide Denial Laws," *Northwestern Journal of International Human Rights* 12/2 (2014), pp. 191–213.

This book has been written by a historian, not by a legal scholar. Although we owe to jurists most of what is known about memory laws, in particular with respect to the ongoing debate about the legitimacy of that legislation, history has an important contribution to make to the legal dispute that I will review later in this introduction. I hold that the expansion of memory laws, which is characteristic of the present-day political climate, is gradually changing their nature. Over recent decades, memory laws have become a historical phenomenon with its own logic of development, which has led legislators in many European countries far beyond the original intentions of the authors of the first new-generation memory laws. Initially conceived as a means of maintaining peace, these laws have instead become one of the preferred instruments of the memory wars within and between many European countries.

The book is the first study to offer a complete overview of the laws criminalizing statements about the past in Europe, including in Russia.[25] Most of the existing literature deals with memory laws in the West. Their more recent Eastern European, and especially Russian and Ukrainian, analogues are far less well known, for all that they are critical in assessing the role of memory laws as a device of the present-day politics of history and in understanding the polarity of the two main forms of European memory.[26]

Although adopted largely on the initiative of the European Union and in compliance with its recommendations, some Eastern European memory laws differ significantly from their Western prototypes. I argue that in

[25] Texts of most memory laws are available in English in Talia Naamat, Nina Osin and Dina Porat, eds., *Legislating for Equality: A Multinational Collection of Non-Discrimination Norms*, vol. 1: Europe (Leiden: Martinus Nijhoff, 2012). Pedro Lima Marcheri, *Legislação europeia de combate ao nazismo, doutrinas de ódio e discriminação racial* (Editora Cio Do Ebook, 2015) quotes those laws in original languages as well. However, both books give only the laws' last versions as amended by 2012 and 2015, respectively. Thomas Wandres' *Die Strafbarkeit des Auschwitz-Leugnens* (Berlin: Duncker and Humblot, 2000) and Robert A. Kahn's *Holocaust Denial and the Law: A Comparative Study* (New York: Palgrave Macmillan, 2004) were the first monographical studies of memory laws (to 2000 and 2004 respectively). Matuschek's *Erinnerungsstrafrecht* focuses on German, French, and Polish cases. Other useful overviews include Michael Whine, "Expanding Holocaust Denial and Legislation Against It," in *Extreme Speech and Democracy*, eds. Ivan Hare and James Weinstein Oxford: Oxford University Press, 2009), pp. 538–556; Luigi Cajani, "Criminal Laws on History: The Case of the European Union," *Historein* 11 (2011), pp. 19–48; Cajani, "Diritto penale et libertà dello storico," in *Riparare, Risarcire, Ricordare: Un dialogo tra storici e giuristi*, eds. Georgio Resta and Vinzenzo Zeno-Zencovich (Napoli: Editoriale Scientifica, 2012), pp. 371–410; and *Law and Memory: Towards Legal Governance of History*, eds. Uladzislau Belavusau and Aleksandra Gliszczyńska-Grabias (Cambridge University Press, forthcoming).

[26] On the perception of Eastern Europe "as a marginal [and] supplementary" issue in memory studies, see Małgorzata Pakier and Johanna Wawrzyniak, "Introduction: Memory and Change in Eastern Europe: How Special?" in *Memory and Change in Europe: Eastern Perspectives* (New York, Oxford: Berghahn Books, 2016), p. 1.

Eastern Europe, legislation on the issues of the past is often used to give the force of law to narratives centered on the history of the nation-states, which is the opposite of what such laws were meant to achieve in Western Europe and what the European Union intends to accomplish by promoting them. The latter's goal is to create a common European memory centered on the memory of the Holocaust as a means of integrating Europe, combating racism, and averting the national and ethnic conflicts[27] that national narratives are likely to stimulate.

The Russian case is central to my book because it convincingly demonstrates the changing nature of legislation on the issues of the past and its transformation into an instrument of memory wars that can potentially lead to shooting wars. The Russian law adopted in the midst of the Ukraine crisis in May 2014 penalizes "dissemination of knowingly false information on the activities of the USSR during the Second World War."[28] This document is almost unique among memory laws, which normally protect the memories of the victims of state policy. Russian legislators claim that their law differs in no way from Western memory laws; but what they are actually seeking to do is protect the memory of the Stalin regime against the memory of its victims. The law gives legal protection to the cult of World War II (or the Great Patriotic War, as the Russians typically call it) that under Putin has become the myth of the origins of post-Soviet Russia. This cult includes the notion of the Yalta System and legitimizes the Soviet occupation of Eastern Europe in the aftermath of the war. However, as radical as it is, the Russian case points to broader tendencies in the evolution of the legislation of memory, which is now being widely used in promoting nationalistic goals. (Edoardo Grendi's notion of exceptional/normal[29] could almost have been coined to account for the peculiarity of this country, where world-wide trends often take extreme forms whose study helps us better understand those trends themselves.) I will, in particular, show that memory laws were an important instrument in the memory war between Russia and Ukraine, which laid the groundwork for the Russian annexation of Crimea and the war in Donbass.[30] Fans of "the French sport" need to be aware of its potential dangers.

---

[27] Klas-Göran Karlsson, "The Uses of History and the Third Wave of Europeanisation," in *A European Memory? Contested Histories and Politics of Remembrance*, eds. Małgorzata Pakier and Bo Stråth (New York: Berghahn Books, 2010), pp. 38–46.

[28] See below, Chapter 6.

[29] Edoardo Grendi, "Microanalisi e storia sociale," *Quaderni storici* 35 (1977), p. 512.

[30] Cf. Georgiy Kasianov, "How a War for the Past Becomes a War in the Present," *Kritika: Explorations in Russian and Eurasian History* 16/1 (2015), pp. 149–156.

Memory Laws and the Rise of Memory

Alongside the role of memory laws in present-day politics, my second concern in this book is with their cultural meaning, and more specifically with what they reveal about the changing forms of modern historical consciousness and political legitimation. In other words, I will consider memory laws in the context of the rise of memory in the late twentieth and early twenty-first centuries.

The memory boom is perhaps the most salient feature of the present-day historical consciousness. Here too, the proliferation of new concepts signals some important changes that have been taking place in recent decades. Such expressions as "historical memory," "identity," "politics of history," and "memory wars" are relative newcomers to the vocabulary of the social and human sciences. Before the 1980s, the concept of memory, and of historical memory in particular, was only occasionally used by historians, political scientists, sociologists, anthropologists, or literary scholars.[31] But since then, memory has become "perhaps the leading term" in cultural history and "a central concept in the humanities and the social sciences" in general.[32] The notion of identity (in the sense of personal identity) was coined in the 1950s, but came to prominence only with the emergence of interest in memory, with which its meaning largely overlaps.[33] Indeed, memory, both individual and collective, is often viewed as

---

[31] Maurice Halbwachs' groundbreaking research on collective memory (*Les cadres sociaux de la mémoire* [Paris: Félix Alcan, 1925]) had little influence before the 1980s. See Philippe Joutard, *Histoire et mémoires, conflits et alliance* (Paris: La Découverte, 2013), pp. 12–13. Joutard's own study of the memory of the Camisard insurrection in France and George Duby's book on the memory of the battle of Bouvines were the first signs of the emerging interest in historical memory in France. See George Duby, *Le dimanche de Bouvines: 27 juillet 1214* (Paris: Gallimard, 1973), and Joutard, *La légende des Camisards: Une sensibilité au passé* (Paris: Gallimard, 1977). Frances A. Yates' *The Art of Memory* (London: Routledge and Kegan Paul, 1966) marked the discovery of this problematic in English-language historiography. But it was not until the publication of Yosef H. Yerushalmi's *Zakhor: Jewish History and Jewish Memory* (Seattle: University of Washington Press, 1982), David Lowenthal's *The Past Is a Foreign Country* (London: Cambridge University Press, 1985), and especially Pierre Nora's *Les lieux de mémoire* (Paris: Gallimard, 1984–1992, vols. 1–7) that historical memory has become a central preoccupation for historians.

[32] Alon Confino, "Collective Memory and Cultural History: Problems of Method," *American Historical Review* 102/5 (1997), p. 1386; Wulf Kansteiner, "Finding Meaning in Memory: A Methodological Critique of Collective Memory Studies," *History and Theory* 41/2 (2002), p. 180; and William G. Rosenberg, "Is Social Memory a 'Useful Category of Historical Analysis'?," in *Rossiya i SShA: Poznavaya drug druga* [Russia and the United States: Coming To Know One Another], ed. V.V. Noskov et al. (Saint Petersburg: Nestor-Istoriya, 2015), p. 300.

[33] The identity discourse became central to the German conservatives' attempts to rehabilitate the national past after the publication of philosopher Hermann Lübbe's 1976 speech on identity-building as history's principal function. See Edgar Wolfrum, *Geschichte als Waffe: Vom Kaiserreich bis zur Wiedervereinigung* (Göttingen: Vandenhoeck & Ruprecht, 2001), p. 126; Hermann Lübbe,

the custodian of identity.[34] The term "politics of history" (*Geschichtspolitik*) was invented in 1986 in the context of the West German *Historikerstreit* ("the historians' debate" over the uniqueness of the Holocaust), although the adjective *geschichtspolitisch* was occasionally used in the early twentieth century to denounce politically biased interpretations of the past.[35] The notion of memory wars came to be widely used as recently as the 1990s and 2000s, not because there had previously been no heated political disagreements over the past but because they had not been conceptualized as a form of conflict typifying the age of memory.

The study of memory laws is a promising entry into the problematic of present-day historical consciousness, memory, and identity. As already mentioned, laws that regulate collective representations of the past are not a new phenomenon, but laws that criminalize certain statements about the past are. Even the USSR, with its formidable system of censorship, had no memory laws in the narrow sense, notwithstanding the importance of history to the communist ideology. The emergence of memory laws in the strict sense shows that in the age of memory, the past has become even more important for cultural identity and political legitimation than it was in the age of history-based political ideologies. It also demonstrates the ongoing "juridification" [*Verrechtlichung*] of our societies (in Jürgen Habermas' sense of "the tendency towards an increase in formal... law").[36]

Understanding how the present-day historical consciousness differs from that of the age of ideologies entails recognizing not only the novelty of the laws that penalize statements about the past but also the kinds of

"Zur Identitätspräsentationsfunktion von Historie," in *Identität*, eds. Odo Marquard and Karlheinz Stierle (Munich: W. Fink, 1979), pp. 277–292.

[34] "The modern conception of the self has memory at its core," as Michael S. Roth and Charles G. Salas put it. See their "Introduction," in *Disturbing Remains: Memory, History, and Crisis in the Twentieth Century* (Los Angeles, Calif.: Getty Research Institute, 2001), p. 2. Anthony Smith claims: "One might almost say: no memory, no identity; no identity, no nation." See his "Memory and Identity: Reflections on Ernst Gellner's Theory of Nationalism," *Nations and Nationalism* 2/3 (1996) p. 383.

[35] Harald Schmid, "Vom publizistischen Kampfbegriff zum Forschungskonzept: Zur Historisierung der Kategorie 'Geschichtspolitik,'" in *Geschichtspolitik und kollektives Gedächtnis: Erinnerungskulturen in Theorie und Praxis* (Göttingen: Vandenhoeck & Ruprecht, 2009), p. 65; Stefan Troebst, "Geschichtspolitik," Docupedia-Zeitgeschichte, 04.08.2014: http://docupedia.de/zg/Geschichtspolitik; Troebst, "Geschichtspolitik: Politikfeld, Analyserahmen, Streitobjekt," in *Geschichtspolitik in Europa seit 1989: Deutschland, Frankreich und Polen in internationalen Vergleich*, eds. Étienne François, Kornelia Kończal, Robert Traba, and Troebst (Göttingen: Wallstein Verlag, 2013), pp. 17–19. In English, the term "politics of history" was occasionally used with regard to publicly engaged historical research. See Howard Zinn, *The Politics of History* [1970], 2nd ed. (Urbana-Champaign: University of Illinois Press, 1990).

[36] Jürgen Habermas, *The Theory of Communicative Action*, vol. 2, *Lifeworld and System: A Critique of Functionalist Reason* [1981] (Boston: Beacon Press, 1987), p. 357.

statements that this legislation bans. All memory laws without exception prohibit "incorrect" interpretations of concrete historical events, which demonstrates that in the age of memory, Western historical consciousness has become centered not on "master narratives" but on the fragments of the past that symbolically represent national communities and other constituencies.[37] Most of these events are tragedies and traumas that have become central to the ways in which particular communities represent themselves in a context informed by the new culture of victimhood typical of the late twentieth and early twenty-first centuries.[38] It goes without saying that self-victimization often presents as a perverse form of self-glorification.

To appreciate the importance of that shift, we need to return to the theory of historical concepts. As has already been suggested, each historical concept combines aspects of both a general and a proper name, which is why Jean-Claude Passeron calls them semi-proper names.[39] But there are various kinds of historical concepts, some of which are closer to the model of general names while others are closer to that of proper names. In addition, as we will see in Chapter 1, the proportion in which the elements of a common and a proper name typically come together to form a concept's meaning changes over time. Preferencing more general names over more proper ones, or vice versa, entails differing forms of legitimation (reference to universal values versus reference to the ways in which collective individuals such as nations have emerged over time).[40] In his dialogues with René Rémond, François Azouvi claims that "the promulgation of memory laws is happening in the historical and cultural context, which privileges communitarian identities."[41] I will argue that the present-day politics of memory, especially in Russia, tends to privilege concepts that are

---

[37] On nations as "primary memory communities" of the present-day world see Etienne François, "Geschichtspolitik und Erinnerungskultur in Europa heute," in *Geschichtspolitik in Europa seit 1989*, pp. 541–544. To be sure, no hard and fast dividing lines can be drawn between master narratives and the interpretation of singular events. Events acquire their symbolic meaning within broader interpretative frameworks, and we can hardly imagine a master narrative that would not mention concrete events. But there is a clear difference in emphasis between a narrative organized around a philosophy of history and one that explores the symbolic meanings of historical events.

[38] Chris Lorenz, "Unstuck in Time, Or: The Sudden Presence of the Past," in *Performing the Past: Memory, History, and Identity in Modern Europe*, eds. Karin Tilmans, Frank van Vree, and Jay Winter (Amsterdam: Amsterdam University Press, 2010), p. 83. On victimization, see below, Chapter 1.

[39] Passeron, *Le raisonnement sociologique*, pp. 60–61.

[40] See my "The Logic of Democracy," *Le Banquet* 27 (2010), pp. 101–121, and "Collective Singulars: A Reinterpretation," *Contributions to the History of Concepts* 6/1 (2011), pp. 37–62.

[41] Rémond, *Quand l'État se mêle de l'histoire*, p. 82.

closer to proper than to general names. To put it differently, the idea of a special path of historical development (or *Sonderweg*, to use the infamous German notion that has traditionally supported much of the nationalistic thinking in Central and Eastern Europe) has become particularly prominent of late, which presupposes a far more relativistic approach to values and a crisis of democracy conceived as a profoundly universalistic project.

The idea of memory laws was genealogically linked to the notion of universal values. But this idea was overtaken by revived national narratives, not least because its logical form (or event-centeredness) is perfectly compatible with them.[42] The memory boom and the revival of nationalism are not only contemporaneous but also closely interrelated phenomena. Today, concrete historical events symbolizing different communities of memory have acquired an importance that they could never have had earlier, when ideological battles developed around the projects of the future and interpretations of global history.[43]

Memory Laws: Pro et Contra

Various arguments have been put forward for and against the criminalization of certain statements about the past, in terms of both legitimacy and practical utility.[44] As far as legitimacy is concerned, some jurists maintain that memory laws violate freedom of speech (and freedom of historical

[42] On the logical implications of the event-centered historical consciousness, see my "Events, Proper Names and the Rise of Memory," in *Afterlife of Events: Perspectives of Mnemohistory*, ed. Marek Tamm (London: Palgrave Macmillan, 2015), pp. 44–61.

[43] This theory resonates with the claim that the notion of collective memory has replaced those of ideology and myth that were used in the 1960s and 1970s to refer to similar phenomena. See Aleida Assmann, *Der lange Schatten der Vergangenheit: Erinnerungskultur und Geschichtspolitik* (Munich: Beck, 2006), p. 30.

[44] Some scholars explicitly advocate outlawing denial, and some are openly opposed to it. For the first position, see Martin Imbleau, "Denial of the Holocaust, Genocide, and Crimes against Humanity: A Comparative Overview of *Ad Hoc* Statutes," in *Genocide Denials and the Law*, eds. Ludovic Hennebel and Thomas Hochmann (Oxford: Oxford University Press, 2011), pp. 235–277; Whine, "Expanding Holocaust Denial and Legislation against It," pp. 555–556 (the author suggests, though, that "laws alone" are insufficient absent improvements in education on the Holocaust); Jonathan D. Josephs, "Holocaust Denial Legislation: A Justifiable Infringement of Freedom of Expression?" *Série de Working Papers du Centre Perelman de philosophie du droit*, no. 2008/3, pp. 25–28, 61; Pascale Bloch, "Response to Professor Fronza's *The Punishment of Negationism*," *Vermont Law Review* 30/3 (2006), pp. 627–643; and Matuschek, *Erinnerungsstrafrecht*. For the second position, see Emanuela Fronza, "The Punishment of Negationism: The Difficult Dialogue between Law and Memory," *Vermont Law Review* 30/3 (2006), pp. 609–626; Fronza, "The Criminal Protection of Memory: Some Observations About the Offense of Holocaust Denial," in *Genocide Denials and the Law*, pp. 155–181; Peter R. Teachout, "Making 'Holocaust Denial' a Crime: Reflections on European Anti-Negationist Laws from the Perspective of U.S. Constitutional Experience," *Vermont Law Review* 30/3 (2006), pp. 655–692; Laurent Pech, "The Law of

research, historians add). The claim that nothing is more important to democracy than freedom of speech is based on the assumption that only open discussion can lead to truth and justice.

The partisans of memory laws reply that this is a naïve expectation (some ironically call it "the Darwinian theory of free speech"[45]). Freedom of speech is but one of the rights that need to be protected, and in cases where that freedom comes into conflict with right to safety and human dignity, it can be legitimately limited. Moreover, freedoms can be abused, and Holocaust denial is just such an abuse. Deniers are not searching for truth but intentionally misinterpreting facts to promote their anti-Semitic goals. Consequently, the prohibition of negationism is not even a restriction of freedom of research,[46] since this legislation bans knowingly false statements.[47]

The argument based on the abuse of freedom dates back to the concept of militant democracy,[48] according to which democracy is not just about procedures but about certain values, which it must be able to defend (substantial democracy versus procedural democracy). Given that the experience of the Weimar Republic seems to give weight to this claim, it is no wonder that today's Germany is a classic example of militant democracy.[49]

Holocaust Denial in Europe: Toward a (Qualified) EU-Wide Criminal Prohibition," in *Genocide Denials and the Law*, pp. 185–234; Andrew Altman, "Freedom of Expression and Human Rights Law: The Case of Holocaust Denial," in *Speech and Harm: Controversies over Free Speech*, eds. Ishani Maitra and Mary Kate McGowan (Oxford: Oxford University Press, 2012), pp. 24–49; and Stiina Löytömäki, *Law and the Politics of Memory: Confronting the Past* (London: Routledge, 2014).

[45] Stephanie Farrior, "Molding the Matrix: The Historical and Theoretical Foundations of International Law Concerning Hate Speech," *Berkeley Journal of International Law* 14/1 (1996), p. 95.

[46] Kenneth Lasson, "Defending Truth: Legal and Psychological Aspects of Holocaust Denial," *Current Psychology* 26 (2007), p. 265; Martin Imbleau, "Denial of the Holocaust, Genocide, and Crimes Against Humanity," p. 277; Thomas Hochmann, "The Denier's Intent," in *Genocide Denials and the Law*, pp. 279–319; and Israel W. Charny, "A Classification of Denials of the Holocaust and Other Genocides," *Journal of Genocide Research* 5/1 (2003), pp. 11–34.

[47] According to the European Court of Human Rights, the denial of "clearly established historical facts – such as the Holocaust – . . . would be removed from the protection of Article 10 [freedom of expression] by Article 17 [prohibition of abuse of rights] of the ECHR [European Convention on Human Rights] (Lehideux and Isorni v. France, judgment of 23.9.1998)." See Report from the Commission to the European Parliament and the Council on the Implementation of Council Framework Decision 2008/913/JHA on Combating Certain Forms and Expressions of Racism and Xenophobia by Means of Criminal Law, January 27, 2014, p. 5, note 6.

[48] Karl Loewenstein, "Militant Democracy and Fundamental Rights," *The American Political Science Review* 31/3 (1937), pp. 417–432, and 31/4 (1937), pp. 638–658.

[49] Gregory H. Fox and Georg Nolte, "Intolerant Democracies," *Harvard International Law Review* 36/1 (1995), pp. 14–17; Pech, "The Law of Holocaust Denial in Europe," pp. 190–206; Dieter Oberndörfer, "Germany's 'Militant Democracy': An Attempt to Fight Incitement against Democracy and Freedom of Speech through Constitutional Provisions: History and Overall

As a matter of fact, all democracies limit freedoms. Partisans and opponents of memory laws agree in principle that those limits should be as minimal as possible. But what is a reasonable minimum? This is the subject of a never-ending dispute to which the issue of memory laws is quite central, some observers even suggesting that "laws forbidding Holocaust denial are perhaps the most controversial limitation on freedom of expression to have flourished over the past few decades."[50] Many jurists hold that limiting freedom of speech can be legitimate only when its exercise exposes concrete individuals to danger or causes them immediate harm; indeed, some memory laws specify that negationism is a criminal offence only when it is intentional and hazardous to actual individuals. In practice, however, German and French courts, as well as the European Court of Human Rights, assume that denial is always dangerous; the potential danger is so great that it makes no sense to wait until it becomes real.[51] There can also be the belated effects of certain acts that do not create immediate danger today but may strongly contribute to it in the future. Some jurists speak of the accumulation of harm: minor harms of a racist nature, if constantly repeated, can produce pernicious long-term effects (by lowering a person's status, etc.). At this point, their opponents advance a slippery-slope argument in which trying to foresee all possible dangers of all possible abuses of freedom can lead to overreach in limiting those freedoms.[52] But a simple counter-argument is possible here: *abusus non tollit usum* (abuse is not an argument against valid use).

Another important question deals with the type of crimes whose denial can be legitimately prohibited. Some jurists argue that such prohibition should be limited only to crimes committed by the state, which would include genocide, commonly viewed as a state-sponsored crime. Following this logic, the state has no right to prohibit the rehabilitation of entities other than itself.[53] (I find this to be a very strong argument.)

Record," in *Freedom of Speech and Incitement against Democracy*, eds. Davis Kretzmer and Francine Kershman Hazan (Hague: Kluwer Law International, 2000), pp. 235–246.

[50] Erik Bleich, "The Rise of Hate Speech and Hate Crime Laws in Liberal Democracies," *Journal of Ethnic and Migration Studies* 37/6 (2011), p. 920.

[51] Alexander Tsesis, *Destructive Messages* (New York: New York University Press, 2002), p. 145; Pech, "The Law of Holocaust Denial in Europe," pp. 210–222.

[52] Roger W. Smith, "Legislating against Genocide Denial: Criminalizing Denial or Preventing Free Speech?" *Journal of Law and Public Policy* 4/2 (2010), p. 137.

[53] Lawrence Douglas, "The Memory of Judgment: The Law, the Holocaust, and Denial," *History and Memory* 7/2 (1995), p. 103. On the connection between the emergence of modern state and genocides, see Enzo Traverso, *L'Histoire déchirée: Essai sur Auschwitz et les intellectuels* (Paris: Cerf, 1997).

A recurrent objection to memory laws is that not only courts of law but also parliaments have neither the authority nor the competence to judge history or, as articulated by the French opponents of memory laws, "history is not an object of law."[54] However, there are counter-arguments here as well. Can we imagine a state without a minimal official history embodied in its constitution, symbols, rituals, and the like? Should we condemn acts of official repentance, state apologies, and restitution, which are impossible without judging the past?[55] In other words, the principle of state non-interference in issues of the past also labors under certain restrictions. De facto, in most countries including France, history has long been an object of law.[56] But one can of course still claim that although the authorities are entitled to express their official position regarding past events, they have no right to penalize alternative opinions.

The necessity for memory laws can be called into question because denial can be (and on some occasions has been) punished under existing laws against hate speech. What is particularly dangerous about deniers is not denial per se but the intention behind it, the hateful message it conveys. But why do we need special laws prohibiting certain statements about the past if their racist animus is already banned by other laws? However, one can also approach this issue from a different angle, by asking if it really matters which law is used to punish certain statements. The real question, therefore, might be not whether we need special laws to punish denial, but whether it should be punished at all.

Confronted with these difficulties, some jurists have tried a different tactic. There can scarcely be any absolute answers to the question of the legitimacy of memory laws in a democratic society, because democracies vary: "Free speech rights are highly culturally contingent."[57] Thus, American democracy gives priority to freedom of expression, while German tradition privileges human dignity and public order.[58] In principle,

---

[54] "Liberté pour l'histoire," *Libération*, December 13, 2005; Rémond, *Quand l'État se mêle de l'histoire*, p. 51.

[55] Elazar Barkan, *The Guilt of Nations: Restitution and Negotiating Historical Injustices* (New York: W.W. Norton, 2000); Antoine Garapon, *Peut-on réparer l'histoire? Colonisation, esclavage, Shoah* (Paris: Odile Jacob, 2008).

[56] Baruch, *Des lois indignes?*, pp. 99–169.

[57] Ronald J. Krotoszynski, Jr., *The First Amendment in Cross-Cultural Perspective* (New York: New York University Press, 2006), p. 214, and Linda O. Smiddy, "An Essay on Professor Fronza's Paper: Should Holocaust Denial Be Criminalized?," *Vermont Law Review* 30/3 (2006), p. 653.

[58] Robert A. Kahn, "Informal Censorship of Holocaust Revisionism in the United States and Germany," *George Mason University Civil Rights Law Journal* 9/1 (1998), pp. 125–149; John C. Knechtle, "Holocaust Denial and the Concept of Dignity in the European Union," *Florida State University Law Review* 36 (2008), pp. 41–66.

communitarianism favors restrictions on free speech, while libertarianism protects it.[59] As a rule, it is easier to limit freedom of expression in civil law countries than in common law countries. The latter (the United States, the United Kingdom, Canada) consistently resist the idea of criminalizing statements about the past, as is also true of those civil law countries that have been strongly influenced by the common law tradition (the Scandinavian countries, for example). However, some jurists believe that "the prohibition of some denials of crimes against humanity... is constitutional in most of the legal systems" that have other laws limiting freedom of expression.[60] The fact that many countries refuse to criminalize denial because they have other laws that provide for its punishment is a strong argument in support of this position.

This approach looks appealing, although relativizing democratic principles beyond certain limits risks undermining the very idea of democracy. The difficulty arises when we remember that legal frameworks can and do undergo permanent change. The First Amendment liberalism that is considered fundamental to the American legal tradition is in fact a recent development in the United States, where "periods of libertarian tendencies have alternated with periods of sharp regulation of speech."[61] One had to wait until the 1960s to see "First Amendment absolutism" emerging as a part of the broad cultural movement that liberalized American society.[62] The Brandenburg doctrine that embodies First Amendment absolutism regarding Holocaust denial was formulated in 1969.[63] What prevents us from supposing that this "absolutism" may not have triumphed permanently? This demonstrates the limits of legal relativism: we need criteria to determine what is acceptable in a democratic society.

[59] Ian Cram, *Contested Words: Legal Restrictions on Freedom of Speech in Liberal Democracies* (Aldershot: Ashgate, 2006), pp. 1–9, 97–138.

[60] Ludovic Hennebel and Thomas Hochmann, "Introduction: Questioning the Criminalization of Denials," in *Genocide Denials and the Law*, p. li. See also Fox and Nolte, "Intolerant Democracies"; Michel Troper, "La loi Gayssot et la constitution," *Annales: Histoire, Sciences Sociales* 54/6 (1999), pp. 1239–1255.

[61] Robert A. Kahn, "Cross-Burning, Holocaust Denial, and the Development of Hate Speech Law in the United States and Germany," *University of Detroit Mercy Law Review* 83/3 (2006), p. 166.

[62] Antony Lewis, "Keynote Address: Freedom of Speech and Incitement against Democracy," in *Freedom of Speech and Incitement against Democracy*, pp. 3–10; Knechtle, "Holocaust Denial and the Concept of Dignity in the European Union," pp. 46–47; Teachout, "Making 'Holocaust Denial' a Crime," pp. 677–678.

[63] Brandenburg doctrine holds that speech can be punished only if it "is directed to inciting or producing imminent lawless action and is likely to incite or produce such action." See Altman, "Freedom of Expression and Human Rights Law: The Case of Holocaust Denial," pp. 34–35.

Contextualizing the phenomenon of memory laws has yet another aspect, which is that similar acts committed in different societies are not necessarily considered equally dangerous. The recent history of certain types of crimes, or the lack of such history, affects the acceptance of prohibitions on the denial of those crimes.[64] Fascist movements have, as a rule, been more robust in civil law countries than in common law countries, and it therefore comes as no surprise that civil law countries are more apt to prohibit Holocaust denial, memory laws being widely perceived as an expression of state repentance.

The efficacy of memory laws is another difficult question. We have no reliable data to measure that efficacy, and localized examples have proven rather inconclusive. Thus, the deniers' activity in Germany decreased very considerably after the adoption of the memory law of 1994. But its center moved to the United States and Canada, and denial websites there are easily accessible from Germany. Moreover, in the 2000s, denial reemerged in popular music, especially in the former German Democratic Republic (GDR).[65] What does this tell us about the efficacy of memory laws?

From the 1980s on, the adoption of memory laws has been justified by "the growing assault on truth and memory" (to borrow from Deborah Lipstadt's title).[66] Is this assault still growing, though? If it is not, perhaps those limitations on freedom are no longer needed. But if it is (and far-right movements are indeed rising throughout the world), what should our conclusion be: that we need more laws to stop the assault or that laws cannot stop it? Perhaps it makes sense to concentrate efforts not on legislation but, rather, on education? "Memory and identity battles can hardly be resolved by legal engagement," writes Stiina Löytömäki.[67] Other researchers also believe that "genocide allegations may increase hostility, not diminish it."[68] Emanuela Fronza suggests that "European states should consider proceeding down the *long route* of encouraging

---

[64] Knechtle, "Holocaust Denial and the Concept of Dignity in the European Union," p. 52.

[65] Anthony Long, "Forgetting the Führer: The Recent History of the Holocaust Denial Movement in Germany," *Australian Journal of Politics and History* 48/1 (2002), pp. 72–84; Michael J. Bazyler, "Holocaust Denial Laws and Other Legislation Criminalizing Promotion of Nazism," p. 5: http://beta.genocidepreventionnow.org/Portals/0/docs/Bazyler-GPN-Original.pdf.

[66] Deborah Lipstadt, *Denying the Holocaust: The Growing Assault on Truth and Memory* (New York: Free Press/Macmillan, 1993).

[67] Stiina Löytömäki, "Law and Memory: The Politics of Victimhood," *Griffith Law Review* 21/1 (2012), pp. 1, 19.

[68] Robert M. Hayden, "'Genocide Denial' as Secular Heresy: A Critical Analysis with Reference to Bosnia," *Slavic review* 67/2 (2008), p. 406; Teachout, "Making 'Holocaust Denial' a Crime," pp. 689–91.

remembrance and commemoration rather than the short route of criminalizing negationism."[69]

A skeptical evaluation of law as an instrument for use by the politics of memory draws upon the idea of the incompatibility of legal truth and the "broader and more profound issues studied by historians."[70] This has to do in particular with the two differing ways of assessing the evidence: "History aims to tell the whole truth – jurisdictional concepts and procedural rules affect the creation of a complete historical record. ... A historian... would surely be more interested in the real truth than in the 'trial truth.'"[71] In addition, "whereas legal judgment is final..., neither memory nor history has any strong interest in finality."[72] Unsurprisingly, some historians have refused to give testimony at war criminals' trials because (they argue) their knowledge bears not upon the individuals in question but upon the historical phenomena.[73] As for the deniers' trials, their impact is questionable: one of the chief arguments against memory laws is that those trials help deniers propagate their theories.

Having examined arguments for and against memory laws, a historian might conclude that jurists are much more convincing in showing the complexity of the issue than in justifying any one solution for it. As I have already suggested, taking into account the evolution of the laws prohibiting certain statements about the past seems to back the critics of this legislation. Assessing memory laws historically may be important in the context of "the proliferation of new local hate speech laws" when "the 'minimalist' approach is losing out under a growing, punitive trend that is introducing new speech bans into national criminal codes."[74] Understanding where this "punitive trend" may lead cannot be a matter of purely legal analysis.

---

[69] Fronza, "The Punishment of Negationism," p. 625. See also her "The Criminal Protection of Memory," p. 181, and Ash, "Trials, Purges and History Lessons," p. 281.

[70] David Frazer, "Law's Holocaust Denial: State, Memory, Legality," in *Genocide Denials and the Law*, p. 7; Yan Thomas, "La vérité, le temps, le juge et l'historien," *Le Débat* 102/5 (1998), pp. 17–36; Antoon De Baets, "Conceptualising Historical Crimes," *Historein* 11 (2011), pp. 59–68.

[71] Fergal Gaynor, "Uneasy Partners – Evidence, Truth and History in International Trials," *Journal of International Criminal Justice* 10 (2012), pp. 1258, 1260.

[72] Mark Osiel, *Mass Atrocity, Collective Memory, and the Law* (New Brunswick, N.J.: Transaction Publishers, 1997), pp. 217, 220. Osiel believes it possible to "cultivate liberal memory" by legal means. On "the conflict between the 'time of jurisdiction' and the 'time of history'" see Berber Bevernage, *History, Memory, and State-Sponsored Violence: Time and Justice* (New York, London: Routledge, 2012).

[73] Henry Rousso, *The Haunting Past: History, Memory, and Justice in Contemporary France* (Philadelphia: University of Pennsylvania Press, 2002); Olivier Dumoulin, *Le rôle social de l'historien: De la chair au prétoire* (Paris: Albin Michel, 2003); Richard J. Evans, "History, Memory, and the Law: The Historian as Expert Witness," *History and Theory*, 41/3 (2002), pp. 326–345.

[74] Miklos Haraszti, "Foreword: Hate Speech and the Coming Death of the International Standard before It Was Born (Complaints of a Watchdog)," in *The Content and Context of Hate Speech:*

Assessing Memory Laws and Understanding the Rise of Memory

In many cases, a positive or negative assessment of memory laws by a given author correlates with his or her understanding of the rise of memory. This is particularly true of the historians' take on the issue. Most historians protest memory laws in the name of freedom of research, which they feel is endangered by such "Stalinist" regulations.[75] In contrast, those historians who welcome memory laws argue that this legislation does nothing to restrain their freedom.[76] (This said, though, even in France there have been cases in which professional historians with nothing in common with deniers were persecuted for their opinions of the issues of genocide.[77]) Another typical criticism of memory laws by historians is that they tend to be used in the interests of a manipulative kind of memory politics. Timothy Garton Ash imagines the "horse-trading behind closed doors in Brussels (Polish official to French counterpart: 'OK, we'll give you the Armenian genocide if you give us the Ukrainian famine.') Pure Gogol."[78] Yet, the main reason behind some of the historians' protests against these laws seems to lie elsewhere.

We will see in Chapter 1 that the rise of the memory of the Holocaust was crucial to the emergence of the age of memory, although the present-day fascination with the past has been conditioned by other factors of equal importance as well. Initially, the rise of memory was widely perceived as a sign of the growing emancipation of individuals and (especially subaltern) social groups from (often nationalist) state-sponsored history-based ideologies, as a powerful instrument for exploring one's own

---

Rethinking Regulation and Responses, eds. Michael Herz and Peter Molnar (Cambridge: Cambridge University Press, 2012), pp. xiv–xv.

[75] Timothy Garton Ash, "The Freedom of Historical Debate Is under Attack by the Memory Police," *Guardian*, October 16, 2008.

[76] Baruch, *Des lois indignes?*, p. 319.

[77] Those cases include the condemnation, in 1995, to a symbolic fine of one franc of Bernard Lewis, the eminent American historian of the Near East, for having rejected the qualification of the 1915 massacre of the Armenians as a genocide; and a 2005 case against a leading French historian of the slave trade Olivier Pétré-Grenouilleau, who argued that this phenomenon did not fall within the scope of the concept of genocide as defined in international law (see below, Chapter 2).

[78] Ash, "The Freedom of Historical Debate." Georges Mink suggests that by replacing "history" with "memory" in Paul Valéry's famous dictum, "History is the most dangerous product evolved from the chemistry of the intellect," one would "obtain... a fairly accurate representation of how memory manifests itself and is used at the present time." See his "Geopolitics, Reconciliation and Memory Games: For a New Social Memory Explanatory Paradigm," in *Clashes in European Memory: The Case of Communist Repression and the Holocaust*, eds. Muriel Blaive, Christian Gerbel, and Thomas Lindenberger (Innsbruck: Studien Verlag, 2011), p. 255.

subjectivity and identity.[79] Promoting the memory of the victims of past crimes and injustices was an important item on the agenda of the left, which includes a significant – and in many countries even predominant – segment of the historical profession. Originally, the obsession with the duty of memory and a broad support for Holocaust denial laws came largely from that political and cultural contingent. Characteristically, in France, most of those who in the 2000s became ardent opponents of laws about the past had hailed the adoption of the Gayssot Act in 1990.[80]

From the outset, however, some historians protested memory laws, while others doubted that the rise of memory was such a healthy phenomenon. In the 1980s and 1990s, the founding fathers of memory studies, David Lowenthal and especially Pierre Nora, had developed ironic narratives about the "heritage crusade" and the "era of commemoration."[81] Both diagnosed an obsessive nostalgia for the past as a hallmark of their time but were themselves nostalgic about the intellectual culture of the era that had preceded the memory boom. It was not by chance that they both saw the rise of memory as a consequence of the crisis of history (or the crisis of the future). In a sense, memory studies were born of cultural pessimism, although they were very soon overrun by devotees of the coming age of memory.

A few years later, when the rise of memory had already become a fait accompli, new voices began expressing concerns about its possible consequences. On the one hand, Tony Judt powerfully argued in 1992 that the postwar recovery in Europe had been made possible only by a tacit yet universal agreement to leave the past in the past and focus on building a better future.[82] This historical observation had an obvious implication: for all its humanistic intentions, focusing on the past may not always be an efficient cultural and political strategy – a claim that might sound overly Nietzschean, although for Judt it was essentially pragmatic. On the other hand, Charles C. Maier, famous in particular for his persuasive critical examination of the unwillingness of right-wing German politicians and

---

[79] To quote Michael S. Roth, "Memory seems to promise immediacy." See his *The Ironist's Cage: Memory, Trauma, and the Construction of History* (New York: Columbia University Press, 1995), p. 9.

[80] Rémond, *Quand l'État se mêle de l'histoire*, p. 14.

[81] In addition to the works quoted above, see Lowenthal, *The Heritage Crusade and the Spoils of History* (New York: Free Press, 1996).

[82] Tony Judt, "The Past is Another Country: Myth and Memory in Postwar Europe," *Daedalus* 21/4 (1992), pp. 83–118, and Judt, *Postwar: A History of Europe since 1945* (New York: Penguin Books, 2005), pp. 803–831.

intellectuals to face the legacy of the Nazi past head on,[83] unambiguously condemned what he labeled a "surfeit of memory":

> The surfeit of memory is a sign not of historical confidence but of a retreat from transformative politics. It testifies to the loss of a future orientation, of progress toward civic enfranchisement and growing equality. It reflects a new focus on narrow ethnicity as a replacement for encompassing communities based on constitutions, legislation and widening attributes of citizenship. The program for this new ethnicity... aspires preeminently to the recognition by other groups of its own sufferings and victimhood.[84]

As we see, criticism of the rise of memory, and not just fascination with it, was apt to emanate from the left. Since that time, the problem of too much versus not enough memory has become a recurrent theme of public debates and academic explorations.[85] Maier's denunciations were largely in line with Nora's analysis of the pernicious impact of the rise of memory on democracy and national identity in France. To Nora, the present-day memory is no longer a natural memory transmitted from one generation to another, but an "artificial hyper-reality" created by various agents of memory in the interests of political manipulation. Being essentially fragmented, this manipulative artificial memory can only divide a nation internally and undermine its identity.[86] More than that, since particularistic memories emphasize past tragedies, they deprive France of its "positive relation" to its history and stimulate a "national masochism" in the name of multiculturalism.[87]

This "anti-multimemorism" has largely informed the protest movement against memory laws in France. (By multimemorism, I mean a mnemonic situation typical of the age of multiculturalism, when multiple memories of historical events co-exist, and struggle for official recognition, in our societies.) It also explains why the declarative memory laws of the 2000s,

---

[83] Charles C. Maier, *The Unmasterable Past: History, Holocaust, and German National Identity* (Cambridge, Mass.: Harvard University Press, 1988).

[84] Charles C. Maier, "A Surfeit of Memory? Reflections on History, Melancholy and Denial," *History and Memory* 5/2 (1993), pp. 136–152.

[85] Gil Eyal, "Identity and Trauma: Two Forms of the Will to Memory," *History and Memory* 16/1 (2004), pp. 5–36; Ariana Macaya, "Un passé qui ne passe pas: les enjeux juridiques de la 'mémoire historique' en France et en Espagne," *Jurisdoctoria* 3 (2009), pp. 65–95.

[86] Pierre Nora, "General Introduction: Between Memory and History" [1984], in *Realms of Memory*, ed. Lawrence D. Kritzman (New York: Columbia University Press, 1996–1998), vol. 1, pp. 1–20; Rémond, *Quand l'État se mêle de l'histoire*, pp. 82–83.

[87] Nora, "Malaise dans l'identité historique," pp. 20, 23; Andreas Huyssen, "International Human Rights and the Politics of Memory: Limits and Challenges," *Criticism* 53/4 (2011), pp. 607–624; David Rieff, *In Praise of Forgetting: Historical Memory and Its Ironies* (New Haven, Conn.: Yale University Press, 2016).

rather than the normative Gayssot Act, were its main target. The Holocaust being perceived as a universal symbol of suffering, the law that
protected its memory could be said to express the nation's adherence to
universal values and its repentance for its part in this crime. By contrast,
laws recognizing other crimes were often viewed in the context of the
fragmentation of national identity rather than in terms of the nation's
access to universal values. René Rémond's answer to François Azouvi's
question about the potential dangers of the "legitimate recognition of
diversity" (read: the expansion of memory laws) makes this logic absolutely
obvious: "The process becomes dangerous when attachment to the particular overrides adherence to the general and prevents [a nation] from
opening toward the universal."[88] From this vantage point, the main
problem with the Gayssot Act was that it had created a precedent for the
proliferation of memory laws. Characteristically, those French historians
who supported (albeit with reservations) the memory laws insisted that all
of them "had been adopted in the name of universal values."[89]

   Similar objections to memory laws have also been raised outside
France.[90] Seeing the multiplication of memory laws through the lens of
a competition of victims naturally leads to their assessment as manipulative
electoral devices and their dismissal as a legitimate tool of democratic
history politics. But are there good grounds for such a gloomy view of
the present-day historical memory? Does not the memory boom, on the
contrary, hold out the promise of modern man's more human and democratic relationships with the past? In my first chapter, I will try to answer
those questions before turning to an analysis of memory laws in the
chapters that follow.

---

[88] Rémond, *Quand l'État se mêle de l'histoire*, p. 86.   [89] Baruch, *Des lois indignes?*, p. 319.
[90] Löytömäki, "Law and Memory: The Politics of Victimhood," pp. 1, 19.

CHAPTER I

The Rise of Memory and the Origins of Memory Laws

The Delaware Indians called the Hudson "the river that flows two ways," and salt water can in fact be pushed upriver well beyond the estuary, especially when the wind blows from the east. History is similar to the Hudson: just as water from the ocean continues to flow into the river for some time after the wind has changed direction, so the forces of inertia can act powerfully in history, even after the wind has begun to freshen from a different quarter.

The story of laws criminalizing statements about the past that this book is going to tell shows the Hudson River effect in action. This legislation came into being in the 1980s and 1990s and further developed in the 2000s and 2010s under the combined impact of factors that "logically" pertain to at least two different periods in the history of democracy. Indeed, the triumphant rise of liberal democracy in the 1960s and 1970s gave place to a far more complex development, which since the 1980s has involved both its further expansion and its incipient erosion. The factors that influenced the emergence and dissemination of memory laws include the end of the era of class struggle, the formation of the new culture of victimhood, and the triumph of the "last utopia" (as Samuel Moyn called the ideology of human rights);[1] the democratic revolution in historiography, the decay of "master narratives," and the rise of memory; and the fall of communism, the end of the postwar social-liberal consensus, and the emergence of neoliberalism, neoconservatism, and ethno-populism. This chapter will examine these quite heterogeneous factors whose interconnections have yet to be sufficiently appreciated, highlighting in particular the links between the evolution of Western historical consciousness and the emergence of laws criminalizing statements about the past.

---

[1] Samuel Moyn, *The Last Utopia: Human Rights in History* (Cambridge, Mass.: Belknap Press, 2010).

The need for memory laws is usually justified by the growth of Holocaust denial and the persisting fascist danger.[2] In 1982, the first draft of the first German memory law (adopted in 1985) specifically referred to a recent "substantial increase" of "right-extremist, especially neo-Nazi activities."[3] It would be a simplification, however, to project this *pragmatic* reasoning onto history and explain the origins of memory laws exclusively by the upsurge of far-right movements in the 1980s (and beyond). That said, this factor no doubt had a role to play. The criminalization of denial gradually developed in the 1970s and 1980s in response to a "growing assault on truth and memory," to use Deborah Lipstadt's expression.[4] But that was not the only *historical* cause of this legislation.

To be sure, in the second half of the 1970s denial became far more widespread and aggressive than ever before.[5] Its expansion was an indicator of important political and ideological changes and showed that anti-Semitism had found a new, apparently more "academic" form of expression. This was obviously linked to the rise of the neo-fascist movement, including the emergence of new far-right parties such as the French *Front National* whose leader, Jean-Marie Le Pen, was twice convicted of denial (in 1999 in Germany and in 2006 in France). However, denial was by no means a new phenomenon. It dates back, rather, to World War II, when it emerged in both far-right and far-left circles. It manifested again in the 1950s and 1960s in several scandalous episodes that Lipstadt considers in her book. But it was at that point a relatively marginal issue that attracted little public attention. It was not until the 1970s and 1980s that the Holocaust began to be commonly viewed as "the crime of crimes." Not until then would denial become a real political problem.

"Negationism... negates the ethical-political universe born after the Second World War," as Emanuela Fronza puts it.[6] But the formation of

---

[2] Michael Whine, "Expanding Holocaust Denial and Legislation against It," in *Extreme Speech and Democracy*, eds. Ivan Hare and James Weinstein (Oxford: Oxford University Press, 2009), p. 538.

[3] Quoted in Eric Stein, "History against Free Speech: The New German Law against the 'Auschwitz' – and Other – 'Lies'," *Michigan Law Review* 85/2 (1986), p. 305.

[4] Deborah Lipstadt, *Denying the Holocaust: The Growing Assault on Truth and Memory* (New York: Free Press/Macmillan, 1993).

[5] In 1975, Richard Harwood published his *Did Six Million Really Die?* Arthur Butz's *The Hoax of the Twentieth Century* and David Irving's *Hitler's War* came out in 1977. In 1978, Willis Carto founded the Institute for Historical Review, which was to become a leading center of the revisionist movement. In France, the same year witnessed the beginning of one of the most scandalous cases of Holocaust denial, *l'affaire Faurisson*, which ultimately led to the adoption, in 1990, of the Gayssot Act.

[6] Emanuela Fronza, "The Punishment of Negationism: The Difficult Dialogue between Law and Memory," *Vermont Law Review* 30/3 (2006), p. 625. See also Regula Ludi, *Reparations for Nazi Victims in Postwar Europe* (Cambridge: Cambridge University Press, 2012), p. 14.

that universe, which was largely rooted in the tragedies of war, was an outcome of several later developments rather than the war's direct consequence.

It is obvious that memory laws defend state-sponsored memories and that they initially came into being as a means of protecting the memory of the Holocaust. Consequently, the increasingly significant role of historical memory in present-day politics and the formation of a Holocaust-centered historical consciousness were sine qua non preconditions of memory laws. Had the Holocaust not emerged as an important historical symbol it would make little sense to criminalize its denial.[7]

The rise of memory in general (the "memory boom") and the rise of the memory of the Holocaust in particular informed the evolution of historical consciousness in the West in the 1970s and 1980s. Arguably, the feeling that the newly emerging form of Western historical consciousness had to be defended against all insults or even doubts was the most important impetus behind the memory laws.

Although the memory boom is a much broader phenomenon than the rise of the memory of the Holocaust, the latter was crucial to the emergence of the former. The memory boom includes the memories of the other tragic events of the twentieth century (e.g., the Gulag) as well as the growing interest in cultural heritage and the "heritage industry," which also dates back to the 1960s and especially the 1970s.[8] All these topics have been objects of scrupulous research and passionate debates. I will briefly summarize here the studies that are immediately relevant to a full understanding of the origins of memory laws.

The Memory of the Shoah

It is often claimed that "the Holocaust [is] at the heart of much of the current concern with memory."[9] The Shoah became central in the

---

[7] Cf. Tim Cole, *Selling the Holocaust: From Auschwitz to Schindler: How History Is Bought, Packaged, and Sold* (New York: Routledge, 1999), p. 188.

[8] Pierre Nora, *Les lieux de mémoire* (Paris: Gallimard, 1984–1992), vols. 1–7; David Lowenthal, *The Past Is a Foreign Country* (London: Cambridge University Press, 1985); Michael Kammen, *Mystic Chords of Memory: The Transformation of Tradition in American Culture* (New York: Alfred A. Knopf, 1991); Saul Friedländer, *Memory, History, and the Extermination of the Jews of Europe* (Bloomington: Indiana University Press, 1993); Kerwin L. Klein, "On the Emergence of Memory in Historical Discourse," *Representations* 69/1 (2000), pp. 127–150; and Jay Winter, "The Generation of Memory: Reflections on the 'Memory Boom' in Contemporary Historical Studies," *Bulletin of the German Historical Institute*, Washington DC, 27/3 (Fall 2000), 69–92.

[9] Jan-Werner Müller, "Introduction: The Power of Memory, the Memory of Power and the Power over Memory," in *Memory and Power in Post-War Europe: Studies in the Presence of the Past*, ed.

Western historical consciousness simultaneously with the beginning of the memory boom in the 1970s and 1980s. It was during this time that Nazism began to be viewed in a new way; perhaps surprisingly, the interpretation of Nazi crimes articulated during the Nuremberg trial was somewhat different from the way they are usually perceived today. In Jeffrey C. Alexander's words, "In the beginning, in April 1945, the Holocaust was not the 'Holocaust.'"[10] In the 1940s, "German guilt" was often seen through the prism of World War I and deemed to be a consequence of Prussian militarism.[11] At Nuremberg, emphasis was placed on the unleashing of an aggressive war rather than on crimes of a racist nature. Characteristically, the French prosecutor François de Menthon, who "was uncomfortable with the very concept of 'crimes against humanity'" and "preferred 'crimes against peace,'" "neglected to include [in his report] the annihilation of European Jewry as one of the Nazis' principal offenses."[12] This did not prevent the Tribunal from establishing the fact of the Holocaust, but the extermination of the Jews was by no means central to the Nuremberg notion of Nazi crimes. In the 1940s, the Shoah was, rather, perceived as one of the war's many tragedies.[13]

The advent of the Cold War made it difficult to publicize the fact of the Holocaust and, more generally, the idea of the unique enormity of Nazi crimes, one reason for that being the need to incorporate the Federal Republic of Germany into the system of anti-communist alliances.

Jan-Werner Müller (Cambridge: Cambridge University Press, 2002), p. 14; Andreas Huyssen, *Present Pasts: Urban Palimpsests and the Politics of Memory* (Stanford, Calif.: Stanford University Press, 2003), p. 99.

[10] Jeffrey C. Alexander "On the Social Construction of Moral Universals: The Holocaust from War Crime to Trauma Drama," *European Journal of Social Theory* 5/1 (2002), p. 6.

[11] Dan Diner, *Beyond the Conceivable: Studies on Germany, Nazism, and the Holocaust* (Berkeley: University of California Press, 2000), p. 176.

[12] Tony Judt, *Postwar: A History of Europe Since 1945* (New York: Penguin Books, 2005), p. 805; Peter Novick, *The Holocaust in American Life* (Boston: Houghton Mifflin, 2000), p. 29; Lawrence Douglas, "The Memory of Judgment: The Law, the Holocaust, and Denial," *History and Memory* 7/2 (1995), pp. 105–106; Daniel Levy and Nathan Sznaider, *The Holocaust and Memory in the Global Age* (Philadelphia: Temple University Press, 2006), p. 58; Michael Marrus, "The Holocaust at Nuremberg," *Yad-Vashem Studies* 26 (1998), p. 10. The Soviet prosecutor Roman Rudenko also avoided mentioning Jews and spoke instead of "Soviet citizens." See Nathalie Moine, "Defining 'War Crimes against Humanity' in the Soviet Union: Nazi Arson of Soviet Villages and the Soviet Narrative on Jewish and Non-Jewish Soviet War Victims, 1941–1947," *Cahiers du monde russe* 52/2 (2011), pp. 456–458. See also Donald Bloxham, *Genocide on Trial: War Crimes Trials and the Formation of Holocaust History and Memory* (Oxford: Oxford University Press, 2001), pp. 57–92, and Tony Kushner, *The Holocaust and the Liberal Imagination: A Social and Cultural History* (Oxford, Cambridge, Mass.: Blackwell, 1994).

[13] Omer Bartov, "The Holocaust as Leitmotif of the Twentieth Century," in *The Holocaust in International Perspective*, ed. Dagmar Herzog (Evanston, Ill.: Northwestern University Press, 2006), pp. 3–4.

Denazification began being curtailed in the late 1940s, and the rejection of Nazi ideology was paradoxically accompanied by "the political and social rehabilitation of former Nazis,"[14] although a handful of intellectuals such as Karl Jaspers and social democratic politicians such as Kurt Schumacher were still calling on Germans to reflect upon their guilt. But despite their efforts, the dominant memory of the war in Adenauer's Germany centered on German sufferings and the glorious deeds of the Wehrmacht. The Nazi leadership alone was blamed for the country's defeat and the war crimes, of which Germans were fully aware. The main goal of Adenauer's politics of memory was to "normalize" German history and break with the anti-Western tradition of German conservatism.[15] But by and large, the country's tragic past attracted relatively little attention. When referring to it, conservative and liberal politicians alike used the term "totalitarianism" or even "fascism" instead of "Nazism," to avoid any allusion to the unique character of German guilt.[16]

The final defeat did not prevent Germans from developing heroic memories of the war, as had also happened after World War I. This was not without parallels in other countries (including France), no matter how different their experience of the war had been. In France, as well as in other European countries that were occupied by the Nazis and owed their liberation to Russia, the United Kingdom, and the United States, the goal of the postwar politics of memory was "to turn the Allied victory of 1945 into a national victory."[17] This was not an easy task for many

[14] Devin O. Pendas, *The Frankfurt Auschwitz Trial, 1963–1965: Genocide, History, and the Limits of the Law* (Cambridge: Cambridge University Press, 2006), p. 17; Norbert Frei, *Adenauer's Germany and the Nazi Past: The Politics of Amnesty and Integration* [1996] (New York: Columbia University Press, 2002).

[15] Karl Jaspers in particular wrote: "We... should not pity ourselves as victims." See his *The Question of German Guilt* [1946] (New York: Capricorn Books, 1961), pp. 21, 114; Anson Rabinbach, *In the Shadow of Catastrophe: German Intellectuals between Apocalypse and Enlightenment* (Berkeley: University of California Press, 1997), pp. 129–165. See also Jeffrey Herf, *Divided Memory: The Nazi Past in the Two Germanys* (Cambridge, Mass.: Harvard University Press, 1997); Edgar Wolfrum, *Geschichte als Waffe: Vom Kaiserreich bis zur Wiedervereinigung* (Göttingen: Vandenhoeck & Ruprecht, 2001); Eric Langenbacher, "Changing Memory Regimes in Contemporary Germany?," *German Politics and Society* 21/3 (2003), pp. 46–68; Eric Langenbacher and Friederike Eigler, "Introduction: Memory Boom or Memory Fatigue in 21st Century Germany?" *German Politics and Society* 23/3 (2005), pp. 1–15; Jeffrey K. Olick, *In the House of the Hangman: The Agonies of German Defeat, 1943–1949* (Chicago, Ill.: The University of Chicago Press, 2005), particularly pp. 234–269; Alf Lüdtke "'Coming to Terms with the Past': Illusions of Remembering, Ways of Forgetting Nazism in West Germany," *Journal of Modern History* 65/3 (1993), pp. 542–572.

[16] Helmut Dubiel, *Niemand ist frei von der Geschichte: Die nationalsozialistische Herrschaft in den Debatten des Deutschen Bundestages* (Munich: Carl Hanser, 1999), p. 75.

[17] Pieter Lagrou, *The Legacy of Nazi Occupation: Patriotic Memory and National Recovery in Western Europe, 1945–1965* (Cambridge: Cambridge University Press, 2000), pp. 15, 29.

reasons, including the communists' attempts to capitalize on their central role in the resistance, to shift the blame for fascism onto capitalism, and to underline the USSR's decisive role in the victory over Germany.

In France, Charles de Gaulle promoted the myth of the French people united in its struggle for liberation. In that narrative, there was no place for more than a handful of collaborators or for the complicity of the French state and ordinary citizens in the extermination of the Jews.[18] Typologically, this heroic memory was similar to traditional war myths, including the memory of the Great War.[19] Those myths usually centered on patriotism, glory, sacrifices, brotherhood in arms, and the like, and, not surprisingly, the self-congratulatory narratives of both world wars tended to merge in the Gaullist resistance myth.[20] However, this "patriotic amalgamation of the two wars" was not without its problems, for World War II could not be viewed solely through the lens of the Great War.[21] In Italy, a similar narrative, focused on "the Christian community of those fallen for the fatherland," came to dominate public memory, as the Christian Democrats established their monopoly over official commemorations of the war.[22] A little later, it was complemented by the narrative of the resistance to fascism, which was promoted by Italian communists. Patriotic resistance myths also developed in Austria (officially recognized by the Allies as Hitler's first victim as early as 1943), Belgium, Denmark, Norway, the Netherlands, and even neutral Switzerland.[23] In Sweden,

---

[18] Henry Rousso, *The Vichy Syndrome: History and Memory in France since 1944* (Cambridge, Mass.: Harvard University Press, 1994); Johann Michel, *Gouverner les mémoires: Les politiques mémorielles en France* (Paris: Presses Universitaires de France, 2010); Olivier Wieviorka, *La Mémoire désunie: Le souvenir politique des années sombres, de la Libération à nos jours* (Paris: Seuil, 2010).

[19] On the origins of romantic images of the war and their transformations in the twentieth century, see Omer Bartov, *Murder in Our Midst: The Holocaust, Industrial Killing, and Representation* (Oxford: Oxford University Press, 1996), pp. 15–50.

[20] Serge Barcellini, "L'État républicain, acteur de la mémoire: Des morts pour la France aux morts à cause de la France," in *Les guerres de mémoire*, eds. Pascal Blanchard and Isabelle Veyrat-Masson (Paris: La Découverte, 2008), p. 213.

[21] Lagrou, *The Legacy of Nazi Occupation*, p. 3; Jay Winter, *Sites of Memory, Sites of Mourning: The Great War in European Cultural History* [1995] (Cambridge: Cambridge University Press, 2014), p. 229; George L. Mosse, *Fallen Soldiers: Reshaping the Memory of the World Wars* (New York: Oxford University Press, 1990), pp. 201–225; and Rémi Dalisson, *Les guerres et la mémoire: Enjeux identitaires et célébrations de guerre en France de 1870 à nos jours* (Paris: CNRS Éditions, 2013).

[22] Claudio Fogu, "*Italiani brava gente*: The Legacy of Fascist Historical Culture on Italian Politics of Memory," in *The Politics of Memory in Postwar Europe*, eds. Richard Ned Lebow, Wulf Kansteiner, and Claudio Fogu (Durham, N.C.: Duke University Press, 2006), pp. 152–153.

[23] Heidemarie Uhl, "From Victim Myth to Co-Responsibility Thesis: Nazi Rule, World War II, and the Holocaust in Austrian memory," in *The Politics of Memory in Postwar Europe*, pp. 41, 47, 57; Regula Ludi, "What Is So Special about Switzerland? Wartime Memory as a National Ideology," *ibid.*, p. 212; Lagrou, *The Legacy of Nazi Occupation*; Lagrou, "The Victims of Genocide and

which also stood outside the war, the self-congratulatory narrative of the "small-country realism" occasionally implied a "heroicisation of adjustment" to Nazi Germany.[24] A cult of fallen soldiers was also typical of Israel, where "the hero fallen on a battlefield to protect his country [became] the central figure of the Israeli renaissance.... The genocide was silenced, because it undermined the glorious image of a victorious and rapidly developing people."[25]

Of course, tragedies of war were not, and could hardly be, totally erased from memory when the wounds were still so fresh; the main function of those tragedies in the context of heroic myths, rather, was to highlight heroism, while the heroic myths themselves made tragedies meaningful by presenting them as sacrifices.[26]

In the 1950s and even 1960s, whitewashing the national past was still a prevailing strategy of the ruling elites, which remained attached to nineteenth-century national narratives. The choice of that strategy was facilitated by the fact that during the "thirty glorious years" of postwar economic growth, most Europeans were inclined to leave the past in the past and concentrate on the "production" of the future, which promised to exceed their most optimistic expectations. A focus on the crimes of the past was scarcely compatible with the optimism of the future-oriented postwar generation and hardly possible in the framework of traditional national narratives. In the United States, paying too much attention to German war

National Memory: Belgium, France, and the Netherlands, 1945–1965," *Past and Present* 154 (1997), pp. 181–222; Lagrou, "The Politics of Memory: Resistance as a Collective Myth in Post-War France, Belgium and the Netherlands, 1945–1965," *European Review* 11/4 (2003), pp. 527–549; Henrik Stenius, Mirja Österberg, and Johan Östling, eds., *Nordic Narratives of the Second World War: National Historiographies Revisited* (Lund: Nordic Academic Press, 2011).

[24] Bo Stråth, "Nordic Foundation Myths after 1945: A European Context," in *Nordic Narratives of the Second World War*, p. 159. See also Johan Östling, "The Rise and Fall of Small-State Realism: Sweden and the Second World War," *ibid.*, pp. 127–148.

[25] Esther Benbassa, "Politisation de la mémoire du génocide des Juifs en Israël et en diaspora": http://centrealbertobenveniste.org/formail-cab/uploads/Politisation-de-la-memoire-du-genocide-des-Juifs-en-Israel-et-en-diaspora.pdf; Benbassa, *La Souffrance comme identité* (Paris: Fayard, 2007); Amos Elon, "The Politics of Memory," *New York Review of Books*, October 7, 1993. According to Elon, in the 1950s, the Holocaust was perceived as a shameful aspect of Jewish history. Cf. Michel Chaumont, *La concurrence des victimes* (Paris: La Découverte, 1997), chapter 1: "The Time of Shame (1945–1967)."

[26] Characteristically, Israel "constituted in 1959 a national Remembrance Day for the Holocaust and its Heroism." See Alon Confino, "Remembering the Second World War, 1945–1965: Narratives of Victimhood and Genocide," *Cultural Analysis* 4 (2005), p. 48; Cole, *Selling the Holocaust*, p. 122; Mikael Tossavainen, "Calendar, Context and Commemoration: Establishing an Israeli Holocaust Remembrance Day," in *Echoes of the Holocaust: Historical Cultures in Contemporary Europe*, eds. Klas-Göran Karlsson and Ulf Zander (Lund: Nordic Academic Press, 2003), pp. 81–114.

crimes could also be seen as inappropriate in the context of memories of the atomic bombs dropped on Hiroshima and Nagasaki.[27]

This does not, however, mean that the Holocaust was forgotten in the aftermath of the war. On the contrary, recent research has convincingly demonstrated that information about the Shoah was widely available in the late 1940s and the 1950s, and some important testimonies (such as Anne Frank's *Diary*) were published and widely read. Meanwhile, the memory of the Holocaust was gradually deflating the heroic myths of the war.[28] In 1961, Eichmann's trial in Jerusalem attracted the attention of international public opinion to the extermination of the Jews as one of the main Nazi crimes.[29] But by and large the Holocaust, although by no means ignored, remained peripheral to Western memories of the war.[30]

Historians disagree on whether this relative lack of attention to the Holocaust was also characteristic of European and American Jews and whether Holocaust survivors typically opted to remain silent about their traumatic experience because willing audiences were hard to find. Most likely, the situation varied from place to place, and in many Jewish communities (e.g., in Brooklyn) the topic of the Holocaust was by no means kept under wraps.[31] But drawing attention to the specificity of the Jewish case might impede the integration of the Jews into national communities, a goal that in the aftermath of the war was still to be achieved in both the United States and Western Europe. And society at large was, in

---

[27] Lawrence Baron, "The Holocaust and American Public Memory, 1945–1960," *Holocaust and Genocide Studies* 17/1 (2003), p. 63.

[28] Enzo Traverso, *Le Passé, mode d'emploi: Histoire, mémoire, politique* (Paris: La Fabrique éditions, 2005), p. 86.

[29] Lawrence Douglas, *The Memory of Judgment: Making Law and History in the Trials of the Holocaust* (New Haven, Conn.: Yale University Press, 2001), pp. 97–182.

[30] Saul Friedländer, "History, Memory, and the Historian: Facing the Shoah," in *Disturbing Remains: Memory, History, and Crisis in the Twentieth Century*, eds. Michael S. Roth and Charles G. Salas (Los Angeles: The Getty Research Institute, 2001), p. 273; Friedländer, "History, Memory, and the Historian: Dilemmas and Responsibilities," *New German Critique* 80 (2000), p. 5; Novick, *The Holocaust in American Life*.

[31] Baron, "The Holocaust and American Public Memory, 1945–1960"; Hasia R. Diner, *We Remember with Reverence and Love: American Jews and the Myth of Silence after the Holocaust, 1945–1962* (New York: New York University Press, 2009); David Cesarini and Eric J. Sundquist, eds. *After the Holocaust: Challenging the Myth of Silence* (London: Routledge, 2012); Alon Confino, *Germany as a Culture of Remembrance: Promises and Limits of Writing History* (Chapel Hill: University of North Carolina Press, 2006), p. 239; Levy and Sznaider, *The Holocaust and Memory in the Global Age*, p. 70; Johann Michel, *Gouverner les mémoires: Les politiques mémorielles en France* (Paris: Presses Universitaires de France, 2010), p. 75–76; Annette Wieviorka, *Déportation et génocide: Entre la mémoire et l'oubli* (Paris: Hachette, 2000); François Azouvi, *Le Mythe du grand silence: Auschwitz, les Français, la mémoire* (Paris: Fayard, 2012); and Henry Rousso, *Face au passé: Essais sur la mémoire contemporaine* (Paris: Belin, 2016), p. 38–40.

turn, not ready to recognize the Jews as the main victims of Nazism, not least because anti-Semitism remained relatively strong in the West in the immediate postwar years.

In many respects, the 1950s closely resembled the interwar period with its furious class struggles, nationalism, and the looming threat of world war. New historical forces such as postwar economic growth, the social-liberal consensus, the welfare state, and the "never again" mentality[32] were already operative, but the old habits of thought and behavior remained strong. The age of class struggle in Western history was gradually receding into the past, but the wars in Korea and Algeria, McCarthyism, the Soviet invasion of Hungary, and the Cuban missile crisis showed that this past was not about to make a speedy exit.

By the 1960s, the social-liberal consensus began bearing fruit, as the democratization of political, social, and cultural life entered a decisive (although still very difficult) stage. Symptomatically, the development of anti-fascist legislation, which had begun in the 1940s but had been interrupted by the Cold War, resumed in the 1960s. That decade also witnessed a rising awareness of the Holocaust in Western Europe and America.[33] But it was not until the 1970s and 1980s that the Shoah began to be perceived as "the crime of crimes," in step with the development of a much more democratic and humanistic form of historical consciousness. Holocaust-centered historical narratives were born in the United States, Germany, and France, before spreading to other countries. The "Americanization" of the Holocaust (its integration into the American national memory) was largely responsible for its transformation into a universal symbol of horror and for the emerging recognition of the unique character of the Shoah.[34] But in some

[32] On "the distinction between the two postcatastrophic epochs" that followed the first and second world wars, see Rabinbach, *In the Shadow of Catastrophe*.
[33] Samuel Moyn, *A Holocaust Controversy: The Treblinka Affair in Postwar France* (Waltham, Mass.: Brandeis University Press, 2005).
[34] Alvin Rosenfeld, "The Americanization of the Holocaust," in *Thinking about the Holocaust after Half a Century* (Bloomington: Indiana University Press, 1997), pp. 119–150. For Rosenfeld, the Americanization of the Holocaust creates the danger of relativizing it and transforming it into an "empty and all but meaningless abstraction" (p. 131). See also his *The End of the Holocaust* (Bloomington: Indiana University Press, 2011). Other scholars have a more positive view of the Americanization of the Holocaust. Daniel Levy and Nathan Sznaider argue that "Holocaust memories have taken on a cosmopolitan scope because they enable diverse oppressed groups to recognize themselves in the role of Jewish victims." See their *The Holocaust and Memory in the Global Age*, pp. 12, 46. See also David B. MacDonald, *Identity Politics in the Age of Genocide: The Holocaust and Historical Representation* (London: Routledge, 2008), p. 36 and Efraim Sicher, "The Future of the Past: Countermemory and Postmemory in Contemporary Post-Holocaust Narratives," *History and Memory* 12/2 (2000), pp. 56–91.

countries, most notably in Scandinavia, patriotic narratives remained almost undisturbed until the 1990s.[35]

Various factors contributed to the belated rise of the memory of the Shoah. Some historians explain this change by a return of a previously suppressed traumatic memory, which is described as occurring typically in the second generation.[36] One of the strengths of this approach is that it postulates an internal dynamic in the memory of the Holocaust, which could also aid in explaining broader phenomena such as the collapse of future-oriented ideologies, the postmodern crisis of rationality, and the rise of memory. From this vantage point, the rise of the memory of the Shoah presents as a critically important aspect in, if not the cause of, the memory boom. The hypothesis that the tragic experience of World War II and the totalitarian regimes has undermined belief in human nature and the progress of reason seems very plausible indeed.[37] The centrality of the debates over the Holocaust, trauma, victims, and testimonies at the wellsprings of the memory boom adds credence to this explanation.[38]

---

[35] A Holocaust-centered memory emerged in Scandinavia under the influence of the European Union's politics of memory, the Stockholm International Forum on the Holocaust in 2000 marking an important turning point. See Henrik Stenius, Mirja Österberg, and Johan Östling, "Introduction," in *Nordic Narratives of the Second World War*, pp. 16–17.

[36] Alexander and Margarete Mitscherlich, in their *The Inability to Mourn* [1967] (New York: Grove Press, 1975), provide a classical psychological explanation of the fact that in the aftermath of the war, most Germans demonstrated a "diffuse indifference" with regard to the past and instead of "working [it] out" focused their energies on "the explosive development of German industry." However, speaking about the 1960s, they emphasize "a markedly improved ability to sympathize with other nations" (pp. 10, 13, 17, 26). See also Cathy Caruth, *Unclaimed Experience: Trauma, Narrative and History* (Baltimore, Md.: Johns Hopkins University Press, 1996); Michael S. Roth, *Memory, Trauma, and History: Essays on Living with the Past* (New York: Columbia University Press, 2012), pp. 77–103; Dominick LaCapra, *Representing the Holocaust: History, Theory, Trauma* (Ithaca, N.Y.: Cornell University Press, 1994); LaCapra, *History and Memory after Auschwitz* (Ithaca, N.Y.: Cornell University Press, 1998); LaCapra, *Writing History, Writing Trauma* (Baltimore, Md.: John Hopkins University Press, 2001); Helen Epstein, *Children of the Holocaust: Conversations with Sons and Daughters of Survivors* [1979] (New York: Penguin Books, 1988); and Aaron Hass, *In the Shadow of the Holocaust: The Second Generation* (Ithaca, N.Y.: Cornell University Press, 1990).

[37] Gabrielle M. Spiegel, "Orations of the Dead/Silences of the Living: The Sociology of the Linguistic Turn," in *The Past as Text: The Theory and Practice of Medieval Historiography* (Baltimore, Md.: Johns Hopkins University Press, 1997), pp. 29–43; Alexander, "On the Social Construction of Moral Universals," pp. 30–32. Cf. Alan Milchman and Alan Rosenberg, "Postmodernism and the Holocaust," in *Postmodernism and the Holocaust* (Amsterdam: Rodopi, 1998), pp. 1–22, and Robert Eaglestone, *The Holocaust and the Postmodern* (Oxford: Oxford University Press, 2004). The view of the Holocaust as a "caesura in civilization" (*Zivilisationsbruch*) harkens back to the works of Theodor Adorno and Hannah Arendt, but the expression itself became popular only in the 1980s. See Dan Diner, "Den Zivilisationsbruch erinnern: Über Entstehung und Geltung eines Begriffs," in *Zivilisationsbruch und Gedächtniskultur: Das 20. Jahrhundert in der Erinnerung des beginnenden 21. Jahrhunderts*, ed. Heidemarie Uhl (Innsbruck: StudeinVerlag, 2003), pp. 17–34; *Zivilisationsbruch: Denken nach Auschwitz*, ed. Dan Diner (Frankfurt am Main: Fischer, 1988).

[38] Annette Wieviorka, *The Era of the Witness* [1998] (Ithaca, N.Y.: Cornell University Press, 2006).

To be sure, the chronological gap between the discovery of Nazi crimes in the 1940s and the crisis of the future in the 1970s could call this hypothesis into doubt. The idea of a suppression/return cycle has appeal precisely because it solves that difficulty. But another issue remains: the internalist explanation of the memory of the Holocaust is based on the psychologically *necessary* character of this cycle, which presumably implies a sharp contrast between the phases of suppression and return. However, as already mentioned, in light of the recent research this contrast does not appear as sharp or as universal in scope as some historians have believed. And the very use of the concept of trauma with regard to collective historical phenomena also, of course, remains problematic.[39] Many scholars question the psychoanalytic account of Western historical consciousness and maintain that the formation of the Shoah-centered memory can be better explained by social, political, and cultural causes, including generational change and the struggle between competing narratives about the past.[40]

According to Peter Novick, the 1970s marked a profound change in American culture, namely "the decline... of the integrationist ethos (which focused on what Americans have in common and what unites us) and its replacement by a particularist ethos (which stresses what differentiates and divides us)."[41] Various ethnic and cultural groups became much more interested in the issues of identity, while at the same time religion(s) and traditional culture(s) were in decay. According to Novick, the

---

[39] Wulf Kansteiner, "Genealogy of a Category Mistake: A Critical Intellectual History of the Cultural Trauma Metaphor," *Rethinking History* 8/2 (2004), pp. 193–221; Andreas Huyssen, *Present Pasts*, p. 8; Confino, "Remembering the Second World War, 1945–1965," p. 50; and Confino, *Germany as a Culture of Remembrance*, p. 236. Confino, if I read him correctly, doubts that psychological explanations are useful in history in general, but he also has a strong argument regarding the concrete case of postwar German memory: for repression to occur, there has to be a consciousness of guilt to be repressed, while most Germans did not feel any guilt in the aftermath of the war but viewed themselves as victims. See also Régine Robin-Maire "The Bifurcations of Memory," in *Politics of Collective Memory: Cultural Patterns of Commemorative Practices in Post-War Europe*, eds. Sophie Wahnich, Barbara Lasticova, and Andrej Findor (Vienna: LIT Verlag, 2008), p. 30. "Internalist" interpretations of the dynamics of the memory of the Shoah do not have to be framed in psychoanalytical terms: emphasis can simply be laid on the impossibility of forgetting atrocities. See Gavriel D. Rosenfeld, "A Looming Crash or a Soft Landing? Forecasting the Future of the Memory 'Industry,'" *The Journal of Modern History* 81/1 (2009), pp. 126, 128, 130; Aleida Assmann, *Der lange Schatten der Vergangenheit: Erinnerungskultur und Geschichtspolitik* (München: C.H. Beck, 2006), p. 28.

[40] Herf, *Divided Memory*, p. 374; Novick, *The Holocaust in American Life*; Eric Langenbacher, "Changing Memory Regimes in Contemporary Germany?," pp. 49–51; Harold Marcuse, *Legacies of Dachau: The Uses and Abuses of a Concentration Camp, 1933–2001* (Cambridge: Cambridge University Press, 2001), pp. 290–325.

[41] Novick, *The Holocaust in American Life*, pp. 6–7.

Holocaust, seen as "the only common denominator of American Jewish identity," "has filled a need for a consensual symbol." The Holocaust's enhanced status in memory was also suggested by an emerging "victim culture," defined as "a change in the attitude toward victimhood from a status all but universally shunned and despised to one often eagerly embraced."[42] The new form taken by the Jewish memory of the Holocaust was embraced by society at large because it corresponded to the new cultural climate. In this interpretation, the rise of the memory of the Holocaust appears as a consequence, not the cause, of the memory boom.

Novick was rightly criticized for having exaggerated the manipulative aspects of the Jewish focus on the memory of the Shoah since the 1970s and for having overestimated the contrast between the postwar "silence" about the Holocaust and its more recent promotion to the forefront of Western memory.[43] But his theory does reveal the links between the transformations of the memory of the Holocaust and several other cultural and political processes such as the evolution of Jewish identity in the United States, the emergence of the new victim culture, and the memory boom. Most importantly, it opens the way to an understanding of the memory of the Holocaust not as a "German (or European) story," but, rather, in the context of global transformations such as decolonization, the civil rights movement, and the growing significance of the problem of racism. As Michael Rothberg argues,

> Early Holocaust memory emerged in dialogue with the dynamic transform-ations and multifaceted struggles that define the era of decolonization. The period between 1954 and 1962 contains both the rise of consciousness of the Holocaust as an unprecedented form of modern genocide and the coming to national consciousness and political independence of many of the subjects of European colonialism.[44]

However, European colonialism and American slavery were by no means two unrelated stories. In the United States, the second half of the 1960s and the 1970s did indeed witness a rise of particularism in which

---

[42] *Ibid.*, pp. 7–8.
[43] Hasia R. Diner, *We Remember with Reverence and Love*, p. 8; Cesarini and Sundquist, eds., *Challenging the Myth of Silence.*
[44] Michael Rothberg, *Multidirectional Memory: Remembering the Holocaust in the Age of Decolonization* (Stanford, Calif.: Stanford University Press, 2009), pp. 7, 309. See also Huyssen, *Present Pasts*, p. 11. However, as Confino argues, parallels between the Holocaust and colonialism were, until very recently, difficult to draw, largely because of the emphasis on the Holocaust's uniqueness. See his *Foundational Pasts: The Holocaust as Historical Understanding* (Cambridge: Cambridge University Press, 2012), pp. 29–30.

various racial, ethnic, and religious communities refused to embrace the
strategy of integration into the "melting pot" of American society, one of
the reasons for that being that the price to be paid for integration could
include the loss of group identity. The first successes of the civil rights
movement in the United States in 1964 and 1965 were of fundamental
importance to Jewish organizations, which borrowed some of the language
and approaches of African-American leaders, who had in their turn been
influenced by the historical experience of American Jewry, which they
often perceived as a paradigmatic minority.[45] Some researchers even speak
of a "grand alliance of the Jews and the Blacks in their struggle for civil
rights in the 1950s and early 1960s."[46]

The new particularist ethos was by no means exclusively typical of
American Jews. For most of them, moreover, the quest for integration
did not directly involve a repudiation of the group identity (although there
was some tension between these two tendencies). The Holocaust could
thus be conceived simultaneously as a universal symbol of evil and as the
unique tragedy of the Jewish people, a combination that remains an
important feature of the memory of the Shoah. Particularism probably
had more to do with the rise of memory in general than with the memory
of the Holocaust. The memory boom entailed a gradual divorce between
the universal and the particular with regard to the ways in which the
problems of identity were confronted. Unsurprisingly, the concept of
identity became popular in the West only with the beginning of the
memory boom. In this context, the memory of the Holocaust appears as
a refuge for universal values, even if the particularist ethos had, paradoxically, influenced its development.

The links between the civil rights movement, the evolution of the
American Jewish identity, and the memory of the Holocaust were critically
important to the changing notion of Nazi crimes, which were coming to
be seen as crimes of a racist nature rather than as war crimes. There were,
furthermore, obvious parallels between the American civil rights movement and the national liberation movements in Third World countries.
The collapse of the colonial empires made the problems of memory and

---

[45] Eric Goldstein, *The Price of Whiteness: Jews, Race, and American Identity* (Princeton, N.J.: Princeton
University Press, 2006), pp. 211–216, 223–225; Marc Dollinger, *Quest for Inclusion: Jews and
Liberalism in Modern America* (Princeton, N.J.: Princeton University Press, 2000), pp. 5, 10.

[46] Nicole Lapierre, *Causes communes: Des Juifs et des Noirs* (Paris: Stock, 2011), p. 3. See also
MacDonald, *Identity Politics in the Age of Genocide*, pp. 19–20. This alliance did not last forever,
though, and already in the mid-1960s there were signs of a growing misunderstanding, and
occasionally even hostility, between the two groups.

identity central for newly emerging states (although the Cold War, which stimulated thinking in terms of binary oppositions, provisionally tempered those developments).[47] And the formation of the post-colonial system foregrounded racism as one of the central issues requiring resolution, which was no easy task. Anti-racist laws were, predictably, passed in many countries in the 1960 and 1970s, to prohibit discrimination and insulting behavior with allusion to race, nationality, and religion. This legislation was an extension of the anti-fascist laws of the 1940s. The Shoah became central to the new notion of Nazi crimes in the context of the worldwide struggle against racism, and its memory was a powerful argument in favor of the anti-racist laws that laid the groundwork for Holocaust denial legislation. Tellingly, most memory laws are today incorporated into the parts of the penal codes that forbid hate speech and intolerant behavior that alludes to race and/or nationality.

The Social-Liberal Consensus and the Culture of Victimhood

Let us now turn to victim culture, which Novick sees as an important premise of Holocaust-centered memory. Other scholars suggest the opposite, that the memory of the Shoah was crucial to the emergence of the new culture of victimhood.[48] I believe it would be fair to say that sympathies toward victims have their origins in much broader social transformations, for all that the Holocaust did provide an iconic model of victimhood that has informed and legitimized the emerging victim culture (and what Jeffrey K. Olick calls a "public culture of collective remorse").[49] In the 1960s and 1970s, various minorities began taking pride in their subaltern status and asserting claims for the reparation of historical injustices. These subaltern groups included categories as different as women, gays, lesbians, ethnic communities, and entire nations, which claimed the status of victims of gender inequality, colonialism, slavery, war crimes, deportations, occupation, and so on.

---

[47] For Huyssen, the memory boom rooted in the decolonization process of the 1960s was "energized" at the turn of the 1980s "by the ever-broadening debate about the Holocaust." See his *Present Pasts*, p. 12.

[48] Müller, "Introduction: The Power of Memory, the Memory of Power and the Power over Memory," p. 14. See also Carolyn J. Dean, *The Fragility of Empathy after the Holocaust* (Ithaca, N.Y.: Cornell University Press, 2004), p. 4. On the origins of the culture of victimhood, see Robert Elias, *The Politics of Victimization: Victims, Victimology, and Human Rights* (Oxford: Oxford University Press, 1986).

[49] Jeffrey K. Olick, *The Politics of Regret: On Collective Memory and Historical Responsibility* (New York: Routledge, 2007), p. 13.

The formation of the victim culture was part of the democratization of Western societies and the rise of the welfare state, which was based upon a new form of "social contract" otherwise known as the social-liberal consensus. This "class compromise between labor and capital"[50] in the leading capitalist countries owed much to the danger of socialist revolutions that could be supported by the Soviet Union, whose power and international prestige peaked in the aftermath of the war. As a result of the postwar economic growth and the redistribution of national income in the interests of the middle, and to some extent the lower, classes, the epoch of class struggle in the West came to an end. Never before had the proportion of national income controlled by the upper classes been as low as during those "thirty glorious years."[51] The fear of, and disdain toward, the oppressed classes[52] were as immaterial in the new context as calls for revolutionary violence and indifference toward its victims. The stockpiles of social hatred that had accumulated over the course of centuries and largely determined the political climate in the interwar period and the immediate postwar years were rapidly diminishing in the West. Humanistic attitudes, including compassion for the disadvantaged, became far more prominent in Western public life than they had ever been before. A little later, in the somewhat different climate of the 1970s, these attitudes gave rise to the ideology of human rights. Parallel to that, the politics of détente began a significant "warming" of the international Cold War climate.

In the nineteenth and the first half of the twentieth centuries, class inequality was normally considered the main form of social injustice, Marxism supplying the most elaborate theoretical foundation of this view. Although diversification of the forms of victimhood and multiplication of victim categories since the 1960s implied both rejection of the class-centered revolutionary theory and continuation of the struggle of subaltern groups to assert their interests, the victimization discourse was largely framed in Marxism-inspired terms. In the 1960s and 1970s, many Marxists too reconsidered their narrow economic focus, in light of which all social distinctions presented as a result of class inequalities. Identity, culture, and subjectivity replaced the dictatorship of the proletariat as the Marxists' new battle cries, in yet another manifestation of the democratic

[50] David Harvey, *A Brief History of Neoliberalism* (Oxford: Oxford University Press, 2005), p. 10.

[51] Thomas Piketty, *Capital in the Twenty-First Century* (Cambridge, Mass., London: Belknap Press, 2014).

[52] On the educated elites' traditional disdain toward the oppressed classes, see Yegor Gaidar, *Russia: A Long View* (Cambridge, Mass.: MIT Press, 2012), p. 25.

and humanistic spirit that typified the period following the age of class struggle.[53]

The subaltern groups' movements contributed powerfully to the memory boom, an essential component of which were formerly suppressed "counter-memories."[54] The new concept of victimhood was quite broad and referred to victims of state-sponsored violence, social inequalities, and ordinary crimes (including rapes),[55] and was at the same time strongly associated with collective identities and cultural traumas. A sine qua non of the new victim culture was the victimization of the past, which is why memory laws can be seen as the ultimate expression of this culture. Most raise the memory of the victims to the rank of a nation's official memory and protect it against the memory of the perpetrators. Johann Michel describes the current form of French historical consciousness, which came to replace the postwar patriotic narratives in the 1970s, as a *régime victimo-mémoriel*,[56] a coinage that aptly emphasizes the connection between the rise of memory and the culture of victimhood.[57] With regard to World War II, victims replaced heroes as central protagonists of war narratives in the West.[58]

A corollary of the victims' rise to prominence was that some countries and social groups had to accept the role of perpetrators. Thus, "in the 1980s... a critical mass of Germans in positions of public influence... accepted that their national collective had been perpetrators, not victims."[59] The "guilt of nations" was more and more characteristically acknowledged (although not without strong resistance) by those nations themselves. Public apologies by state leaders for those states' past crimes

---

[53] Perry Anderson, *Considerations on Western Marxism* [1976] (London: Verso, 1979), pp. 75–94.

[54] Marc Ferro, *L'histoire sous surveillance: Science et conscience de l'histoire* (Paris: Calmann-Lévy, 1985), pp. 71–131.

[55] Alyson M. Cole, *The Cult of True Victimhood: From the War on Welfare to the War on Terror* (Stanford, Calif.: Stanford University Press, 2007).

[56] Johann Michel, "L'institutionalisation du crime contre l'humanité et l'avènement du régime victimo-mémoriel en France," *Canadian Journal of Political Science* 43/3 (2011), pp. 663–684.

[57] Alon Confino views heroic myths and the victimization of the past as two main aspects of the memory of World War II rather than two consecutive stages of its development. See his "Remembering the Second World War, 1945–1965," p. 52, 48. However, the relative importance of heroism and tragedies changed over time, and prior to the emergence of the new culture of victimhood in the 1960s and 1970s, tragedies were, in the light of heroic war myths, typically interpreted as sacrifices.

[58] Olivier Wieviorka, *La Mémoire désunie*, pp. 154–155, 186. Martin Sabrow also speaks about "the post-heroic age of memory." See his "The Post-Heroic Memory Society: Models of Historical Narration in the Present," in *Clashes in European Memory: The Case of Communist Repression and the Holocaust*, eds. Muriel Blaive, Christian Gerbel, and Thomas Lindenberger (Innsbruck: Studien Verlag, 2011), p. 92.

[59] Marcuse, *Legacies of Dachau*, p. 372.

became a typical expression of the cultural and political climate of the "age of apologies" (Jacques Chirac's 1995 speech on France's responsibility for the deportations of Jews being perhaps the best-known example).[60] The politics of retribution for past injustices that began in the aftermath of the war reached an unprecedented scale in the 1990s and 2000s.[61]

In the 1990s, there emerged a powerful anti-victimization discourse that some scholars view as an aspect of the neoliberal criticism of the welfare state. Here, victimization is presented as a form of perverse narcissism. Anti-victimizers claim that instead of concentrating on overcoming their underprivileged status individually, the partisans of the politics of victimization invent collective traumas and claim reparations. By doing so they undermine universal values, destroy national communities, and impose a heavy burden on national economies.[62] A more moderate version of this criticism holds, relative to the rise of memory, that "modern American politics... has become a competition for enshrining grievances. Every group claims its share of public honor and public funds by pressing disabilities and injustices."[63] Similar attitudes also exist in Europe.[64]

The typical criticism of the criminalization of the past goes in step with this anti-victimization discourse. Some scholars argue that "legal engagements in memory and identity politics tend to give rise to competition between victims..., leading to further polarization of particular groups against each other and the state."[65] There is some truth to this claim, especially given that the victimization of the past has become an important strategy of nationalist movements. The rise of memory and that of nationalism are interrelated phenomena, although historical memory cannot legitimately be reduced to the ways in which nationalists use it. One has therefore to appreciate the complexity of the phenomenon of victimization, and see both its humanistic and manipulative sides.

---

[60] Marc Olivier Baruch, *Des lois indignes? Les Historiens, la politique et le droit* (Paris: Tallandier, 2013), pp. 75–80.
[61] Elazar Barkan, *The Guilt of Nations: Restitution and Negotiating Historical Injustices* (New York: W.W. Norton, 2000); John Torpey, "'Making Whole What Has Been Smashed': Reflections on Reparations," *Journal of Modern History* 73/2 (2001), pp. 333–361.
[62] Cf. Cole, *The Cult of True Victimhood*; Dean, *The Fragility of Empathy after the Holocaust*; Dean, *Aversion and Erasure: The Fate of the Victim after the Holocaust* (Ithaca, N.Y.: Cornell University Press, 2010).
[63] Charles C. Maier, "A Surfeit of Memory? Reflections on History, Melancholy and Denial," *History and Memory* 5/2 (1993), p. 147.
[64] Chaumont, *La concurrence des victimes.*
[65] See Stiina Löytömäki, "Law and Memory: The Politics of Victimhood," *Griffith Law Review* 21/1 (2012), pp. 1, 19.

The Democratic Revolution in Historiography

The formation of the new culture of victimhood was inseparable from the democratic revolution in postwar historiography. This revolution consisted in the emergence of social (and, a little later, cultural) history or "history from below," which was willing to give "the silent majority," or ordinary people, the place they deserved in accounts of the past, which had been refused them by the traditional political history that was focused on the glorious deeds of "great men." This process began at the turn of the twentieth century, accelerated in the postwar decades, and reached its apogee in the 1960s and 1970s. The emergence of the French *Annales* School at the turn of the 1930s and its achievement of international prominence after the war were crucial to it.[66] From its early stages, social history was an expression of empathic interest in the life and culture of the underprivileged classes. It was influenced partly by Marxism and partly by the broader leftist sympathies of a growing part of the historical profession.

The silent majority favored by "history from below" could be considered losers or victims (in the broad, social, rather than psycho-analytical, sense) of the "big history" of state politics and the ruling classes. Sympathy toward, and identification with, the victims of the historical process therefore became the dominant moral standpoint for a broad segment of the historical profession. Indeed, many democratically minded historians thought of themselves as participants in the oppressed classes' struggle for liberation.[67] This reorientation of historiography actually had a strong anti-nationalist component. The study of the past ceased to be centered on state politics and national glory. A little later, the program of social history was expanded to include cultural history, which was soon to become the prevailing focus of avant-garde historiography. By the 1980s, in yet another sign that the age of class struggle was over, social history began to be seen as too dependent on simplistic macro-sociological theories, including Marxist notions of classes. But although the cultural turn (which in France was known as the *tournant vers les mentalités* and began as

---

[66] Peter Burke, *The French Historical Revolution: The* Annales *School, 1929–89* (Stanford, Calif.: Stanford University Press, 1990) and André Burguière, *The* Annales *School: An Intellectual History* (Ithaca, N.Y.: Cornell University Press, 2009).

[67] Geoff Eley, *A Crooked Line: From Cultural History to the History of Society* (Ann Arbor: University of Michigan Press, 2005), pp. 13–60; William H. Sewell Jr., *Logics of History: Social Theory and Social Transformation* (Chicago, Ill.: University of Chicago Press, 2005), pp. 22–80; Ronald Grigor Suny, "Back and Beyond: Reversing the Cultural Turn?" *The American Historical Review* 107/5 (2002), pp. 1477–1482.

early as the 1960s) came about partly in opposition to social history, it often also entailed a deepening of historians' interest in the silent majority of the underprivileged. Historians now sought to restore to them their subjectivity and agency rather than describe their "objective" living conditions and their class struggle. Class struggle now, in fact, was widely perceived as a road leading toward the totalitarian annihilation of the individual. Culture, not social relationships, came to be seen as the essence of humanity.[68]

From the vantage point of historiography, the memory boom was part of this attempt to restore subjectivity to history's rank-and-file actors. In one of its most popular definitions, culture is nothing other than "the nonhereditary memory of the community,"[69] or collective memory, and the memory boom was, not surprisingly, part of this cultural turn. In another popular interpretation, memory forms the core of personal (and collective) identity, so that without memory there can be no subjectivity and no agency.[70] At the same time, master narratives and history-based ideologies fell under suspicion along with historians' pretensions to the uncovering of objective truths. And before long, postmodernism was making counter-memories look like a resource for the democratic subversion of academic historiography, whose false objectivity was said to mask its function of promoting social discipline.[71] The upsurge of counter-memories was thus accompanied by a decomposition of global history, a crucial fact to which we will return later in this chapter.

All this was, of course, conceivable only in the context of relative social peace that, ironically, had been achieved through class conflict. The expansion and diversification of the notion of victimhood was a natural corollary of this triumph of democracy and humanism at the very juncture that was revealing the first signs of their future decline. The winds of

---

[68] See my "Sowjetische Historiographie, Marxismus und Totalitarismus: Zur Analyse der mentalen Grundlagen der Historiographie," *Österreichische Zeitschrift für Geschichtswissenschaften* 2/1 (1991), pp. 41–66.

[69] Yuri M. Lotman and Boris A. Uspensky, "On the Semiotic Mechanism of Culture," *New Literary History* 9/1 (1971), p. 213.

[70] John R. Gillis, "Memory and Identity: The History of a Relationship," in *Commemorations: The Politics of National Identity* (Princeton, N.J.: Princeton University Press, 1994), pp. 3–24. See also Michael S. Roth and Charles G. Salas, "Introduction," in *Disturbing Remains: Memory, History, and Crisis in the Twentieth Century* (Los Angeles, Calif.: Getty Research Institute, 2001), p. 2, and Anthony Smith, "Memory and Identity: Reflections on Ernst Gellner's Theory of Nationalism," *Nations and Nationalism* 2/3 (1996), p. 383.

[71] For a critique of "academic historiography," see Sande Cohen, *Historical Culture: On the Recoding of an Academic Discipline* (Berkeley: University of California Press, 1986).

history had shifted direction, but the forces of inertia remained at work, partly informing the new developments.

The triumph of social and cultural history marked an important change in the political function of the study of the past. In 1973, Paul Kennedy proclaimed "the decline of nationalistic history in the West," by which he meant the history of the nation-states.[72] The concept of the West and the project of a United Europe, which came to prominence in the postwar decades, were invented to overcome the legacy of classical nationalisms that had brought the European nations to the battlefields of two world wars. For almost two centuries, national history, or "the national romance" (Pierre Nora), was a major instrument of nation-building.[73] That history was written from the point of view of the national elites to which most historians belonged. But considered from the vantage point of history from below, those national romances were couched instead as criminal chronicles,[74] which were centered on the crimes of the ruling classes, whether genocide, dictatorship, inequality, or colonialism. The genocide-centered historical memory was a clear expression of this approach to history. Although largely rooted in the socio-psychological experience of the age of class struggle, it became predominant only after that age had ended, in the new atmosphere marked by the triumph of the humanistic attitudes toward the victims of history.

History from below and the victimization of the past were two crucial components of the new democratic culture of memory that emerged in the West in the 1960s and especially the 1970s, and firmly established itself in the 1980s and 1990s. The adoption of the first Holocaust denial laws created by the spirit of this culture was an important sign of its growing importance to the official politics of history in many European states. But even those Western countries that for various reasons chose not to pass memory laws (e.g., Great Britain and the Scandinavian countries) promoted the democratic culture of memory by nonlegislative means (such as commemorations, educational programs, etc.,). However, the triumph of this culture came as the political and social forces that had brought it into being were manifestly eroding.

[72] Paul Kennedy, "The Decline of Nationalistic History in the West, 1900–1970," *Journal of Contemporary History* 8/1 (1973), pp. 77–100.
[73] Stefan Berger, *The Past as History: National Identity and Historical Consciousness in Modern Europe* (Basingstoke: Palgrave Macmillan, 2015).
[74] Pierre Nora has ironically summarized this attitude thus: "History is nothing more than a lengthy series of crimes against humanity." See his "Malaise dans l'identité historique," in Nora and Françoise Chandernagor, *Liberté pour l'histoire* (Paris: CNRS Editions, 2008), p. 14.

Human Rights, the Crisis of the Future, and the Historic Turn

The formation of the democratic culture of memory centered on (though not limited to) the memory of the Shoah coincided with the human rights revolution that Samuel Moyn dates to the second half of the 1970s, although the groundwork was clearly laid by the civil rights movement, anti-racist legislation, and other developments of the 1960s.[75] The first peak in the discussion of human rights issues in the US press took place in 1976 and 1977, immediately after the signing of the Helsinki Accords in 1975. Human rights violations became one of the central themes of American criticism of the USSR, which ill-advisedly pledged in Helsinki to respect democratic freedoms. Indeed, the ideology of human rights provided the most common language for denouncing communist rule throughout the entire Soviet empire. And after the collapse of communism, this ideology became an important foundation of the post–Cold War order.

Moyn probably underestimates the historical roots of the human rights ideology, which can be traced back to the Enlightenment and also has various twentieth-century antecedents.[76] But what he does demonstrate is that since the 1970s, human rights issues have acquired an unprecedented importance in Western public discourse and practical politics.

According to Moyn, "Holocaust memory was peripheral to the explosion of human rights in the crucial era of the 1970s."[77] He speaks of "the amazingly belated integration of genocide consciousness as a human rights concern," something he believes to have happened only in the 1990s. However, as we have seen, the 1970s saw not only the ascendency of the human rights ideology, but also the growing centrality of the memory of the Shoah in Western historical consciousness. The coincidence is hardly fortuitous. Arguably, the same "spirit of the age" influenced both the rise of the memory of the Holocaust and the formation of the ideology of human rights, even though they were for a time largely separate processes.[78]

---

[75] Moyn, *The Last Utopia*, p. 231. See also Andreas Huyssen, "International Human Rights and the Politics of Memory: Limits and Challenges," *Criticism* 53/4 (2011), pp. 607–624.

[76] Lynn Hunt, *Inventing Human Rights: A History* (New York: W.W. Norton, 2007); Kirsten Sellars, *The Rise and Rise of Human Rights* (Stroud: Sutton, 2002).

[77] Moyn, *The Last Utopia*, p. 220.

[78] Levy and Sznaider, *The Holocaust and Memory in the Global Age*, p. 5; Andreas Huyssen, "Memory Culture and Human Rights: A New Constellation," in *Historical Justice and Memory*, eds. Klaus Neumann and Janna Thompson (Madison: University of Wisconsin Press, 2015), p. 27–28.

This ideology became predominant in the West in the period marked by the decay of traditional master narratives. Moyn suggests that "it is crucial to link the emergence of human rights to the history of utopianism" and "the crisis of other utopias" (such as communism or the welfare state).[79] We see here another connection between the rise of memory and the triumph of human rights. Indeed, the crisis of utopias is but an aspect of a broader process that has been described variously as the decay of ideologies, the crisis of the future, the collapse of the Enlightenment project, the end of history, and the emergence of present-mindedness (*présentisme*). According to François Hartog, *présentisme* characterizes our *régime d'historicité*, which is our way of perceiving the relationship between past, present, and future.[80] From the eighteenth century through the 1970s, various projects for the future (communist, liberal, nationalist, social-democratic) were applied to explain the course of history and give meaning to present and past. The collapse of those projects made "the eternal present" central to our consciousness of time and transformed the "omnipresent" past into an incoherent body of memories. It was therefore the crisis of the future that brought about the memory boom (as Charles S. Maier puts it, "The fault is not with memory, but with our current balance of past and future").[81] Unsurprisingly, then, "the last utopia" became focused on "the grievances of the past." But if the rise of the human rights ideology was indeed a consequence of the evaporation of the Enlightenment project, should we consider it the triumph of democracy or democracy's rearguard action?

The evaporation of the future-oriented ideologies has often been said to have caused a "crisis of history," which became an important topic of discussion among historians in the 1980s and 1990s. This notion had two main components: the crisis of objectivity and the fragmentation of historical discourse (or the collapse of global history). On the one hand, the proponents of the linguistic turn held that our representations of the past represent only the "linguistic protocols" in our own minds.[82]

---

[79] Moyn, *The Last Utopia*, pp. 220, 213.

[80] Hartog, *Regimes of Historicity: Presentism and Experiences of Time* [2003] (New York: Columbia University Press, 2015), and Hartog, *Croire en l'histoire* (Paris: Flammarion, 2013), pp. 225–285. See also Helga Nowotny, *Time: The Modern and Postmodern Experience* (Cambridge: Polity Press, 1994).

[81] Chalres S. Maier, "A Surfeit of Memory?," p. 150. On "the crisis of the future," see Krzysztof Pomian, "La crise de l'avenir," *Le Débat* 7 (1980), p. 5–17; Pierre-André Taguieff, *L'effacement de l'avenir* (Paris: Galilée, 2000); *Breaking up Time: Negotiating the Borders between Present, Past and Future*, eds. Chris Lorenz and Berber Bevernage (Göttingen: Vandenhoeck & Ruprecht, 2013).

[82] Hayden White, *Metahistory: The Historical Imagination in Nineteenth-Century Europe* (Baltimore, Md.: Johns Hopkins University Press, 1973).

Objectivity is but a "noble dream," which masks history's real goal of legitimizing existing power relationships.[83] On the other hand, many observers noted "the crumbling of history,"[84] or the historians' growing disappointment with "big structures, large processes, [and] huge comparisons" (to borrow Charles Tilly's expression).[85] An obvious explanation of the link between the two aspects of the crisis was that ideologies were the only way of arranging the facts of history in meaningful configurations. To generalize about the past, we have no choice but to use historical concepts, which are rife with ideologies. Many historians were quick to conclude that the best they could do was interpret the subjective meanings (including memories) that had supposedly guided the actions of individual actors. Of course, memory studies could only profit from these methodological discussions.[86]

In the 2000s, historians have largely overcome the crisis of objectivity by integrating the discoveries of the linguistic turn into the theory of practice.[87] But the fragmentation of historical discourse remains an unresolved problem. Attempts to create a "new paradigm" that would provide historians with more reliable instruments of generalization failed in the 1990s.[88] Since then, the question of generalization has disappeared from the historians' agenda, perhaps because it is commonly perceived as unresolvable.[89] This marked if not the much-discussed end of history, then at least the end of the two most ambitious projects of global history in twentieth-century historiography: Marxism and the French *Annales* School.

The interconnection between the crisis of history and the rise of memory has been commonplace in memory studies since the pioneering works of Pierre Nora and David Lowenthal.[90] Memory and history are often seen as two different ways of dealing with the past,[91] but this is a

[83] Peter Novick, *That Noble Dream: The "Objectivity Question" and the American Historical Profession* (Cambridge: Cambridge University Press, 1988).

[84] François Dosse, *New History in France: The Triumph of the* Annales [1987] (Urbana: University of Illinois Press, 1994).

[85] Charles Tilly, *Big Structures, Large Processes, Huge Comparisons* (New York: Russell Sage Foundation, 1984).

[86] Klein, "On the Emergence of *Memory* in Historical Discourse."

[87] Gabrielle M. Spiegel, "Introduction," in *Practicing History: New Directions in Historical Writing after the Linguistic Turn* (New York, London: Routledge, 2005), pp. 9–26; Sewell, *Logics of History*.

[88] Most of these attempts were undertaken in France and are known as "the pragmatic turn." See François Dosse, *Empire of Meaning: The Humanization of the Social Sciences* [1995] (Minneapolis: University of Minnesota Press, 1999).

[89] See my *De l'imagination historique* (Paris: Éditions de l'EHESS, 2009), pp. 105, 157.

[90] See the works cited in note 8. See also Kushner, *The Holocaust and the Liberal Imagination*, pp. 274, 277.

[91] Jacques Le Goff, *History and Memory* [1988] (New York: Columbia University Press, 1996).

grossly exaggerated opposition, if only because history and memory are not clearly delineated phenomena but concepts with complex and largely intersecting meanings.[92] The rise of memory, the decline of faith in the objectivity of historical knowledge, and the crumbling of global history, at least, were most certainly interdependent phenomena.

The rise of memory can be described as such only if we understand the word "memory" in a largely counterintuitive sense. "Memory" refers, first and foremost, to a property of the human mind and hence is regarded as authentic and reliable. Similarly, collective memory can be defined as "communicative memory,"[93] which is the natural transmission of skills and knowledge from one generation to another. This is not, however, the sense in which we use the term while speaking about the rise of memory. What has happened to the "natural" transmission of social skills in the twentieth century is often described as "the death of the past."[94] Thus, discussing the rise of memory, Pierre Nora famously argued that "memory is constantly on our lips because it no longer exists."[95] Nora goes even further, to claim that "our form of memory... is nothing but history." And, elsewhere: "What we call memory today is... not memory but already history."[96] Yet he also uses the term "memory" to refer to "historicized memory" and "memory transformed by its passage through history."[97] The "transformed memory" is characterized by fragmentation and alienation, because the passage through history destroys its natural continuity: "We used to know whose children we were; now we are the children of no one and everyone."[98] In other words, according to Nora (and I believe that he has every justification for claiming this) the present-day historical memory is an "artificial hyper-reality" that seems to be rooted in natural transmission of knowledge but is in fact produced (often intentionally) by various agents of memory, including states, public associations, mass media, historians, and journalists. Fragmentation presents as a common feature of both academic history and collective representations of the past.

---

[92] In addition, those concepts refer to different classes of phenomena because (as Jay Winter rightly observes) "History is a discipline [while] memory is a faculty." See Jay Winter, "The Performance of the Past: Memory, History, Identity," in *Performing the Past: Memory, History, and Identity in Modern Europe*, eds. Karin Tilmans, Frank van Vree, and Winter (Amsterdam: Amsterdam University Press, 2010), p. 12.

[93] Jan Assmann, "Collective Memory and Cultural Identity," *New German Critique* 65 (1995), pp. 125–133.

[94] John H. Plumb, *The Death of the Past* (London: Macmillan, 1969).

[95] Pierre Nora, "General Introduction: Between Memory and History" [1984], in *Realms of Memory*, ed. Lawrence D. Kritzman (New York: Columbia University Press, 1996–1998), vol. 1, p. 1.

[96] *Ibid.*, pp. 2, 8.   [97] *Ibid.*, pp. 10, 8.   [98] *Ibid.*, pp. 14, 12.

From the eighteenth century on, democratically interpreted global history was a narrative of human liberation. After the crisis of master narratives, the rise of memory, and the triumph of the human rights utopia, historical consciousness has become largely focused on particular misdeeds committed against particular groups, and memory laws are one of the most salient manifestations of this new form of historical consciousness: no single memory law actually bans any philosophy of history. They prohibit only misinterpretations of individual historical events that are regarded as sacred symbols of different "imagined communities" (to borrow Benedict Anderson's term).[99]

Amidst the postmodernist assault on objectivity, some historians claim that a "historic turn" is happening across the social and human sciences, from literary criticism to institutional economics. They argue that history, not social theory, has become our major device for explaining social phenomena because we have come to prefer complex contextual explanations over theoretical models.[100] Other historians assert that "we live in an expanding historical culture," which is of course another way of saying that we inhabit an age of memory.[101] From this vantage, the crisis of global history and the rise of memory appear as an expansion, rather than a crisis, of modern historical consciousness.

I believe that both diagnoses are correct and that the past-dependency of present-day culture entails a profound change in historical consciousness – namely, a crisis of global history and of the very idea of progress. We are now thinking more historically in a world that has lost confidence in history as a powerful and largely benevolent force laying the groundwork for our future. Traditional historicism (which was born in the eighteenth century and can be broadly defined as a philosophy that emphasizes the historicity of being)[102] presupposed a certain idea of global history. Within its framework, legitimation through history implied a reference to universal history, which allowed for the demonstration of the concrete historical

---

[99] Benedict Anderson, *Imagined Communities: Reflections on the Origins and Spread of Nationalism* (London: Verso, 1983).

[100] Terrence J. McDonald, ed., *The Historic Turn in the Human Sciences* (Ann Arbor: University of Michigan Press, 1996).

[101] Raphael Samuel, *Theatres of Memory*, vol. 1: *Past and Present in Contemporary Culture* (London: Verso, 1994), p. 25.

[102] Friedrich Meinecke, *Historism: The Rise of a New Historical Outlook* [1936] (New York: Herder and Herder, 1972); Friedrich Jaeger and Jörn Rüsen, *Geschichte des Historismus: Eine Einfürung* (Munich: C.H. Beck, 1992); Otto Gerhard Oexle, *Geschichtswissenschaft im Zeichen des Historismus: Studien zu Problemgeschichten der Moderne* (Göttingen: Vandenhoeck & Ruprecht, 1996); Frederick C. Beiser, *The German Historicist Tradition* (Oxford: Oxford University Press, 2011).

place and the universal meaning of a given historical phenomenon. The modern idea of history was based on a balance of – and a tension between – historical relativism and universalism embodied in the concept of global history. But if the latter is no more, can we now define contemporary historicism as a historicism without global history?[103]

The rise of memory is heavily exploited by nationalist and populist movements throughout the world. It leads to memory wars within and between many countries. Is the critical awareness of roots and contexts propagated by the historic turn compatible with obvious misuses of the past for the purposes of political manipulation? I believe that they can be seen as the positive and negative aspects of the same "reorientation of Western social thought" (to borrow Stuart Hughes' classical formula).[104] The memory boom is a manifestation of the continuing historicization of the modern worldview. But it has also contributed to the rise of ahistorical "mythical thinking" and particularist identities, which are often seen in essentialist rather than historical terms. This reorientation becomes most obvious if one considers the changing semantic structures of historical concepts, to which we will return later in this chapter.

How are memories of the Holocaust related to this picture? If Holocaust commemoration is part of, and one of the reasons for, the memory boom, should the latter be viewed in exclusively somber terms? Does not the claim that the Shoah has become "a generalized symbol of human suffering and moral evil" (Jeffrey C. Alexander) contradict the theory according to which the rise of memory favors particularistic identities? Daniel Levy and Nathan Sznaider propose to overcome this contradiction by distinguishing "between memories that refer back to the past and ones that point to the future," Holocaust commemoration being the main example of "the future-oriented cosmopolitan memory" typical of the age of globalization. Crucial to their argument is the concept of Second Modernity as developed by German sociologist of globalization Ulrich Beck, who describes it as a reflexive modernity that critically examines ("modernizes") "its own foundations."[105] From this vantage point, Levy and Sznaider

---

[103] Cf.: "It is safest to grasp the concept of the postmodern as an attempt to think the present historically in an age that has forgotten how to think historically in the first place." See Fredric Jameson, *Postmodernism, Or, The Cultural Logic of Late Capitalism* (Durham, N.C.: Duke University Press, 1991), p. VII. It is hard to imagine what the second part of this phrase means, if not the collapse of global history.

[104] Henry Stuart Hughes, *Consciousness and Society: The Reorientation of European Social Thought, 1890–1930* (New York: Knopf, 1958).

[105] Levy and Sznaider, *The Holocaust and Memory in the Global Age*, pp. 6, 195. Cf. Ulrich Beck, *What is Globalization?* (Cambridge: Polity Press, 2000).

criticize scholars such as Anthony Smith and Pierre Nora who (they claim) overemphasize the *Gemeinschaft* vs. *Gesellschaft* dichotomy and "regard mediated representations as something that dissolves collective memory." Levy and Sznaider praise as "a self-reflective culture of recollection" just what Smith and Nora condemn as "timeless global culture" or "artificial hyper-reality." In contrast to First Modernity, "collective memory in Second Modernity is freed from naturalized categories (e.g., the nation) and turns toward symbols (e.g., the Holocaust) to try to come to terms with an uncertain future rather than to celebrate a certain past."[106] The Holocaust has become central to the new cosmopolitan culture of remembrance by virtue of its Americanization and the emergence of "de-territorialized compassion" as a result of globalization.[107] Levy and Sznaider view this transformation as typical of Second Modernity, when "forms of remembrance become displaced from their original ground-specific (or religious) context and are transformed into a widely disseminated set of common values."[108] They conclude by saying that "the bitterest reminder of the consequences of national self-certainty in First Modernity" – the future-oriented cosmopolitan memory of the Holocaust – "can become part of the foundation for an emerging global civil society."[109]

In their analysis of the Holocaust's transformation in a universal symbol Levy and Sznaider depend on Jeffrey C. Alexander's idea that "a specific and situated historical event" becomes a universal symbol capable of providing "the basis for psychological identification" due to its "separation from the specifics of any particular time or space."[110] However, Alexander develops a totally different understanding of the perception of historical time that was involved in the constructing of the Holocaust as "a moral universal." For him, "the Jewish mass killings were not an end but a beginning" of the history of the Holocaust within what he calls a "progressive narrative frame," or the postwar liberal narrative that saw the Holocaust as a concrete historical event and "suggested confidence that things would be better over time." Alexander continues:

> By contrast, the newly emerging world-historical status of the mass murders suggested that they represented an end point, not a new beginning,... a cause for despair, not the beginning of hope.... In the new tragic

---

[106] Levy and Sznaider, *The Holocaust and Memory in the Global Age*, pp. 31–32, 36, 195.

[107] *Ibid.*, pp. 132, 179–181. To be sure, they also claim that, in Second Modernity, universalism and particularism presuppose each other, which explains how a particular event can stand for a universal value (pp. 7, 49, 154).

[108] *Ibid.*, p. 80. [109] *Ibid.*, pp. 197, 203.

[110] Alexander, "On the Social Construction of Moral Universals," pp. 6, 30.

understanding of the Jewish mass murder, suffering, not progress, became the telos toward which the narrative was aimed.

In this tragic narrative of sacred-evil, the Jewish mass killings become not an event in history but an archetype, an event out of time.... The tragedy of the Holocaust challenged the ethical self-identification, the self-esteem, of modernity.

[T]he tragic framing of the Holocaust fundamentally contributed to postmodern relativism and disquiet [rather than to "Second Modernity"].[111]

Alexander was justifiably criticized for having underestimated the pragmatic political reasons behind the memory of the Holocaust (in contrast to Novick, who has overemphasized the importance of those reasons).[112] Nevertheless, I believe that his theory – which is fully compatible with the notion of the memory boom as a manifestation of the past-dependent historical consciousness – better grasps the temporal underpinnings of Holocaust commemoration, although I also sympathize with some of Levy and Sznaider's claims. Despite its obvious link to a tragic vision of human nature, the memory of the Shoah has indeed had a "utopian" component, as did the human rights ideology in Samuel Moyn's analysis. Of course, the very expression "future-oriented memory" can be dismissed as a *contradictio in terminis*, but here we can safely replace "memory" with the somewhat broader concept of historical consciousness. In fact, what provides memory with a sense of hope can be best described as the optimistic philosophy of history that it implicitly contains, so that the Holocaust acquires its present-day meaning within the framework of the liberal master narrative, even though it has powerfully contributed to problematizing it. One may not believe in redemption, but would one argue that remembering the Shoah is irrelevant to making the world a better place?

Although events and philosophies are closely intertwined, the emphasis matters, and the fact that the liberal master narrative is now often celebrated indirectly, through Holocaust commemoration, reveals event-centeredness as a hallmark of contemporary historical consciousness.

Neoliberalism, Neoconservatism, and the Memory Boom

To fully understand the meaning of the memory boom, one has to contextualize it in terms of the rise of neoliberalism and

---

[111] *Ibid.*, pp. 30–32.
[112] Robert Manne, "On the Political Corruptions of a Moral Universal," in Jeffrey C. Alexander et al., *Remembering the Holocaust: A Debate* (Oxford: Oxford University Press, 2009), p. 142.

neoconservatism.[113] The formation of neoliberalism and the rise of memory are two strictly contemporaneous phenomena. Both began to take shape in the 1970s and surfaced powerfully in cultural and political life at the turn of the 1980s. By the 1970s, the Western elites had realized that they no longer had to fear socialist revolutions (although that decade witnessed some ruthless rearguard battles of the age of class struggle). The onset of recession provided those elites with arguments against the welfare state that they used to justify a redistribution of national income that above all else benefited them. In fact, my understanding of neoliberalism is not as an economic theory but rather as a set of policies, arguments, and rhetorical devices that have been leveraged by social elites since the end of the 1970s to ensure that redistribution. As for "neoconservatism," I use it to refer not to American theorists of the US-dominated world but to a broad cultural and political movement that was born in the 1960s and 1970s, in both Europe and the United States, as a reaction to the emerging cultural hegemony of the left. Although neoliberalism and neoconservatism are not the same thing, they partly overlap, since neoconservatives typically disapprove of social programs while neoliberals often embrace "traditional values."

The near-contemporaneous election of three neoconservative governments (Margaret Thatcher's in 1979, Ronald Reagan's in 1980, and Helmut Kohl's in 1982) was a turning point in postwar politics. It marked the beginning of a period characterized by the reversal, "on two continents," of a "century-long tendency of limiting the inequality of revenues and fortunes."[114] In parallel fashion, France, Great Britain, and Brazil, independently from each other, declared 1980 the Year of Heritage; this declaration is often seen as the symbolic beginning of the memory boom. A new historical period and a new form of historical consciousness were born simultaneously.

The neoconservatives' coming to power was followed by an ideological campaign aimed at putting an end to the cultural liberalism of the

---

[113] Harvey, *A Brief History of Neoliberalism*; Christoph Butterwegge, Bettina Lösch, and Ralf Ptak, *Kritik des Neoliberalismus* (Wiesbaden: VS Verlag für Sozialwissenschaften, 2008); Serge Audier, *Néo-libéralisme(s): Une archéologie intellectuelle* (Paris: Grasset, 2012); Michael Thompson, ed., *Confronting the New Conservatism: The Rise of the Right in America* (New York: New York University Press, 2007); Justin Vaïsse, *Neoconservatism: The Biography of a Movement* (Cambridge, Mass.: Belknap Press, 2010); and Adam L. Fuller, *Taking the Fight to the Enemy: Neoconservatism and the Age of Ideology* (Lanham, Md.: Lexington Books, 2011).

[114] Pierre Rosanvallon, *La société des égaux* (Paris: Editions du Seuil, 2011), p. 14. See also Luc Boltanski and Ève Chiapello, *Le nouvel esprit du capitalisme* (Paris: Gallimard, 1999) and Piketty, *Capital in the Twenty-First Century*.

1960s and 1970s, including doing away with history from below. In particular, the neoconservatives endeavored to restore the "national romances" and halt the victimization of the past.[115] Thatcher's government was the first to attempt to regulate history textbooks (also seeking to revive the cult of Queen Victoria, whose image appealed to the Prime Minister), with Reagan and Kohl following suit.[116] All three tried to mobilize groups of right-wing intellectuals to counterbalance the "subversive" work of left-wing historians. By and large, though, this did not work, since most historians refused to go along with the proposed "whitewashing" of the national past. It turned out to be impossible to recreate, late in the twentieth century, the superannuated cults of nation-states. In particular, during the *Historikerstreit* of 1986–1987, German and international public opinion condemned any attempt to relativize the Holocaust and provide Germans with a more comforting past.[117] As a result of this failure, the neoconservative governments chose a twofold strategy: to endorse the leftist victimization of history, including the struggle against Holocaust negationism, and to stimulate the development of "cultural patriotism" by promoting the notion of national heritage and the heritage industry. The fall of communism made the inclusion of the political tradition of the left in the post–Cold War order far less risky for the ruling elites.[118] Most remarkably, in Germany, a revived cult of *Heimat* ("homeland," a concept that expresses "an apolitical representation of the nation") – in other words, a fascination with

---

[115] Harvey J. Kaye, *The Powers of the Past: Reflections on the Crisis and the Promise of History* (New York: Harvester, 1991); Frank Füredi, *Mythical Past, Elusive Future: History and Society in an Anxious Age* (London: Pluto Press, 1992); Richard J. Evans, *In Hitler's Shadow: West German Historians and the Attempt to Escape from the Nazi Past* (New York: Pantheon Books, 1989), pp. 118–128; Konrad Hugo Jarausch and Michael Geyer, *Shattered Past: Reconstructing German Histories* (Princeton, N.J.: Princeton University Press, 2009), pp. 50–54; and Stefan Berger, "A Return to the National Paradigm? National History Writing in Germany, Italy, France, and Britain from 1945 to the Present," *The Journal of Modern History* 77/3 (2005), pp. 650–657.

[116] In Germany, the neoconservative offensive began around 1976–1977, several years before Kohl came to power, under the slogan of retrieving the country's "lost identity," but Kohl's energetic support was crucial to its progress. Characteristically, the rise of interest in "heritage and tradition" in the GDR was strictly contemporaneous with those West German developments. See Wolfrum, *Geschichte als Waffe*, pp. 123–128.

[117] Charles S. Maier, *The Unmasterable Past: History, Holocaust, and German National Identity* (Cambridge, Mass.: Harvard University Press, 1997); Ian Buruma, *The Wages of Guilt: Memories of War in Germany and Japan* (New York: Farrar, Straus, and Giroux, 1994); Wulf Kansteiner, *In Pursuit of German Memory: History, Television and Politics after Auschwitz* (Athens, Ohio: Ohio University Press, 2006).

[118] This is not to say that there have been no attempts since then to revitalize the "national romances." See Berger, "A Return to the National Paradigm?" pp. 662–672.

"authentic" Germanness as reflected in "local history, nature, and ethnography" – has developed powerfully since the 1980s.[119]

We will consider the recent politics of memory in greater detail in Chapter 2, because it explains the context in which the first memory laws were adopted. Here I will discuss the impact of neoliberalism and neoconservatism on the changing perceptions of historical time, the emergence of presentism, and the rise of memory.

Today, the dominance of neoliberal ideology finds expression in a largely shared vision of the principles that any government has to follow in its economic policy. More generally, this ideology determines our *Weltanschauung*, which is a worldview typified by a culture marked by present-mindedness that would be inconceivable absent a profound change in our consciousness of historical time. A particular attitude toward history is both a foundation and a consequence of neoliberalism, so that without present-mindedness, there would be no neoliberalism, and vice versa.

The hypothesis of the interconnection between "late capitalism" and the crisis of history harks back to the works of Fredric Jameson, David Harvey, Perry Anderson, and William H. Sewell. For them, the advent of postmodernism was caused by the "political failure" of the left in the 1960s, including the "defeat of organized labour and student rebellion," "the erosion of working class confidence and identity," and disillusionment with the utopias of social liberation.[120] All of this can be more succinctly described as the end of the age of class struggle. Indeed, those "failures" occurred in the context of an unprecedented improvement of living standards for the vast majority in the West. I find appeal in the hypothesis

---

[119] Confino, *Germany as a Culture of Remembrance*, p. 44. Confino views Edgar Reitz's tremendously successful television series *Heimat* (1984) as the key moment of the renewed cult of national heritage in Germany. The Heimat ideology, which had emerged in the late nineteenth century, was brought back by Reitz in response to the American 1978 television miniseries *Holocaust* (broadcast in Germany in 1979), which played a key role in the emergence of the memory of the Shoah in Germany. The return to Heimat ideology was for him a means of regaining a sense of authentic Germanness in a time that had "Americanized" memory and transformed it into a commodity. The acceptance of the international memory of the Holocaust in Germany and the emphasis on national heritage appear as two sides of the same coin. Confino draws an interesting parallel between Reitz's *Heimat* and Pierre Nora's *Les lieux de mémoire* (also of 1984), viewing the latter as a parallel attempt to explore French nationhood by means of a new form of historiography (pp. 57, 70–71). On the origins of the Heimat ideology, see Confino, *The Nation as a Local Metaphor: Württemberg, Imperial Germany, and National Memory, 1871–1918* (Chapel Hill: University of North Carolina Press, 1997), and Celia Applegate, *A Nation of Provincials: The German Idea of* Heimat (Berkeley: University of California Press, 1990); Wulf Kansteiner, *In Pursuit of German Memory*, pp. 109–153.

[120] Jameson, *Postmodernism*, p. XV; Perry Anderson, *The Origins of Postmodernity* (London: Verso, 1998), pp. 81–82, 91, 104, 116.

according to which the fragmentation of history was partially rooted in the social-psychological experience of the passage from Fordism to post-Fordism, or in other words in the transition "from mass production to smaller batch, more niche-oriented production" aimed at "creating and commercially exploiting a multitude of consumer 'lifestyles.'"[121] Jameson and others are, however, far less convincing when they seek to establish a nexus between late capitalism and changes in the perception of historical time. Jameson speaks of the spatialization of time in postmodernist culture, which according to him is "increasingly dominated by space and spatial logic."[122] But he overlooks the fact that the modern idea of history was already crucially dependent on the spatial imagination and that the time of global history was a deeply spatialized form of temporality.[123]

The concept of the *cité marchande* (or market order) developed by French sociologists Luc Boltanski and Laurent Thévenot throws light on this interconnection. For them, the *cité marchande* is a worldview produced by the "economic ideology" (or political economy) of the late eighteenth and the nineteenth centuries. Boltanski and Thévenot speak of several "cities," or models of social relationships, that co-exist in our societies, including the *cité industrielle* and the *cité domestique*, and those differing worldviews entail differing perceptions of historical time. In the market order, "human beings must be mobile, without attachments or past histories,"[124] because what matters in this "city" is rational behavior driven by the individual's desire to possess certain objects. Boltanski and Thévenot continue:

> Market arrangements are not conductive to the integration of a temporal perspective; by contrast, industrial arrangements allow for the possibility of projection into the future. . ., while domestic arrangements make it possible to establish links with the past and allow specific assets to put down local roots.[125]

---

[121] Sewell, *Logics of History*, p. 56.   [122] Jameson, *Postmodernism*, p. 24.

[123] Koposov, *De l'imagination historique*.

[124] This clearly echoes Marxist theory, according to which capitalism annihilates history by reifying social relationships and alienating products of labor from the individuals involved in their production. And, as Max Horkheimer and Theodor Adorno famously put it, "all reification is a forgetting." See their *Dialectic of Enlightenment: Philosophical Fragments* [1947] (Stanford, Calif.: Stanford University Press, 2002); György Lukács, *History and Class Consciousness: Studies in Marxist Dialectics* [1922] (London: Merlin Press, 1971), pp. 11, 157; Martin Jay, *Marxism and Totality: The Adventures of a Concept from Lukacs to Habermas* (Berkeley: University of California Press, 1984), pp. 223–240; and Richard Terdiman, *Present Past: Modernity and the Memory Crisis* (Ithaca, N.Y.: Cornell University Press, 1993), pp. 12–13, 57. Boltanski and Thévenot avoid reducing modernity to a single "cultural logic." Moreover, for them ahistoricity is a property of an "economic ideology," rather than of the capitalist mode of production.

[125] Luc Boltanski and Laurent Thévenot, *On Justification: Economies of Worth* [1991] (Princeton, N.J.: Princeton University Press, 2006), pp. 8–9.

To simplify, political economy tends to annihilate history as a dimension of human experience by presenting economic laws as perennial and transcultural. By contrast, the *cité industrielle* is based on the idea of technological progress and consequently on the notion of change, while the *cité domestique* values tradition above all else. The plurality of "cities" explains why the "naturalizing" logic of the market order could co-exist in the nineteenth- and early twentieth-century historical consciousness with the idea of global history and nostalgic complaints about "temporal disorientation" and lost links with the past.

According to my hypothesis, neoliberalism has taken the *cité marchande* logic to its extreme by assimilating economy to a mathematical model, which can work well only if social groups (seen as "redistribution coalitions") do not intervene into its operation. Within this framework, history viewed as the struggle of human collectivities to assert their own interests presents as irrelevant, if not detrimental, to a society's wellbeing. It can only corrupt the purity of the principal economic law, as neoliberals understand it, which is that the less the state weighs on an economy, the more investors invest and the faster the economy grows. This law can be illustrated by arbitrarily chosen historical examples, but it is hardly compatible with the notion of global history seen as a narrative of human liberation.

That is why history – and above all social history with its collective actors – has no place in the neoliberal "order." The new form of economic ideology has successfully undermined traditional history-based ideologies. Other "orders" and perceptions of historical time, including the idea of global history, have not, of course, disappeared; rather, they have been repressed and marginalized. But alternative ways of dealing with the past had to be found to replace the modern idea of history. Paradoxically, the traditionalism of the *cité domestique* seems to be the most natural counterpart of the neoliberal annihilation of history, and this largely explains the connection between neoliberalism and neoconservatism as well as the fact that the rise of memory coincided chronologically with the crisis of history. The ostracized narrative of human liberation has returned in the form of fragmented memories, including those of particular subaltern communities. Or, as Michael S. Roth puts it, "Trauma has replaced utopia in providing overriding legitimation."[126]

As we have seen, the victimization of history presents a problem for neoliberalism. But it is a minor problem in comparison with the

---

[126] Roth, *Memory, Trauma, and History*, p. 96.

sociological and historical critique of social inequalities, which would call the validity of abstract economic models into question. As long as those models went unquestioned, the problem of retribution for past injustices with regard to particular victim groups could be safely tackled with within the "limits of the possible" that are determined by those selfsame models. Fragmented and subjective memories do not challenge the existence of capitalism, as some versions of global history did.

Memory Laws and the Logic of Proper Names

The formation of the new form of historical consciousness brought about important changes in the style of our thinking, including the accepted forms of political legitimation. This evolution manifested in the changing semantic structures of basic historical concepts.

According to Reinhart Koselleck, the formation, in the eighteenth century, of the modern system of social and political concepts (or basic historical terms) was closely interconnected with the emergence of future-oriented thinking and the modern idea of history.[127] In particular, semantic structures of the basic historical concepts were deeply influenced by this style of thought. The semantic structure of every historical concept, Koselleck believes, contains two elements differently oriented in historical time, which he calls "the horizon of expectations" and "the space of experience." The space of experience determined the meaning of the concepts that prevailed in premodern societies, including the medieval West. These "old" concepts described fragmented realities of particularistic societies, which gradually developed over time without any preconceived plan. In contrast, in the late eighteenth and early nineteenth centuries, the horizon of expectations came to dominate the semantic structures of social and political concepts. That period that Koselleck calls *Sattelzeit* ("saddle time") witnessed the emergence of a new type of historical concept that since then has formed the core of our modern conceptual system. This reorientation in time made social and political concepts more abstract than they had previously been, since the "new" notions served to express a vision of history dominated by (often conflicting) images of the future and thus to legitimize a given universal principle of social organization.

---

[127] Koselleck, *Futures Past: On the Semantics of Historical Time* (Cambridge, Mass.: MIT Press, 1985); Koselleck, *The Practice of Conceptual History* (Stanford, Calif.: Stanford University Press, 2002); Koselleck, "Geschichte/Historie," in *Geschichtliche Grundbegriffe: Historisches Lexikon zur politisch-sozialen Sprache in Deutschland*, eds. Otto Brunner, Werner Conze, and Koselleck (Stuttgart: Klett-Cotta, 1972–1997), vol. 2, pp. 593–717.

In light of Koselleck's theory, we can return now to the hypothesis according to which historical concepts refer simultaneously to universal ideas and concrete occurrences and function as *semi-noms propres* (semi-proper names), which contain aspects of both general and proper names.[128] The unstable balance between the two aspects of their meaning can change over time. One might expect that, following the decline of the future-oriented ideologies, the universal and abstract component of basic historical concepts would gradually lose its importance, while reference to particular experiences would become central to historical thought and political legitimation. And that, I believe, is precisely what is happening today,[129] as the logic of proper names comes to prevail over the logic of general names. The more a concept can be understood as a proper name, the better its chances of being used by the politics of memory.

Memory laws as an instrument of the politics of history correspond to a certain stage in the development of Western historical consciousness. This stage is in particular characterized by a focus on concrete historical events that serve as sacred symbols of various communities of memory. The emphasis on the particular as one of the characteristic features of the age of memory separates it from the age of ideologies, of which universalist claims embodied in the philosophies of history were a hallmark. It is by no means a coincidence that some practitioners of the politics of memory claim that, after the collapse of the traditional ideologies, "the politics of history will become the standard of politics as such."[130] As we will see, the focus on the particular is manifest in the vocabulary of the politics of memory, including that of certain memory laws.

---

[128] Jean-Claude Passeron, *Le raisonnement sociologique: L'espace non-popperien du raisonnement naturel* (Paris: Nathan, 1991), pp. 60–61.

[129] See my "Collective Singulars: A Reinterpretation," *Contributions to the History of Concepts* 6/1 (2011), pp. 37–62.

[130] Gleb Pavlovskiy, "Plokho s pamyatyu – Plokho s politikoy [Bad with Memory – Bad with Politics]," *Russkiy Zhurnal,* December 9, 2008: www.russ.ru/pole/Ploho-s-pamyat-yu-ploho-s-politikoj. Pavlovskiy was at the time of this article one of the leading "political technologists" in the service of Vladimir Putin.

CHAPTER 2

Memory Laws in Western Europe

In this chapter, I will show how the notion of criminalizing statements about the past gradually developed in postwar Europe in the framework of human rights laws, including the anti-fascist legislation of the late 1940s and early 1950s and the anti-racist legislation of the 1960s and the following decades. I will then review the first Holocaust denial laws of the 1980s and 1990s that applied the approaches of anti-racist legislation to the issues of historical memory, which became a highly sensitive political topic as a result of the "memory boom." I will also consider the emergence of memory laws as a European phenomenon and their extension from the memory of the Holocaust to other traumatic memories, as well as the emergence of the protest movement against the "judicialization" of the past.

The Emergence of Anti-Fascist Legislation

Laws enacted in numerous countries of the postwar world to combat the resurgence of fascist parties and criminalize racism, in response to the atrocities of the world wars, the totalitarian regimes, and colonialism, were an important predecessor of Holocaust denial legislation. The concepts of crimes against humanity and genocide were critical to this development. Memory laws might never have come into being had these concepts not previously become central to Western political and legal thinking.

The first attempts to introduce the notion of crimes against humanity in international law and to try those deemed guilty of them were undertaken during and in the aftermath of World War I. The Allied Joint Declaration of May 24, 1915, condemning the massacre of the Armenians in the Ottoman Empire ("those new crimes of Turkey against humanity and civilization") was the first official international document to use the notion of crimes against humanity as different from, although related to, war crimes.[1] The classical definition of crimes against humanity given in the Charter of the Nuremberg Tribunal in August 1945 was largely based on the understanding of those crimes formulated during the Paris Peace Conference of 1919 with regard to the Armenian genocide.[2] The treaties of Versailles (1919) and Sèvres (1920) stipulated that German and Turkish war criminals would be tried for their crimes. However, the implementation of those agreements was ineffective. In Germany, several lower-ranking officers were brought to trial in Leipzig in 1921 and were either acquitted or sentenced to relatively short terms of imprisonment. In Turkey, the Kemalist revolution put an end to the trials that Turkish nationalists saw as acts of continuing foreign aggression.[3] However, these largely failed attempts at retributive justice prepared the ground for the trials of Nazi and Japanese war criminals after World War II and helped shape the memory of the Armenian genocide.

The 1940s were decisive for the emergence of anti-fascist legislation and of the concepts of genocide and crimes against humanity. The Charter of the Nuremberg Tribunal attached to the London Agreement of August 8, 1945, defined three categories of Nazi crimes: crimes against peace, war crimes, and crimes against humanity. Crimes against peace were understood as "planning, preparation, initiation or waging of a war of aggression, or a war in violation of international treaties." War crimes were defined as

---

[1] The text of the declaration is available at www.armenian-genocide.org/Affirmation.160/current_category.7/affirmation_detail.html. The notion of crimes against humanity dates back to the late eighteenth century, when Condorcet and other abolitionists called slavery a "crime against the human species." See Gilles Manceron, "La loi: régulateur ou acteur des guerres de mémoires?" in *Les guerres de mémoires: La France et son histoire: Enjeux politiques, controverses historiques, stratégies médiatiques*, eds. Pascal Blanchard and Isabelle Veyrat-Masson (Paris: La Découverte, 2008), p. 248.

[2] The declaration and the proceedings of the Paris Peace Conference used the formulas "crimes against humanity and civilization" and "crimes against the laws of humanity." See Sévane Garibian, "From the 1915 Allied Joint Declaration to the 1920 Treaty of Sèvres: Back to an International Criminal Law in Progress," *The Armenian Review* 52/1–2 (2010), pp. 87–102. Arguably, the term "Holocaust" was first used to refer to mass killings in a *New York Times* article of September 10, 1895, dealing with the massacre of the Armenians in 1894 and 1895. See David M. Crowe, "War Crimes and Genocide in History, and the Evolution of Responsive International Law," *Nationalities Papers* 37/6 (2009), p. 771.

[3] Crowe, "War Crimes and Genocide in History," pp. 770–773; William A. Schabas, *Genocide in International Law: The Crime of Crimes* (Cambridge: Cambridge University Press, 2009), pp. 16–22; James E. Willis, *Prologue to Nuremberg: The Politics and Diplomacy of Punishing War Criminals of the First World War* (Westport, Conn.: Greenwood, 1982); Alan Kramer, "The First Wave of International War Crimes Trials: Istanbul and Leipzig," *European Review* 14/4 (2006), pp. 441–455; Aram Kuyumjian, "The Armenian Genocide: International Legal and Political Avenues for Turkey's Responsibility," *Revue de Droit: Université de Sherbrooke* 41 (2011), pp. 247–305; and Jean-Baptiste Racine, *Le génocide des Arméniens: Origine et permanence du crime contre l'humanité* (Paris: Dalloz-Sirey, 2006).

"violations of the laws or customs of war," including "murder, ill-treatment or deportation... of civilian population..., murder or ill-treatment of prisoners of war... or devastation not justified by military necessity." Finally, the term "crimes against humanity" referred to "murder, extermination, enslavement, deportation, and other inhumane acts committed against any civilian population...; or persecutions on political, racial or religious grounds."[4]

This classification replaced much less precise language in previous international agreements and declarations, which used such terms as "atrocities," "slaughters," "abominable deeds," etc.[5] To be sure, the notion of crimes against humanity was still closely linked to that of war crimes (characteristically, the murder and deportation of civilians were included in both categories). And unsurprisingly, some lawyers preferred the notion of war crimes to that of crimes against humanity, partly because of their unwillingness to emphasize the racist dimension of Nazi crimes.[6] However, persecution on racist grounds is explicitly mentioned in the Charter as a crime against humanity, which makes this category substantially different from the traditional notion of war crimes.

The concept of genocide proposed by Raphael Lemkin in 1944 also aided in conceptualizing Nazi atrocities as crimes of a racist nature. This concept was used in the drafts of the Charter of the Nuremberg Tribunal and occasionally during the trial itself. In December 1946, the General Assembly of the United Nations passed a resolution recognizing genocide as a crime under international law. The term "genocide" was then clearly defined in the United Nations Convention on the Prevention and Punishment of the Crime of Genocide (1948).[7]

---

[4] Charter of the International Military Tribunal, Article 6: http://avalon.law.yale.edu/imt/imtconst .asp.

[5] Joint Four-Nation Declaration ["Moscow Declaration"], October 1943: http://avalon.law.yale.edu/ wwii/moscow.asp.

[6] See Chapter 1.

[7] Raphael Lemkin, *Axis Rule in Occupied Europe: Laws of Occupation, Analysis of Government, Proposals for Redress* (Washington DC: Carnegie Endowment for International Peace, 1944). Article 2 of the 1948 Convention reads: "In the present Convention, genocide means any of the following acts committed with intent to destroy, in whole or in part, a national, ethnical, racial or religious group, as such: (a) Killing members of the group; (b) Causing serious bodily or mental harm to members of the group; (c) Deliberately inflicting on the group conditions of life calculated to bring about its physical destruction in whole or in part; (d) Imposing measures intended to prevent births within the group; (e) Forcibly transferring children of the group to another group." See Convention on the Prevention and Punishment of the Crime of Genocide, December 9, 1948; Schabas, *Genocide in International Law*, pp. 24–101; Anson Rabinbach, "The Challenge of the Unprecedented: Raphael Lemkin and the Concept of Genocide," *Simon Dubnow Institute Yearbook* 4 (2005), pp. 397–420; and John Q. Barrett, "Raphael Lemkin and 'Genocide' at Nuremberg," in *The Genocide Convention*

Several other international documents adopted in the aftermath of World War II, such as the Universal Declaration of Human Rights (1948) and the European Convention for the Protection of Human Rights and Fundamental Freedoms (1950), developed a broader legal framework within which Nazi offenses could be conceived as violations of basic human rights, or crimes against humanity. The fundamental principles of human rights were therefore formulated as an explicit response to Nazi crimes.[8]

The emergence of human rights legislation was accompanied by the adoption of several national laws prohibiting fascist parties, symbols, and ideology, which were adopted in the early postwar years in countries willing to break with their fascist past.[9] The process of denazification, all its inconsistencies notwithstanding, implied a condemnation of fascism as a political and historical phenomenon. In Austria, the Provisional Government passed legislation banning the Nazi party and any affiliated organizations. The "Prohibition Law" (*Verbotsgesetz*) was adopted in May 1945, amended in February 1947,[10] and further revised in 1992, by adding Holocaust denial to the roster of prohibited activities. In occupied Germany, the Allied Control Council ordered the liquidation of Nazi organizations in October 1945, and in January 1946, Article 86a penalizing the production and distribution of written materials and symbols of the prohibited organizations was added to the German Criminal Code.[11] After the founding of the Federal Republic of Germany, the ban of Nazism was reaffirmed. Article 21.2 of the 1949 Basic Law declares unconstitutional "parties that, by reason of their aims or the behaviour of their adherents, seek to undermine or abolish the free, democratic basic order."[12]

Similar measures were undertaken in postwar Italian law. Disposition XII of the Transitional and Final Provisions of the Constitution of

---

Sixty Years after Its Adoption, eds. Christoph J.M. Safferling and Eckart-Alexander Conze (Hague: T.M.C. Asser Press, 2010), pp. 35–54.

[8] Schabas, *Genocide in International Law*, p. 5; Mark Mazover, "The Strange Triumph of Human Rights, 1933–1950," *The Historical Journal* 47/2 (2004), pp. 382, 387–388.

[9] Claudia Pohl, "European States Dealing with Extremist Political Parties: Prohibition of Political Parties as an Instrument of Repressive State Policy," *Fascism, Communism, and the Consolidation of Democracy: A Comparison of European Dictatorships*, eds. Gerhard Besier, Francesca Piombo, and Katarzyna Stoklosa (Berlin: Lit Verlag, 2006), pp. 95–110.

[10] Verfassungsgesetz vom 8. Mai 1945 über das Verbot der NSDAP (Verbotsgesetz); Bundesverfassungsgesetz vom 6. Februar 1947 über die Behandlung der Nationalsozialisten (Nationalsozialistengesetz).

[11] German Criminal Code, Article 86a. Article 86 of the Code penalizes the "dissemination of propaganda material of unconstitutional organizations."

[12] Basic Law for the Federal Republic of Germany, Article 21.2.

1947 forbade reorganizing, "under any form whatever, the dissolved fascist party."[13] In 1952, on the initiative of the Interior Minister Mario Scelba, the Italian parliament passed the most comprehensive postwar anti-fascist law, which introduced criminal liability for organizing fascist associations and participating in their activities. The Scelba Law also prohibited *apologia del fascismo* or "propaganda aimed at creating a [fascist] association, movement, or group." Under this law, "publicly exalting proponents, principles, deeds, and methods of fascism, or its antidemocratic purposes" became punishable by up to two years of imprisonment (and up to three years if such *apologia* concerned the fascists' "racist ideas and methods").[14] Later, in October 1978, a Law on Fascist Organizations was also adopted in Portugal in the aftermath of the revolution of 1974, which put an end to Salazar's *Estado Novo*. That legislation banned all "organizations that adhere to fascist ideology."[15]

Of course, regulating historical memory was not the main goal of those laws and international agreements; they had far more practical political objectives, not to mention that in the aftermath of the war, "the international human rights project was basically future-oriented"[16] and focused on the prevention of further crimes rather than on the victimization of the past. But all the laws do display some indirect linkage with historical memory. They implied a highly negative legal assessment of fascism and offered a vocabulary for conceptualizing it. And in so doing, they framed the memory of fascism (even if, as Andrea Mammone convincingly argues, "mainstream politics worked to avoid any serious debate regarding recent history," so that the assessment of fascism in the aftermath of the war remained somewhat ambiguous).[17]

Some of these documents contained no reference to actual historical experience. Thus, the German Basic Law used quite general terms to prohibit parties seeking to "undermine... the... democratic order." In

[13] Constitution of the Italian Republic, Section Transitional and Final Provisions, Disposition XII.
[14] Legge 20 guigno 1952, n. 645 (legge Scelba) "Norme di attuazione della XII disposizione transitoria e finale (comma primo) della Costituzione," Article 4; Talia Naamat, Nina Osin and Dina Porat, eds., *Legislating for Equality: A Multinational Collection of Non-Discrimination Norms*, vol. 1: Europe (Leiden, Boston: Martinus Nijhoff, 2012), pp. 231–232; Stefano Ceccanti and Francesco Clementi, "Italy," in *The 'Militant Democracy' Principle in Modern Democracies*, ed. Markus Thiel (Farnham: Ashgate, 2009), pp. 209–218.
[15] *Legislating for Equality*, p. 363.
[16] Regula Ludi, *Reparations for Nazi Victims in Postwar Europe* (Cambridge: Cambridge University Press, 2012), p. 2. Ludi shows that the problem of reparations for Nazi victims was being intensively discussed as early as the 1950s (pp. 95, 115).
[17] Andrea Mammone, *Transnational Neofascism in France and Italy* (New York: Cambridge University Press, 2015), p. 36.

this case, the vagueness was due to the fact that the law was meant to be, and actually was, used as a "two-edged sword... directed as much against recently defeated National Socialism as against really-existing state Socialism."[18] However, most of these documents contained historical references ranging from the rather indefinite to the very concrete. The Universal Declaration of Human Rights refers almost explicitly to Nazism when it states that "disregard and contempt for human rights have resulted in barbarous acts which have outraged the conscience of mankind."[19] And the Austrian and Italian anti-fascist laws, contrary to that passed in Germany, explicitly forbade fascist parties.

Several anti-fascist laws criminalized not only concrete actions, including membership in neo-fascist parties, but also statements about fascist politics. Some condemned exclusively performative utterances such as "direct and public incitement to commit genocide"[20] or "propaganda aimed at creating a [fascist] association."[21] But the Scelba Law also prohibited purely descriptive utterances that assessed the fascist regime and its politics in a positive way. The Portuguese law of 1978 also contained an indirect ban on statements about the past: it viewed "the idealization of persons most related to [fascist] regimes" as a criterion for assessing an organization as being fascist (Article 3.1).[22]

To this legislation, one has to add the trials of the German and Japanese war criminals in Nuremberg, Tokyo, and elsewhere. These trials unambiguously condemned fascist regimes and their leaders and played an important role in the molding of the memory of fascism as well as in the development of international law.

Much like the entire postwar arrangement (the "Yalta System") in general, the Nuremberg trials represented a compromise between the United States, Britain, and Stalin's Russia. In 1948, the UN Convention on genocide had defined its subject rather narrowly under pressure from the USSR. The Soviet leadership could certainly not accept a broader interpretation of genocide that would include extermination not only of racial or ethnic groups, but also of social classes. And the Western Allies, and even more so the USSR, had no interest in publicizing the complexity

[18] Peter Niesen, "Anti-Extremism, Negative Republicanism, Civic Society: Three Paradigms for Banning Political Parties," in *Europe's Century of Discontent: The Legacies of Fascism, Nazism, and Communism*, eds. Shlomo Avineri and Zeev Sternhell (Jerusalem: The Hebrew University Magnes Press, 2003), p. 250.
[19] The Universal Declaration of Human Rights, December 10, 1948, Preamble.
[20] Convention on the Prevention and Punishment of the Crime of Genocide, Article 3c.
[21] Legge n. 645 del 1952 (legge Scelba), Article 4. [22] *Legislating for Equality*, p. 363.

of the prewar situation, including problematic actions of their own that had contributed to the outbreak of the war. This is why references to the Nuremberg trials today raise numerous complex historical and legal issues.[23] All of this said, though, the foundations of anti-fascist legislation were indeed laid in the immediate postwar years.

Israel passed its own "Nazis and Nazi Collaborators (Punishment) Law" in August 1950.[24] This law introduced the death penalty for crimes against the Jewish people, crimes against humanity, and war crimes committed under the Nazi regime (Article 1a). It also provided long terms of imprisonment for those "who held any post or exercised any function" in an organization declared criminal by the Nuremberg Tribunal and who denounced the Jews to those organizations (Articles 4, 5, and 6). The definitions of crimes against humanity and war crimes provided by the law (Article 1b) used the language of the Charter of the Nuremberg Tribunal, while the definition of crimes against the Jewish people was a word-for-word borrowing from the 1948 Convention on genocide. Significantly, the Israeli law added two points to the UN definition: "(6) destroying or desecrating Jewish religious or cultural assets or values" and "(7) inciting to hatred of Jews." This law was one of the first attempts to criminalize hate speech by allusion to race and nationality.

The Development of Anti-Racist Legislation

The Cold War, however, temporarily suspended the development of anti-fascist legislation, and even the 1948 Convention on genocide was not ratified in some Western countries until the 1970s and 1980s, largely because they were not yet fully prepared to deal with the colonial legacy and racial inequality.[25] As already discussed, the memory of the Holocaust (and Nazi crimes in general) remained peripheral in the immediate post-war decades. It was not until the late 1950s and early 1960s that the first signs of a changing political climate appeared, several of which are particularly relevant to our topic. The Eichmann trial in Jerusalem in 1961 reanimated the Nuremberg notion of crimes against humanity and drew the

---

[23] See Chapter 6.

[24] The Nazis and Nazi Collaborators (Punishment) Law of August 1, 1950; Michael J. Bazyler and Julia Y. Scheppach, "The Strange and Curious History of the Law Used to Prosecute Adolf Eichmann," *Loyola of Los Angeles International and Comparative Law Review* 34/3 (2012), pp. 417–461.

[25] Karen E. Smith, *Genocide and the Europeans* (Cambridge: Cambridge University Press, 2010), pp. 43, 65–104. Great Britain ratified it in 1970 and the United States in 1985.

attention of international public opinion to the extermination of the Jews.[26] The Frankfurt trial of concentration camp personnel ("the Auschwitz trial") of 1963–1965 and other similar trials in Germany, Israel, and the USSR reinforced the effect of the Eichmann case. With regard to the Federal Republic of Germany, Devin O. Pendas speaks of "a juridification of the Nazi legacy" in the 1960s and underlines the importance of trials as "the dominant forum for dealing with the Nazi past" in the period of transition from the rehabilitation of Nazism in the 1950s to its condemnation in the 1970s (although he underlines the Germans' "significant 'inner resistance' to Nazi trials" during that period).[27] The Six-Day War of 1967 also contributed greatly to the rise of the Holocaust awareness in Israel and among American and European Jews. And at the same time, the civil rights movement in the United States, the formation of the postcolonial system, and issues related to the integration into European societies of immigrants from former colonies were bringing the problem of racism increasingly to the fore in the West. Manifestations of anti-Semitism, crimes against immigrants, and race riots came to be perceived as three aspects of a single problem.

The connection between racism and anti-Semitism was an obvious one. The memory of Nazi crimes served as a powerful argument in favor of protecting racial, ethnic, and religious minorities, while the political importance of the problem of racism contributed to a rising awareness of the Holocaust. In the 1960s and 1970s, the anti-fascist legislation of the 1940s gradually developed into a set of more far-reaching anti-racist laws. The emerging anti-racist legislation became an important component of the "legislation for equality" (or anti-discriminatory legislation) aimed at protecting a variety of subaltern groups.

Prior to World War II, anti-racist legal initiatives were rare, the best-known being the proposal to include a racial equality clause in the Covenant of the League of Nations put forward by Japan during the Paris Peace Conference of 1919. Of great importance for our purposes is France's Marchandeau Act of April 1939 of which the "archetypal" memory law, the Gayssot Act of 1990, was a direct descendent. Paul Marchandeau was a Radical Socialist politician and Minister of Justice in the left-wing government of Édouard Daladier. The law in question was

---

[26] Lawrence Douglas, *The Memory of Judgment: Making Law and History in the Trials of the Holocaust* (New Haven, Conn.: Yale University Press, 2001), pp. 97–182; David Cesarani, ed., *After Eichmann: Collective Memory and Holocaust Since 1961* (Abingdon: Routledge, 2005).

[27] Devin O. Pendas, *The Frankfurt Auschwitz Trial, 1963–1965: Genocide, History, and the Limits of the Law* (Cambridge: Cambridge University Press, 2006), pp. 21, 255.

adopted in response to the proliferation of anti-Semitism in France on the eve of World War II. At that time, anti-Semitism was a sign of pro-German sympathies and a weapon of the radical right in its struggle against the left (in which the latter was accused of anti-patriotism). The March-andeau Act prohibited "defamation and insults against a group of persons belonging by their origin to a particular race or religion, which have for their purpose to incite hatred against citizens or residents."[28] ("Residents" referred here to Jewish immigrants from Germany and Eastern Europe.) In August 1940, however, the law was repealed by the puppet Pétain government. That abrogation, along with all other acts of the Vichy regime, was in its turn declared null and void by de Gaulle's Provisional Government in August 1944. And to this very day "the... Marchandeau law continues to occupy a central place in contemporary French legal discourse around racism and discrimination."[29]

In Denmark, Article 244b was introduced in the penal code in 1939, in response to the growing anti-Semitism emanating from Germany. The article stated that

> Any person who, publicly or with the intention of wider dissemination, makes a statement or imparts other information by which a group of people are threatened, insulted or degraded on account of their race, colour, national or ethnic origin or religion shall be liable to a fine or to imprisonment for any term not exceeding two years.[30]

In light of this law, one can better understand the outstanding support that Danish Jews received from their compatriots during World War II. These examples (and some other cases, such as the English Public Order Act of 1936)[31] show that the struggle against anti-Semitism was crucial to

---

[28] Décret du 21 avril 1939 modifiant les articles 32, 33 et 60 de la loi du 29 juillet 1881 sur la liberté de la presse, ["Loi Marchandeau"]; Julie C. Suk, "Denying Experience: Holocaust Denial and the Free Speech Theory of the State," in *The Content and Context of Hate Speech: Rethinking Regulation and Responses*, eds. Michael Herz and Peter Molnar (Cambridge, New York: Cambridge University Press, 2012), p. 155.

[29] Suk, "Denying Experience," p. 158.

[30] *Legislating for Equality*, p. 129. See also Lene Johannessen, "Racist Snakes in the Danish Paradise," in *Striking a Balance: Hate Speech, Freedom of Expression and Non-Discrimination*, ed. Sandra Coliver (London: Article 19, International Centre against Censorship/Human Rights Center, University of Essex, 1992), p. 140.

[31] The Public Order Act of 1936 is sometimes considered "the first legislative response to a steady increase of incidents of incitement to racial hatred." See Kenneth Lasson, "Racism in Great Britain: Drawing the Line on Free Speech," *Boston College Third World Law Journal* 7/2 (1987), p. 165. Joanna Oyediran calls it "the first parliamentary attempt to deal with racist speech" ("The United Kingdom's Compliance with Article 4 of the International Convention on the Elimination of All Forms of Racial Discrimination," in *Striking a Balance*, p. 246). However, that law does not specifically forbid actions or statements of a racist nature: more generally, it criminalizes the use

the emergence of the anti-racist legislation. But notwithstanding these early developments, it took the crisis of the colonial system to create a robust momentum in favor of anti-racist legislation. Even the international law of the late 1940s was confronting the problem of racism in a rather general way, by proclaiming the equality of human beings and condemning genocide.

The 1960s witnessed the beginning of a new stage of development in international human rights law.[32] In 1960, the United Nations Declaration on the Granting of Independence to Colonial Countries and Peoples declared colonialism ("the subjection of peoples to alien subjugation, domination and exploitation") to be "a denial of fundamental human rights." It advocated "bringing to a speedy and unconditional end colonialism in all its forms and manifestations."[33]

The International Convention on the Elimination of all Forms of Racial Discrimination of 1965 marked the turning point in the drafting of human rights legislation. It stated that "any doctrine of superiority based on racial differentiation is scientifically false, morally condemnable, socially unjust and dangerous." The Convention also provided that "Each State Party shall prohibit and bring to an end, by all appropriate means, including legislation as required by circumstances, racial discrimination by any persons, group or organization."[34] Article 4 of this Convention

---

of "threatening, abusive or insulting words or behaviour with intent to provoke a breach of the peace or whereby a breach of the peace is likely to be occasioned" (Article 5). More importantly, it focused on the specific form in which the fascist movement manifested itself in Britain in the mid-1930s. It prohibits participation in "quasi-military organizations" as well as the wearing "in any public place or at any public meeting [of a] uniform signifying [a person's] association with any political organization." See Public Order Act 1936: An Act to prohibit the wearing of uniforms in connection with political objects and the maintenance by private persons of associations of military or similar character; and to make further provision for the preservation of public order on the occasion of public processions and meetings and in public places. 18 December 1936. This law was largely a response to Oswald Mosley's anti-Semitic speeches and the rallies of English fascists, and banned racism only indirectly. A similar law was adopted in France in January 1936 to stop the activities of the fascist "combat groups" (also known as *ligues*). See Loi du 10 janvier 1936 sur les groupes de combat et milices privées. Both acts had the very concrete political goal of preventing a possible fascist coup.

[32] On the stages of human rights legislation, see Jean L. Cohen, "Rethinking Human Rights, Democracy, and Sovereignty in the Age of Globalization," *Political Theory* 36/4 (2008), pp. 579–581.

[33] Declaration on the Granting of Independence to Colonial Countries and Peoples, December 14, 1960.

[34] International Convention on the Elimination of All Forms of Racial Discrimination, December 21, 1965, Article 2d.

directly addressed the issue of hate speech, calling for a legal ban on racist utterances and public associations based on racist ideas:

> States Parties...
> (a) Shall declare an offence punishable by law all dissemination of ideas based on racial superiority or hatred, incitement to racial discrimination...;
> (b) Shall declare illegal and prohibit organizations..., which promote and incite racial discrimination, and shall recognize participation in such organizations or activities as an offence punishable by law.

The Convention therefore committed its signatories to pass laws penalizing racial discrimination and hate speech. Most countries complied and in some cases had done so even prior to the adoption of the Convention,[35] but more typically they procrastinated, often because prohibiting hate speech was seen as an infringement of freedom of expression. Given that laws against hate speech now exist in most democratic countries,[36] the difficulties attendant on their birth may too readily be forgotten. Here, then, are some examples to illustrate the complexity of the process.

In postwar Britain, the question of racism was becoming increasingly acute due to immigration issues and the race riots of 1958. However, the Conservative government voted down an anti-discrimination bill in 1962 and other similar initiatives. It was not until 1965 that Harold Wilson's Labour government passed the first British anti-racist law – the Race Relations Act, which prohibited discrimination on racial grounds in certain public places (such as hotels and restaurants), created the offense of "incitement to racial hatred," and established the Race Relations Board to monitor cases of discrimination.[37] As in Germany several years earlier, a series of anti-Semitic acts and utterances had prompted the adoption of

---

[35] Thus, the US Civil Rights Act of 1964 outlawed "discrimination or segregation on the ground of race, color, religion, or national origin." See Public Law 88–352, Title 2.

[36] *Striking a Balance*; Sionaidh Douglas-Scott, "The Hatefulness of Protected Speech: A Comparison of the American and European Approaches," *William & Mary Bill of Rights Journal* 7/2 (1999), pp. 305–346; Michel Rosenfeld, "Hate Speech in Constitutional Jurisprudence: A Comparative Analysis," *Cardozo Law Review* 24/4 (2003), pp. 1523–1567; Erik Bleich, *Race Politics in Britain and France: Ideas and Policymaking since the 1960s* (Cambridge: Cambridge University Press, 2003); Bleich, "The Rise of Hate Speech and Hate Crime Laws in Liberal Democracies," *Journal of Ethnic and Migration Studies* 37/6 (2011), pp. 917–934; Alexander Tsesis, "Dignity and Speech: The Regulation of Hate Speech in a Democracy," *Wake Forest Law Review* 44 (2009), pp. 497–532; and Roni Cohen, "Regulating Hate Speech: Nothing Customary about It," *Chicago Journal of International Law* 15/1 (2014), pp. 229–255.

[37] Lasson, "Racism in Great Britain," pp. 165–167; Bob A. Hepple, "The British Race Relations Acts, 1965 and 1968," *The University of Toronto Law Journal* 19/2 (1969), pp. 248–257; Bleich, *Race Politics in Britain and France*, pp. 35–87; Bleich, "The Rise of Hate Speech and Hate Crime Laws in Liberal Democracies," p. 919.

anti-racist legislation in the United Kingdom. (In 1963, for example, Colin Jordan, the leader of the far-right National Socialist Movement, was opining publicly that "Hitler [had been] right" in his campaign against "world Jewry."[38])

The law of 1965 was, however, generally seen as incoherent and inefficient. In 1968, another Race Relations Act prohibited discrimination with regard to housing and employment. The third Race Relations Act that followed in 1976 amended the Public Order Act of 1936 by including an article criminalizing incitement to hatred against a racial group. In all these laws, the term "racial group" was understood very broadly as "a group of persons defined by reference to colour, race, nationality [including citizenship] or ethnic or national origins."[39] In 1986, the new Public Order Act criminalized a broad spectrum of actions, from using "threatening, abusive, or insulting words" and circulating inappropriate publications to recording and broadcasting racist visual and audio materials, provided that those acts were committed by those intending "to stir up racial hatred" or if "racial hatred is likely to be stirred up thereby."[40] British authorities refer to this legislation to explain why Britain does not need a memory law, since the racist agendas of deniers are already subject to punishment on the basis of laws already on the books. However, Britain is notorious for applying its hate speech laws seldom and very selectively.[41]

In 1960, in response to a series of desecrations of synagogues and Jewish cemeteries, the German parliament modified Article 130 of the Penal Code, making it a criminal offense to "incite hatred against parts of the population [and] curse, maliciously malign or defame them" "in a manner that is capable of disturbing the public peace and assaulting the human dignity of others."[42] This article replaced the old Article 130 of the Penal Code of 1871, which provided a penalty of up to two years' imprisonment for "anyone who [would] publicly, in a manner dangerous to the public peace, incite different classes of the population to acts of violence against

---

[38] Lasson, "Racism in Great Britain," p. 165.   [39] Race Relations Act 1976, part 9, section 70 (6).
[40] Public Order Act 1986, part 3, articles 18–23.   [41] Cohen, "Regulating Hate Speech," p. 252.
[42] Sechstes Strafrechtsänderungsgesetz vom 30. Juni 1960, Article 2; Benedikt Rohrßen, *Von der "Anreizung zum Klassenkampf" zur "Volksverhetzung" (§ 130 StGB): Reformdiskussion und Gesetzgebung seit dem 19. Jahrhundert* (Berlin: De Gruyter Recht, 2009), pp. 162–166; Eric Stein, "History against Free Speech: The New German Law against the 'Auschwitz' – and Other – 'Lies,'" *Michigan Law Review* 85/2 (1986), pp. 282–285, 322. According to Harold Marcuse, 1960, with its "wave of anti-Semitic vandalism," marked "a clear watershed" in German Holocaust remembrance. See his *Legacies of Dachau: The Uses and Abuses of a Concentration Camp, 1933–2001* (Cambridge: Cambridge University Press, 2001), p. 205. However, he also underlines that this change was prepared by earlier developments (p. 200).

each other."[43] The law of 1960 replaced the word "classes" with the expression "parts of the population," which covered racial, ethnic, and religious groups. The German law of 1960 was one of the first to de facto criminalize hate speech with allusion to race or nationality, although it did not actually use those words.[44]

The 1960 law emphasized human dignity, an idea that was one of the German constitutional tradition's central concepts. Indeed, Article 1.1 of the Basic Law of 1949 reads: "Human dignity shall be inviolable. To respect and protect it shall be the duty of all state authority."[45] The law of 1960 added to that by making it possible to prosecute Holocaust denial, and a little later was actually used for that purpose. Also in 1960, the Austrian Insignia Act forbade the wearing and display of Nazi uniforms, emblems, and symbols.[46]

The importance of Germany's resolute stand against anti-Semitism becomes clear in the context of Adenauer's politics of memory, which emphasized the Nazi leadership's responsibility for war crimes in order to exculpate ordinary Germans, presenting them as victims rather than perpetrators. This policy crucially depended on showing that ordinary Germans had nothing to do with tenets of Nazi ideology such as anti-Semitism, which was perceived "as a threat to the national identity of Germany as a normal nation."[47] However, the law of 1960 sought to prevent generally anti-Semitic acts, rather than focusing specifically on Holocaust denial. Interestingly, it was also intended as part of Adenauer's policy aimed at counterbalancing the growing emphasis on the memory of Nazi crimes in the German Democratic Republic.[48] In 1973, the German parliament amended Article 131 of the Penal Code to expand the ban on

[43] *The Criminal Code of the German Empire*, trans. Geoffrey Drage (London: Chapman and Hall, 1885), p. 221. Banning hate speech by allusion to class distinctions was also typical of the French legislation of the nineteenth century. Thus, a law on freedom of the press of September 9, 1835, prohibited "incitement to hatred between different classes of society." The same article criminalized also "attacks against property [and] the respect which is due to laws." See Loi sur les crimes, délits, et contraventions de la presse et des autres moyens de publication, in *Les codes français: conformes aux textes officiels*, ed. C. Bourguignon, new edition by P. Royer-Collard (Paris: G. Thorel et Joubert, 1844), p. 26. For other similar legal provisions, see Achille Morin, *Répertoire général et raisonné du droit criminel* (Paris: A. Durand, 1851), vol. 2, pp. 548–550.

[44] The notion of racial hatred first appeared in German legislation in the Law Against Writings Endangering Youth of June 1953. See Stein, "History against Free Speech," p. 285, note 33.

[45] Basic Law for the Federal Republic of Germany, Article 1.1.   [46] *Legislating for Equality*, p. 31.

[47] Robert A. Kahn, "Cross-Burning, Holocaust Denial, and the Development of Hate Speech Law in the United States and Germany," *University of Detroit Mercy Law Review* 83/3 (2006), p. 168.

[48] Mutual influences and competition were typical of the two Germanies. See Tobias Hochscherf, Christoph Laucht, and Andrew Plowman, eds., *Divided, But Not Disconnected: German Experiences of the Cold War* (New York: Berghahn Books, 2010).

the "representation of violence [and] instigating race hatred," by criminalizing the dissemination and public exhibition of

> Writings... that incite to race hatred or describe cruel or otherwise
> inhuman acts of violence against humans in a manner, which glorifies or
> minimizes such acts of violence or represents the cruel or inhumane aspects
> of the occurrence in a manner offending human dignity.[49]

That was, of course, an indirect ban on negationism. Somewhat later,
the notion of "glorifying or minimizing" inhuman acts entered the lexicon
of Holocaust denial laws.

Italy passed a law on the prevention and prohibition of the crime of
genocide in 1967. Article 8 of that law made the public incitement to, and
justification of, genocide a crime punishable by imprisonment for three to
twelve years.[50] The International Convention on the Elimination of All
Forms of Racial Discrimination was ratified there as late as 1975 by a law
that criminalized the dissemination of "ideas based on racial superiority or
hatred" and incitement to discrimination or acts of violence on the
grounds of a person's belonging to a particular "national, ethnic, or racial
group."[51] In June 1993, in response to the increasing activity of the
far-right movement, including a neo-fascist rally held in 1992 to commemorate the seventieth anniversary of the March on Rome, the Italian
parliament passed a law on Urgent Measures in Matters of Racial, Ethnic
and Religious Discrimination. That document, commonly known as the
Mancino Law, amended the aforementioned laws of 1967 and 1975,
restated the ban on organizations "whose own goals are to incite to
discrimination or to violence because of racial, ethnic, national or religious
reasons," and criminalized the wearing of the emblems or symbols of those
organizations at public meetings.[52] The adoption of this law triggered a
massive enforcement operation against skinheads, whose larger cells were
shut down in the following months.[53]

---

[49] German Criminal Code, Article 131; Stein, "History against Free Speech," pp. 322–323.
[50] Legge 9 ottobre 1967, n. 962, Prevenzione e repressione del delitto di genocidio; *Legislating for Equality*, p. 231.
[51] Legge 13 ottobre 1975, n. 654, Ratifica ed esecuzione della convenzione Internazionale sull'eliminazione di tutte le forme di discriminazione razziale, aperta alla firma a New York il 7 marzo 1966.
[52] Technically, the Mancino Act gave the force of law to the Government's decree on issues of non-discrimination of April 26, 1993. See Legge 25 giugno 1993, n. 205, Conversione in legge, con modificazioni, del decreto-legge 26 aprile 1993, n. 122, recante misure urgenti in materia di discriminazione razziale, etnica e religiosa; *Legislating for Equality*, p. 233.
[53] Rebecca Clifford, *Commemorating the Holocaust: The Dilemmas of Remembrance in France and Italy* (New York: Oxford University Press, 2013), p. 150.

The circumstances of the adoption, in 1972, of France's Pleven Act clearly show that the memory of World War II was facilitating the development of anti-racist legislation. The right- and left-wing parties unanimously and enthusiastically voted to approve the new law, referring to the enormity of Nazi crimes as the most tragic manifestation of racism.[54] The Pleven Act banned racial discrimination and amended the 1881 law on freedom of the press by making it a criminal offense to "provoke to discrimination, hatred or violence with regard to a person or a group of persons by reason of their origin and their membership or non-membership of an ethnic group, a nation, a race, or a religion." The law provided the same penalty of up to one year of imprisonment for defamation of a person or a group of people with regard to their race, religion, or nationality, and banned the public distribution of written or printed materials that could provoke such defamation.[55] Similar bills were also passed in other countries.[56]

The introduction of the principle of the imprescriptibility of crimes against humanity was another important aspect of the growing corpus of human rights legislation. Although the twenty-year term for crimes committed during World War II would expire in 1965, war criminals were still being tried. Initiatives regarding the extension of those time limits came mostly from the countries of the Eastern Bloc and especially from Poland, where most of the extermination camps had been located during the war. In 1968, the Convention on the Non-Applicability of Statutory Limitations to War Crimes and Crimes against Humanity was adopted by the UN General Assembly, committing party states to continue prosecuting, "irrespective of the date of their commission," war crimes, crimes against humanity, genocide, and "inhuman acts resulting from the policy of apartheid."[57] Russia,

[54] Marc Olivier Baruch, *Des lois indignes? Les Historiens, la politique et le droit* (Paris: Tallandier, 2013), p. 61.
[55] Loi no. 72–546 du 1 juillet 1972 relative à la lutte contre le racisme; Suk, "Denying Experience," pp. 149–150; and Bleich, *Race Politics in Britain and France*, pp. 114–141.
[56] Following the ratification of the UN 1965 Convention in 1971, the Netherlands amended Section 137 of its Criminal Code ("Crimes against Public Order") by prohibiting the deliberate "public expression of views insulting to a group of persons on account of their race, religion or conviction or sexual preference" and incitement to hatred, discrimination, and violence on racial and religious grounds. See Ineke Boerefijn, "Incitement to National, Racial and Religious Hatred: Legislation and Practice in the Netherlands," in *Striking a Balance*, p. 202. Belgium's law of July 30, 1981, criminalized incitement to discrimination, hatred, or violence against a person "on the grounds of his nationality, alleged race, skin color, ancestry, or national or ethnic origin." Loi no. 1981-07-30/35 du 30 juillet 1981 tendant à réprimer certains actes inspirés par le racisme ou la xénophobie, articles 3, 20.
[57] Convention on the Non-Applicability of Statutory Limitations to War Crimes and Crimes against Humanity adopted by the General Assembly on November 26, 1968. In its Preamble, the

Ukraine, Poland, Hungary, and Romania were among the first to ratify the Convention. Attempts to introduce the principle of imprescriptibility in Western countries had been successful to varying degrees. Thus, there were four *Verjärungsdebatten* (debates on imprescriptibility) in the West German parliament before the time limitation was entirely abolished in 1979. In every case, Social Democrats pushed for continuing the persecution of the Nazi war criminals, while a gradually decreasing proportion of liberals and conservatives claimed that this would be an ex post facto enactment.[58] The French parliament, by contrast, adopted the principle of imprescriptibility as early as 1964, largely because the *Bundestag* was so obviously hesitant to do so, which was one of the first signs of the emergence of the new victim-centered memory regime in France.[59]

The expansion of legislation on the issues of racism and xenophobia prepared the way for the Holocaust denial laws of the 1980s and 1990s. Some anti-fascist and anti-racist enactments allowed for the prosecution of Holocaust revisionism and were indeed used for this purpose, although the regulation of historical memory was not their main goal. In any event, they created a legal framework for the criminalization of statements about the past by making hate speech a punishable offense. Characteristically, the Gayssot Act of 1990 was an amendment to the Pleven Act of 1972, while the German memory law of 1994 was a modification of the law of 1960, which had introduced criminal liability for the incitement of hatred with allusion to race or nationality. Penalizing Holocaust negationism was a logical next step that further developed anti-racist legislation in the context provided by the rise of memory.

The Point of Departure: The German Memory Law of 1985

The first attempt to specifically criminalize Holocaust denial was undertaken in Germany in 1982 on the strength of a long evolution of German

Convention refers to UN resolutions of 1966 condemning the policy of apartheid, which is another indication that the legacy of colonialism and World War II were being approached as two sides of the same coin.

[58] In 1960, the Social Democrats' initiative was rejected; in 1965, the time limit was moved from May 1965 (the twentieth anniversary of the Victory Day) to May 1969 (the twentieth anniversary of the Federal Republic); in 1969, it was changed from twenty to thirty years, which extended it to 1979. See Jeffrey Herf, *Divided Memory: The Nazi Past in the Two Germanys* (Cambridge, Mass.: Harvard University Press, 1997), pp. 339–342; Helmut Dubiel, *Niemand ist frei von der Geschichte: Die nationalsozialistische Herrschaft in den Debatten des Deutschen Bundestages* (Munich: Carl Hanser, 1999), pp. 103–110, 160–174.

[59] Johann Michel, "L'institutionalisation du crime contre l'humanité et l'avènement du régime victimo-mémoriel en France," *Canadian Journal of Political Science* 43/3 (2011), pp. 668–669.

legislation and legal practice. In the 1960s and 1970s, deniers were prosecuted in Germany mostly on the basis of Articles 130 and 131, which prohibited hate speech and dissemination of pro-Nazi literature, and Article 185, which protected personal honor. Typically, local courts hesitated to use those provisions against deniers, but the Supreme Court insisted on their applicability.

The 1970s witnessed the formation, in Germany as elsewhere, of a Holocaust-centered memory regime.[60] The events of 1968 and the election of Willy Brandt's Social-Democratic government in 1969 marked a new stage in the democratization of West German society. The new chancellor called for the abandonment of postwar revanchism, the acceptance of the country's new boundaries, and the normalization of its relationships with Eastern Europe. Brandt's *Kniefall* ("kneeling") before the monument to the Warsaw Ghetto Uprising in 1970 was a symbolic expression of German repentance for Nazi crimes committed in Eastern Europe.[61] The generational change, the end of the postwar recovery, and the emergence of Germany as the economic engine of Europe explained the massive (albeit not unanimous) support in Germany for the new *Ostpolitik*, which was continued under Brandt's successor, Helmut Schmidt. That politics was widely viewed in the Federal Republic as an essential part of a new, future-oriented democratic Germany that was liberating itself from the burden of the past and questioning inherited authorities and traditions.[62]

But building trust with Poland and Russia was not the only reason behind the Social Democrats' politics of memory. In the East, the predominant interpretation of the war ignored the extermination of the Jews, because the memory of the Shoah was seen as an "irritating competitor" to the Soviet war myth.[63] Nonetheless, Brandt and Schmidt persisted in emphasizing the memory of the Holocaust; the rise of that memory in the United States and Israel had arguably exerted a significant influence on

---

[60] Eric Langenbacher, "Changing Memory Regimes in Contemporary Germany?," *German Politics and Society* 21/2 (2003), p. 55.

[61] Herf, *Divided Memory*, p. 345.

[62] Edgar Wolfrum, *Geschichte als Waffe: Vom Kaiserreich bis zur Wiedervereinigung* (Göttingen: Vandenhoeck & Ruprecht, 2001), pp. 86–87; Marcuse, *Legacies of Dachau*, pp. 290–325. Anthony Dirk Moses underlines the role of the generation of '68 in challenging the generally forgiving postwar attitudes toward Nazism, but also the importance of the revision of "German intellectual traditions" by the generation of '45, which prepared the ground for the formation of "cultural modernity" in Germany after 1968. See his *German Intellectuals and the Nazi Past* (Cambridge: Cambridge University Press, 2007), pp. 8, 66, 69.

[63] Herf, *Divided Memory*, p. 381.

the perception of the past in the Germany of the 1970s. In particular, reaching a common understanding of the Shoah was a sine qua non condition for developing a partnership with Israel, which was a priority of the Federal Republic's foreign policy.[64] Brandt's *Kniefall* resonated with both narratives, on the Holocaust and on the resistance to Nazism (especially because the Warsaw Ghetto Uprising "symbolize[d] the whole Holocaust" in light of Israel's national story of heroic resistance).[65]

During their time in power (1969–1982) the Social Democrats succeeded in building a broad consensus around the Holocaust as the central event of the war, while the German-centered historical memory of the Adenauer era was marginalized, though by no means eliminated.[66]

The criminalization of negationism was a natural consequence of the new attitude toward the Nazi past. In 1979, the Civil Chamber of the Federal Court of Justice ruled Holocaust denial to be defamatory of, and insulting to, German Jews (and consequently punishable as an offence against their human dignity).[67] Robert A. Kahn concludes: "Since the 1970s Holocaust revisionism has been illegal in Germany."[68]

The plan to enact the first memory law was proposed by Helmut Schmidt's Social Democratic government in 1982, two days before its fall. It was not enough, the authors of the draft argued, to consider denial merely an insult to the individual honor of citizens, inasmuch as it is also a crime against public peace.

Helmut Kohl's new center-right government proved to be far less supportive of the bill. Kohl's politics of memory was simultaneously

---

[64] On German-Jewish dialogue over the legacy of the war, see Mary J. Gallant and Harry M. Rhea, "Collective Memory, International Law, and Restorative Social Processes after Conflagration: The Holocaust," *International Criminal Justice Review* 20/3 (2010), pp. 265–279.

[65] Mikael Tossavainen, "Calendar, Context and Commemoration: Establishing an Israeli Holocaust Remembrance Day," in *Echoes of the Holocaust: Historical Cultures in Contemporary Europe*, eds. Klas-Göran Karlsson and Ulf Zander (Lund: Nordic Academic Press, 2003), p. 70.

[66] Wulf Kansteiner, *In Pursuit of German Memory: History, Television and Politics after Auschwitz* (Athens, Ohio: Ohio University Press, 2006), pp. 109–153.

[67] "The Jews living in the Federal Republic... are entitled, as a component of their personal self-image, to be viewed as a part of a group, singled out by fate, to which all others owe a particular moral responsibility, and that is an aspect of their honor. The respect of this self-image constitutes for every one of them one of the guarantees against a repetition of discrimination and a basis of their life in the Federal Republic. Whoever attempts to deny these events [i.e., the Holocaust] deprives each and every one of them of the personal worth to which they are entitled. For the affected person such denial means a continuation of the discrimination against the group of people to which he belongs, and simultaneously a direct discrimination against his own person." The Court considered this status to be exclusively typical of the Jews. See Stein, "History against Free Speech," p. 303.

[68] Robert A. Kahn, "Informal Censorship of Holocaust Revisionism in the United States and Germany," *George Mason University Civil Rights Law Journal* 9/1 (1998), p. 140.

innovative and traditionalist. On the one hand, he was one of the first
Western leaders to realize the growing political importance of the past.
A trained historian, Kohl practiced the politics of memory far more
systematically than any of his predecessors.[69] On the other hand, especially
at the beginning of his mandate, the new chancellor attempted to return to
Adenauer's interpretation of the war. Kohl's "quest for normality," or
rather for "liberation from anti-national sentiments" and the dismantling
of "the Germans' stigma"[70] entailed relativizing, if not silencing, Nazi
crimes. His neoconservative cultural offensive was in line with the attempts
of Margaret Thatcher and Ronald Reagan to revamp their own respective
"national romances." Although Kohl's efforts initially proved unproduct-
ive, they have largely succeeded in the long run, when after the fall of
communism and the reunification of Germany he developed a new
approach to the politics of history that would embrace the memory of
the Holocaust as the symbol of Nazi rule.

In 1982, Kohl still considered the memory of the Holocaust part of the
political arsenal of the left, which is why he opposed the introduction of a
Holocaust denial bill. The project had been turned down several times
before the governing coalition proposed a compromise, which was to
outlaw not only Holocaust denial, but also the denial of "any genocide,"
including the expulsion of the German population from Eastern Europe
after 1945.[71] But even this was not enough to usher the bill to passage. To
save what could be saved from the project, another compromise was agreed
upon: continue considering Holocaust denial an insult to personal honor;
maintain the reference to other criminal regimes; but also allow the state to
persecute denial ex officio, without a private petition being needed to
initiate the suit.[72] This enabled the bill to pass.

---

[69] Dubiel, *Niemand ist frei von der Geschichte*, p. 190.

[70] Christian Wicke, *Helmut Kohl's Quest for Normality: His Representation of the German Nation and
Himself* (New York: Berghahn Books, 2015), p. 5.

[71] Stein, "History against Free Speech," p. 307. On the painful memories of this expulsion, which
many Germans saw as a crime against humanity comparable to the Holocaust, see Robert G.
Moeller, *War Stories: The Search for a Usable Past in the Federal Republic of Germany* (Berkeley:
University of California Press, 2001).

[72] Article 194 of the Penal Code provided: "Persecution for insult shall be instituted only upon
petition." The 1985 law added the following clause: "A petition is not required, if the insulted
person was persecuted as a member of a group under the National Socialist or another violent and
arbitrary dominance, if the group is part of the population and the insult is connected with such
persecution." See Einundzwanzigstes Strafrechtsänderungsgesetz von 13. Juni 1985, Article 4;
Stein, "History against Free Speech," p. 323; Thomas Wandres, *Die Strafbarkeit des Auschwitz-
Leugnens* (Berlin: Duncker and Humblot, 2000), pp. 110–112.

The significance of this episode becomes obvious in light of the Bitburg scandal, which was sparked by Ronald Reagan's 1985 visit, in connection with the celebration of Victory Day, to a German military cemetery that contained, among others, the bodies of former SS soldiers. The visit was initially conceived by its German organizers as a recognition of "the shared comradeship of arms, the sacrifices on both sides now to be hallowed as historical 'tragedy.'"[73] And that symbolism – which was denounced by the media worldwide as an attempt to rehabilitate the Reich – was not much different from what Kohl's party sought to achieve (in the same year) by banning denial of genocides other than the Holocaust.

The Bitburg scandal was followed by the *Historikerstreit*, in which Germany's leading intellectuals, including Jürgen Habermas, became embroiled in a heated debate that was widely covered by the international media. Historian Ernst Nolte had developed a "soft form" of historical revisionism. While not denying Nazi crimes, he tried to relativize them through comparison and by shifting the responsibility for the "European civil war" of 1917–1945 to Bolshevism.[74] Nolte was almost openly supported by Helmut Kohl, who sympathized with his attempts to provide Germans with a more positive national identity. But the majority of intellectuals, in Germany and worldwide, condemned any attempt to relativize the Holocaust.

With regard to the politics of memory, the *Historikerstreit* was the central event of the neoconservative cultural offensive of the 1980s. The failure of right-wing governments to rehabilitate the history of the nation-states explains the turn that the politics of memory took in the 1980s and 1990s. The fall of communism, the reunification of Germany, and the prospect of German leadership of a united Europe were contributory factors.[75] Germany would be unlikely to achieve its goal if it did not embrace the Holocaust-centered vision of the war, given the anxieties that its reunification was provoking in several European countries, including

[73] Charles S. Maier, *The Unmasterable Past: History, Holocaust, and German National Identity* (Cambridge, Mass.: Harvard University Press, 1997), p. 10; Geoff Eley, "Nazism, Politics and the Image of the Past: Thoughts on the West German *Historikerstreit*, 1986–1987," *Past and Present* 121 (1988), pp. 171–208; Ian Buruma, *The Wages of Guilt: Memories of War in Germany and Japan* (New York: Farrar, Straus, and Giroux, 1994); Herf, *Divided Memory*, pp. 334–372; and Kansteiner, *In Pursuit of German Memory*, pp. 54–85, 248–279.

[74] Peter Baldwin, ed., *Reworking the Past: Hitler, the Holocaust, and the Historians' Debate* (Boston: Beacon Press, 1990); Ernst Nolte, *Three Faces of Fascism: Action Française, Italian Fascism, National Socialism* (New York: Holt, Rinehart, and Winston, 1966); Nolte, *Der europäische Bürgerkrieg 1917–1945: Nationalsozialismus und Bolschewismus* (Berlin: Propyläen Verlag, 1987).

[75] Bill Niven, *Facing the Nazi Past: United Germany and the Legacy of the Third Reich* (London: Routledge, 2002).

France. The fall of communism made "conservative politicians [realize] that properly displayed historical guilt could be a source of cultural as well as economic capital," which is why many of them (including Kohl) eventually rallied and "challenged the Holocaust monopoly of the Left."[76] Building social consensus (and European identity) around the legacy of anti-fascism was important to the integration of the political tradition of the left into the post–Cold War order (which was gradually shifting to the right).

Helmut Kohl's politics of memory of the 1990s reflected that shift. Notwithstanding his enduring reservations about the memory of the Shoah and the attempts of the right to promote the memory of communist crimes committed in the GDR,[77] the official German memory became centered on the extermination of the Jews, with an emphasis on the shared responsibility for the Shoah ("the new Europeanization of the Holocaust"). This model found support throughout Europe. By the mid-1990s, Kohl's revised politics of memory had proved overwhelmingly successful,[78] as the Holocaust was integrated into the official historical narrative of a Germany-dominated Europe. Shortly thereafter, however, the theme of German victimhood returned in the German public debate.[79] German conservative intellectuals did, to be sure, continue to call for overcoming the "leftist German self-hatred."[80] But by and large the warnings regarding the eventual re-nationalization of the past in united Germany, of which there was no shortage in the early 1990s,[81] have proven exaggerated, because "even amongst a majority of [German] conservative historians there is still a clear commitment to the European Union and the West."[82]

[76] Kansteiner, *In Pursuit of German Memory*, pp. 251, 262–263.
[77] Niven, *Facing the Nazi Past*, pp. 41–61.
[78] Wulf Kansteiner, "Losing the War, Winning the Memory Battle: The Legacy of Nazism, World War II, and the Holocaust in the Federal Republic of Germany," in *The Politics of Memory in Postwar Europe*, eds. Richard Ned Lebow, Wulf Kansteiner, and Claudio Fogu (Durham, N.C.: Duke University Press, 2006), p. 127.
[79] Gavriel D. Rosenfeld, *Hi Hitler! How the Nazi Past Is Being Normalized in Contemporary Culture* (Cambridge: Cambridge University Press, 2015), pp. 36–42; Robert G. Moeller, "Germans as Victims? Thoughts on a Post-Cold War History of World War II's Legacies," *History and Memory* 17/1–2 (2005), pp. 147–194; Omer Bartov, "Germany as Victim," *New German Critique* 80 (2000), pp. 29–40.
[80] Irene Götz, "The Rediscovery of 'the National' in the 1990s – Contexts, New Cultural Forms and Practices in Reunified Germany," *Nations and Nationalism*, DOI: 10.1111/nana.12171, p. 6.
[81] Anson Rabinbach, "From Expulsion to Erosion: Holocaust Memorialization in America since Bitburg," *History and Memory* 9/1–2 (1997), p. 236.
[82] Stefan Berger, *The Search for Normality: National Identity and Historical Consciousness in Germany since 1800* (New York: Berghahn Books, 1997), pp. 111, 182.

In this context, the German parliament adopted, in 1994, a new memory law modeled after France's Gayssot Act of 1990.[83] In the late 1990s, Germany and France became the main driving force behind the efforts to transform the memory of the Holocaust into an official memory of the European Union and promote the criminalization of denial throughout Europe. The ethnic cleansings in Europe and elsewhere in the 1990s also contributed to "the... integration of genocide consciousness as a human rights concern."[84]

But let us return to the mid-1980s. Israel was soon to follow Germany by passing a bill of its own to criminalize Holocaust denial.[85] The memory of the Holocaust became central to the Israeli identity in the late 1960s and 1970s, largely due to the wars of 1967 and 1973. The law was adopted in the context of the legislative reform undertaken in response to the electoral success of the far-right Kach party, which was founded by Rabbi Meir Kahane in 1971 and entered the Knesset in 1984. In 1985, the Knesset amended the Basic Law to forbid any political party from participating in elections "if its aims or deeds explicitly or implicitly deny the existence of the State of Israel as the State of the Jewish people, deny the democratic character of the State, or incite to racism."[86] In 1986, the Knesset amended the Penal Code and criminalized any publication performed "with the purposes of stirring up racism" (Article 144B). And the Holocaust denial law of 1986 provided that

> A person who, in writing or by word of mouth, publishes any statement denying or diminishing the proportions of acts committed in the period of the Nazi regime, which are crimes against the Jewish people or crimes against humanity, with intent to defend the perpetrators of those acts or to express sympathy or identification with them, shall be liable to imprisonment for a term of five years.[87]

The same punishment was ordered for publishing "any statement expressing praise or sympathy" for Nazi crimes (Article 3). For definitions

---

[83] See below in this chapter.

[84] Samuel Moyn, *The Last Utopia: Human Rights in History* (Cambridge, Mass.: Belknap Press, 2010), p. 220.

[85] Luigi Cajani considers the 1986 Israeli act to be the first Holocaust denial law and not without reason, since the German law of 1985 was a partial failure. See his "Diritto penale et libertà dello storico," in *Riparare, Risarcire, Ricordare: Un dialogo tra storici e giuristi*, eds. Georgio Resta and Vinzenzo Zeno-Zencovich (Napoli: Editoriale Scientifica, 2012), p. 373.

[86] Quoted in Elieser Lederman and Mala Tabory, "Criminalization of Racial Incitement in Israel," in *Striking a Balance*, p. 182. This ban was confirmed in 1992. See Joshua Schoffman, "Legislation against Racist Incitement in Israel: A 1992 Appraisal," in *Striking a Balance*, pp. 193–197.

[87] Denial of Holocaust (Prohibition) Law 5746–1986 of July 8, 1986, Article 2.

of crimes against the Jewish people and crimes against humanity, the 1986 law referred to the Nazis and Nazi Collaborators (Punishment) Law of 1950. This ban on negationism was far more explicit than it had been in the German law of 1985. However, the 1986 law could not serve as a model for other countries because it was too deeply rooted in the Israeli legal tradition.

The Classical Memory Law: The French Gayssot Act of 1990

The expansion of memory laws began in 1990 with the adoption of France's Gayssot Act, which set the standard for several international agreements and national laws. By 1990, all necessary preconditions for expanding that legislation were in place: the human rights ideology and the memory of the Holocaust were firmly established in the West. The deniers' movement was also attracting considerable public attention due to several protracted scandals such as the Zündel and Faurisson cases, which enjoyed extensive press coverage for many years. But attempts to rehabilitate national histories had failed, and many conservative politicians found it wiser to support initiatives from the left to criminalize the denial, while at the same time promoting a soft "cultural patriotism" and a cult of national heritage. In other words, by 1990, the Holocaust-and-heritage model of Western historical consciousness had largely taken its final form.

In the 1970s and 1980s, the Holocaust-centered memory regime came to replace the myth of the French people united in their struggle against fascism that Charles de Gaulle had promoted in the aftermath of the war and during his tenure as President of the Republic (1958–1969).[88] The memory of the Holocaust, focused then on deportations of French Jews to the death camps, was already quite present in France in the 1950s, and the 1960s witnessed its gradual expansion.[89] The French Jewish memory was strongly influenced by the pro-Israeli mobilization during and after the Six-

---

[88] On the politics of memory in France, see Johann Michel, *Gouverner les mémoires: Les politiques mémorielles en France* (Paris: Presses Universitaires de France, 2010); Henry Rousso, *The Vichy Syndrome: History and Memory in France since 1944* (Cambridge, Mass.: Harvard University Press, 1994); Rousso, *The Haunting Past: History, Memory, and Justice in Contemporary France* (Philadelphia: University of Pennsylvania Press, 2002); and Rousso, *Face au passé: Essais sur la mémoire contemporaine* (Paris: Belin, 2016).

[89] Annette Wieviorka, "Shoah: Les étapes de la mémoire en France," *Les guerres de mémoires: La France et son histoire*, p. 113; Wieviorka, *Déportation et génocide: Entre la mémoire et l'oubli* (Paris: Hachette, 2000); Joan B. Wolf, *Harnessing the Holocaust: The Politics of Memory in France* (Stanford, Calif.: Stanford University Press, 2004); and Samuel Moyn, *A Holocaust Controversy: The Treblinka Affair in Postwar France* (Waltham, Mass.: Brandeis University Press, 2005).

Day War of 1967, which proved especially powerful due to the French government's continuing support for the Arab countries.[90] De Gaulle's fall in 1969 contributed to the undermining of his war myth: with his departure, the epoch of French history whose main event was the Resistance seemed to have ended. The events of 1968 had made a greater impression on France than on other Western countries and contributed to the left-wing intellectuals' disillusionment with the prospects of a "radiant future." The "Solzhenitsyn effect" (the shock produced by the publication of a French translation of *The Gulag Archipelago* in Paris in 1974) drove a crucial wedge between French fellow travelers and Soviet Communism, and contributed to the crisis of the future and the memory boom.

The *affaire Faurisson* shaped the immediate context in which the Gayssot Act was adopted. Robert Faurisson, professor of French at the University of Lyon, surfaced as the central figure of French negationism in 1978, when his article denying the existence of gas chambers was published in *Le Monde*. The debate around the Faurisson case, the best-known junctures of which were Noam Chomsky's articles in support of Faurisson's "right to say it" and Pierre Vidal-Naquet's passionate repudiation of the applicability of the principle of freedom of speech to Holocaust negationism, had a potent international dimension.[91]

Chomsky's position found few supporters. If the *Historikerstreit* had prompted international public opinion to resolutely condemn the relativization of the Holocaust, the *affaire Faurisson* resulted in a widely shared consensus that the search for truth was not the deniers' intent. Negationism came to be unambiguously considered a form of hate speech that could be legitimately banned. In 1981, Faurisson was sentenced, after civil litigation, to a symbolic fine of 1 franc for the improper conduct of historical research and causing harm to the plaintiff (several anti-racist associations), a judgment that was widely perceived as a failure of the French legal system to face the challenge of negationism. Although the French law required the plaintiff to prove the accusation in court, which implied demonstrating the reality of the Holocaust, neither the plaintiff nor the court was eager to engage in such an exercise. The former did not

---

[90] Robert Gildea, "Myth, Memory and Policy in France since 1945," in *Memory and Power in Post-War Europe: Studies in the Presence of the Past*, ed. Jan-Werner Müller (Cambridge: Cambridge University Press, 2002), p. 64; Wolf, *Harnessing the Holocaust*, pp. 25–50.

[91] Noam Chomsky, "His Right to Say It," *The Nation*, February 28, 1981; Pierre Vidal-Naquet, "On Faurisson and Chomsky" [1981], in *Assassins of Memory: Essays on the Denial of the Holocaust* (New York: Columbia University Press, 1992), p. 71; Valérie Igounet, *Histoire du négationnisme en France* (Paris: Seuil, 2000), pp. 231–405.

want to acknowledge Holocaust denial as a position worthy of discussion, while the latter felt it had "neither the authority nor the competence to judge History."[92] The idea of passing a special law that would facilitate the fight against denial naturally emerged from this context.

In the 1980s, several new factors contributed to the growing popularity of this idea, including the electoral successes of the French National Front and the trial of Klaus Barbie, a former Gestapo head in Lyon deported from Bolivia to France in 1983 and convicted of crimes against humanity in 1987. The extent to which ordinary Frenchmen were involved in collaboration with Nazism, including the deportation of the Jews, became a passionately debated political topic, as did the Fifth Republic's responsibility for the crimes committed by "the French State" (the official name of the puppet regime of Marshal Pétain). Notwithstanding that many French politicians, including François Mitterrand, claimed that there had been no continuity between the Vichy regime and postwar France, and that consequently it would be pointless for the French president to apologize for the deportations, the opposite attitude came to prevail in French public opinion (one of the first acts of Mitterrand's successor, Jacques Chirac, upon taking the office in 1995 was in fact to recognize the French nation's responsibility for the deportations).[93]

The idea of passing a memory law in France was originally suggested in 1987 by Charles Pasqua, a long-time de Gaulle supporter and the Minister of the Interior in Jacques Chirac's right-wing cohabitation government. A year later, Socialist Georges Sarre submitted a project criminalizing "insults to the memory and honor of the victims of the Nazi Holocaust by negating it or minimizing its importance."[94] The text of the adopted bill was authored by Jean-Claude Gayssot, an influential communist deputy, which is another indication that the criminalization of denial was rooted in the political tradition of the left. But it was obviously also compatible with the Gaullist tradition. Indeed, anti-fascism was essential to both Gaullism and communism. However, the unanimity with which the French parliament had adopted the Pleven Act of 1972 was absent in

---

[92] Quoted in Robert A. Kahn, *Holocaust Denial and the Law: A Comparative Study* (New York: Palgrave Macmillan, 2004), p. 34.

[93] Baruch, *Des lois indignes?*, pp. 66–80. Arguably, Mitterrand's resistance to the idea of presenting apologies for the deportations was partly due to his covert anti-Semitism and his ambiguous attitudes toward Vichy. See Richard J. Golsan, "The Legacy of World War II in France: Mapping the Discourse of Memory," in *The Politics of Memory in Postwar Europe*, p. 84.

[94] Madeleine Rébérioux, "Le Génocide, le juge et l'historien," *L'Histoire* 138 (November 1990), pp. 92–94; Baruch, *Des lois indignes?*, pp. 27–64.

1990: the Holocaust could now no longer be seen as an exclusively "German guilt" in which the French nation was in no way implicated. Like most memory laws, the Gayssot Act involved the nation's repentance for crimes that not everyone was prepared to acknowledge.

Certainly, the French politics of memory in 1981 to 1995 differed from that in the United States, Great Britain, and Germany: France had a socialist president (even though the government was controlled by the right for a part of that period) and the neoconservative cultural offensive, including attempts to rehabilitate the "national romance," was restrained there in comparison with the efforts of Thatcher, Reagan, and Kohl. To be sure, a "soft version" of cultural patriotism and a cult of national heritage (*patrimoine*) did come to typify France at that time,[95] which was by no means incompatible with the memory of the Holocaust. In the 2000s, France became the center of the international movement among historians against memory laws. But by the turn of the 1990s, an overwhelming majority of French intellectuals (with some notable exceptions such as Pierre Vidal-Naquet and Madeleine Rebérioux) supported the criminalization of untoward statements about the past.

The Faurisson case had demonstrated the reluctance of French judges to become involved in establishing "the truth of the past." To relieve the courts of this obligation, legislators took the responsibility on themselves and unambiguously criminalized denial. All that the courts now had to prove was the fact of the denial, not the fact of the Holocaust. The Gayssot Act (titled "a law seeking to repress any racist, anti-Semitic, or xenophobic act") was conceived as a continuation of existing anti-racist legislation, including the 1939 Marchandeau Act and the 1972 Pleven Act. It reiterated the ban introduced by the Pleven Act with reference to "discrimination based on belonging or not belonging to an ethnic group, a nation, a race or a religion" but added that:

> Whoever should have disputed... the existence of one or many crimes against humanity, as they were defined in Article 6 of the Statute [Charter] of the International Military Tribunal annexed to the London Agreement of 8 August 1945, that were committed by members of an organization declared criminal by the application of Article 9 of the mentioned Statute, or by a person declared guilty of such crimes by a French or an international jurisdiction shall be punished with [one year imprisonment and a fine of 45,000 euros or one of the punishments only].[96]

---

[95] Baruch, *Des lois indignes?*, pp. 247–280.
[96] Loi no 90–615 du 13 juillet 1990 tendant à réprimer tout acte raciste, antisémite ou xenophobe. The English translation is quoted from *Legislating for Equality*, pp. 156–157. See also Kahn,

Strictly speaking, the reference to the Charter of the Nuremberg Tribunal, which was later reflected in several other memory laws throughout Europe, is used here to *define* the term "crimes against humanity"; but it can also be interpreted as prohibiting denial of the crimes *established* by the Tribunal.

In fact, determining exactly which crimes the Gayssot Act forbids the denial of is not easy. Article 9 of the Nuremberg Charter, to which it refers, allowed the International Military Tribunal to declare criminal any organization whose members were convicted of crimes against peace, crimes against humanity, and war crimes; the Charter further stipulated that, upon such declaration, any member of such organization would "be entitled to apply to the Tribunal for leave to be heard by the Tribunal upon the question of the criminal character of the organization" (the Tribunal, though, was given a right to reject those applications).[97] In other words, the Charter conceded "the other side" the right to be heard, which was intended to give more weight to the Tribunal's decisions. The Tribunal has indeed declared groups and organizations such as the Nazi party leadership, the SS, and the Gestapo criminal, on the basis of the conviction of their members.[98] The notion of specific crimes perpetrated by those groups and organizations is, of course, more concrete than the blanket term "Nazi crimes," but one is still entitled to wonder if all the crimes ever attributed to them actually happened as reported.[99] Reference to documents that *establish* the fact of those crimes seems hard to avoid if legislators seriously intend to define what exactly they consider to be absolutely true and legally undeniable.

Unsurprisingly, the Gayssot Act also uses the notion of crimes committed by persons convicted "by a French or an international jurisdiction," which is an even more concrete notion than crimes perpetrated by criminal organizations. But by doing so, it substitutes the truth of the trial for historical truth, and as we know, serious doubts have been voiced as to whether those truths are fully fungible. In addition, the international jurisdictions to which the law refers obviously include the Nuremberg Tribunal itself. However, the reference is made here to the individual

Holocaust Denial and the Law, pp. 101–118, and Roberto D'Orazio, "La memoria doverosa: L'Esperienza francese delle *lois mémorielles*," in *Riparare, Risarcire, Ricordare*, pp. 411–445.
[97] Charter of the International Military Tribunal, Article 9: http://avalon.law.yale.edu/imt/imtconst .asp.
[98] Judgment of the International Military Tribunal, section "The Accused Organizations": http:// avalon.law.yale.edu/imt/judorg.asp.
[99] See Chapter 6.

sentences handed down by the Tribunal rather than to its Judgment as a whole. Indeed, the Judgment of the Nuremberg Tribunal is a document whose use entails complex historical and legal interpretation, and the French lawmakers were clearly aware of that. That is why they made such an effort to avoid a straightforward reference to the Nuremberg Judgment.

In fact, despite the seemingly technical language of the law, it simply prohibits the denial of "facts of common knowledge," for which the Nuremberg Tribunal itself had a right not to "require proofs," as stated in Article 21 of its Charter. Although that is, of course, by no means an ideal solution, the point is that the Gayssot Act does not endorse every single statement in the Nuremberg Judgment (unlike Russia's 2014 memory law, which unambiguously affirms that Judgment, as it is seen in Russia as being protective of the official Soviet narrative of war).

The adoption of the Gayssot Act enabled the conviction of Faurisson and of several other deniers. It was, however, criticized for limitations it apparently placed on freedom of research. During Faurisson's 1996 appeal case, several members of the UN Human Rights Committee expressed the following individual opinion: "The Gayssot Act is phrased in the widest language and would seem to prohibit publication of bona fide research connected with matters decided by the Nuremberg Tribunal."[100] However, over the past twenty-five years, there seems not to have been a single case when "bona fide" historical research was indeed prevented by that law, while several deniers (including Roger Garody) have been convicted on its basis. Several attempts have recently been made to replace the Gayssot Act with a broader interdiction of negationism in regard to other crimes against humanity, to which we will return later in this chapter.

The Internationalization of Holocaust Denial Legislation

Shortly after the adoption of the Gayssot Act, Austria, Switzerland, Belgium, and Spain also criminalized Holocaust denial. The shaping of Holocaust awareness in Austria largely followed the same tempo as in Germany, although the rise of the far right in the 1990s proved particularly noteworthy there.[101] Still, in Austria as in Germany, the groundwork was laid for the criminalization of denial by anti-fascist and anti-racist

[100] Quoted in Ludovic Hennebel and Thomas Hochmann, "Introduction: Questioning the Criminalization of Denials," in *Genocide Denials and the Law* (Oxford: Oxford University Press, 2011), p. XXXIII.

[101] Heidemarie Uhl, "From Victim Myth to Co-Responsibility Thesis: Nazi Rule, World War II, and the Holocaust in Austrian memory," *The Politics of Memory in Postwar Europe*, pp. 40–72.

legislation. In February 1992, Article 3h was added to Austria's Prohibition Law of 1945/1947. This article stipulated that

> A person shall also be liable to [imprisonment of one to ten years] if, in print or in a broadcast or in some other medium, or otherwise publicly in any manner accessible to a large number of people, he denies the National Socialist genocide or other National Socialist crimes against humanity, or seeks to minimize them in a coarse manner or consents thereto or to justify them.[102]

The Austrian law provides an exceptionally stern penalty for denial. As for the definition of what exactly may not be denied, it clearly refers to the Nazi genocide as a "fact of common knowledge."

In Switzerland, the official resistance myth survived until the scandals of the 1990s, which were rooted in the discovery of the Swiss banks' wartime collaboration with the Nazis. At this point, the problem of Swiss Holocaust bystanders became central to national and international debates.[103] However, the decision to pass a Holocaust denial law had been taken in Switzerland prior to the Nazi assets scandal, which probably explains its very broad wording and the absence of any explicit reference to the Shoah. The criminalizing of negationism was, rather, part of a broader anti-racist law that was passed by the parliament on June 18, 1993, and enacted in January 1995. This new legislation amended the Penal Code of 1937 and outlawed the denial of genocide in general, not restricting penalties to the Nazi genocide:

> Any person who publicly incites hatred or discrimination against a person or a group of persons on the grounds of their race, ethnic origin or religion...; or any person who on any of these grounds denies, trivialises or seeks justification for genocide or other crimes against humanity... is liable to a custodial sentence not exceeding three years or to a monetary penalty.[104]

Given the spreading criminalization of denial, the German government had no choice but to follow suit, amending Article 130 of the Criminal Code in 1994, shortly after the Supreme Court had ruled that the existing version of that article (introduced in 1960) banned Nazi propaganda but

---

[102] Bundesverfassungsgesetz [No. 148/1992 of March 19, 1992], mit dem das Verbotsgesetz geändert wird (Verbotsgesetz-Novelle 1992), Article 4; *Legislating for Equality*, p. 31.

[103] Regula Ludi, "What Is Special about Switzerland? Wartime Memory as a National Ideology in the Cold War Era," in *The Politics of Memory in Postwar Europe*, pp. 210–248; Ludi, *Reparations for Nazi Victims in Postwar Europe*, pp. 145–184.

[104] Swiss Criminal Code of 21 December 1937, Article 261*bis*; *Legislating for Equality*, pp. 463–464; and ECRI Report on Switzerland, 1998, p. 8.

not "a bare denial of gas chambers."[105] Denial was now banned as a crime against public peace rather than against individual honor. The following section (130.3) was added to the Criminal Code:

> Whoever publicly or in a meeting approves of, denies or downplays an act committed under the rule of National Socialism of the kind indicated in Section 220a Subsection 1 [the article on genocide], in a manner capable of disturbing the public peace shall be punished with imprisonment for not more than five years or a fine.[106]

By adopting this bill, Germany considerably upgraded its Holocaust denial legislation in line with the new pan-European trend. Belgium was the next country to follow that trend, whose trajectory from a heroic war myth to the Shoah-centered memory regime had been influenced in large part by the evolution of historical memory in France.[107] In 1995, Belgium followed the French example by passing an ad hoc Holocaust denial law:

> Whosoever, [publicly] denies, grossly minimizes, attempts to justify or approves of the genocide committed by the German National-Socialist regime during the Second World War shall be punished by a prison sentence of eight days to one year, and by a fine of twenty six francs to five thousand francs.[108]

Spain also criminalized Holocaust denial. In the early post-Franco decades, the crimes of the Civil War and the subsequent dictatorship remained a taboo topic in Spain, which refused to countenance the

---

[105] Robert A. Kahn, "Cross-Burning, Holocaust Denial, and the Development of Hate Speech Law in the United States and Germany," *University of Detroit Mercy Law Review* 83/3 (2006), p. 190.

[106] Gesetz zur Änderung des Strafgesetzbuches... (Verbrechensbekämpfungsgesetz) von 28. Oktober 1994, Article 7. A reference to the definition of genocide given in the Code of Crimes against International Law later replaced the reference here to Section 220a: *Legislating for Equality*, p. 181. In 2005, Paragraph 4 was added to Section 130. It provides that "Whosoever publicly or in a meeting disturbs the public peace in a manner that violates the dignity of the victims by approving of, glorifying or justifying National Socialist rule of arbitrary force shall be liable to imprisonment not exceeding three years or a fine." Section 189 of the Criminal Code ("Violating the memory of the dead") stipulates: "Whosoever defames the memory of a deceased person shall be liable to imprisonment not exceeding two years or a fine" (*Legislating for Equality*, p. 183). See also Wandres, *Die Strafbarkeit des Auschwitz-Leugnens*, pp. 113–121, and Rohrßen, *Von der "Anreizung zum Klassenkampf" zur "Volksverhetzung,"* pp. 194–208.

[107] On the postwar heroic narrative in Belgium, see Pieter Lagrou, "The Victims of Genocide and National Memory: Belgium, France, and the Netherlands, 1945–1965," *Past and Present* 154 (1997), pp. 181–222, and Lagrou, *The Legacy of Nazi Occupation: Patriotic Memory and National Recovery in Western Europe, 1945–1965* (Cambridge: Cambridge University Press, 2000).

[108] Loi du 23 mars 1995 tendant à réprimer la négation, la minimisation, la justification ou l'approbation du génocide commis par le régime national-socialiste allemand pendant la seconde guerre mondiale, Article 1; *Legislating for Equality*, p. 58; Pieter Lagrou, "Sanctionner pénalement les négationnistes?," *Politique: Revue de débats* 47 (December 2006), pp. 15–17.

discussion of fascism's legacy in general. In fact, the 1977 Amnesty Law forbade the persecution of crimes committed under the Franco regime.[109] During the period of transition, however, Spain gradually adopted several anti-discriminatory laws, in which it followed the example of other EU countries.[110] In particular, Article 607.2 of the new Penal Code of 1995 (in force since 1996) stated:

> Any dissemination of ideas or doctrines that deny or justify the crimes specified in the above paragraph of this article [namely, genocide], or that pretend to rehabilitate regimes or institutions that promote such practices, by any means, shall be punished with imprisonment for a period of one to two years.[111]

But this provision was partly invalidated in 2007 as a violation of freedom of expression, following the lengthy trial of Pedro Varela, the leading Spanish denier. According to the Constitutional Court, justification of the Holocaust may be criminalized, but its denial may not.[112]

However, the 1995 code also included Article 510, which forbade incitement to racial discrimination, hatred, and violence and, in its second part, provided a penalty up to three years of incarceration for disseminating defamatory information against racial or other groups "with knowledge of its falseness or reckless disregard for the truth." In principle, this article could also be used against deniers, and it is hardly surprising that, during the 2015 revision of the Penal Code, it was amended to reintroduce a ban on negationism (which the European Council had been persistently encouraging Spain to do). The new legislation has introduced a punishment of from one to four years of incarceration for those who

> Publicly deny, seriously trivialize, or extol the crimes of genocide, crimes against humanity or against persons or goods protected in the event of armed conflict, or extol the perpetrators of those crimes, when they had been committed against a group or a part thereof, or against a person determined by reason of his belonging to such group, for racist, anti-

[109] Ley 46/1977, de 15 de octubre, de Amnistía.
[110] Maria Miguel Sierra, "Anti-Discrimination Legislation in EU Member States: Spain," www.pedz .uni-mannheim.de/daten/edz-b/ebr/02/ART13_Spain-en.pdf.
[111] Ley Orgánica No. 10/1995, de 23 de noviembre, del Código Penal; *Legislating for Equality*, p. 438; ECRI Report on Spain, 1999, p. 8.
[112] See ECRI Report on Spain (fourth monitoring cycle), 2010, p. 11; Laurent Pech, "The Law of Holocaust Denial in Europe: Toward a (Qualified) EU-Wide Criminal Prohibition," in *Genocide Denials and the Law*, pp. 206–209; Stephen E. Atkins, *Holocaust Denial as an International Movement* (Westport, Conn.: Praeger Publishers, 2009), pp. 131–132; Jonathan D. Josephs, "Holocaust Denial Legislation: A Justifiable Infringement of Freedom of Expression?," Série des Working Papers du Centre Perelman de philosophie du droit, no. 2008/3, pp. 15–16.

Semitic, or other reasons related to ideology, religion, or beliefs, family situation or membership of an ethnic group, race or nation, national origin..., sexual orientation..., gender, disease or disabilities, when [by those actions] a climate of violence, hostility, hatred or discrimination against them is promoted or encouraged.[113]

The Code now also provides for up to two years imprisonment for those who, for the same reasons, "infringe the dignity of people" or "extol or justify by any means of public expression or dissemination [the aforementioned] crimes" (articles 510.2.A and B).

The 2015 Spanish memory law is part of the most recent wave of Western European legislation criminalizing the past, including the 2016 Italian and the 2017 French statutes, which we will discuss later in this chapter. For now, though, let us return in the late 1990s, when such Western Europe countries as Luxembourg (1997) and Liechtenstein (1999)[114] also criminalized Holocaust negationism. The 1997 Luxembourgian statute introduced into the Criminal Code Article 457–3:

> 1. Whoever... had contested, minimized, justified or denied the existence of one or of many crimes against humanity or war crimes, as defined by Article 6 of the Statute of the International Military Court, annex to the London Agreements of 8 August 1945, that were committed by members of an organization considered criminal in application of Article 9 of the same Statute, or by a person considered culpable of such crimes by a Luxembourgian or by a foreign or an international instance, shall be punished with imprisonment from eight days to six months and with a fine from 10,001 to 1,000,000 francs, or with one of both punishments alone.
>
> 2. Whoever... had contested, minimized, justified or denied the existence of one or of many of the genocides, as defined by Law of 8 August 1985 on the Punishment of Genocide and recognized by a Luxembourgian or by an international instance, shall be punished with the same punishments or with one of both punishments alone.[115]

---

[113] Código Penal (Ley Orgánica N° 10/1995, de 23 de noviembre, modificada por la Ley Orgánica N° 4/2015 de 27 de abril), Article 510.1.C. Article's 607.2 ban on genocide denial was suppressed in the 2015 Code.

[114] Article 283, as amended in December 1999 (given the force of law in 2000), of the Penal Code of 1987 says: "A person shall be punished with imprisonment of up to two years, if the person... (2) publicly disseminates ideologies aimed at a systematic disparagement or defamation of members of a race, ethnicity or religion;... (5) publicly denies, grossly plays down the harm of, or attempts to justify genocide or other crimes against humanity." See *Legislating for Equality*, p. 260, and ECRI Second Report on Liechtenstein, 2002, p. 9.

[115] Loi du 19 juillet 1997 complétant le code pénal en modifiant l'incrimination du racisme et en portant incrimination du révisionnisme..., Article 3; *Legislating for Equality*, pp. 277–278; ECRI

In its first part, the Luxembourgian law reproduces almost verbatim the Gayssot Act in penalizing denial (and, in contrast to its French model, justification) of Nazi crimes against humanity. But it was also the first law to ban the denial of Nazi war crimes, which several later acts also did. Also, in its second part, it forbids the negation of other genocides and crimes against humanity. For the first time, norms prohibiting denial of Nazi crimes and of other genocides were included as two separate bans in one and the same legislation, an approach that later became paradigmatic in the European Union and found its expression in the 2008 Framework Decision and several national laws. Both innovations pointed to a tendency toward expanding the scope of memory laws. Several factors could account for that. First, war crimes had become a politically urgent topic in light of the Yugoslav wars and the activities of the International Criminal Tribunal for the Former Yugoslavia (created in 1993 but in operation since the autumn of 1994). Second, in 1996, the European Union endorsed the notion of criminalizing the past and directly connected the struggle against negationism with combating racism and xenophobia. This connection was, of course, also obvious to French, German, Austrian, and Belgian authors of memory laws, but their laws were more immediately influenced by the debates about those countries' national pasts. All this makes the Luxembourgian case (together with the 1998 Polish law, the first memory law per se to be adopted in Eastern Europe) a milestone in the development of the legislation about history. With the adoption of all these bills Holocaust denial legislation was becoming a pan-European phenomenon.

The late 1990s witnessed the beginning of a new period in the development of Holocaust denial legislation. It was characterized by the further internationalization of the movement and its expansion across Eastern Europe; the role of the European Council in promoting it; the extension of memory laws to new topics (the Armenian genocide, communist crimes, the slave trade); and a rising tide of protest against them.

The 1990s witnessed the culminating stage of European integration and a mounting concern that the united Europe should be grounded in

---

Second Report on Luxembourg, 2002, p. 8. The law also renamed the chapter (chapter 6) of the code of which this article was part titling it "On Racism, Revisionism, and Other [Forms of] Discrimination" (instead of "On Certain Other Crimes against Persons"). In 2011 and 2012, Article 457–3 was amended: the sanctions were increased to up to two years of incarceration and a reference to the definition of crimes against humanity in the Statute of the International Criminal Court (in 2011) and in the new articles 136.2, 136.3, and 136.5 of the Penal Code was added. See Loi du 13 février 2011 portant modification de l'article 457–3 du Code pénal and Loi du 27 février 2012 portant adaptation du droit interne aux dispositions du Statut de Rome de la Cour pénale internationale.

common values and memories. This created conditions favorable for the reanimation of the initial anti-fascist inspiration of the European project, which was of particular importance given the consolidation of neo-fascist movements in the region. Several new challenges, such as the increasing use of the internet by deniers and the attacks on the memory of the Shoah from Islamic countries (especially Iran), also influenced the Holocaust denial legislation of the 2000s.[116]

Under the influence of Germany and France, the European Council became the major driving force behind the adoption of the new memory laws. The EU Joint Action of July 1996, which aimed to harmonize policies adopted to confront racism and xenophobia, invited the member states, in clear emulation of the Gayssot Act, to criminalize "public denial of the crimes defined in Article 6 of the Charter of the International Military Tribunal."[117] In 2001, Germany initiated the European Council Framework Decision on combating racism and xenophobia. This document committed member states to make Holocaust denial a punishable offense.[118] Many countries had difficulty subscribing to this decision and claimed that an explicit ban on denial would limit freedom of expression and that the already existing anti-racist legislation provided for the punishment of deniers. The negotiations dragged on for seven years. Meanwhile, in 2003, the European Council adopted an Additional Protocol to the Convention on Cybercrime and encouraged the Party States to criminalize

> Distributing or otherwise making available, through a computer system to the public, material which denies, grossly minimizes, approves or justifies acts constituting genocide or crimes against humanity, as defined by international law and recognized as such by final and binding decisions of the International Military Tribunal, established by the London Agreement of 8 August 1945, or of any other international court established by relevant international instruments and whose jurisdiction is recognized by that Party.[119]

---

[116] David Fraser, "'On the Internet, Nobody Knows You're a Nazi': Some Comparative Legal Aspects of Holocaust Denial on the WWW," in *Extreme Speech and Democracy*, eds. Ivan Hare and James Weinstein (Oxford: Oxford University Press, 2009), pp. 511–537.

[117] 96/443/JHA: Joint Action of 15 July 1996, title 1; Mark Bell, *Racism and Equality in the European Union* (Oxford: Oxford University Press, 2008), pp. 157–177; Luigi Cajani, "Diritto penale et libertà dello storico," pp. 379–391.

[118] *Combating Racism and Xenophobia through Criminal Legislation*, p. 24; Laurent Pech, "The Law of Holocaust Denial in Europe: Toward a (Qualified) EU-Wide Criminal Prohibition," in *Genocide Denials and the Law*, pp. 223–234.

[119] Additional Protocol to the Convention on Cybercrime, Concerning the Criminalization of Acts of a Racist and Xenophobic Nature Committed through Computer Systems, Strasbourg, January 28, 2003, Article 6.1.

Once again, the wording here has been influenced by the Gayssot Act, although the Additional Protocol refers not only to the definition of Nazi crimes given by international law, but also to concrete decisions by the Nuremberg Tribunal that, the document emphasizes, are "final and binding," which is not far from endorsing any given statement of the Nuremberg Judgment. Not coincidentally, the formula "final and binding" (with regard to that Judgment) is typically used in Russian official documents; in 2003 the prospects for EU–Russia cooperation were still looking bright. The ongoing discussion within the EU and the absence of a shared position regarding the criminalization of denial is manifest in a clause that allowed a signatory to "reserve the right not to apply, in whole or in part," the aforementioned provision (Article 6.2). However, several countries did introduce memory laws that complied with it (Slovenia and Macedonia in 2004, Andorra in 2005,[120] Cyprus in 2006,[121] and Portugal in 2007). Article 240.2 of the Portuguese Penal Code, for instance, stipulated that

> Whosoever, in a public meeting, in a written manner intended for dissemination or by any other means of social communication or through an informational system... insults or injures a person or a group of persons because of their race, colour, ethnic or national origin, religion, gender or sexual orientation, specifically denial of war crimes or crimes against peace and humanity...; with the intention to incite to racial or religion discrimination or to encourage it, shall be punished with imprisonment of a period of 6 months to 5 years.[122]

"Denial of war crimes or crimes against peace and humanity" is obviously a partial duplication of the Nuremberg classification of Nazi crimes. However, the formula used in the Portuguese law is broad enough to cover the denial of other genocides as well.

---

[120] Article 458 of the Penal Code of Andorra of 2005 stipulated: "Whosoever denies, through the media, the existence of facts described as genocide in this chapter, which are declared and tested by a jurisdiction, shall be punished with imprisonment for up to two years." This law is interesting because of the reference to the courts' decisions recognizing certain events as genocides, which was most likely inspired by the Gayssot Act. Article 457 criminalized "transmit[ting], by any means, ideologies or doctrines aimed at justifying genocide or justifying regimes, parties or organizations that practiced or supported it." See Llei 9/2005, del 21 de febrer, qualificada del Codi penal and *Legislating for Equality*, p. 14.

[121] The case of Cyprus is somewhat special. ECRI Report on Cyprus (fourth monitoring cycle, 2011, p. 11) states: "In March 2006, the law ratifying the Additional Protocol to the Convention on Cybercrime concerning the criminalization of acts of a racist or xenophobic nature committed through a computer system [Section 7], created new criminal offences on issues such as Holocaust denial and dissemination of racist material through the Internet. There is no case law yet invoking this law." Such law was passed in 2011.

[122] Lei no. 59/2007 de 4 de Setembro [2007] (Vigésima terceira alteração ao Código Penal); *Legislating for Equality*, p. 365.

The Framework Decision that was finally adopted by the European Union in November 2008 formally obliged Member States to punish

> c. Publicly condoning, denying or grossly trivialising crimes of genocide, crimes against humanity and war crimes as defined in Articles 6, 7 and 8 of the Statute of the International Criminal Court, directed against a group of persons or a member of such a group defined by reference to race, colour, religion, descent or national or ethnic origin when the conduct is carried out in a manner likely to incite to violence or hatred against such a group or a member of such a group;
> d. Publicly condoning, denying or grossly trivialising crimes of genocide, crimes against humanity and war crimes as defined in the Statute of the International Criminal Court (Articles 6, 7 and 8) and crimes defined in Article 6 of the Charter of the International Military Tribunal, when the conduct is carried out in a manner likely to incite violence or hatred against such a group or a member of such a group.[123]

By contrast to the 2003 Additional Protocol, the Framework Decision refers only to the definition of Nazi crimes given by international law, not to the documents establishing them. After the 2004 EU enlargement, and especially given the memory wars between Russia and its Eastern European neighbors (2008 was also the year of the Prague Declaration), it was not feasible to refer to the Nuremberg Judgment as establishing full historical truth in an EU official document.

The Council's expectation was that all parties would penalize the denial of Nazi crimes as well as that of other genocides, but most countries preferred to adopt one solution or the other.[124] And even then, not all member states agreed to pass memory laws, having reached a common understanding that punishing deniers on the basis of anti-racist laws was an acceptable alternative.

Following the Framework Decision, several countries passed memory laws (Malta[125] and Latvia in 2009; Hungary, Lithuania, and Montenegro

---

[123] European Council Framework Decision 2008/913/JHA of 28 November 2008 on Combating Certain Forms and Expressions of Racism and Xenophobia by Means of Criminal Law, Article 1; Luigi Cajani, "Criminal Laws on History: The Case of the European Union," *Historein* 11 (2011), pp. 27–35

[124] Report from the Commission to the European Parliament and the Council on the Implementation of Council Framework Decision 2008/913/JHA on Combating Certain Forms and Expressions of Racism and Xenophobia by Means of Criminal Law, Brussels, January 27, 2014, pp. 4–5.

[125] Article 82B of the Criminal Code of Malta as amended in 2009 says: "Whosoever publicly condones, denies or grossly trivializes genocide, crimes against humanity and war crimes directed against a group of persons or a member of such a group defined by reference to race, color, religion, descent or national or ethnic origin when the conduct is carried out in a manner (a) likely to incite

in 2010; Cyprus in 2011;[126] Greece in 2014; and Italy in 2016). We will discuss the Greek and the Italian cases here and consider the Eastern European laws in the following chapter.

Greece passed the first broad anti-racist law in 1979, shortly after the fall of the military dictatorship and the establishment of democracy in 1974. This law, adopted in preparation for the country's accession to the European Union, banned the "expression of offensive ideas aimed at racial discrimination."[127] A bill criminalizing Holocaust denial submitted in February 2011 by the Ministry of Justice was rejected by the parliament in January 2012, because the influential far-right Popular Orthodox Rally (LAOS) Party was strongly opposed to it.[128] But a second attempt in September 2014 proved successful. The new law provided that

> Anyone who intentionally, either orally, through the press, online, or by any other means or methods, condones, trivialises, or denies the existence or seriousness of the crimes of genocide, war crimes, crimes against humanity, the Holocaust, or Nazi crimes, when those crimes have been established by international court decisions or the Greek Parliament, if this conduct is directed against a group of persons or a member of such a group defined by race, colour, religion, descent, national or ethnic origin, sexual orientation, or gender identity and in a manner that is likely to incite hatred or violence or is of a threatening or insulting nature against such a group or one of its members, will be punished by the punishments indicated above [i.e., imprisonment of three months to three years and a fine of 5,000 to 20,000 euros].[129]

to violence or hatred against such a group or a member of such a group; (b) likely to disturb public order or which is threatening, abusive or insulting, shall, on conviction, be liable to imprisonment for a term from eight months to two years." Article 82C provides the same punishment for denying or trivializing crimes against peace. See Act No. XI of July 17, 2009, An Act Further to Amend the Criminal Code, Article 3 and *Legislating for Equality*, pp. 298–299.

[126] Law no. 134 (I) of 21 October 2011 on Combating Certain Forms and Expressions of Racism and Xenophobia by Means of Criminal Law was enacted within the framework of the transposition of the Framework Decision of 28 November 2008. See *Legislating for Equality*, p. 108, and Corina Demetriou, Executive Summary: Country Report Cyprus 2013 on measures to combat discrimination, January 1, 2014, pp. 4–5: www.non-discrimination.net/countries/cyprus.

[127] Nasos Theodorides and Ioannis N. Dimitrakopoulos, "Analytical Report on Legislation: Greece," Antigone Information and Documentation Centre, Athens 2004, pp. 19–29: http://fra.europa.eu/sites/default/files/fra_uploads/300-R4-LEG-EL.pdf.

[128] Theresa Papademetriou, "Greece: New Proposal on Fighting Racism and Xenophobia," March 7, 2011: www.loc.gov/lawweb/servlet/lloc_news?disp3_l205402556_text.

[129] Law no. 4285/2014, Article 2, quoted in Theresa Papademetriou, "Greece: New Law Criminalizes Denial of Genocide, Hate Speech, and Other Acts of Racism," September 24, 2014: http://www.loc.gov/lawweb/servlet/lloc_news?disp3_l205404129_text; ECRI Report on Greece (fifth monitoring cycle), February 24, 2015, pp. 13–14.

This law reproduces the wording of the Framework Decision, although it refers not to the definition of those crimes in international law but to the decisions of international courts and the Greek parliament establishing the truth of the past.

In Italy, Holocaust-centered memory emerged as late as the 1990s, which is not surprising given the country's relatively limited involvement in the extermination of the Jews during the war. Paradoxically, the formation of the Holocaust-centered memory regime coincided with the emergence of a powerful trend toward the normalization of the past. After the fall of communism and the dramatic decrease in the Communist Party's popularity, the legacy of anti-fascism came under attack from the new right, which included Silvio Berlusconi's Forza Italia party. The new right's "anti-anti-fascist" project of national "reconciliation" presupposed that fascism and anti-fascism had to be viewed as two equally extremist movements.[130]

The tension between the "European" approach and its new nationalist counterpart manifested itself in a conflict over proposed memory legislation. The first attempt to criminalize denial failed in 2007, when the Italian parliament rejected initiatives from the Romano Prodi center-left government to bring national anti-racist legislation more in line with the EU standards (Prodi was one of the main promoters of European standards in Italy).[131] Determined opposition by Italian historians, who protested the limitation of the freedom of research, played its role in the failure of that project.[132] After the fall of the Berlusconi government in 2011, the new center-left coalition, referring to the Framework Decision of 2008, returned to the idea of a memory law. A new draft (known as "On Negationism") was introduced into the parliament in March 2013, approved by the Senate in February 2015, and adopted in June 2016. It amends a law of 1975 that ratified the International Convention on the Elimination of All Forms of Racial Discrimination by introducing the following provision:

> The penalty is two to six years' imprisonment, if propaganda, public instigation, and public incitement [to discrimination or violence], carried out in a way that creates a real danger of their dissemination, is based in whole or in part on denial of the *Shoah* or of crimes of genocide, crimes

---

[130] Clifford, *Commemorating the Holocaust*, p. 143.
[131] ECRI Report on Italy (fourth monitoring cycle), 2011, p. 15.
[132] Luigi Cajani, Presentation given at the General Assembly of *Liberté pour l'histoire*, June 2, 2012.

against humanity and war crimes, as defined in articles 6, 7 and 8 of the Statute of the International Criminal Court.[133]

Holocaust denial is thus viewed here as an aggravating circumstance in hate-speech cases, which is a way of emphasizing that negationism is indeed a form of hate speech. And, as Luigi Cajani emphasizes, the law, unlike the Framework Decision, forbids only the denial, not the trivialization, of the Holocaust.[134]

Expanding the Criminalization of the Past to Other Topics

A growing corpus of law recognizes cases of mass murder other than the Holocaust as genocides and sometimes criminalizes their denial, fully in line with the official recommendations of the European Council. Following the rise of the memory of the Holocaust and its emergence as the EU's official narrative, other communities of memory also began laying claim to the legal protection of their interpretations of the past.

In 1987, at a time when Gorbachev's perestroika was liberating formerly repressed memories of communist crimes, the European Parliament recognized the Armenian genocide. Additionally, the influential Ukrainian diaspora began pressing for the recognition of the Holodomor (literally "extermination by starvation"; the deliberately induced famine of 1932–1933 in Soviet Ukraine), which was one of the most tragic episodes in the history of Stalin's repressions. The rise of memories of colonialism also found expression in numerous memory law initiatives. We will consider attempts to criminalize the denial of communist crimes in the following chapters, which cover Eastern European memory laws. Here I will briefly review the legislation regarding the memory of colonialism and of the Armenian genocide.

There are striking similarities and characteristic differences between the memory of the Holocaust and that of the Armenian genocide.[135] Both events were promptly officially categorized as crimes against humanity (in

---

[133] Legge 16 giugno 2016, n. 115, modifiche all'articolo 3 della legge 13 ottobre 1975, n. 654, in materia di contrasto e repressione dei crimini di genocidio, crimini contro l'umanità e crimini di guerra, come definiti dagli articoli 6, 7 e 8 dello statuto della Corte penale internazionale.

[134] Luigi Cajani, "Italy and the Law on Denialism": http://freespeechdebate.com/en/2015/04/italy-and-the-law-on-denialism/.

[135] Klas-Göran Karlsson, "Memory of Mass Murder: The Genocide in Armenian and Non-Armenian Historical Consciousness," in *Collective Traumas Memories of War and Conflict in 20th-Century Europe*, eds. Conny Mithander, John Sundholm, and Maria Holmgren Troy (Brussels: Peter Lang, 2012), pp. 13–46.

1915 and 1945, respectively); but soon thereafter both were, if not forgotten, then at least marginalized in international opinion, and their memories were nurtured mostly in Jewish and Armenian communities. But the stigma of the memory of the Armenian genocide lasted much longer, and its ultimate removal owed almost everything to the great strides made in preserving the memory of the Holocaust.

Two factors contributed to the delay. On the one hand, information on the Armenian genocide was intentionally and systematically suppressed by the Turkish government. For Turkey, it was an undesirable feature of the country's historical record.[136] For most of the twentieth century, the Kemalist revolution was seen in Turkey as a radical break with the Ottoman past; the modernized Turkish Republic claimed to have nothing in common with the imperial legacy. In addition, the unitary nationalist vision of the Turkish Republic excluded any discussion of its mosaic ethnic structure.[137] Turkey's support of the Allies during World War II and its subsequent membership of NATO turned the memory of the 1915 massacre into a "forgotten genocide." And on the other hand, Armenia was a Soviet republic, and as such had little freedom in designing its own politics of memory, while for the Kremlin, ethnic cleansing was of secondary importance to class conflict. Even more significantly, the genocide of 1915 had every likelihood of becoming a symbol of Armenian identity, while Moscow was striving – and not without success – to promote Soviet identity at the expense of local and ethnic selfhood.

Nevertheless, the first signs of the rising memory of the Armenian genocide appeared in the 1960s, almost simultaneously with changing attitudes to the Holocaust.[138] In 1965, a few days before the fiftieth anniversary of the genocide, Uruguay passed a law declaring April 24, the date accepted as the beginning of the massacre, a Day of Remembrance

[136] As Prime Minister of Turkey Erdoğan, speaking at London School of Economics in 2005, put it, "everyone should know that the history of Turkey is by no means a history of mass extermination." Quoted in Nikolaus Schrodt, *Modern Turkey and the Armenian Genocide: An Argument about the Meaning of the Past* (Heidelberg: Springer, 2014), p. 5. See also Ronald Grigor Suny, "*They Can Live in the Desert but Nowhere Else*": *A History of the Armenian Genocide (Human Rights and Crimes against Humanity)* (Princeton, N.J.: Princeton University Press, 2015), and Vicken Cheterian, *Open Wounds: Armenians, Turks and a Century of Genocide* (Oxford: Oxford University Press, 2015).
[137] Esra Özyürek, ed., *The Politics of Public Memory in Turkey* (Syracuse, N.Y.: Syracuse University Press, 2007).
[138] Richard G. Hovannisian, "The Armenian Genocide: Remembrance and Denial," in *Remembrance and Denial: The Case of the Armenian Genocide* (Detroit, Mich.: Wayne State University Press, 1999), p. 16.

for the Armenian Martyrs.[139] This was one of the first manifestations of the rise of memory as a worldwide phenomenon. However, the recognition of the Armenian genocide was a slow process. Cyprus was only the second country to sign on, ten years later, in April 1975. In the United States, April 24 was also instituted as a National Day of Remembrance of Man's Inhumanity to Man in 1975, to commemorate the sixtieth anniversary of the tragedy that was explicitly qualified as genocide in the Joint Resolution of the Congress.[140] And in the 1970s, Turkey began an international propaganda campaign designed to minimize the scale of the extermination, deny the responsibility of the Turkish state, and negate the categorization of the massacre as a genocide. The events of 1915 were presented by Turkey as a violent ethnic conflict, deplorable but understandable given the circumstances of the war, in which, it was claimed, Armenians massively supported Russia against Turkey. This trivialization of the Armenian genocide is readily comparable to Holocaust denial.[141]

The recognition of the Armenian genocide by the European Parliament in 1987 was crucial to the shaping of its memory (the fact that the first draft of this resolution dates from 1983 shows that the decision to pass it was not an easy one). The resolution stated that

> [The Parliament] believes that the tragic events in 1915–1917 involving the Armenians living in the territory of the Ottoman Empire constitute genocide within the meaning of the convention on the prevention and the punishment of the crime of genocide.[142]

The resolution called on Turkey to recognize "this historical event as an act of genocide." It stressed that "the present Turkey cannot be held responsible for [this] tragedy," so that "neither political nor legal or material claims against present-day Turkey can be derived from [such] recognition." But, although Turkey's official disavowal of its responsibility for the Ottoman crimes was accepted by the European Parliament, the latter did not balk at putting undisguised pressure on Istanbul:

> [T]he refusal by the present Turkish Government to acknowledge the genocide against the Armenian people... together with the lack of true

---

[139] Law no. 13.326 of April 20, 1965, Day of Remembrance for the Armenian Martyrs.
[140] Joint Resolution to Designate April 24, 1975, as "National Day of Remembrance of Man's Inhumanity to Man." See also Harut Sassounian, "US Recognized Armenian Genocide in 1951, World Court Document Reveals," *Asbarez*, June 13, 2008.
[141] Richard G. Hovannisian, "Denial of the Armenian Genocide in Comparison with Holocaust Denial," in *Remembrance and Denial: The Case of the Armenian Genocide*, pp. 201–236.
[142] European Parliament. Resolution on a political solution to the Armenian question, 18 June 1987.

parliamentary democracy and the failure to respect individual and collective freedoms... in that country are insurmountable obstacles to consideration of the possibility of Turkey's accession to the Community. (Article 4)

Since then, the question of Turkey's accession to the European Union has been firmly linked to the issue of the Armenian genocide, which was acknowledged by several other European and Latin American countries in the 1990s and 2000s. Its recognition in 1991 was one of the first acts of a newly independent Armenia. To date, more than twenty countries, including Argentina (1993), Russia (1995), Greece (1996), France (1998), Belgium (1998), Italy (2000), Austria (2015), and Germany (2016) have officially recognized the events of 1915 as a genocide. Characteristically, the Bundestag resolution also mentions "the inglorious role of the German Reich, Turkey's main military ally in the First World War," which "made no attempt to stop those crimes against humanity," although it had "unambiguous information" about them.[143] This is certainly in line with the culture of repentance for historical misdeeds. Most of those countries adopted parliamentary resolutions, but some instead passed special laws, usually purely declarative. For example, France's "Armenian" law of 2001, adopted after three years of passionate debate, states that "France publicly recognizes the Armenian Genocide of 1915."[144] An Argentinian law of 2004 instructs that school and university curricula must cover the Armenian genocide. The Uruguay law of the same year restates the aforementioned provision of the law of 1965 and provides that "radio and television services have the duty on this date [April 24] to allocate part of their programming to the said events."[145] However, some Holocaust negationism laws are also formulated in such a way as to encompass denial of the Armenian genocide. Such laws were adopted, for example, in Switzerland, Liechtenstein, Portugal, Slovenia, Andorra, Greece, and Cyprus.[146] In

---

[143] Resolution of June 2, 2015, "Erinnerung und Gedenken an den Völkermord an den Armeniern und anderen christlichen Minderheiten in den Jahren 1915 und 1916": http://dip21.bundestag .de/dip21/btd/18/086/1808613.pdf.

[144] Loi no. 2001–70 du 29 janvier 2001 relative à la reconnaissance du génocide arménien de 1915.

[145] Ley N° 17.752 de 26 de março de 2004 "Día de recordación de los mártires armenios."

[146] The Cypriot case is particularly interesting. The law criminalizing the denial of the Armenian genocide was passed there in commemoration of the centenary of the tragedy in April 2015. Since 2011 Cyprus had had a law criminalizing the denial of crimes against humanity recognized by international courts, but, since the Armenian genocide did not fall within the scope of that definition, the parliament amended the law to include the formula "unanimously recognized by a resolution of the Cyprus parliament." The Cypriot House of Representatives actually had unanimously adopted a resolution recognizing the Armenian genocide in 1975. See Siranush Ghazanchyan, "Cyprus Set to Criminalize Armenian Genocide Denial This Week," March 31, 2015: www.armradio.am/en/2015/03/31/cyprus-set-to-criminalize-armenian-genocide-denial-

Belgium, the parliament passed a bill recognizing the Armenian genocide in 1998, but refused to penalize its denial in 2005.

In France, several proposals to criminalize certain statements about the past, including the denial of the Armenian genocide, were introduced into the parliament between 2002 and 2006, shortly after the adoption of the "Armenian" law (and the Taubira Act, which recognized the slave trade as genocide) in 2001. Five of those proposals expanded the scope of the Gayssot Act by penalizing the denial of other genocides recognized as such in French law or the decisions of international courts, of which the massacre of the Armenians was considered a paradigmatic example; and it was, in fact, invoked by the explanatory notes attached to those bills, although they also (or even primarily) targeted slave trade denial.[147] If adopted, they would have made the denial of the Armenian genocide a criminal offense. In addition, Socialist deputies led by Didier Migaud (the author of the 2001 law recognizing the Armenian genocide) proposed two drafts specifically aimed at penalizing the denial of the Armenian genocide.[148] The second, the one ultimately approved by the National Assembly on October 12, 2006, amended the 1881 law on freedom of the press by providing the penalties foreseen by the Gayssot Act for "those who would contest. . . the existence of the Armenian genocide of 1915."[149]

By that time, however, French public opinion had become hypersensitive to memory laws, which prompted the parliament to follow the

---

this-week/; "Cyprus Criminalizes Denial of 1915 Armenian Genocide by Turks," April 2, 2015: www.reuters.com/article/2015/04/02/us-cyprus-armenia-turkey-idUKKBN0MT0YS20150402.

[147] See bills No. 479 of December 18, 2002; No. 1359 of January 15, 2004; No. 2135 of March 3, 2005; No. 2278 of December 22, 2005; and No. 2854 of February 8, 2006. See also Rapport fait au nom de la commission des lois constitutionnelles, de la législation et de l'administration générale de la République sur la proposition de loi (n. 3030) de M. Didier Migaud. . ., complétant la loi n. 2001–70 du 29 janvier 2001 relative à la reconnaissance du génocide arménien de 1915, par M. Christophe Masse: www.assemblee-nationale.fr/12/rapports/r3074 .asp. All those proposals were declined on the grounds that the denial of "other genocides" can be prosecuted on the basis of anti-racist legislation but cannot be banned following the model of the Gayssot Act, in which reference to the Charter of the Nuremberg Tribunal is essential. Other French memory law projects include two bills proposing that the suppression of the 1793–1794 Vendée uprising be officially recognized as a genocide. See drafts No. 3754 of February 27, 2007 and No. 4441 of March 6, 2012 and D'Orazio, "La memoria doverosa," p. 421. Indeed, some historians consider those events the first modern genocide. See Reynald Secher, *A French Genocide: The Vendée* [1986] (Notre Dame, Ind.: University of Notre Dame Press, 2003).

[148] See drafts No. 1643 of June 8, 2004; and No. 3030 of April 12, 2006.

[149] Proposition de loi no. 3030 adoptée par l'Assemblée Nationale en première lecture, tendant à réprimer la contestation de l'existence du génocide arménien. The law is sometimes called the *loi Masse*, because it was adopted following a report (see above) presented by Christophe Masse, who strongly supported the bill but was not its author. See also David Fraser, "Law's Holocaust Denial: State, Memory, Legality," in *Genocide Denials and the Law*, pp. 39–47.

recommendations of the Accoyer Commission and postpone sine die the expansion of the legislation (especially given Turkey's harsh reaction to the 2006 draft). Nevertheless, in 2011, Nicolas Sarkozy supported the notion of criminalizing denial of the 1915 genocide during his run for the presidency, in order to win the vote of the powerful Armenian diaspora. In December, the parliament adopted a new Armenian bill authored by Valérie Boyer, an MP from Sarkozy's Union for a Popular Movement and deputy mayor of Marseilles, which is one of the main centers of the Armenian diaspora in France. Characteristically, Boyer won her 2007 election in the Bouches-du-Rhône district against socialist Christophe Masse, the key supporter of the 2006 Armenian law (*loi Masse*).[150] Obviously, both the left and the right considered the memory of the 1915 tragedy to be important political leverage. More recently, Valérie Boyer became also known for her proposals to amend the French constitution by including a reference to the Christian roots of the French Republic and to pass a declarative law recognizing the 1915 genocide of Assyrians in the Ottoman Empire.[151]

The 2011 Boyer Act, like several previous drafts, criminalized the denial of both the Armenian genocide and the slave trade by extending the norms of the Gayssot Act to other genocides officially recognized in France. It introduced the following article (Article 24 *ter*) into the 1881 law on freedom of the press:

> The penalties provided by Article 24 *bis* [the Gayssot Act] will apply to those who contest or grossly minimize... the existence of one or many crimes of genocide defined in Article 211.1 of the penal code and recognized as such by French law.[152]

However, in February 2012, the Constitutional Council declared the statute unconstitutional on the grounds that "legislation that has as its object the recognition of a crime of genocide does not in itself possess the normative character essential to law."[153] This statement obviously echoes the argument that, with the exception of the Gayssot Act, all memory

---

[150] Résultats des élections législatives, 2007, Bouches-du-Rhône: www.lexpress.fr/resultats-elections/legislatives-2007-bouches-du-rhone-8eme-circonscription_299864.html.

[151] Amendement 112 au Projet de loi constitutionnelle de protection de la Nation, no. 3381 du 2 février 2016 (rejected by the parliament) and Proposition de loi no. 2642 relative à la reconnaissance du génocide assyrien de 1915, March 11, 2015 (still under consideration at the time of writing).

[152] Proposition de loi 3842 visant à réprimer la contestation de l'existence des génocides reconnus par la loi, adoptée par l'Assemblée Nationale le 22 décembre 2011.

[153] Conseil constitutionnel. Décision no. 2012–647 DC du 28 février 2012.

laws are declarations rather than real laws because they have created no new norms.

The Constitutional Council further developed its understanding of the difference between Holocaust negationism and the denial of other crimes against humanity in its decision of January 8, 2016. This time, the key question addressed to the council was whether the ban on Holocaust denial only violates the principle of equality before the law and implicitly establishes a hierarchy of victims. The council restated its argument that "the denial of facts qualified as crimes against humanity by a decision of a French or an international jurisdiction recognized by France differs from the denial of facts qualified as crimes against humanity by any other jurisdiction or by a law," a claim that might seem pointlessly formalist. Arguably, the underlying idea was that establishing the truth of the past and introducing sanctions for calling it into question cannot be a prerogative of one and the same body.[154] In any event, the council does not limit itself to a purely formal analysis and argues that Holocaust negationism is different from that of other genocides in that it "constitutes in itself an incitement to racism and anti-Semitism" and consequently is an abuse of freedom of speech, not least because the extermination of the Jews "took place in part on the [French] territory."[155] That is why "no other denial of crimes against humanity... would carry an equivalent symbolic violence in our society."[156] In other words, what has to be compared are discourses about genocides rather than genocides themselves. These arguments were similar to the 2013/2015 decision of the European Court of Human Rights (ECtHR) that we will consider later in this chapter.

---

[154] Bertrand Mathieu and Anne Levade, "Le législateur ne peut fixer des vérités et en sanctionner la contestation," *La Semaine juridique* 2/14 (2012), pp. 680-684.

[155] Conseil constitutionnel. Décision no. 2015-512 QPC du 8 janvier 2016. M. Vincent R[eynouard] (Délit de contestation de l'existence de certains crimes contre l'humanité). See also Marion Tissier-Raffin, "La constitutionnalité enfin confirmée de la loi Gayssot: Liberté d'expression et négationnisme (Art. 11 DDHC)," *La revue des droits de l'homme*, February 2016: https://revdh.revues.org/1789; Nathalie Droin, "Le glas sonne-t-il pour la 'loi Gayssot'? A propos de l'arrêt de la Cour de Cassation du 6 octobre 2015 n° 15-84335," *Revue des droits et libertés fondamentales* 26 (2015): www.revuedlf.com/droit-penal/le-glas-sonne-t-il-pour-la-loi-gayssot-a-propos-de-larret-de-la-cour-de-cassation-du-6-octobre-2015-n15-84335/; and Daniel Kuri, "L'incrimination de la contestation de l'existence de crimes contre l'humanité de la loi dite 'Gayssot' confortée par le Conseil constitutionnel, commentaire sur la décision n° 2015-512 QPC du 8 janvier 2016": www.lagbd.org/index.php/L'incrimination_de_la_contestation_de_l'existence_de_crimes_contre_l'humanité_de_la_loi_dite_«Gayssot»_confortée_par_le_Conseil_constitutionnel,_commentaire_sur_la_décision_n°_2015-512_QPC_du_8_janvier_2016_(fr).

[156] Conseil constitutionnel. Commentaire: Décision no. 2015-512 QPC du 8 janvier 2016, p. 23.

Let us return in 2012. Although the Constitutional Council's decision was hailed as "the end for the historical memory laws,"[157] both right-wing politicians and the newly elected Socialist president, François Hollande, spoke on many occasions in favor of penalizing the denial of the Armenian genocide. In the years that followed, both parties also came up with their own bills. In 2014, Valérie Boyer and her colleagues proposed an amendment to the Penal Code (Article 213.6), which she thought could replace the Gayssot Act (the latter to remain in force only with regard to crimes committed prior to the adoption of the new legislation) and ban denial of any crimes against humanity:

> Systematically contesting, denying..., banalizing, grossly minimizing, and attempting to justify crimes against humanity and genocides of the twentieth century as defined by articles 211.1 and 212.2 of the Penal Code and/or by the statute of the International Criminal Court, are punishable with... five years of incarceration and a fine of 45,000 euros.[158]

The penalty was considerably more stringent than that in the Gayssot Act. The new bill foresees several conditions under which an act of denial can be considered an offense: it has to be public, use falsified evidence, profit from the audience's ignorance, silence obvious arguments in favor of considering an event a genocide, and "call into question [its] assessment by lawyers [working for] international organizations," all of this presumably being intended to ensure that the behavior in question is not a bona fide piece of research, which is protected in the draft. With regard to the question of exactly which kinds of negation it prohibits, the draft provides an unusually detailed list that includes crimes recognized by the French government; by an international convention ratified by France; by an international organization in which France participates; by a national or international jurisdiction; by experts designated by a court; and, most curiously, by no less than one twelfth of the UN party states. Taken all together, this would, of course, have opened the door to the almost unlimited criminalization of statements about the past, which explains why the bill was sent to the parliament's legal commission and buried there. However, as the 2017 elections approached, Boyer submitted a new draft, which returned to the notion of amending the 1881 law on freedom

---

[157] Robert Badinter, "Is This the End for the Historical Memory Laws?": www.lph-asso.fr/index.php?option=com_content&view=article&id=182%3A-intervention-de-robert-badinter-a-lassemblee-generale-de-liberte-pour-lhistoire-2-juin-2012&catid=53%3Aactualites&Itemid=170&lang=en.

[158] Proposition de loi no. 2276 [du 14 octobre 2014] visant à réprimer la négation des génocides et des crimes contre l'humanité du XXème siècle.

of the press and expanding the norms created by the Gayssot Act to the denial of other genocides:

> The penalties provided by Article 24 *bis* will apply to those who have systematically contested, denied... or tried to justify the existence of one or many crimes of genocide or... crimes against humanity as defined respectively in articles 211.1 and 212.1 of the penal code.[159]

The new bill, like the 2014 proposal, foresees a number of conditions, including that to be viewed as an offense, an act of denial should be based on falsified information and directly or indirectly incite to violence, while the crimes in question should have been recognized by an international treaty signed by France, by a judgment of a national (non-French) jurisdiction under which they had been perpetrated, or by an international court created with France's participation. Obviously, the draft remains (as Boyer herself called her previous project) "legally fragile"; unsurprisingly, it has also been redirected to the parliament's legal commission for improvement. But in the meanwhile, President Hollande himself took the initiative of criminalizing the denial of the Armenian genocide, which has made the prospects of Boyer's bill even less secure.

Boyer's proposal was registered in the parliament on January 19, 2016. On January 28, Hollande announced that he had commissioned Jean-Paul Costa, a former president of the European Court of Human Rights, to find "a solid, incontestable [legal] way that would allow us to protect [historical] memory."[160] In June, the government proposed an amendment to the draft law on equality and citizenship, which was then under consideration in the parliament. The Gayssot Act (more exactly, Article 24 *bis* of the 1881 law on freedom of the press) was to be replaced with the following provision:

> Will punish with a one-year imprisonment and a fine of 45,000 euros those who... justify, deny, contest, or grossly minimize crimes against humanity as... defined in (1) Article 7 of the statute of the International Criminal Court...; (2) Article 212.1 of the penal code; (3) Article 6 of the Statute [Charter] of the International Military Tribunal...; (4) Article 1 of Law no. 2001–434 of May 21, 2001 recognizing the slave trade and slavery as a crime against humanity.[161]

---

[159] Proposition de loi no. 3411 [du 19 janvier 2011] visant à réprimer la négation des crimes de génocide et des crimes contre l'humanité.

[160] Quoted in Jacques Pitou, "Les avatars d'une proposition de limitation de la liberté d'expression: La loi sur la pénalisation de la 'négation du génocide arménien' (2011–2012)": http://j.poitou.free.fr/pro/html/cens/genarm-a.html.

[161] Projet de loi no. 3851 [du 17 juin 2016] relatif à l'égalité et à la citoyenneté, article 38 *ter*. The bill was initially proposed by the government in April 2016: Projet de loi [no. 3679 du 13 avril 2016] Egalité et citoyenneté. See also Amendement no. 1559 du 27 juin 2016.

The draft builds upon Boyer's initiatives but incorporates them into an almost unassailable project designed to considerably extend the rights of victims of what Hollande's Prime Minister, Manuel Walls, condemned, in the aftermath of the terrorist attacks of January 2015, as "a territorial, social, and ethnic apartheid" in French suburban communities.[162] The bill uses the broadest possible language, thus making it possible to prohibit the denial of several different genocides. The denial of the Armenian genocide in particular could be subsumed under the new regulation, but its center of gravity has clearly shifted to the slave trade (which may be less uncomfortable for Turkey). The bill was approved by the parliament in December 2016 (and signed into law in January 2017), although in a different form. Instead of replacing Article 24 *bis* of the 1881 law on freedom of the press, the new enactment amended it by adding the following paragraph:

> Will be punished with the same penalties those who have denied, minimized or grossly trivialized. . . the existence of a crime of genocide other than those mentioned in the first paragraph of this article, of another crime against humanity, of a crime of enslavement, or of a war crime as defined in Articles 6, 7 and 8 of the Statute of the International Criminal Court. . . and in Articles 211.1 to 212.3, 224.1A to 224.1C and 461.1 to 461.31 of the penal code, when
>
> 1. This crime has been condemned by a French or an international jurisdiction;
> 2. Or when the negation, minimization, or trivialization of this crime constitutes an incitement to violence or to hatred
>
> against a group of persons or a member of such group defined by alleged race, color, religion, descent, or national origin.[163]

In the context of the law aimed in particular at ensuring equality between the memories of different genocides the Constitutional Council did not dare to straightforwardly insist upon Holocaust denial being the only punishable form of negationism. Nevertheless, it modified the new provision and minimized the potential extension of its scope. The council retained the reference to French or international courts, the importance of which it had emphasized in its former rulings, but declared unconstitutional the second condition under which denial can be considered a criminal offense.[164] As we know, the council believes that only

[162] "Manuel Valls évoque 'un apartheid territorial, social, ethnique' en France," *Le Monde*, January 20, 2015: www.lemonde.fr/politique/article/2015/01/20/pour-manuel-valls-il-existe-un-apartheid-territorial-social-ethnique-en-france_4559714_823448.html.

[163] Loi n° 2017-86 du 27 janvier 2017 relative à l'égalité et à la citoyenneté, Article 173.

[164] Conseil constitutionnel. Décision no. 2016=745 DC du 26 janvier 2017. Loi relative à l'égalité et à la citoyenneté, Considérations 191-197.

Holocaust negationism constitutes in itself an incitement to hatred. However, the facts of the Armenian genocide and of slavery have not been "condemned by a French or an international court." Consequently, the new law does not criminalize their denial, although it does criminalize, say, that of the Rwandan genocide (which is far from being a hot topic in French debates).[165] Nevertheless, the law has considerably changed the French "memory régime," undermined the unique legal status of Holocaust negationism, and marked an important step toward establishing "multimemorism" as the foundation of French history politics.

Laws criminalizing the denial of the Armenian genocide are very infrequently applied, the best known case being that of Turkish nationalist Doğu Perinçek, who was convicted of racially motivated genocide denial by a Swiss court in 2007. He claimed that the massacre of 1915 was not a genocide and was in any event justified by the Armenians' support for Russia during World War I. He was sentenced to ninety days of imprisonment and a fine. In December 2013, the European Court of Human Rights ruled that his conviction had violated the freedom of expression guaranteed by Article 10 of the European Convention on Human Rights. According to the ECtHR decision, "the rejection of the legal characterization as 'genocide' of the 1915 events was not such as to incite hatred against the Armenian people." The Court stated that "Mr. Perinçek had never questioned the massacres and deportations.... Nor had he expressed contempt for the victims of the events."[166]

According to Paolo Lobba, this ruling "represents a turning point in the ECtHR approach to the broader phenomenon of 'negationism,'" demonstrating a propensity toward a narrow understanding of anti-denial legislation:

> The [ECtHR] judgment suggests that, from a legal viewpoint, denial of the Shoah remains unique, such that it may justify restrictions on free speech that the denial of other grave crimes may not. Whereas the denial of the Shoah is *presumed* to be nothing other than a subtle form of anti-Semitism – as such warranting an *ad hoc* legal regime – other types of negationism do

[165] Daniel Kuri, "Brèves observations sur la décision n° 2016-745 DC du 26 janvier 2017 du Conseil constitutionnel, ou Les surprises du Conseil constitutionnel à propos des modifications de l'article 24 *bis* de la loi du 29 juillet 1881 sur la presse": www.unilim.fr/iirco/2017/05/05/breves-observations-decision-n-2016-745-dc-26-janvier-2017-conseil-constitutionnel/
[166] European Court of Human Rights. Press Release. ECHR 370 (2013), December 17, 2013: "Criminal conviction for denial that the atrocities perpetrated against the Armenian people in 1915 and years after constituted genocide was unjustified."

not necessarily entail comparable harm, thereby calling for a case-specific analysis.[167]

As we see, the ECtHR's position is quite similar to that of the French Constitutional council. In October 2015, the decision of the ECtHR was confirmed by its Great Chamber:

> The applicant's statements, read as a whole and taken in their immediate and wider context, cannot be seen as a call for hatred, violence or intolerance towards the Armenians.[168]

In a striking paragraph, the Grand Chamber claims that

> The justification for making [Holocaust] denial a criminal offence lies not so much in that it is a clearly established historical fact but in that, in view of the historical context in the States concerned... [such as] Austria, Belgium, Germany and France..., its denial, even if dressed up as impartial historical research, must invariably be seen as connoting an antidemocratic ideology and anti-Semitism.
>
> By contrast, it has not been argued that there was a direct link between Switzerland and the events that took place in the Ottoman Empire in 1915 and the following years. [169]

The quote invites three comments. First, the notion of state repentance for state-sponsored crimes largely determines the decision's logic (as well as that of the 2016 ruling of the French Constitutional Council). Second, the decision calls into question one of the main arguments in support of memory laws, namely, that they ban intentionally false statements. Third, just as the French Constitutional Council, the Grand Chamber tries to separate the question of the unique legal status of Holocaust negationism from the discussion of the uniqueness of the Shoah, arguably because both institutions see the latter claim as less tenable.

The decision of the Grand Chamber will probably have important consequences for European legislation on issues of the past. However, the aforementioned French developments may have an even stronger impact on European approaches to the uniqueness of Holocaust negationism, which would work in the opposite direction. The question of whether

---

[167] Paolo Lobba, "The Fate of the Prohibition against Genocide Denial," February 5, 2014: www.lph-asso.fr/index.php?option=com_content&view=article&id=194%3Ale-destin-de-la-penalisation-du-negationnisme-par-paolo-lobba&catid=53%3Aactualites&Itemid=170&lang=en.

[168] European Court of Human Rights. Grand Chamber. Case of Perinçek v. Switzerland (Application no. 27510/08). Judgment. Strasburg, 15 October 2015, paragraph 239.

[169] *Ibid.*, paragraphs 243 and 244.

multimemorism will replace the Holocaust-centered memory regime in the West remains open.

In Turkey, calling the 1915 massacre a genocide is deemed an insult to the country's dignity. On several occasions, Turkey reacted to official recognitions of the Armenian genocide by warning the respective countries about the potential repercussions on bilateral relations and by recalling Turkish ambassadors (e.g., from France in 2011, from Austria in 2015, and from Germany in 2016). There are many reasons for this rigid position.

After a long period of modernization and Westernization, nationalism and conservatism began to revive in Turkey during the 1980s. The rise of memory, including that of the Ottoman Empire, accompanied this anti-Western turn, so that neo-Ottomanism was a leading feature of Turkish political and cultural life by the end of the twentieth century. That movement, which was founded by Turgut Özal (Prime Minister in 1983–1989, President in 1989–1993), was continued by the Justice and Development Party that came to power in 2002.[170] As bipolar alliances began to crumble and fall, Turkey realized that it had the potential to become a major independent political player, which promptly sparked concerns about its imperial heritage. But the memory boom in Turkey also had other dimensions, including the revival of ethnic nationalisms, most notably among the Kurds.[171] Nationalist movements were becoming influential as early as the 1960s and 1970s and, although the National Security Council moved decisively against them in 1980–1983, they survived. The restored democracy had to find a way of coping with this nationalist resurgence. The idea of softening the principles of the unitary nation state, accepting the ethnic and cultural diversity of Turkey, and returning to some of the imperial traditions was particularly appealing in the wake of disappointment with Western-style modernism and a new interest in conservative values. Since the 1990s, the rise of neoconservatism has been accompanied by an Islamist revival.

The collapse of Soviet rule in the Balkans and the Caucasus rendered imperial pluralism even more attractive to Turkey, because it offered a model for a stronger Turkish presence in these regions. The proponents of

---

[170] Yilmaz Çolac, "Ottomanism vs. Kemalism: Collective Memory and Cultural Pluralism in 1990s Turkey," *Middle Eastern Studies* 42/2 (2006), pp. 587–602; Ömer Taspinar, "Turkey's Middle East Policies: Between Neo-Ottomanism and Kemalism," Carnegie Papers, Carnegie Middle East Center 10 (September 2008): http://carnegieendowment.org/files/cmec10_taspinar_final.pdf.

[171] Henri J. Barkey and Graham E. Fuller, *Turkey's Kurdish Question* (Lanham, Mass.: Rowman and Littlefield, 1998), pp. 15–16.

neo-Ottomanism (as well as some scholars) deny its neo-imperial agenda, insist on its pragmatic character, and underline Turkey's natural role as a bridge between the West and the Islamic world. For them, neo-Ottomanism is a manifestation of multiculturalism rooted in nostalgia for an ethnically diverse world in which each group could treasure its own traditions. But Turkey's official position on the Armenian genocide shows that the real picture may be less reassuring.

The politics of neo-Ottomanism explains why Istanbul has taken such an uncompromising stand on the Armenian genocide. The European Parliament's resolution of 1987 invited Turkey to profit from its proclaimed break with the Ottoman Empire at the very point when the country's leadership had begun to reestablish links with the Ottoman past in order to exploit the imperial legacy for both domestic and international purposes. Acknowledgment of a genocide would corrode the image of peaceful co-existence among various ethnic and religious groups under Ottoman rule and call into question the reputation of the Turkish state, with which none of Turkey's political regimes has been willing to meddle.[172]

And so, in response to the international recognition of the Armenian genocide Turkey passed a law criminalizing any affront to the Turkish nation and its government, which would include calling the massacre of 1915 "a genocide":

> Any person who publicly denigrates the Turkish nation, the State of the Turkish Republic, the Grand National Assembly of Turkey or the judicial bodies of the state shall be sentenced to six months to two years of imprisonment.[173]

The law provides the same punishment for defaming Turkish "military or security structures." Its terms were added, as Article 301, to the Penal

---

[172] For a typical exchange between Armenian and Turkish scholars on the issue of the Armenian genocide, see Vahagn Avedian, "State Identity, Continuity and Responsibility: The Ottoman Empire, the Republic of Turkey and the Armenian Genocide," *European Journal of International Law* 23/3 (2012), pp. 797–820, and Pulat Tacar and Maxime Gauin, "A Reply to Vahagn Avedian – State Identity, Continuity, and Responsibility: The Ottoman Empire, the Republic of Turkey and the Armenian Genocide," *European Journal of International Law* 23/3 (2012), pp. 821–835.

[173] The quotation is taken from the Penal Code as amended in 2008. See *Legislating for Equality*, p. 478; Schrodt, *Modern Turkey and the Armenian Genocide*, p. 19; Jahnisa Tate, "Turkey's Article 301: A Legitimate Tool for Maintaining Order or a Threat to Freedom of Expression?," Georgia Journal of International and Comparative Law 37 (2008), pp. 181–217; and Bülent Algan, "The Brand New Version of Article 301 of Turkish Penal Code and the Future of Freedom of Expression Cases in Turkey," German Law Journal 9/12 (2008), pp. 2237–2252.

Code in 2005, and its wording was amended and broadened in 2008. Although it has provided the basis for the conviction of several dozen people over the years,[174] this is not technically a memory law, because it does not explicitly criminalize statements about the past. However, the law's main goal was to give legal protection to the *denial* of the Armenian genocide. That is why I believe it to be a borderline instance in the category of memory laws (a de facto memory law). Ultimately, laws recognizing the Armenian genocide and the Turkish law protecting the official Turkish historical narrative have been important instruments in the memory conflicts between Turkey and other nations (especially France).

France has several memory laws that deal with the legacy of colonialism, although in different ways (some of which we encountered while discussing denial of the Armenian genocide).[175] In May 2001, shortly after the adoption of the "Armenian" law, the French parliament passed the Taubira Act, named after the socialist MP Christiane Taubira, which recognized "both the transatlantic and Indian Ocean Negro slave trade, on the one hand, and slavery itself, on the other, that were practiced from the 15th century... as constituting crimes against humanity."[176] The law also instituted the commemoration of slavery's victims and stipulated that "school curricula and research projects in the fields of history and the human sciences will accord to the subjects of the Negro slave trade and slavery the important place they deserve" (Article 2). As I have already shown, several attempts were made in the years that followed to criminalize the denial of the slave trade (along with the 1915 massacre of Armenians) as a genocide, but none of them has proven successful by the time of writing.

In 2005, the law on repatriated people was initiated by Hamlaoui Mekachera, the Deputy Minister of Defense for Veterans' Affairs. The bill expressed France's official opinion on certain aspects of the Algerian war, in which Mekachera had taken part. The memory of the Algerian war is almost as painful in France as that of the deportations; it has become a

---

[174] ECRI Report on Turkey (fourth monitoring cycle), February 8, 2011, p. 15.
[175] Löytömäki, *Law and the Politics of Memory;* Eadem, "Legislation of the Memory of the Algerian War in France," *Journal of the History of International Law* 7 (205), pp. 157–179; Jan Jansen, "Politics of Remembrance, Colonialism, and the Algerian War of Independence in France," in *A European Memory? Contested Histories and Politics of Remembrance*, eds. Małgorzata Pakier and Bo Stråth (New York: Berghahn Books, 2010), pp. 275–293.
[176] Loi no. 2001–434 du 21 mai 2001 tendant à la reconnaissance, par la France, de la traite et de l'esclavage en tant que crime contre l'humanité, article 1.

symbol of crimes against humanity perpetrated by the French army. The fate that befell French nationals living in Algeria who were repatriated to France and of Algerians who had served as auxiliaries in the French army (the *harkis*) was another aspect of the tragedy. The *harkis* had not been allowed to escape to France after the end of the war and became victims of the victors' vengeance. The law's goal, therefore, was to acknowledge the merits and sufferings of the repatriated Frenchmen and the *harkis*, and to protect their memory:

> The Nation expresses its gratitude to the women and men who participated in the achievements of France in the former French departments of Algeria, Morocco, Tunisia and Indochina.... It acknowledges the sufferings and sacrifices of the repatriated persons, former members of the auxiliary and other similar units, the missing, and the civil and military victims of the events linked to the process of independence of these departments and territories, and pays solemn tribute to them and their families.[177]

The law extended to the deportees, the *harkis*, and all "victims of the massacres" committed by Algerians the homage due to French soldiers "fallen for France" in Northern Africa (Article 2). It also envisaged the creation of a foundation to commemorate the Algerian war (Article 3) and financial compensation for former *harkis* and their families (Article 6). Finally, it forbade "any insult or defamation with regard to a person or a group of persons on the grounds of their real or supposed status of *harki*, former member of auxiliary or similar units," as well as "any apologia for crimes perpetrated against the *harkis* or members of auxiliary units after the Évian Accords" (Article 5). (In the Évian Accords of March 18, 1962, France had recognized Algeria's independence in exchange for guarantees of non-discrimination for all Algerians including the *harkis*.) In other words, the law of 2005, while not prohibiting denial, did ban any apologias for crimes committed by the supporters of the Algerian independence after their victory. And, although introducing no changes to the criminal law, it made provision for this ban to be implemented "within the framework of the existing laws."

The language of the Mekachera Act leaves no doubt that its goal was to protect the memory of French colonialism. The bill does not mention any crime committed by the French in Northern Africa before or during the Algerian war, but makes several references to the crimes of Algerians (without, however, classifying them as crimes against humanity). During

---

[177] Loi no. 2005–158 du 23 février 2005 portant reconnaissance de la Nation et contribution nationale en faveur des Français rapatriés, article 1.

the discussion of the bill in the parliament, the MPs added to it an article stipulating that research programs should pay due attention to the history of the "French presence overseas," which is a euphemism for colonialism. The new article also included the following provision: "School curricula [shall] recognize in particular the positive role of the French presence overseas, including Northern Africa." This provision provoked a scandal and was repealed by President Chirac in February 2006 under pressure from public opinion.[178] However, other articles of the enactment remain in force.

Spain's Historical Memory Law (*Ley de la Memoria Histórica*) of 2007 is another interesting case of legislation dealing with issues of the past, in that it recognizes the atrocities of the Civil War and the Franco regime without criminalizing their denial. Under Franco, the public memory of the Civil War was efficiently suppressed by the regime with the complicity of the population, although hidden memories survived on both sides. As has happened in many countries, modernization in the 1950s and 1960s contributed to the nation's desire to leave the past in the past. The "time of silence" gave way to what is known as the "pact of forgetting" (*pacto de olvido*): during the transition to democracy "the experience of the Civil War was deliberately played down" with the support of a broad consensus on both the left and the right. The goal of this policy was to prevent a resurrection of old resentments, "to break away from an ancestral tradition of civil confrontations," and "to prevent a repetition of the tragedy of 1936."[179] According to Gregorio Alonso and Diego Muro, silencing the past was "the key pillar of the transition."[180] And Salvador Cardús i Ros claims that "the Transition depended on the erasure of memory and the reinvention of a *new* [democratic] political tradition".[181] The Amnesty Law of 1977 granted a pardon for all crimes committed by both sides during the Civil War and under the Franco regime.

---

[178] Michel, *Gouverner les mémoires*, pp. 145–162.

[179] Carlos Jerez-Farrán and Samuel Amago, "Introduction," in *Unearthing Franco's Legacy: Mass Graves and the Recovery of Historical Memory in Spain* (Notre Dame, Ind.: University of Notre Dame Press, 2010), p. 2; Paloma Aguilar Fernández, *Memory and Amnesia: The Role of the Spanish Civil War in the Transition to Democracy* (New York: Berghahn Books, 2002), pp. XX, 210, 213; Karsten Humlebaek, "The 'Pacto del Olvido,'" in *The Politics and Memory of Democratic Transition: The Spanish Model*, eds. Diego Muro and Gregorio Alonso (New York: Routledge, 2011), pp. 183–198.

[180] Alonso and Muro, "Introduction," in *The Politics and Memory of Democratic Transition*, p. 5.

[181] Cardús i Ros, "Politics and the Invention of Memory: For a Sociology of the Transition to Democracy in Spain," in *Disremembering the Dictatorship: The Politics of Memory in the Spanish Transition to Democracy*, ed. Joan Ramon Resina (Amsterdam: Rodopi, 2000), p. 19.

It was not until the 1990s that a "time of memory" emerged in Spain, with writers and filmmakers being the first to explore the painful past.[182] The discovery, in 2000, of a mass grave of the Civil War period in Priaranza del Bierzo marked the beginning of an obsession with the tragic past and initiated waves of exhumations, which – alongside exhumation photography – became a characteristic feature of the Spanish politics of memory.[183] In the same year, the Association for the Recovery of Historical Memory (*Asociación para la Recuperación de la Memoria Histórica*) was founded with the goal of identifying places of execution, excavating burial sites, and identifying and reburying victims of the Civil War and the Franco regime (to date, hundreds of graves have been discovered and tens of thousands of victims reburied).

Spain's belated rendezvous with its unmasterable past coincided with a new stage in the democratization process, when it became obvious that without facing the past, "Spain's transition to democracy [would] look strangely unfinished."[184] For all its specificity, the Spanish politics of memory was heavily influenced by the pan-European memory of the Holocaust. In 1995, when the memory of the Civil War was just about to be rediscovered, an article criminalizing Holocaust negationism was included in the new Criminal Code, many other articles of which were also consistent with EU norms. But this particular provision was declared unconstitutional in 2007 and reintroduced in 2015, as mentioned earlier.

In Spain, as in many other Western countries, initiatives involving the confrontation of the tragic past most often came from the left. After the victory of the Spanish Socialist Workers' Party in the 2004 elections, the government of José Luis Rodríguez Zapatero announced its intention to develop a broad historical memory agenda. In Madrid, the last remaining Franco statue was taken down in 2005. In March 2006, the Parliamentary Assembly of the Council of Europe adopted a resolution condemning "the extensive and wide-ranging human rights abuses

[182] José M. Gonzáles, "Spanish Literature and the Recovery of Historical Memory," *European Review* 17/1 (2009), p. 179.

[183] Jerez-Farrán and Amago, "Introduction," p. 4. See also Francisco Ferrándiz, "The Intimacy of Defeat: Exhumations in Contemporary Spain," in *Unearthing Franco's Legacy*, pp. 304–324

[184] Sebastian Faber, "The Price of Peace: Historical Memory in Post-Franco Spain, A Review-Article," *Revista hispanica moderna* 58 (June–December 2005), p. 212; Alison Ribeiro de Menezes, *Embodying Memory in Contemporary Spain* (New York: Palgrave Macmillan, 2014), pp. 3–4, 27–58.

committed by the Franco regime in Spain from 1939 to 1975."[185] The Spanish parliament also declared 2006 the Year of Historical Memory, while the government initiated the adoption of a bill "to recognize and extend the rights of, and to establish measures in favor of, those who suffered persecution or violence during the Civil War and the dictatorship."[186]

Although the bill was inspired by "the spirit of reconciliation and concord" and recognized the victims on both sides of the Civil War, it subscribed to the "condemnation of Francoism" pursuant to the Council of Europe's resolution and declared illegitimate all politically or ideologically motivated sentences and judgments entered during the Civil War and the dictatorship (Article 3). It also prohibited "coats of arms, paraphernalia, plaques, or other commemorative objects or mentions aimed at the exaltation... of the uprising, the Civil War, or the repressions of the dictatorship." The bill obliges local administrations to remove those objects from public spaces (Article 15). The core of the law provides financial compensation for various victim categories and material support for the development of the memory of the Civil War and the dictatorship, including the creation of a documentation center and financial backing for the discovery of the burial sites (after the fall of the socialist government in 2011, the law was not repealed but many of its provisions have remained unmet).

Resistance and Failures

In the 1990s, the notion that criminalizing statements about the past serves to promote democracy received broad support among European politicians and intellectuals and was adopted as an official position by the EU. Various communities of memory also consider criminal law a desirable means of securing their historical narratives and identities. But there are also sources of resistance to memory laws.

---

[185] Council of Europe. Parliamentary Assembly. Recommendation 1736, March 17, 2006, Need for international condemnation of the Franco regime.

[186] Ley 52/2007, de 26 de diciembre [2007], por la que se reconocen y amplían derechos y se establecen medidas en favor de quienes padecieron persecución o violencia durante la guerra civil y la dictadura; Mónica López Lerma, "The Ghosts of Justice and the Law of Historical Memory," *Converieries mémorielles* 9 (2011): http://cm.revues.org/840?lang=en; Patrizia Violi, "Memories in Transition: The Spanish Law of Historical Memory," in *Historical Justice and Memory*, eds. Klaus Neumann and Janna Thompson (Madison: University of Wisconsin Press, 2015), pp. 114–129; and Michael Hamphrey "Law, Memory, and Amnesty in Spain," *Macquarie Law Journal* 13 (2014), pp. 25–40.

The adoption of memory laws has never been an easy process. Many laws were long in the making, and many drafts have never been approved. Some acts (such as the 1995 Spanish law and France's 2011 "Armenian" law) were invalidated by constitutional courts. In ideological terms, the criminalization of the past is usually promoted by the left, while right-wing parties (not to mention the far right groups that feel threatened by it) tend to resist it. There are, of course, exceptions to this rule, since some right-wing parties (such as the Gaullists in France) have tended to support Holocaust denial legislation. As time passed, many right-wing politicians began to appreciate the advantages to be gained from victimizing the past, creating a momentum that helped secure the growing popularity of memory laws in the 1990s and 2000s. As we will see in the next chapter, some nationalists, especially in Eastern Europe, are among the most devoted partisans of memory laws.

Attitudes toward memory laws also depend on a country's legal tradition. Common law countries such as the United States, Canada, and the United Kingdom, which tend to value freedom of expression above other freedoms, do not have memory laws. Interestingly, those common law countries have also never had fascist regimes, which may be another important reason for their unwillingness to penalize Holocaust denial.

However, unlike the United States, where the criminalization of statements about the past is usually seen as contradicting First Amendment liberalism, the United Kingdom has no such concerns, which has opened the door to initiatives to criminalize negationism in Britain. In particular, a Holocaust Denial Act was presented to the House of Commons in February 1997 by Labour MP Michael Gapes shortly before the elections of May 1997. Tony Blair, then the leader of the opposition, publicly expressed his support of the bill[187] amid a growing Holocaust awareness in Britain after the "Nazi gold" controversy of 1995 and the 1996 David Irving trial.[188] Gapes was one of the most pro-European British politicians,

---

[187] *The Independent* quoted Blair as saying: "There is a very strong case that denial of the Holocaust should be a specific offence. This will stand alongside our commitment to strengthen the laws against incitement to racial hatred." See "Blair May Outlaw Denial of Holocaust," *The Independent*, January 30, 1997. See also Ian Cram, *Contested Words: Legal Restrictions on Freedom of Speech in Liberal Democracies* (Aldershot: Ashgate, 2006), p. 125; Andy Pearce, *Holocaust Consciousness in Contemporary Britain* (New York, Abingdon: Routledge, 2014), p. 136; and Douglas-Scott, "The Hatefulness of Protected Speech," p. 318.

[188] This was the case of Irving versus Penguin Books and Deborah Lipstadt, in which the court ruled that Lipstadt's description of Irving as a Holocaust denier was not a defamation. See Lipstadt, *History on Trial: My Day in Court with David Irving* (New York: HarperCollins, 2005).

which partly explains his initiative. He proposed to amend the 1986 Public Order Act by introducing the following provision:

> Any words, behavior or material which purport to deny the existence of the policy of genocide against the Jewish people and other similar crimes against humanity committed by Nazi Germany ("the Holocaust") shall be deemed to be intended to stir up racial hatred.[189]

This provision is similar to the rulings of the German and Dutch supreme courts that negationism falls within the scope of hate speech legislation. Defending his draft, Gapes reportedly said:

> Some people will say, "what about freedom of speech?" But the fact is we have got other laws which are constraining. We've got incitement to racial hatred laws and a blasphemy law in this country. There is no such thing as absolute freedom of speech.[190]

This claim suggests that the penalization of Holocaust denial would not be unconstitutional in Britain. Nevertheless, the bill was not adopted prior to the elections that brought Blair's government to power. The Labour Party had every intention of promoting Holocaust consciousness, but it preferred to achieve that aim through educational reform and the museification of the memory of the Shoah,[191] not least because experts in Britain have generally taken a dim view of the criminalization of denial.[192] Moreover, in 1998, Britain passed the Crime and Disorder Act to expand the anti-racist legislation under which, as the British authorities persistently claim, Holocaust denial can be punished (although that in fact has yet to happen).[193]

The Scandinavian countries and the Netherlands do not have memory laws either. Their legal systems, which are based on civil law, have been strongly influenced by the English and American approaches, but those countries had a far more complex experience of fascism than the United Kingdom or the United States. Denmark, Norway, and the Netherlands were actually occupied by Nazi Germany, whereas Sweden remained

---

[189] Described as "A Bill to make it a criminal offence to claim, whether in writing or orally, that the policy of genocide against the Jewish people committed by Nazi Germany did not occur," in Combating Holocaust Denial through Law in the United Kingdom, Institute for Jewish Policy Research, Report No. 3, June 23, 2000: www.bjpa.org/Publications/downloadFile.cfm?FileID=4240.

[190] "Attempt to Ban Genocide Denial," *The Independent*, December 23, 1996.

[191] Pearce, *Holocaust Consciousness in Contemporary Britain*, p. 72.

[192] Josephs, "Holocaust Denial Legislation," and Combating Holocaust Denial through Law in the United Kingdom.

[193] Crime and Disorder Act 1998, Part II, articles 28–33.

formally neutral while closely collaborating with the Nazis both politically and economically. In all these countries, influential political forces openly sympathized with Nazism, and the Netherlands in particular had a robust fascist movement. Therefore, although the Netherlands has no memory law per se, it may not be fortuitous that Holocaust denial is de facto criminalized there: on November 25, 1997, the Supreme Court of the Netherlands ruled that "the denial of the Holocaust amounts to *belediging* [insult or defamation] of Jews" and thus falls within the scope of Article 137c of the Penal Code.[194] While of course not an ad hoc memory law, this ruling could perhaps be viewed as a borderline instance within that category.

Self-congratulatory resistance myths of the war (including the Finnish narrative of the Continuation War)[195] prevailed in the Nordic countries into the 1990s and even the 2000s, when the Holocaust-centered memory regime emerged there under EU influence. The Nordic countries rediscovered the problematic aspects of their wartime experience, including their direct or indirect participation in the Holocaust (with the exception of Denmark, since Danes rescued Danish Jews and moved them to Sweden in October 1943). This "moral turn" in the perception of the war became a part of the official narratives. However, those countries refused to criminalize Holocaust denial on the grounds that anti-racist laws were already on the books.

The 2000s witnessed a growing resistance to memory laws on the part of the historical profession, especially in France, the classical homeland of memory laws. Few historians had protested the Gayssot Act in 1990, but a wave of indignation arose against the Mekachera law of February 2005, more specifically, against the clause regarding the "positive effects" of French colonialism. In March, a petition signed by a thousand historians

[194] *Combating Racism and Xenophobia through Criminal Legislation*, p. 81; *Legislating for Equality*, p. 336.
[195] Finland's case is probably the most complex because it entered the war on the German side, due in some degree to the Finnish elites' sympathies with Nazism. But there was another reason for the alliance with Germany, in that it gave Finland a chance to recover territories occupied by the Soviets during the Winter War of 1939–1940. The official post-1945 Finnish conception of the war calls the Russo-Finnish hostilities of 1941–1944 a "separate war" (also known as the Continuation War), a claim that simplifies the historical reality. See Henrik Meinander, "A Separate Story? Interpretations of Finland in the Second World War," in *Nordic Narratives of the Second World War: National Historiographies Revisited*, eds. Henrik Stenius, Mirja Österberg, and Johan Östling (Lund: Nordic Academic Press, 2011), pp. 55–78. World War II remains a painful aspect of the Finnish national memory, much like the Civil War of 1918, whose legacy had for several generations divided the descendants of the Reds and the Whites.

called for the abrogation of this clause and for a halt to the imposition of an "official history."[196] Soon thereafter, in June 2005, historian Olivier Pétré-Grenouilleau, the author of a fundamental study of the slave trade, said in an interview: "The Negro slave trade was not a genocide. The goal of the slave trade was not to exterminate a people.... The genocide of the Jews and the Negro slave trade were two different processes."[197] Although Pétré-Grenouilleau denied neither the scale of the slave trade nor its inhumane character, a group of activists, the *Collectif des Antillais, Guyanais, Réunionnais*, with support from Christiane Taubira, accused him of denying a crime against humanity, citing both the Gayssot Act and the Taubira Act. The *Collectif* initiated criminal and civil lawsuits against Pétré-Grenouilleau and called for him to be suspended from teaching as a revisionist.[198]

This attempt to use memory laws to censor historical research contributed further to the historians' mobilization. In June 2005, a group of historians founded the Committee for Vigilance on the Public Uses of History. The Committee's manifesto of June 17, 2005, stated that "The increasing intervention of political power and the media in historical questions tends to impose value judgments to the detriment of critical analysis." The authors see competition of victims as a major factor leading to manipulative uses of history and "refuse to be used to arbitrate the polemics on the 'true' victims of the atrocities of the past."[199]

Somewhat later, on December 13, a group of nineteen historians representing *la fine fleur* of the French historical profession published a manifesto entitled "For the Freedom for History":

> History is not a religion. Historians accept no dogma, respect no prohibition, ignore every taboo. Historical truth is different from morals. The historian's task is not to extol or to blame, but to explain. History is not the slave of current issues. History is not memory. History is not a juridical issue. In a free state, neither the Parliament nor the judicial courts have the right to define historical truth.[200]

[196] "Colonisation: Non à l'enseignement d'une histoire officielle," *Le Monde*, Mars 24, 2005.
[197] Quoted in Baruch, *Des lois indignes?*, p. 16.
[198] Löytömäki, *Law and the Politics of Memory*, pp. 97–98.
[199] "Manifeste du Comité de Vigilance face aux usages publics de l'histoire (CVUH)," *Cahiers d'histoire: Revue d'histoire critique* 96/97 (2005), pp. 191–194, available in English at http://cvuh.blogspot.com/2007/02/manifesto-of-comite-de-vigilance-face.html. See also Mary Stevens, "Public Policy and the Public Historian: The Changing Place of Historians in Public Life in France and the UK," *The Public Historian* 32/3 (2010), pp. 123, 132.
[200] "Liberté pour l'histoire: Une pétition pour l'abrogation des articles de loi contraignant la recherche et l'enseignement de cette discipline," *Libération*, December 13, 2005. The English translation is

Among the signatories, one finds the names of Pierre Nora, René Rémond, Paul Veyne, Pierre Vidal-Naquet, and other distinguished historians. They were obviously protesting the politicization of history in the name of their discipline's ideal image as a positivistic science pursuing objective truths. Interestingly, some of the signatories, most notably Pierre Nora and Paul Veyne, had previously spared no efforts to undermine this image in the course of their long and distinguished intellectual careers, developing instead constructivist approaches to the study of the past.[201] However, once confronted with this novel politics of memory, the historians felt that the "noble dream" of objectivity was their only resort.

The petition (which was ultimately signed by one thousand historians in France and abroad) called for the abrogation of all memory laws, including the Gayssot Act. However, not all historians – and intellectuals more generally – were ready to subscribe to this claim. A petition tellingly entitled "Let Us Not Mix Everything" (December 20, 2005) insisted that there was a profound difference between the first three memory laws, which "recognize firmly established facts of genocide and crimes against humanity in order to struggle against their denial," and the law of 2005, which limited academic freedom by imposing a politically biased interpretation of the past.[202] The signatories of this petition included Claude Lanzmann, whose documentary *Shoah* (1985) was a milestone in the molding of Holocaust consciousness in France, and Serge Klarsfeld, who with his wife Beate played the central role in documenting Nazi crimes against humanity in France.

The members of the Vigilance Committee also found the *Liberté pour l'histoire* petition "excessive." For them, it was enough to abrogate the unfortunate clause of the Mekachera Act (regarding the positive effects of French colonialism). They claimed that "We cannot ignore universal values in the name of which [memory] laws were passed" (as the reader will remember, the opponents of memory laws in France tend to believe that only the Gayssot Act has been adopted in the name of those values, while the other laws are, rather, manifestations of the competition between victims).[203]

---

quoted from www.lph-asso.fr/index.php?option=com_content&view=article&id=2&Itemid=13&lang=en.

[201] Thus, Paul Veyne, in his seminal work *Writing History: Essay on Epistemology* [1971] (Middletown, Conn.: Wesleyan University Press, 1984), p. IX, asserted that "History is not [a] science." See Dina Khapaeva, "Des lois historiques aux lois mémorielles: 19 historiens français pour la liberté de l'histoire," *Le Banquet* 24 (2007), pp. 131–148.

[202] Baruch, *Des lois indignes?*, pp. 320–321   [203] *Ibid.*, p. 319.

In February 2006, the undesirable clause of the Mekachera law was repealed, and the *Collectif des Antillais, Guyanais, Réunionnais* withdrew its complaint against Pétré-Grenouilleau. However, the question was still not closed. The *Liberté pour l'histoire* signatories formed an association under the same name with the objective of defending the historian's freedom of expression. The association, whose primary goal is to combat memory laws, has in recent years been chaired by Pierre Nora. In 2008, protesting against the EU Framework Decision, the association published a manifesto known as the "Blois Appeal," which was signed by a group of the world's leading historians including Carlo Ginzburg, Eric Hobsbawm, and Jacques Le Goff. The document stated:

> History must not be a slave to contemporary politics nor can it be written on the command of competing memories. In a free state, no political authority has the right to define historical truth and to restrain the freedom of the historian with the threat of penal sanctions. . . .
>
> We ask government authorities to recognize that, while they are responsible for the maintenance of the collective memory, they must not establish, by law and for the past, an official truth. . . .
>
> In a democracy, liberty for history is liberty for all.[204]

To be sure, the *Appel de Blois* protests not only criminalization of the past but also a government's right to articulate its official assessment of historical events. As we know, though, its actual targets were declarative memory laws, which could potentially become "real laws," and it sought to present the halting of all attempts to legislate on the past as an appealing option.

Historians in other countries are also protesting memory laws. Soon after the Belgian parliament failed to pass a bill criminalizing denial of the Armenian genocide in 2005, one hundred fifty Belgian historians published a manifesto against memory laws, using the language of *Liberté pour l'histoire*:

> History is not at the service of politics. . . . It accepts no dogma and can be disturbing. . . . Instead of the duty of memory, which is so much invoked, we would prefer to see the duty of history and knowledge invoked more often. . . . The growing judicialization of historical debate constitutes an infringement on the freedom of expression and of research.[205]

---

[204] "Appel de Blois," *Le Monde*, October 10, 2008. The English translation is quoted from www.lph-asso.fr/index.php?Itemid=14&id=47&lang=en&option=com_content&view=article.

[205] "Pléthore de mémoire: quand l'État se mêle d'histoire. . ." *La Libre Belgique*, January 25, 2006, and *Le Soir*, January 25, 2006. See also Pieter Lagrou, "Sanctionner pénalement les négationnistes?,"

To these common themes referring to the opposition between scientific history and manipulative memory, the Belgian manifesto adds an important motif that is absent from both the *Liberté pour l'histoire* petition and the *Appel de Blois*, although it is strongly present in the writings of the leaders of the French movement: "History is not a new catechism of multiculturalism."

In connection with the introduction of an Italian Holocaust denial bill of 2007, the Italian Society for the Study of Contemporary History (*Società italiana per lo studio della storia contemporanea*) launched a petition warning about the dangers of introducing "a state truth on issues of the historical past" and claiming that denial can be effectively marginalized only through open discussion.[206] The petition, which was signed by several hundred historians, arguably played a role in the bill's failure.

The debates around the European Council's Framework Decision of 2008 generated new protests from historians. In September 2007, the general assembly of the International Committee of Historical Sciences expressed its concern with criminalization of the past,[207] and in November, the American Historical Association had published its own statement against the proposed Framework Decision:

> [I]t can never be in the public interest... to forbid the publication of particular historical theses. Any limitation on freedom of research or expression, however well intentioned, violates a fundamental principle of scholarship: that the researcher must be able to investigate any aspect of the past and to report without fear what the evidence reveals.[208]

As we see, the arguments put forward by historians in different countries are quite similar. They are based on the idea of autonomy of the historical profession. The historians' struggle against the criminalization of the past has become an international phenomenon. Indeed, support from abroad strengthened the positions of the *Liberté pour l'histoire* association in the domestic debate. In March 2008, the National Assembly created a special commission on issues of historical memory, with Bernard Accoyer, president of the lower house, as its chair. Upon careful examination of the arguments pro and contra, the commission declared that regulating

Politique: Revue de débats 47 (December 2006), pp. 15–17, and Gilles Manceron, "La loi: régulateur ou acteur des guerres de mémoire?," p. 242.

[206] "Noi storici contro la legge che punisce chi nega la Shoah," *L'Unità*, January 23, 2007.

[207] Luigi Cajani, "Criminal Laws on History," p. 30.

[208] AHA Statement on the Framework Decision of the Council of the European Union on the Fight against Racism and Xenophobia, in *Perspectives on History*, November 2007.

historical memory is not parliament's legitimate function[209] and recommended that it refrain from adopting any new memory laws. But the commission also decided from the outset not to call into question any existing laws, including the Gayssot Act.[210]

As a result, both partisans and opponents of memory laws could claim victory.[211] In fact, although the *Liberté pour l'histoire* association was protesting all memory laws, many of its members had mixed feelings about the Gayssot Act, which most historians had welcomed in 1990 and which is not usually seen as a case of electoral manipulation. As for other laws, they were purely declarative and consequently less important. The main goal of the *Liberté pour l'histoire* association was to prevent the further criminalization of history, which was exactly what the Accoyer Commission recommended.

In practical terms, the decision of the Accoyer Commission jeopardized the prospects of only the "Armenian" law. Yet, notwithstanding the commission's advice, the struggle over memory laws in France continues. In Western Europe, France remains the main point of growth for legislation on issues of the past, as well as the center of the protest movement against it.

To conclude this chapter, let us take a closer look at what exactly Western European memory laws penalize. Using differing language, they are all almost exclusively focused on the denial of acts of genocide and other crimes against humanity, which are typically viewed as crimes of a racist nature. However, although they are usually labeled "Holocaust denial laws," the term "Holocaust" is almost entirely absent from them.[212] Some acts forbid the denial of Nazi crimes against humanity[213] while others more broadly outlaw denial of any genocide or other crimes against

[209] "Le rôle du Parlement n'est pas d'adopter des lois qualifiant ou portant une appréciation sur les faits historiques, à fortiori lorsque celles-ci s'accompagnent de sanctions pénales." See *Assemblée Nationale. Rapport d'information no 1262: Rassembler la Nation autour d'une mémoire partagée* (Paris: Assemblée Nationale, 2008), p. 181. As Robert Badinter, former president of the Constitutional Council, puts it, "Constitutionally, the French Parliament has not been assigned the power to recognise the existence of genocide." See Badinter, "Is This the End for the Historical Memory Laws?"

[210] Baruch, *Des lois indignes?*, p. 173; Nicolas Offenstadt, *L'Histoire bling-bling: Le retour du roman national* (Paris: Stock, 2009), pp. 99–117.

[211] President's Report, Presented by Pierre Nora, President of Liberté pour l'Histoire, to the Association's Annual Meeting, June 2012: www.lph-asso.fr/index.php?option=com_content&view=article&id=181%3Aune-lourde-annee-pour-les-lois-memorielles&catid=53%3Aactualites&Itemid=170&lang=en. Cf. Baruch, *Des lois indignes?*, p. 174.

[212] With the exception of the 2014 Greek law and the Italian law of 2016 (the latter uses the word "Shoah").

[213] The 1990 French law, the 1992 Austrian law, the 1994 German law, the 1995 Belgian law, and the 1997 Luxembourgian law, as well as the 1986 Israeli law.

humanity.[214] In the 1990s, references to war crimes were rare (e.g., the 1997 Luxembourgian law), which is characteristic of the Holocaust-centered memory regime, but they have become more typical since the end of the 2000s,[215] in line with the expanding scope of this legislation. As defined in the Charter of the Nuremberg Tribunal, in fact, war crimes are quite close to, and partly overlap with, crimes against humanity. The 2007 Portuguese law is the only Western act to ban denial of crimes against peace, which are not considered crimes of racism and currently attract far less attention than they did in the aftermath of the war.

Most memory laws make no attempt to define which facts exactly they view as firmly established and whose denial would be illegal. Obviously, they consider those facts to be commonly known; however, common knowledge is not the most reliable criterion for deciding which utterances about the past are false and which are not. Unsurprisingly, legislators in several countries did endeavor to clarify what they proposed to penalize. Most typically, they referred to the definitions of Nazi crimes in the Charter of the Nuremberg Tribunal and/or the notions of genocide and crimes against humanity in the Statute of the International Criminal Court.[216] But this does not solve the problem of deciding which concrete facts cannot be denied. In some cases, memory laws also reference the verdicts of national and international jurisdictions regarding concrete crimes,[217] which would be a better solution if legal truth and historical truth were the same thing (and many jurists do not believe they are). However, even referring to individual sentences imposed by the Verdict of the Nuremberg Tribunal, no Western European law straightforwardly endorses the Nuremberg Judgment as establishing the truth of the past. I would argue that so far, Western lawmakers have not found a satisfactory way of unambiguously defining which historical utterances cannot be denied (which does not mean to imply, of course, that Holocaust denial is not itself a lie).

---

[214] The 1993 Swiss law, the 1995 and 2015 Spanish laws, the 1999 Liechtensteinian law, the 2005 Andorran law, the 2007 Portuguese law, the 2009 Maltese law, and the 2014 Greek law.

[215] The 2008 Framework Decision, the 2007 Portuguese law, the 2009 Maltese law, the 2015 Spanish law, the 2016 Italian law, and the 2017 French law.

[216] The 1990 French law, the 1997 Luxembourgian law, and the 2008 Framework Decision refer to the Nuremberg definition of Nazi crimes. The latest version of the 1994 German law, the 2011 Luxembourgian law, the 2015 Italian law, and the 2008 Framework Decision refer to the definition given in the Rome Statute.

[217] The 1990 French law, the 2005 Andorran law, and the 2014 Greek law.

CHAPTER 3

Memory Laws in Eastern Europe

In the 2000s, Eastern Europe became an important center, alongside France, of legislative activity concerning the past, which resulted from a confluence of several factors. First, the peak of optimistic expectations about the future, which coincided with a romantic stage of the "capitalist revolution" in the region at the turn of the 1990s, gradually gave place to a more complex perception of historical time that involved both a certain level of self-confident "futurism" and a growing nostalgia for the communist period (known as *Ostalgie*),[1] the relative proportions of those elements

---

[1] *Ostalgie* is a German word coined to refer to nostalgic feelings with regard to the former Eastern Germany. Similar attitudes toward the past are also characteristic of other post-communist countries, and a study of those attitudes confirms Svetlana Boym's understanding of nostalgia as a typically modern reaction to the experience of rapid social change. See Svetlana Boym, *The Future of Nostalgia* (New York: Basic Books, 2001), pp. XIV–XVII. Some scholars propose viewing *Ostalgie* as "one of the few salvage mechanisms available to Eastern Europeans" in their protest against "the hegemony of the West" and "the globalizing capitalism" that tends to deprive them of their "difference," "past," and "identity," rather than as a conservative attachment to communist values and "history without guilt." See Marta Rabikowska, "Introduction: The Memory of the Communist Past – An Alternative Present?" in *The Everyday of Memory: Between Communism and Post-Communism* (Oxford: Peter Lang, 2013), pp. 3, 15, 25. See also other articles in that volume and *Post-Communist Nostalgia*, eds. Maria Todorova and Zsuzsa Gill (New York: Berghahn Books, 2010). The expression "history without guilt" is Michael Kammen's; it is to me an exact characterization of a significant portion of post-communist memories (including some memories of the anti-communist nationalist resistance). See Michael Kammen, *Mystic Chords of Memory: The Transformation of Tradition in American Culture* (New York: Knopf, 1991), p. 688. Post-communist nostalgia is focused on seemingly innocent and at times even moving recollections of the subjects' everyday life under communism, which are largely similar to those that many "ordinary Germans" had of their youth under the Nazi regime. See Martin Broszat, "A Plea for the Historicization of National Socialism," in *Reworking the Past: Hitler, the Holocaust, and the Historians Debate*, ed. Peter Baldwin (Boston: Beacon Press, 1990), pp. 77–87. In both cases, I believe, nostalgia contributes to the normalization of the totalitarian past and the preservation of totalitarian subjectivity, even while containing some features of the "discourse of the losers" with which recent historiography tends to sympathize. For an analysis of *Ostalgie* viewed as "the romantic rediscovery [by Eastern Europe] of its consumer culture" in the late communist period, see Greg Castillo, "East as True West: Redeeming Bourgeois Culture, from Socialist Realism to *Ostalgie*," in *Imagining the West in Eastern Europe and the Soviet Union,* ed. György Péteri (Pittsburgh, Pa.: University of Pittsburgh Press, 2010), p. 104. On the role of nostalgia for Soviet times as the "structuring content of the nationalist consensus" in Russia, see

being largely conditioned by a country's (or a social group's) performance in the "brave new world." The Eastern European "space of experience" (to borrow Reinhart Koselleck's expression) was gradually becoming more and more forcefully determined by the hardships of the transition period, although the prospect of accession to the EU temporarily softened the crisis of historical optimism. By the turn of the twenty-first century, the age of memory, the beginning of which – in this region as elsewhere – dates back approximately to the 1970s, had finally triumphed in Eastern Europe, making historical grievances an increasingly important aspect of Eastern European politics and cultural life.

Second, with the Eastern European countries' gradual entry into the EU, Brussels' official Holocaust-centered politics of memory also expanded eastward. The Council of Europe and the European Commission against Racism and Intolerance (ECRI) have been persistent in encouraging the new member states to bring their legislation fully into line with EU standards. Absent that pressure, there was every likelihood that the banning of Holocaust denial would not have become a priority in the region.

Third, Russia's neo-imperial reconstruction under Putin has brought about numerous conflicts between Russia and its Western neighbors regarding the interpretation of the past, communism being increasingly frequently interpreted in Eastern Europe as a synonym for the Russian occupation, which also served to counterbalance *Ostalgie* and leftist sympathies in the population at large. In contrast to the EU's official memory, the Kremlin supports an interpretation of the war that focuses on the Soviet Union's decisive role in the victory over fascism, and implicitly on Russia's rights to the former Soviet sphere of influence as defined by the 1945 agreements between the USSR, the United States, and Great Britain.

The competition between those two narratives promoted respectively by the EU and Russia is often seen, especially in Moscow, as a battle for Eastern Europe, which of course also has historical memories of its own. Unsurprisingly, then, Eastern European memory landscapes are particularly complex, not least because of the international context in which they have developed.

It goes without saying that, Eastern Europe being a highly diverse region with a long and intricate history, any general characterization of it would be an oversimplification (the same being, of course, equally true of Western Europe). Stefan Troebst has recently argued that Eastern Europe

Madeleine Laruelle, *In the Name of the Nation: Nationalism and Politics in Contemporary Russia* (New York: Palgrave Macmillan, 2009), p. 199.

can be divided into four "meso-regions" with distinctively different "cultures of remembrance," ranging from "societies with a strong anti-communist consensus concerning recent history" (e.g., Estonia, Latvia, and Lithuania) to "societies where communism had not suffered a loss of legitimacy" (such as Belarus, Moldova, and "above all the Russian Federation, where communism is perceived as part of the imperial legacy"). In between, Troebst places those countries that are "ambivalent" (Hungary, Poland, and Ukraine) or even "apathetic" (Bulgaria, Romania, and Serbia) with regard to their communist past.[2] This handy classification is, however, hard to endorse unreservedly: communism has, in fact, "suffered a loss of legitimacy" even in Russia, where the Soviet empire, rather than communism per se, is viewed in light of the Great Power complex (while communism, with its revolutionary rhetoric, is often considered an anti-national force); "ambivalence" about the communist legacy is also not altogether atypical of the Baltic countries, which have considerable Russian minorities and strong socialist parties; and Ukraine can hardly be placed in the same category as Hungary and Poland because it is typologically closer to the model of post-communist transformations characteristic of the Commonwealth of Independent States,[3] and until very recently, Russia's influence there was incomparably stronger than in Poland and Hungary (in the domain of symbolic politics among all else). In addition, attitudes toward communism are but one of the factors that inform the specificity of historical memory in a given country.

   In the first section of this chapter, I will highlight those features of the rise of memory and the politics of history in Eastern Europe that I find characteristic of the region as a whole. Since Eastern European memories can scarcely be understood outside the context of their dialogue (or, if the reader prefers, conflicts) with Russia over the interpretation of the past, we will also look ahead and discuss here some aspects of Russian memory, for all that the Russian case will be explored in greater detail in Chapters 5 and 6. The second and third sections of this chapter examine Eastern European anti-fascist legislation of communist times and the post-1989 de-

---

[2] Stefan Troebst, "Halecki Revisited: Europe's Conflicting Cultures of Remembrance," in *A European Memory? Contested Histories and Politics of Remembrance*, eds. Małgorzata Pakier and Bo Stråth (New York: Berghahn Books, 2010), p. 58; Troebst, "Was für ein Teppich? Postkommunistische Erinnerungskulturen in Ost(mittel)europa," in *Der Kommunismus im Museum: Formen des Auseinandersetzung in Deutschland und Ostmitteleuropa*, eds. Volkhart Knigge and Ulrich Mälert (Cologne: Böhlau, 2005), pp. 31–54.

[3] Anders Åslund, *How Capitalism Was Built: The Transformation of Central and Eastern Europe, Russia, and Central Asia* (Cambridge: Cambridge University Press, 2007), p. 307.

communization laws, two major legislative traditions that exerted considerable influence on approaches to memory laws in the region. Section four considers Eastern European memory laws and their meaning in various national contexts, while the next chapter will offer a case study in the politics of history and legislation on issues of the past in Ukraine.

The Rise of Memory in Eastern Europe

The politics of memory in Eastern Europe is dominated even more powerfully than in the West by the legacy of World War II and the totalitarian regimes. But "the Second World War was not the same for everyone."[4] The "Bloodlands," as Timothy Snyder calls the countries between Stalin's Russia and Hitler's Germany, suffered perhaps more than any other region from the atrocities of those two regimes.[5] The Eastern European experience of the war has been largely determined by the fact that by the end of the war, those countries were conquered by one of the victors with the consent of the others. Obviously, none of the victors' war myths ("liberation from the West" versus "liberation from the East," as Snyder puts it)[6] could be fully shared by most Eastern Europeans.[7] The memory of communism, a regime that lasted much longer than the German occupation, has become their central (although by no means their

---

[4] Tony Judt, "The Past Is Another Country: Myth and Memory in Postwar Europe," *Daedalus* 121/4 (1992), p. 85. See also Stefan Berger, "Remembering the Second World War in Western Europe, 1945–2005," in *A European Memory?* pp. 119–136; Heike Karge, "Practices and Politics of Second World War Remembrance: (Trans-)National Perspectives from Eastern and South-Eastern Europe," in *A European Memory?*, pp. 137–146; Christian Karner and Bram Mertens, eds., *The Use and Abuse of Memory: Interpreting World War II in Contemporary European Politics* (New Brunswick, N.J.: Transaction Publishers, 2013); Frank Biess and Robert G. Moeller, eds., *Histories of the Aftermath: The Legacies of the Second World War in Europe* (New York: Berghahn Books, 2010); Henrik Stenius, Mirja Österberg, and Johan Östling, eds., *Nordic Narratives of the Second World War: National Historiographies Revisited* (Lund: Nordic Academic Press, 2011); and Daniel Chirot, Gi-Wook Shin, and Daniel Sneider, eds., *Confronting Memories of World War II: European and Asian Legacies* (Seattle: University of Washington Press, 2014).

[5] Timothy Snyder, *Bloodlands: Europe between Hitler and Stalin* (New York: Basic Books, 2010).

[6] Timothy Snyder, "European Mass Killing and European Commemoration," in *Remembrance, History, and Justice: Coming to Terms with Traumatic Past in Democratic Societies*, eds. Vladimir Tismaneanu and Bogdan C. Iacob (Budapest: Central European University Press, 2015), pp. 30–31. See also Siobhan Kattago, *Memory and Representation in Contemporary Europe: The Persistence of the Past* (Abington: Routledge, 2016), pp. 32–39.

[7] Such claims of the problematic outcomes of the war for Eastern Europe have contributed to undermining what Gavriel D. Rosenfeld describes as "the good war consensus," or the victors' black-and-white myth of the war. See his *Hi Hitler! How the Nazi Past Is Being Normalized in Contemporary Culture* (Cambridge: Cambridge University Press, 2015), pp. 29–77. However, notwithstanding all the criticism with regard to that myth, it largely continues to inform the "official" narratives of the war, both in the West and in Russia.

only) concern. The upsurge, since the 1980s, of anti-communist memories, which tend to obscure those of Nazi crimes, is seen by some researchers as "the demise of the postwar [anti-fascist] consensus and the revival of previously marginalized ways of thinking"[8] (read: the spread of neo-fascism), while others consider it as a fully legitimate, and even laudable, manifestation of cultural diversity.

The notion of the "asymmetry" of European memory has become a commonplace in memory studies,[9] and my comparison of Eastern and Western European memory laws fully confirms this. However, it is equally important to appreciate similarities between the ways in which the rise of memory occurred in the West and the East, which go far beyond the "hegemonic" imposition of Western narratives in the region.[10] Both the asymmetry and the similarities harken back to the communist times.

---

[8] Dan Stone, *The Holocaust, Fascism, and Memory: Essays in the History of Ideas* (Basingstoke: Palgrave Macmillan, 2013), pp. 176, 173, 175, 179.

[9] Tony Judt, *Postwar: A History of Europe since 1945* (New York: Penguin Books, 2005), p. 826; Harald Wydra, "Dynamics of Generational Memory: Understanding the East and West Divide," in *Dynamics of Memory and Identity in Contemporary Europe*, eds. Eric Langenbacher, Bill Niven, and Ruth Wittlinger (New York: Berghahn Books, 2013), p. 14; Aleida Assmann, "Europe's Divided Memory," in *Clashes in European Memory: The Case of Communist Repression and the Holocaust*, eds. Muriel Blaive, Christian Gerbel, and Thomas Lindenberger (Innsbruck: Studien Verlag, 2011), pp. 270–280; Stefan Troebst, "Jalta versus Stalingrad, GULag versus Holocaust: Konfligierende Erinnerungskulturen im größeren Europa," *Berliner Journal für Soziologie* 15/3 (2005), pp. 381–400; Edgar Wolfrum, *Geschichte als Waffe: Vom Kaiserreich bis zur Wiedervereinigung* (Göttingen: Vandenhoeck & Ruprecht, 2001), pp. 138–139. Emmanuel Droit speaks about an "iron curtain of memory" separating Eastern and Western Europe. See his "Le Goulag contre la Shoah: Mémoires officielles et cultures mémorielles dans l'Europe élargie," *Vingtième Siècle: Revue d'histoire* 94 (2007), pp. 101–120. However, other scholars reject the "asymmetry theory" as a "caricature" and call for a more nuanced approach. See Marie-Claude Maurel, "Introduction: Le passé en héritage," in *L'Europe et ses représentations du passé: Les tournement de la mémoire*, eds. Maurel and Françoise Mayer (Paris: Harmattan, 2008), p. 13. Andrzej Nowak views the "Manichaean opposition between Western and Eastern cultures of remembrance" as a "new Yalta" and a continuation of the "Western construction" of Eastern Europe. See his "Political Correctness and Memories Constructed for 'Eastern Europe,'" in *Memory and Change in Europe: Eastern Perspectives*, eds. Małgorzata Pakier and Johanna Wawrzyniak (New York: Berghahn Books, 2016), pp. 42, 45, 49. However, Nowak – if I read him correctly – only argues for a "peaceful coexistence" of Eastern and Western memory cultures without calling into question their specific differences. See also Slawomir Kapralski, "Ain't Nothing Special," in *Memory and Change in Europe: Eastern Perspectives*, pp. 77–95. See a classical Eastern EuREpean reaction against the opposition (in this case established by Jürgen Habermas and Jacques Derrida) between Core Europe [Kerneuropa] and New Europe: Adam Krzemiński, "First Kant, Now Habermas: A Polish Perspective on 'Core Europe'" [2003], in *Old Europe, New Europe, Core Europe: Transatlantic Relations after the Iraq War*, eds. Daniel Levy, Max Pensky, and John C. Torpey (London: Verso, 2005), pp. 146–152. See also Daniel Levy and Natan Sznaider, *Human Rights and Memory* (University Park: Pennsylvania State University Press, 2010), pp. 122–141.

[10] Wydra, "Dynamics of Generational Memory," p. 15. Eric Langenbacher, "Conclusion," in *Dynamics of Memory and Identity in Contemporary Europe*, p. 212. For a broader post-colonial perspective on understanding Eastern Europe, see Nataša Kovačević, *Narrating Post/Communism: Colonial Discourse and Europe's Borderline Civilization* (London: Routledge, 2008).

Prevalent Eastern European narratives today assert that communist regimes were imposed from the outside, with limited support from local populations. Those accounts, which underline the opposition to communism rather than collaboration with it, resemble the heroic resistance myths typical of postwar Western Europe. Some Eastern European memory laws are rooted in those narratives, which are less false than they are one-sided, given "the heterogeneous nature of communization" that has been highlighted by recent research.[11] In its light, one can safely argue that without the Soviet occupation, communists would have had little chance of coming to power in Eastern Europe. We now have a detailed knowledge of how exactly Eastern European communists, with the support of the KGB, falsified elections (applying technologies that differed little from those currently in use in Putin's Russia) and staged "socialist revolutions" in their countries.[12] This said, however, one should not underestimate the loyalty that the communist regimes, once established, could count upon in the region. Communist socialization was not altogether inefficient, not least because it was imposed by force, and resisting it could be costly indeed. Prior to the 1980s, few Eastern Europeans (and even fewer Russians) thought they would ever see the end of the Soviet empire, no matter how much some of them disliked it.[13] Coming to terms with "reality" often presented as the only option, which was reinforced by the powerful intellectual and psychological appeal of the communist promise of earthly paradise.[14]

At the same time, the communist regimes proved responsive to the interests of those individuals and social groups whose prospects of social mobility they improved. The economic growth and modernization of the

[11] Vladimir Tismaneanu, "Introduction," in *Stalinism Revisited: The Establishment of Communist Regimes in East-Central Europe* (Budapest: Central European University Press, 2009), p. 3.

[12] Nikita Petrov, *Po stsenariyu Stalina: Rol' organov NKVD-MGB SSSR v sovetizatsii stran Tsentral'noy i Vostochnoy Yevropy, 1945–1953 gg.* [Implementing Stalin's Scenario: The Role of the Organs of USSR NKVD-MGB in Sovietizing the Countries of Central and Eastern Europe, 1945–1953] (Moscow: ROSSPEN, 2011), pp. 173, 182–183. Judt, *Postwar*, pp. 129–139; Anne Applebaum, *Iron Curtain: The Crushing of Eastern Europe, 1944–1956* (New York: Anchor Books, 2012). On the staged elections in Western Ukraine and Western Belorussia, which were annexed by the USSR in 1939, see Jan Gross, *Revolution from Abroad: The Soviet Conquest of Poland's Western Ukraine and Western Belorussia* (Princeton, N.J.: Princeton University Press, 2002), pp. 71–113.

[13] As Mark R. Beissinger puts it, "before 1990 the breakup of the Soviet Union remained outside the realm of the conceivable." See his *Nationalist Mobilization and the Collapse of the Soviet State* (New York: Cambridge University Press, 2002), p. 3; Alexei Yurchak, *Everything Was Forever, Until It Was No More: The Last Soviet Generation* (Princeton, N.J.: Princeton University Press, 2005); Andrzej Paszkowski, "Nazism and Communism in Polish Experience and Memory," in *Stalinism and Nazism: History and Memory Compared*, eds. Henry Rousso and Richard J. Golsan (Lincoln: University of Nebraska Press, 2004), pp. 254–257.

[14] François Furet, *The Passing of an Illusion: The Idea of Communism in the Twentieth Century* (Chicago, Ill.: University of Chicago Press, 1999).

1950s and 1960s made many Eastern Europeans think more of the future to come than about past horrors; the phenomenon of a future-oriented postwar generation was not exclusive to the West. Moreover, the end of the era of class struggle could only be a worldwide phenomenon (or at least a Western-and-Eastern-bloc-wide one). Before bringing about the fall of communism, the era of post–class struggle produced, in both West and East, a tendency toward accepting existing regimes on condition that they become more democratic. The broad support that the idea of "socialism with a human face" enjoyed across Eastern Europe shows both that socialism was considered reformable and that any discussion of possible changes could be conducted only in terms of "the socialist choice."

Obtaining more autonomy from Moscow was one of the reformers' important aspirations. Due to the relative liberalization of the Soviet nationalities policy under Khrushchev, the communist elites in Eastern Europe began flirting with nationalism during the 1960s and 1970s, in order to increase their power and secure popular support.[15] However, that flirting was most often limited to bargaining with Moscow over the implementation of common policies and to a cautious "cultural nationalism" that the Soviet leadership was eager to tolerate. Open opponents of socialism and Russian domination were a tiny and persecuted minority, which garnered covert sympathy from some of their compatriots (certain powerful figures among them), while others (probably a majority) considered them pointlessly radical and dangerous. It was not until the 1980s that unambiguous rejection of Soviet rule became predominant in most Eastern bloc countries and certain Soviet republics (especially the Baltic states and Western Ukraine). It replaced the "doublethink" of the previous decades, although without completely overcoming it.

Unsurprisingly, Eastern European historical memory, including that of the war, was (and still is) essentially plural. The communist master narrative that was promoted, with some local variations, by the governing regimes across the entire Soviet empire did not eradicate but clearly marginalized the counter-memories of social, ethnic, and religious groups.

---

[15] Katherine Verdery, *National Ideology under Socialism: Identity and Cultural Politics in Ceauşescu's Romania* (Berkeley, Calif.: University of California Press, 1991). Of course, Ceauşescu's Romania was an extreme case of the "nationalizing" of communism, but even in such a loyal pro-Russian country as the GDR, the politics of national identity was important part of the government's agenda. See Jan Palmowski, *Inventing a Socialist Nation: Heimat and the Politics of Everyday Life in the GDR, 1945–1990* (Cambridge: Cambridge University Press, 2009). See also Martin Mevius, "Reappraising Communism and Nationalism," *Nationalities Papers* 37/4 (2009), pp. 377–400, and Walter A. Kemp *Nationalism and Communism: Eastern Europe and the Soviet Union: A Basic Contradiction?* (Basingstoke: Macmillan/St. Martin's Press, 1999).

The degree to which the official conceptions of history were internalized by the population remains questionable, but some certainly were, the quasi-absent memory of the Holocaust being perhaps the most striking example (we will return to this later). The aforementioned *Ostalgie* would hardly have been possible in recent years were it not for the tenacious traces of "doublethink" and of the communist master narrative.

The chronology of the rise of memory in the East differed from that in the West, although in both cases the 1970s marked an important turning point. Destalinization was resulting in an upsurge of memories of the victims of repressions in Russia and other Eastern European countries as early as the mid-1950s. The communist rulers were quick to realize the dangers of the memories they had provoked by rejecting certain aspects of Stalin's legacy (the "cult of personality" and the "violations of socialist legality"). The authorities therefore typically, and often successfully, tried to control and marginalize memories of the Gulag, especially after the fall of Nikita Khrushchev in 1964.[16] But even under Khrushchev many painful topics were never allowed into the discussion in Eastern Europe – such as, for example, the 1940 massacre of Polish prisoners of war by the Soviets ("the Katyn massacre") or the Holodomor in Ukraine.[17] The reintegration of the victims of repressions into post-Stalinist societies did not come without its problems, and many of them felt it safer to keep silent about their camp experiences, just as many Holocaust survivors also did in the West in the immediate postwar period (although there was no secret police there to impose that silence by force). But the situation in the West began changing in the 1960s with the emergence of the new culture of victimhood, while in the East, the development of that culture was blocked by the communist regimes, whose proclaimed solidarity with the victims of capitalism, colonialism, or fascism co-existed with an all but blanket lack of compassion for those who had suffered from the communists' own policies. In contrast to Nazism, communism had not been

---

[16] On destalinization in Russia, see Polly Jones, *Myth, Memory, and Trauma: Rethinking the Stalinist Past in the Soviet Union, 1953–70* (New Haven, Conn.: Yale University Press, 2013), and Denis Kozlov, *The Readers of Novyi Mir: Coming to Terms with the Stalinist Past* (Cambridge, Mass.: Harvard University Press, 2013).

[17] Inessa Yazhborovskaya, Anatoliy Yablokov, and Valentina Parsadanova, *Katynskiy sindrom v sovetsko-pol'skikh i rossiysko-pol'skikh otnosheniyakh* [The Katyn Syndrome in Soviet-Polish and Russian-Polish Relationships] (Moscow: ROSSPEN, 2009), pp. 189–237; George Sanford, *Katyn and the Soviet Massacre of 1940: Truth, Justice and Memory* (New York: Routledge, 2005), pp. 194–195; and Jacek Chrobaczyński and Piotr Trojański, "Auschwitz and Katyn in Political Bondage: The Process of Shaping Memory in Communist Poland," in *Memory and Change in Europe: Eastern Perspectives*, pp. 246–263. On the memory of the Holodomor, see Chapter 4.

officially condemned by an authoritative international court and remained ascendant in Eastern Europe, which strongly influenced the memory of its crimes. The abortive rise of the memory of Stalin's repressions at the turn of the 1960s thus differed in many ways from the emerging memory of the Holocaust.

In Russia, the late 1960s witnessed the formation of the cult of the Great Patriotic War, which was to become the cornerstone of late Soviet ideology (and, more recently, the foundational myth of the Putin regime). The Soviet war narrative was a typical heroic myth, although for many reasons the authorities were very cautious in promoting it prior to the mid-1960s: Stalin did not want his army generals to use the memory of the victory in legitimizing any political pretensions they may have had,[18] while Khrushchev, for his part, was far more interested in disclosing Stalin's mistakes of 1941 than in celebrating his triumph of 1945. Nevertheless, the core of the Soviet war myth goes back to Stalin's wartime propaganda, which presented the USSR as a peaceful country, a victim of aggression, and humankind's savior from fascism. After the fall of Khrushchev, this patriotic myth became an important instrument that the new Soviet leadership used to partially rehabilitate Stalin and obliterate the memory of the repressions by presenting the victorious war, rather than the terror, as the central event of Soviet history.

In line with the Soviet narrative, Eastern European countries had to develop their own war myths, which became critically important for them as early as the 1950s. The victory over fascism was viewed here as the foundational event of the "people's democracies," while in Russia, the October Revolution of 1917 had long ago been installed as the myth of the origins of the Soviet regime.[19] The Kremlin could, furthermore, use anti-fascist solidarity in consolidating the Eastern bloc, even when it preferred not to encourage the cult of the war inside the country.

The construction of war memorials on the territory of the former Nazi concentration camps Buchenwald (1958), Ravensbrück (1959), and Sachsenhausen (1961) in the GDR was a typical manifestation of the Eastern European war myth.[20] Substantially different from Western Holocaust

---

[18] On the complexity of the postwar struggle around the legacy of the victory over Nazism and on Stalin's "theft of the war," see Jeffrey Brooks, *Thank You, Comrade Stalin! Soviet Public Culture from Revolution to Cold War* (Princeton, N.J.: Princeton University Press, 2000), pp. 195–232.

[19] Frederick C. Corney, *Telling October: Memory and the Making of the Bolshevik Revolution* (Ithaca, N.Y.: Cornell University Press, 2004).

[20] Bill Niven, *Facing the Nazi Past: United Germany and the Legacy of the Third Reich* (London: Routledge, 2002), pp. 19–24. The creation of Holocaust memorials had begun during the war and

memorials, they privileged the theme of anti-fascist resistance and had more to do with the postwar patriotic myths than with the late-twentieth-century culture of victimhood. The celebration of anti-fascist memories in Eastern Germany was obviously linked to the country's claims to be "the only 'truly antifascist' German state."[21] In light of those claims, the Federal Republic came to look almost like a neo-Nazi regime, which meant that Adenauer's politics of memory had to be largely aimed at refuting them (and partly explains the support that he gave to the memory of the Holocaust in 1960).[22]

The Soviet war myth as forged in the late 1960s and the 1970s, under Leonid Brezhnev, was also a heroic resistance myth. As time passed, it came to obscure not only the memory of the repressions but also that of the war's own dark side, including the Soviet defeat of 1941. But there was an important difference between Brezhnev's narrative of the war and the Eastern European anti-fascist resistance myths of the 1950s and early 1960: while the latter legitimized the people's democracies as the project for the region's future, the rise of the Soviet war myth marked the beginning of an important change in the perception of historical time in Russia. As such, it was, rather, an early manifestation of the late-twentieth-century memory boom that accompanied the decay of future-oriented

continued throughout the entire postwar period. However, the East German effort of the late 1950s and early 1960s marked a new stage in this process. Already "the first genuine GDR antifascist monument," the 1958 Buchenwald Memorial, developed the theme of heroism by focusing on "the allegedly victorious uprising in the camp," which became a particularly important juncture in the East German memory of the war, because many German communists, including Ernst Thälmann, had been murdered there. See Susanne Scharnowski, "Heroes and Victims: The Aesthetics and Ideology of Monuments and Memorials in the GDR," in *Memorialization in Germany since 1945,* eds. Bill Niven and Chloe Paver (Basingstoke: Palgrave Macmillan, 2010), pp. 267–275; Harold Marcuse, "Holocaust Memorials: The Emergence of a Genre," *The American Historical Review* 115/1 (2010), pp. 53–89, and James E. Young, ed., *The Art of Memory: Holocaust Memorials in History* (Munich: Prestel, 1994). Typically, in Poland, "the museum in Auschwitz-Birkenau was [until the end of communism] called the Museum of Martyrology of the Polish and Other Nations. . . . The Jewish dimension was concealed, if not outright denied." See Konstanty Gebert, "The Dialectics of Memory in Poland: Holocaust Memorials in Warsaw," in *The Art of Memory: Holocaust Memorials in History,* p. 121.
[21] Devin O. Pendas, *The Frankfurt Auschwitz Trial, 1963–1965: Genocide, History, and the Limits of the Law* (Cambridge: Cambridge University Press, 2006), p. 18; Jeffrey Herf, *Divided Memory: The Nazi Past in the Two Germanys* (Cambridge, Mass.: Harvard University Press, 1997), p. 163.
[22] As we know, 1960 was a turning point in the development of West German legislation regarding hate speech, of which Holocaust denial was assumed to be an instance. In February of the same year, Adenauer visited the Auschwitz-Birkenau concentration camp site and delivered a speech that was very much in line with what his government sought to demonstrate by amending Article 130 of the Penal Code. Adenauer was eager to emphasize that the safety and dignity of German Jews were as well protected in the Federal Republic as those of any other population group. See Harold Marcuse, *Legacies of Dachau: The Uses and Abuses of a Concentration Camp, 1933–2001* (Cambridge: Cambridge University Press, 2001), p. 205.

master narratives. In the USSR, the Khrushchev "Thaw," which witnessed a considerable improvement in living standards and the first impressive achievements in space exploration, was characterized by optimistic expectations about the future. Those expectations, which were the main resource of Khrushchev's symbolic politics, remained important to the Soviet and Eastern European cultural climate for several years after his departure, and they largely informed the project of "socialism with a human face." It was not, in fact, until the Soviet invasion of Czechoslovakia in 1968 that historical optimism began to waver throughout the entire Soviet empire. In Russia, economic reforms were, by and large, abandoned, and the rise in oil prices contributed to the reorientation of Soviet economy toward the export of raw materials after 1973. The myth of the war and the increasingly important role of the past to political legitimation correlated with this change. A ritualistic deference to "the radiant future" could not hide that communism was gradually becoming a past-oriented society, and in the 1980s, it came to be increasingly habitually viewed, on both sides of the Iron Curtain, as a failed social project.

But the crisis of the future took a very special form in Eastern Europe. It was a crisis of the *communist* future, while the idealized capitalism, which by that time had been already "built" in the West, came to be seen as the desired future of all humanity, including the countries of the Soviet bloc (even though until the launching of perestroika it was generally perceived as being scarcely attainable there in practice).[23] The idealization of the West, one of the key features of Eastern European cultures since the eighteenth century that had been provisionally downgraded by the communist experiment, reached its peak in the 1970s and 1980s. Notwithstanding some early developments (such as a renewed interest in national heritage and cultural traditions that in both East and West dates back to the 1960s and especially the 1970s), a full-scale crisis of the future did not come in Eastern Europe (including in Russia) until the mid-1990s, by which time the transition to democracy was proving far more painful than most Eastern Europeans had expected. In contrast, in the late 1980s and early 1990s, the ideal image of the West viewed in light of the liberal master narrative was central to the dismantling of the Soviet empire.

---

[23] See Dina Khapaeva, "L'Occident sera demain," *Annales: Histoire, Sciences Sociales* 50/6 (1995), pp. 1259–1270; Khapaeva, "As the Whole Civilized World," *Social Sciences Information* 34/4 (1995), pp. 687–704; and Khapaeva, "L'Occident dans l'imaginaire russe," *Social Sciences Information* 33/1 (1994), pp. 553–569.

The reader will remember that the democratic revolution in postwar historiography, including the formation of the social and cultural history, played a central role in the emergence of a democratic culture of memory in the West. I have argued elsewhere[24] that some Soviet historians, while still paying lip service to Marxism, made a "cultural turn" in the 1970s similar to that of their French and American colleagues, and some Polish, Hungarian, and other Eastern European historians did the same.[25] Those historians were becoming increasingly influential as time passed, and the impact of Western scholarship, above all of the French *Annales* School, was also rapidly spreading across the region.[26] The fascination with culture was by no means a hallmark of a narrow group of academics living in some ivory tower. Cultural studies enjoyed a remarkable popularity among educated readers, and their message that consisted of the notion of human beings viewed as subjects of culture (*Kulturmenschen*, as Max Weber used to say) rather than as "products" of economic development and class interests resonated with the spirit of the age of post–class struggle. The values of the democratically minded intelligentsia were coming to dominate a growing segment of public opinion on both sides of the Iron Curtain, which was an essential factor in preparing "the decline and fall" of the Soviet empire.[27]

But here again, similarities and differences were intertwined. Thus, the culture of victimhood, crucial to the democratization of historical memory in the West, did not play the same role farther east. The communist ideology had, in fact, always claimed to be the ultimate expression of the aspirations of all who had ever suffered from any form of exploitation. In particular, sympathies toward victims of colonialism, so important in the West, were far less characteristic of Eastern Europe. In Russia, the imperial (and, later, postimperial) syndrome blocked the development of those sympathies, whereas identification with Europe, rather than with its

---

[24] See my "Sowjetische Historiographie, Marxismus und Totalitarismus: Zur Analyse der mentalen Grundlagen der Historiographie," *Österreichische Zeitschrift für Geschichtswissenschaften* 2/1 (1991), pp. 41–66.

[25] E.g., Aaron Gurevich in Russia and Bronislaw Geremek in Poland. See Gourevitch, *Les Catégories de la culture médiévale* [1972] (Paris: Falmmarion, 1983), and Geremek, *Les marginaux parisiens aux XIVe et XVe siècles* [1971] (Paris: Flammarion, 1976).

[26] For useful overviews of post-1989 Eastern European historiographies, which also include information on the communist period, see Sorin Antohi, Balázs Trencsényi, and Péter Apor, eds., *Narratives Unbound: Historical Studies in Post-Communist Eastern Europe* (Budapest: Central European University Press, 2009).

[27] Roger D. Markwick, "Cultural History under Khrushchev and Brezhnev: From Social Psychology to Mentalités," *The Russian Review* 65/2 (2006), pp. 283–301 and my "Sowjetische Historiographie."

colonies, was central to the national consciousness of most other Eastern European countries. (Tellingly, recent attempts to apply post-colonial approaches to the study of the Soviet Empire have met with considerable resistance among Eastern European scholars, insulted as they are by attempts to liken their nations to Third World countries.[28])

As a result, sympathies toward victims of the historical process were typically perceived in Eastern Europe as Marxist hypocrisy. More precisely, only those who were not officially recognized as victims under communist regimes could be accepted as such by a majority of those regimes' subjects. In other words, only victims of the communists' own politics, including the Kremlin's politics of Russification, were typically viewed as "true victims," which partly explains why self-victimization has become so typical of the Eastern European politics with respect to the past.

The communist ideology, and in particular its Soviet version, critically depended on the Marxist conception of history (which in many cases, including that of Soviet Russia, was generously seasoned with nationalist historical mythologies). Unsurprisingly, communism lost its last ideological battle on "the territory of history," when Mikhail Gorbachev's perestroika and his politics of openness triggered a revolt of counter-memories among various social, ethnic, and religious groups against the Soviet master narrative. From the vantage point of the changing perceptions of historical time, that revolt was a complex phenomenon indeed. On the one hand, it was informed by the liberal master narrative and an ideal image of the West, while on the other, it was rooted in a revival of particularistic memories that had made historical grievances a common language for all, from pro-Western liberals to nationalists and religious fundamentalists, who sought to refute "the Soviet experiment."

In the 1990s, the hardships of the period of transition considerably undermined the appeal of the liberal narrative in the former socialist countries, although the situation varied significantly from one country to another. Generally speaking, history lost some of its political relevance after the fall of communism, although (re-)inventing national narratives remained an important item on the agenda of both liberals and nationalists. However, that was no easy task, in part due to the fact that long periods of subjugation to powerful neighbors called into question the "uninterrupted continuity" of the existence of many Eastern European

---

[28] Sorin Antohi, "Narratives Unbound: A Brief Introduction to Post-Communist Historical Studies," in *Narratives Unbound*, p. IX.

countries (Ukraine being the most obvious example of that). In addition, in the eyes of most Eastern European historians, claiming such continuity was methodologically problematic because of the "decline of nationalistic history in the West" (Paul M. Kennedy) and because the notion of rupture, rather than continuity, became central to vanguard historiography amid the postmodernist crisis of rationality. While many Eastern European politicians were still fascinated with their respective national romances, few professional historians demonstrated any strong interest in developing them, which contributed to a relative depoliticization of the past in the 1990s.

As a rule, pro-Western democratic parties and governments tended to pursue a politics of memory that commemorated resistance to communism (which came to be seen as the prehistory of the post-socialist states) as well as the memory of victims of the Nazi, communist, and other violent regimes. Serious "memory work" was also taking place in Eastern Europe (especially in Poland and the Czech Republic). Eastern European countries in many cases succeeded in overcoming some inherited historical conflicts (such as the confrontations over the past between Poland and Lithuania, Poland and Ukraine) by reciprocally acknowledging each other's tragedies and impartially assessing responsibility for them.[29] But by and large, the spectacular attainments of recent history in the region after 1989, discouraging as they were to politicians seeking to cultivate national mythologies, remained of secondary importance for the politics of the past.

However, a considerable portion of post-communist elites in Eastern Europe had no interest in objectively exploring past tragedies (not least because of their own collaboration with the Soviets) and had little to offer by way of projects for their nation's future. Shari J. Cohen calls them "historyless elites."[30] In their politics of oblivion or apathy (to quote Troebst) with regard to the past, "historyless elites" could count on the support of the population, for many Eastern Europeans had been disappointed by market reforms and had grown nostalgic for the life they used

[29] Timothy Snyder, "Memory of Sovereignty and Sovereignty over Memory: Poland, Lithuania and Ukraine, 1939–1999," in *Memory and Power in Post-War Europe: Studies in the Presence of the Past*, ed. Jan-Werner Müller (Cambridge: Cambridge University Press, 2002), pp. 39–58; Tatiana Zhurzhenko, "Memory Wars and Reconciliation in the Ukrainian-Polish Borderlands: Geopolitics of Memory from a Local Perspective," in *History, Memory and Politics in Central and Eastern Europe: Memory Games*, eds. Georges Mink and Laure Neumayer (Basingstoke: Palgrave Macmillan, 2013), pp. 173–192.

[30] Shari J. Cohen, *Politics without a Past: The Absence of History in Post-Communist Nationalism* (Durham, N.C.: Duke University Press, 1999), pp. 4–7. See also Gil Eyal, "Identity and Trauma: Two Forms of the Will to Memory," *History and Memory* 16/1 (2004), pp. 5–36.

to have. Of course, none of that was an obstacle to engaging in the politics of memory, but such engagement would be normally driven by pragmatic considerations. "Historyless elites" could readily accept the – rather abstract – framework of the liberal master narrative or ally themselves with their country's nationalists (or, in some cases, do both).

Indeed, in Eastern Europe as elsewhere, the crisis of the future brought about a revival of nationalism that had begun before the fall of communism and continued after it, especially with the growing disillusionment with Western-style democracy. The rise of nationalism was both a cause and a consequence of the collapse of the communist project.[31] Eastern European nationalism is, however, a special case,[32] partly due to the complex ethno-linguistic composition of most Eastern European countries and to the legacy of three great empires – the Russian, Austro-Hungarian, and Ottoman – whose existence had considerably delayed the formation of nation-states in the region. In addition, one of the main attractions of nationalism consisted in the fact that independence from Moscow would be largely tantamount to the end of communism, which explains the national liberalism (or liberal nationalism) that has become particularly typical of Eastern Europe since the late 1980s. Liberalism and nationalism are certainly not as incompatible as one might believe, but the degree to

[31] Mark R. Beissinger, "Nationalism and the Collapse of Soviet Communism," *Contemporary European History* 18/3 (2009), pp. 331–347. Writing in 1995, Peter F. Sugar characterized nationalism as "the victorious ideology" and "the dominant force" in post-1989 Eastern Europe, and I believe that the claim remains valid today. See his "Nationalism, The Victorious Ideology," in *Eastern European Nationalism in the Twentieth Century*, ed. Sugar (Washington, DC: American University Press, 1995), p. 429. See also Soren Rinder Bollerup and Christian Dons Christensen, *Nationalism in Eastern Europe: Causes and Consequences of the National Revivals and Conflicts in Late-Twentieth-Century Eastern Europe* (Basingstoke: Macmillan, St. Martin's Press, 1997). The authors' prediction that "the ideal of the nation-state and the ideology of nationalism will continue to prevail in Eastern Europe for many years to come" (p. 281) has so far been borne out.

[32] Some researchers, notably Taras Kuzio, claim that "nationalism in the West and East is *not* radically different" and reject "a static model of nationalism contrasting 'Western civic nationalism' with... the backward 'ethnic nationalism' in the East" on the grounds that over the last decades, Eastern European nationalism has also evolved into a Western-style civic nationalism. See Kuzio, "Civic Nationalism and the Nation-State: Towards a Dynamic Model of Convergence," in *Multiplicity of Nationalism in Contemporary Europe*, eds. Ireneusz Pawel Karolewski and Andrzej Marcin Suszycki (Lanham, Md.: Lexington Books, 2010), pp. 9, 25. See also Karolewski and Suszycki, "Nationalism in Contemporary Europe: Multiplicity and West-East Similarity," *Multiplicity of Nationalism in Contemporary Europe*, p. 258. However, the nationalists' political role has been considerably more important in most Eastern European countries over the last several decades than in the West, where they do not normally determine a country's political agenda as is often the case in the East. It would therefore be strange to expect the belated, and in fact very recent, emergence of independent nation-states to have had no influence on the character of national(ist) movements in the region. On the specificity of post-communist nationalism and its predominant focus on the victimization of the past, see Vladimir Tismaneanu, *Fantasies of Salvation: Democracy, Nationalism, and Myth in Post-Communist Europe* (Princeton, N.J.: Princeton University Press, 1998).

which they have merged in the region is somewhat unusual, as is the level of the liberal nationalists' political influence. In particular, their politics of memory has largely informed the ways in which the break with communism was experienced by Eastern European nations: everywhere in the region, the prevailing narratives emphasized both the national liberation component and the "capitalist revolution" component of the fall of communism (although the proportion of those components varied from one national narrative to another).

But there are also other forms of Eastern European nationalism, including the far-right ethno-populism that since the 1980s has spread in both the East and the West.[33] All their similarities notwithstanding, Eastern European ethno-populism still differs from its Western variant, which was also caused by the belated emergence of nation-states in the region. The powerful appeal of liberal nationalism and the notion of national independence as a legitimate concern in former socialist countries with their "post-colonial syndrome" sometimes make Eastern European radical nationalists appear more "respectable" than Western far-right groups in the eyes of both their compatriots and foreign observers. Instances when national liberals and ethno-populists have worked together in Eastern Europe are by no means infrequent, and extreme nationalists have more than once played the role of the "big guns" of national liberation movements, or at least that of "active minorities" whose support the national liberals desperately needed. That, however, is no reason for failing to see differences between liberal nationalists and the far right. To underline those differences, some researchers even speak of national democrats and a national (rather than national*ist*) ideology that they typically view as a romantic fascination with national culture and contrast with "authoritarian," "aggressive," or "ethnic" nationalism.[34] But sometimes there seems to be a continuum of, rather than a clear divide between, various groups of nationalists.

---

[33] Andreas Umland, "Challenges and Promises of Comparative Research into Post-Soviet Fascism: Methodological and Conceptual Issues in the Study of the Contemporary East European Extreme Right," *Communist and Post-Communist Studies* 48/2–3 (2015), pp. 169–181.

[34] Thus, Tismaneanu insists on "the key distinction between anti-liberal, integral nationalism... and liberal or civic, nationalism" (*Fantasies of Salvation*, p. 8). See also Verdery, *National Ideology under Socialism*; Myroslav Shkandrij, *Ukrainian Nationalism: Politics, Ideology, and Literature, 1929–1956* (New Haven, Conn.: Yale University Press, 2015), pp. 2–6; and Lena Surzhko-Harned, "Liberal Nationalism, Nationalist Liberalization, and Democracy: The Cases of Post-Soviet Estonia and Ukraine," *Nationalities Papers* 38/5 (2010), pp. 623–646. In some cases, such reasoning betrays a researcher's sympathies with democrats seeking to achieve their country's independence, while in other cases one might suspect an intent to rehabilitate far-right movements.

Historically, the problem of ethnic minorities has been much more important in Eastern than in Western Europe. In the early decades of the twentieth century, nineteenth-century "romantic nationalism" had gradually given way all across Europe to much more radical and populist tendencies, which had made some nationalist groups the natural allies of Nazism. Two Eastern European countries (Croatia and Slovakia) had, in fact, become nation-states for the first time with the support of Nazi Germany. In this part of the world, extreme nationalism too often presented as the only viable alternative to communism. Finally, antiSemitism, which was widespread in this relatively backward region whose Jewish communities often remained poorly integrated into the society at large, contributed to the local far-right movements' solidarity with the Nazis. That said, many Eastern European nationalists were either traditionally anti-German (which was the case, for example, in Poland) or had had their expectations disappointed by the Nazis and had turned their weapons against them (as did some Ukrainian nationalists).

Collaboration with Nazism was hardly more typical of the far right in Eastern than in Western Europe, but what was special about the region was the scale of the local populations' involvement in the Holocaust. It was by no means by chance that the percentage of the Jews exterminated in most Eastern European countries was much higher than in Western Europe.[35] Even after 1945, Holocaust survivors, upon returning to Poland, Slovakia, or Hungary often became victims of pogroms that far exceeded in cruelty the treatment they might have received in France, Belgium, or the Netherlands (where their reintegration into society was admittedly not without its problems).[36]

Moreover, in contrast to the situation in most Western countries, those facts remained, until recently, publicly unacknowledged and were even intentionally erased from the collective memory. The very concept of the Holocaust is even more recent in the region than it is in the West. In the USSR, "the specificity of the Shoah was deliberately dissolved under the rubric of millions of Soviet victims of all nationalities who suffered

---

[35] Thus, 95% or more of the Jews in the former Soviet republics became victims of the Holocaust, in contrast to one quarter in France. See Snyder, *Bloodlands*, pp. 186–277, and Snyder, *Black Earth: The Holocaust as History and Warning* (New York: Tim Duggan Books, 2015), pp. 179.

[36] In Poland, 1,200 Jews were murdered by local populations between January 1945 and April 1946. See Judt, *Postwar*, pp. 43, 804–808; Piotr Wróbel, "Double Memory: Poles and Jews after the Holocaust," *East European Politics and Society* 11/3 (1997), pp. 560–574; and Jan T. Gross, *Fear: Anti-Semitism in Poland after Auschwitz* (New York: Random House, 2007). On anti-Semitism in Prewar Poland, see Gross, *Neighbors: The Destruction of the Jewish Community in Jedwabne, Poland* (New York: Penguin Books, 2002).

under German fascism."[37] And to quote Zvi Gitelman, "the Holocaust [in the USSR] was treated as regrettable, but merely one small part of the larger phenomenon [of the war]."[38] This interpretation, which was adopted in all socialist countries,[39] differed little from the official position of the Allies during the war, which found expression in the Nuremberg trials. In the East, the inattention given to the Holocaust was largely due to the quasi-official anti-Semitic policies of the late Stalinist period.[40] Anti-Semitism (and the warning not to provoke it by emphasizing the "Jewish dimension" of the war) played its role in the West as well. But in the 1970s and 1980s, as we know, the Holocaust came to be seen in the West as the crime against humanity par excellence, while the Nuremberg interpretation of Nazi crimes continued to prevail in the East. "Fidelity to the spirit of Nuremberg" was partly a consequence of an anti-Israeli Soviet foreign policy, and partly an aspect of the growing cult of the Great Patriotic War.[41] For this cult to fulfill its mission, the Soviet people had to be portrayed as both *the* victim and *the* hero of World War II. That is why "giving the war to the Jews" was seen as equivalent to delegitimizing the Soviet system.[42] Similarly, to quote Piotr Wróbel, "the Poles compete[d] with the Jews for a palm of martyrdom,"[43] for Poland was commonly

[37] Robert S. Wistrich, "Introduction: Lying about the Holocaust," in *Holocaust Denial: The Politics of Perfidy* (Berlin: Walter de Gruyter, Hebrew University Magnes Press, 2012), p. 15. See also Jeffrey Blutinger, "An Inconvenient Past: Post-Communist Holocaust Memorialization," *Shofar: An Interdisciplinary Journal of Jewish Studies* 29/1 (2010), p. 74; Lucy S. Dawidowicz, *The Holocaust and the Historians* (Cambridge, Mass.: Harvard University Press, 1981), pp. 68–87; and Herf, *Divided Memory*, pp. 63–64, 69–72, 106–161.

[38] Zvi Gitelman, "Politics and the Historiography of the Holocaust in the Soviet Union," in *Bitter Legacy: Confronting the Holocaust in the USSR* (Bloomington: Indiana University Press, 1997), p. 20.

[39] Judt, *Postwar*, p. 823.

[40] Joshua Rubenstein and Vladimir P. Naumov, eds., *Stalin's Secret Pogrom: The Postwar Inquisition of the Jewish Anti-Fascist Committee* (New Haven, Conn.: Yale University Press, 2001); G.V. Kostyrchenko, *Taynaya politika Stalina: Vlast' y antisemitizm* [Stalin's Secret Politics: The Authorities and Anti-Semitism] (Moscow: Mezhdunarodnyie otnosheniya, 2003); Kostyrchenko, *Stalin protiv "kosmopolitov": Vlast' y yevreyskaya intelligentsiya v SSSR* [Stalin against the "Cosmopolitans": The Authorities and the Jewish Intelligentsia in the USSR] (Moscow: ROSSPEN, 2010).

[41] Nina Tumarkin, *The Living and the Dead: The Rise and Fall of the Cult of World War II in Russia* (New York: Basic Books, 1994).

[42] Gitelman, "Politics and the Historiography of the Holocaust in the Soviet Union," p. 28; Catherine Merridale, *Ivan's War: The Red Army, 1939–1945* (London: Faber, 2006), pp. 247–258.

[43] Wróbel continues as follows (with the entire period from the postwar years to the present in mind): "Both sides accuse each other of the heinous theft of suffering. Both sides have concentrated on their own martyrdom and do not try to understand each other." See Wróbel, "Double Memory: Poles and Jews after the Holocaust." See also Dawidowicz, *The Holocaust and the Historians*, pp. 88–124, and Michael C. Steinlauf, *Bondage to the Dead: Poland and the Memory of the Holocaust* (Syracuse, N.Y.: Syracuse University Press, 1997).

viewed in the Eastern bloc as having suffered from the Nazis more than any other country (with the exception of the USSR itself), and the official war narrative of "People's Poland" was totally in line with this notion. In contrast to its failure in many other respects, Soviet propaganda was amazingly successful in suppressing the memory of the Holocaust in Eastern Europe precisely because that memory was a serious issue in the region. Most Eastern Europeans preferred to think of themselves as victimized by somebody else's misdeeds (especially those committed by Nazi Germany and the USSR), rather than as complicit in both Nazi and communist crimes.

It was not until the late 1980s and especially the 1990s that the Holocaust began to be recognized in Eastern Europe as the "crime of crimes." In preparation for integration into the European community, several Eastern European countries made attempts to promote the memory of the Shoah, founded Holocaust museums, erected monuments to its victims, and so on. However, the memory of the Shoah in the region is still equivocal. In contrast to the West, where the Holocaust has become the symbol of shared responsibility for the crimes of the past, most Eastern European countries have not fully succeeded in overcoming the legacy of the half-century silence on that subject under the Soviet rule. Even today, the memory of the Holocaust is far less central to historical consciousness in Eastern Europe than in France or Germany.[44]

Worse than that, according to Randolph L. Braham, "the collapse of communism brought about the resurgence of conservative nationalist-populist fervor, reminiscent in its nuances of the 1930s."[45] National

---

[44] John-Paul Himka and Joanna Beata Michlic, eds., *Bringing the Dark Past to Light: The Reception of the Holocaust in Postcommunist Europe* (Lincoln: University of Nebraska Press, 2013). Beata Michlic has recently argued that as a result of the Jedwabne debates, the ethnonationalistic perspective on Polish victimhood typical of the 1990s has given place to a more reflexive and self-critical approach that includes a certain "empathy for the Jews." However, she also underlines the persistence of traditional anti-Semitic and ethnonationalistic attitudes, and recent developments in Poland unfortunately give weight to that assessment. See her "The Path of Bringing the Dark Past to Light: Memory of the Holocaust in Postcommunist Europe," in *Memory and Change in Europe: Eastern Perspectives*, pp. 115–130. See also Małgorzata Pakier, *The Construction of European Holocaust Memory: German and Polish Cinema after 1989* (Frankfurt am Main: Peter Lang, 2013); Marek Haltof, *Polish Film and the Holocaust: Politics and Memory* (New York: Berghahn Books, 2012); Muriel Blaive, "The Memory of the Holocaust and of Communist Repression in a Comparative Perspective: The Cases of Hungary, Poland and Czechoslovakia/the Czech Republic," in *Clashes in European Memory*, pp. 154–172. According to Oliver Rathkolb, Eastern Europeans (with the partial exception of Hungary) typically feel no co-responsibility for the extermination of the Jews. See his "Historical Perceptions of the Repression of the Holocaust in Czech, Polish and Hungarian Public Opinion and the Austrian 'Special Case,'" in *Clashes in European Memory*, pp. 173–191.

[45] Randolph L. Braham, "Anti-Semitism and the Holocaust in the Politics of East Central Europe," in *Anti-Semitism and the Treatment of the Holocaust in Postcommunist Eastern Europe* (New York: Rosenthal Institute for Holocaust Studies Graduate Center/City University of New York and Social

revival resulted in attempts to present as heroes people who had committed anti-Semitic acts (not to mention crimes against other peoples of the region) and to rehabilitate state leaders such as Ion Antonescu in Romania, Miklós Horthy in Hungary, or Father Jozef Tiso in Slovakia.

From 1989 on, the Holocaust denial movement spread across Eastern Europe,[46] usually in the form of "aphasia" or "deflective negationism" (shifting blame for the Holocaust to the Germans or trivializing it through comparison with the Soviet repressions).[47] The *Muzeum Armii Krajowej* (Home Army Museum) in Krakow, founded in 1989, and the *Terror Háza* (House of Terror) in Budapest, founded in 2002, exemplify this tendency.[48] Poles and Hungarians are unambiguously presented in those museums as victims, while fighters against communism are depicted as irreproachable national heroes, no matter what their own misdeeds might have been. Of course, other interpretations of the past, including those that are in line with the EU-promoted memory of the Holocaust, are also present in Eastern Europe, but its regional specificity lies precisely in a more ambiguous attitude toward past atrocities and more straightforward attempts to use history for purposes of nationalist mobilization than are present in the West. And all this cannot but produce tensions, given that creating a historical victimhood of individual nation-states is hardly compatible with promoting a common European memory as a means of overcoming nationalism.[49]

Sciences Monographs, Boulder, 1994), p. 10. Sugar ("Nationalism, The Victorious Ideology," p. 429) also believes that present-day Eastern European nationalism "is the same nationalism" as that which emerged in the early twentieth century. See also William Korey, "Anti-Semitism and the Treatment of the Holocaust in the USSR/CIS," *Anti-Semitism and the Treatment of the Holocaust in Postcommunist Eastern Europe*, pp. 207–224; Tismaneanu, *Fantasies of Salvation*, pp. 88–110, and Ronald G. Suny, *The Revenge of the Past: Nationalism, Revolution and the Collapse of the Soviet Union* (Stanford, Calif.: Stanford University Press, 1993), pp. 120–160.

[46] Michael Shafir, "Denying the Shoah in Post-Communist Eastern Europe," in *Holocaust Denial: The Politics of Perfidy*, pp. 27–65; Stephen E. Atkins, *Holocaust Denial as an International Movement* (Westport, Conn.: Praeger Publishers, 2009), pp. 136–141.

[47] Michael Shafir, "Between Denial and 'Comparative Trivialization': Holocaust Negationism in Post-Communist East Central Europe," in *The Treatment of the Holocaust in Hungary and Romania during the Post-Communist Era*, ed. Randolph L. Braham (New York: The Rosenthal Institute for Holocaust Studies Graduate Center/City University of New York and Social Sciences Monographs, Boulder, 2004), p. 44.

[48] Judt, *Postwar*, p. 827; Blutinger, "An Inconvenient Past," pp. 77–78, 83–91. Blutinger also gives examples of the "open examination" of the memory of the Holocaust in the region (pp. 88–94).

[49] For an interesting comparison between the victimization of the past in Eastern Europe and the "Germans as victims" theme in Germany, see Bill Niven, "German Victimhood Discourse in Comparative Perspective," in *Narratives of Trauma: Discourses of German Wartime Suffering in National and International Perspective*, eds. Helmut Schmitz and Annette Seidel Arpaci (Amsterdam: Rodopi, 2011), pp. 163–180.

The use of history for nationalistic ends has arguably become more typical of Eastern Europe in the 2000s than it was in the 1990s, which is partly explained by such broader tendencies as the continuing rise of nationalism across Europe and the worldwide trend toward a manipulative politics of memory. However, there was also a more immediate cause for those changes, that being the emergence of Putin's authoritarian regime, whose neo-imperialist rhetoric confirmed the Eastern Europeans' worst fears about the Kremlin's real attitude toward their newly acquired independence. In the 2000s, the old Soviet myth of the war, which includes the notion of the Yalta System, has become the core element of "the new Russian ideology." In response, influential political forces in countries such as the Czech Republic, Poland, Ukraine, Lithuania, Latvia, and Estonia began to develop a far more anti-Russian politics of memory, the central point of which consisted in equating communism with Nazism, both phenomena being widely seen there as instances of totalitarian dictatorship. In the late 1980s, the concept of totalitarianism was an important weapon in Eastern European battles over the past, but after the fall of communism, it lost some of its relevance. The resurfacing of the Russian war myth has, however, made it pertinent again.

The 2000s witnessed a series of dramatic confrontations over the past between Russia and its Eastern European neighbors, including the 2007 Russian–Estonian conflict around the relocation of the monument to Soviet soldiers from the center of Tallinn to a military cemetery (which Russian public opinion took as an affront to the myth of the Great Patriotic War).[50] In other words, in part as a result of the reemergence of the Russian war myth, the legacy of World War II has grown considerably in importance to Eastern European politics.[51]

---

[50] Karsten Brüggemann and Andres Kasekamp, "The Politics of History and the 'War of Monuments' in Estonia," *Nationalities Papers* 36/3 (2008), pp. 425–448; Pilvi Torsti, "Why do History Politics Matter? The Case of the Estonian Bronze Soldier," in *The Cold War and the Politics of History*, eds. Juhana Aunesluoma and Pauli Kettunen (Helsinki: University of Helsinki/Edita Publishing, 2008), pp. 19–35; Marek Tamm, "In Search of Lost Time: Memory Politics in Estonia, 1991–2011," *Nationalities Papers* 41/4 (2013), pp. 651–67; Anton Weiss-Wendt, "Victims of History: Perceptions of the Holocaust in Estonia," in *Bringing the Dark Past to Light*, pp. 195–222; Maria Mälksoo, *The Politics of Becoming European: A Study of Polish and Baltic Post-Cold War Security Imaginaries* (London: Routledge, 2010), pp. 106–116; and Meike Wulf, *Shadowlands: Memory and History in Post-Soviet Estonia* (New York: Berghahn Books, 2016), pp. 156–163.

[51] World War II is typically viewed as "the founding event of the European construction" (Chiara Bottici, "European Identity and the Politics of Remembrance," in *Performing the Past: Memory, History, and Identity in Modern Europe*, eds. Karin Tilmans, Frank van Vree, and Jay Winter [Amsterdam: Amsterdam University Press, 2010], pp. 344–345), which certainly explains in part the reasons for the rise of its memory in the 1990s and 2000s, a time of decisive steps in the development of the EU (including its expansion to Eastern Europe). However, fascination with the

Interpretations of the war that emphasize the memory of the Holocaust are sometimes perceived in the region as an obstacle that prevents the West from truly hearing Eastern European stories of Soviet oppression. And condemning Nazism without condemning communism is often seen in Eastern Europe as a manifestation of the West's indifference toward the region's concerns. A widespread opinion holds that the West, which betrayed Eastern Europe in 1945 to please Stalin, has no right to turn a deaf ear to its grievances.[52] But the task to make the West more attentive to the "voices from the East" is not an easy one either.

According to Tony Judt, the idea of revising the traditional interpretation of World War II by including an unequivocal condemnation of Soviet foreign policy "carried uncomfortable implications for the West's own past." The reasons for that, however, are not limited to the fact that "to many Western intellectuals, Communism was a failed variant of a common progressive heritage."[53] Eastern European reinterpretations of the war risk recalling the part that the Western Allies themselves played in starting it and in establishing "spheres of influence" after the victory, which is far from a matter of purely academic interest, not least because the "good war myth" has been widely used in recent decades to justify American and German military interventions.[54]

By 2007 and 2008, the conflicts over the past between Russia and its Eastern European adversaries came to a head. In this context, the negotiations around the 2008 Framework Decision were used by some Eastern European countries to call for a prohibition on the denial of communist crimes as well. But the Council of Europe did not go along with that idea, despite its rapidly growing support in the region. The Prague Declaration on European Conscience and Communism of June 2008 called for "recognition that many crimes committed in the name of Communism should

---

history of World War II is a worldwide phenomenon that cannot be entirely explained by local causes. The rise of memory in general and the memory of the Holocaust in particular, as well as the powerful trend toward the victimization of the past, may not fully account for it either. It might be interesting to explore the interconnections between the fixation on the war and what Dina Khapaeva defines as "the rising cult of death" in the present-day mass culture – in other words, the fascination with horror, atrocities, non-human monsters, and so on. See Khapaeva, *Celebration of Death in Contemporary Culture* (Ann Arbor: The University of Michigan Press, 2017).

[52] On Eastern European discussions of the 1945 Western "betrayal," see Mälksoo, *The Politics of Becoming European*, pp. 83–97. Georges Mink ("Geopolitics, Reconciliation and Memory Games: For a New Social Memory Explanatory Paradigm," in *Clashes in European Memory*, p. 260) calls the "Yalta betrayal" "a major component of 'reactive' Eastern European memory."

[53] Judt, *Postwar*, p. 826.

[54] Maja Zehfuss, *Wounds of Memory: The Politics of War in Germany* (Cambridge: Cambridge University Press, 2007), pp. 7–13; Rosenfeld, *Hi Hitler*, pp. 29–77.

be assessed as crimes against humanity..., in the same way Nazi crimes were assessed by the Nuremberg Tribunal."[55] The European Parliament adopted a similar resolution in 2009 and proclaimed August 23 (the day when Molotov-Ribbentrop pact was signed in 1939) a European Day of Remembrance for Victims of Stalinism and Nazism.[56] That was a gesture of moral support for the Eastern European opponents of Russia's neo-imperialist reconstruction, although the European Union had been careful not to endorse a legal ban on the denial of communist crimes.

The first Eastern European memory laws in the narrow sense of the term had been adopted before the danger threatened by Putin's Russia became an important factor in Eastern European politics. Some of those laws, however, betrayed a tension between the pan-European memory of the Holocaust and the regional concern with the memory of communism. That tension became increasingly pronounced with the eruption of memory wars between Russia and its neighbors, which the more recent Eastern European laws have faithfully reflected.

Anti-Fascism and Law in the People's Democracies

Although the countries of the Soviet bloc had no ad hoc laws criminalizing statements about the past, censorship and repressions against dissidents made it impossible to publicly dispute their official historical narratives. Articles 70 and 190.1 of the Penal Code of the Russian Soviet Federal Socialist Republic (RSFSR) of 1960 (amended in 1966) respectively prohibited "anti-Soviet propaganda and agitation," including "the dissemination of knowingly false and calumnious information that denigrates the Soviet political and social system," and "the systematic dissemination" of such information "in oral form."[57] The penal codes of other Soviet republics contained similar provisions (e.g., articles 62 and 187.1 of the Ukrainian code).[58] Those articles were commonly used against dissidents, including nationalists, and nothing was easier than to subsume any

---

[55] Prague Declaration on European Conscience and Communism of June 3 2008.
[56] European Parliament resolution of 2 April 2009 on European conscience and totalitarianism.
[57] Ugolovnyi kodeks RSFSR ot 27 oktyabrya 1960. The punishment was, respectively, up to seven and up to three years' deprivation of liberty.
[58] Kriminal'niy Kodeks URSR vid 28 grudnya 1960. On October 28, 1989, Article 62 was amended to supplement the ban on anti-Soviet agitation with the proscription of agitation against Ukraine's territorial integrity (Law 8314-XI). On October 11, 1991, the prohibition on anti-Soviet agitation was rescinded, and since then the relevant article has forbidden only incitement to action against the country's territorial integrity (Law 1649-XII).

criticism of Stalinism or Soviet foreign policy during World War II under the rubric of "false and calumnious information."

The Eastern European "people's democracies" also had similar norms. Thus, the Penal Code of the German Democratic Republic included Articles 106, "Anti-State propaganda," and 220, "Slander against the State."[59] But in contrast to the aforementioned passages in the Russian code, those articles of the East German code explicitly criminalized "the glorification [*Verherrlichung*] of fascism or militarism" and public statements of a "fascist or militarist character." In addition, Article 92 of the GDR Penal Code specifically prohibited, alongside incitement to war and racial hatred, "fascist propaganda";[60] other (although not all) Eastern European codes did the same. Thus, the Czechoslovak Penal Code of 1961 stated: "A person who supports or propagates fascism or another similar movement that aims at suppressing the rights and freedoms of citizens or preaches national, racial, or religious hatred, shall be sentenced to a term of imprisonment of from one to five years" (Article 260).[61] The Czechoslovak law also provided a penalty of up to three years of incarceration to "a person who publicly expresses his sympathy with fascism or another similar movement" (Article 261). The 1968 Bulgarian code also forbade "preaching fascist or any other anti-democratic ideology"[62] (by "democratic ideology," Eastern European legislators certainly meant the communist ideology).

One would expect to find in Eastern European legislation of the communist period an even stronger emphasis on the prevention of fascism than in the West, for anti-fascism was one of the key tenets of communist propaganda, but in fact the situation was somewhat more complex. First, in the Soviet-controlled countries, denazification was understood as socialist revolution, because fascism was seen as the dictatorship of the most aggressive and reactionary groups of the bourgeoisie amid a general crisis of capitalism.[63] Typically, the word in use was "fascism" rather than "Nazism,"

---

[59] Strafgesetzbuch der Deutschen Demokratischen Republik vom 12. Januar 1968. The punishment was, respectively, up to five (and ten in case of aggravating circumstances) and two years' deprivation of liberty.
[60] *Ibid.*, Article 92. The punishment was deprivation of liberty for up to ten years if the offense was likely to incite to a crime against humanity.
[61] Zákon č. 140/1961, Trestní zákon ze dne 29. listopadu 1961. Aggravating circumstances could raise the penalty to up to eight years.
[62] Nakazatelen kodeks na Narodna Republika Bulgariya ot 2 April 1968, Article 108. The punishment was deprivation of liberty for up to three years.
[63] A.A. Galkin, "Fascism," in *The Great Soviet Encyclopedia*: http://greatsovietencyclopedia.wikia.com/wiki/Fascism.

and even in the GDR, the Penal Code criminalized (as mentioned earlier) fascist rather than Nazi propaganda, because overemphasizing denazification per se could be seen in this context as a hypocritical and defeatist "bourgeois-liberal" approach. Second, there arguably existed an implicit hierarchy of socialist countries, which in part depended on their respective roles in the struggle against fascism and previous involvement with it. Some Eastern European countries had been German allies during the war and had contributed very little to their own liberation from Nazi rule in its final stages. While public memories of the communist period focused on the victory over fascism, both pro-Soviet authorities and veterans of the anti-Soviet resistance preserved secret memories of collaboration with it.

Since Eastern Germany could not, of course, claim that it had had no involvement with Nazism, its 1949 Constitution (as well as its Penal Code) viewed the struggle against fascism as an important goal for the new regime. Article 13 of that Constitution allowed the existence only of those "associations that, in accordance with their statutes, aim to bring about, on the basis of this Constitution, a democratic organization of public life." (As we know, a similar formula was also used in the West German Basic Law of the same year.) A more straightforward provision was included in Chapter X, "Transitional and Concluding Provisions," of the East German Constitution, which specified that "constitutional liberties and rights may not be used as arguments against past or future measures adopted for the overcoming of National Socialism and militarism, or to redress wrongs caused by them."[64] Twenty years later, in 1968, the new East German Constitution solemnly proclaimed that the GDR "had eradicated German fascism and militarism on its territory," which implied that such eradication had not yet been accomplished on other German "territories."[65] Fascism is clearly viewed here as part of the two Germanies' common legacy, with which the GDR, in contrast to the FRG, had definitively broken. The 1968 Constitution also declared illegal, alongside incitement to racial, national, and religious hatred, "militarist and revanchist propaganda in any form."[66]

Several other Eastern European countries such as Romania and Bulgaria, which had been Germany's allies in World War II, also prohibited not just any parties seeking to undermine their constitutional order, but more specifically organizations that had a "fascist or anti-democratic

[64] Die Verfassung der Deutschen Demokratischen Republik vom 7. Oktober 1949.
[65] Die Verfassung der Deutschen Demokratischen Republik vom 6. April 1968, Article 6.1.
[66] Ibid., Article 6.5.

character"[67] or "promote[d] a fascist or any other anti-democratic ideology,"[68] which is reminiscent of provisions in the 1945/1947 Austrian Prohibition Law and the Italian Constitution of 1947. By contrast, the Polish Constitution contained no special ban on fascist parties, probably because Poland had never allied itself with Germany.[69] As the paradigmatic victim of fascism, Poland took a leading role in the investigation of Nazi crimes and to that end created a special commission in preparation for the Nuremberg trials in 1945 (that commission survived the fall of communism and was transformed into the Institute of National Remembrance in 1998).

Those differences notwithstanding, the constitutions of the Eastern bloc countries referred to the victory over fascism as to their founding event, praised the USSR for its decisive role in that victory, and stated that socialism was the foundation of their social and political system, which was viewed as the only way to dispose of fascism. In the spirit of the Universal Declaration of Human Rights, they also proclaimed illegal any kind of discrimination and inequitable treatment with regard to gender, race, nationality, or religion. Eastern bloc countries were usually among the first signatories of international agreements on human rights, from the Convention on Genocide and the Universal Declaration of Human Rights of 1948 to the 1965 International Convention on the Elimination of All Forms of Racial Discrimination. From the 1960s on, their penal codes typically included articles prohibiting genocide, discrimination, and incitement to hatred by allusion to race or nationality.[70] The reader will remember that the inclusion of similar articles in Western penal codes had in many cases taken far longer and was not completed until the 1970s or even the 1980s. Socialist countries often took the initiative in the prosecution of Nazi war criminals, all the way from the Nuremberg Tribunal, which was created largely in response to Soviet pressure,[71] to

---

[67] Constitutia Republicii Socialiste Romania din 21 august 1965, Article 29.

[68] Konstitutsiya na Narodna Republika Bulgariya ot 18 may 1971, Article 52.3.

[69] The Polish Constitution forbade associations that "threaten[ed] the social and political system or the legal order of the Polish People's Republic." See Konstytucja Polskiej Rzeczypospolitej Ludowej z dnia 22 lipca 1952 r., Article 72.3 (Article 84.3 of the Constitution as amended in 1976). The Hungarian Constitution did not ban fascist parties either; although Hungary had been a German ally until 1944, apparently, the German occupation of 1944 was deemed a rupture of that collaboration. See Act XX of 1949, The Constitution of the Republic of Hungary.

[70] E.g., article 74 of the 1960 Penal Code of the RSFSR, Article 91 of the 1968 Penal Code of the GDR, Article 162 of the 1968 Penal Code of Bulgaria, and Article 259 of the 1961 Penal Code of Czechoslovakia.

[71] Francine Hirsch, "The Soviets at Nuremberg: International Law, Propaganda, and the Making of the Postwar Order," *American Historical Review* 113/3 (2008), pp. 701–730.

the 1968 Convention on the Non-Applicability of Statutory Limitations to War Crimes and Crimes against Humanity, in whose promotion Poland played a central role. Poland, Hungary, Czechoslovakia, Eastern Germany, Bulgaria, and Russia adopted national laws on imprescriptibility, which abolished statutory limitations for those crimes in 1964 and 1965, as did France and Belgium, while Germany's bill along those lines was passed only in 1979. Obviously, an intense rivalry to be seen as the chief force in the anti-fascist and pro-human rights movement was under way between the two blocs. It was not until the late 1970s that the human rights ideology became an "absolute weapon" successfully used by the West against the communist regimes, and as late as 1975, the Soviet leadership was still able to view the Helsinki Accords as its diplomatic triumph.

Eastern European anti-fascist and anti-racist laws, just like their Western analogues in the Cold War period, dealt rather indirectly with the issues of historical memory. However, in contrast to the Western laws, they can hardly be seen as paving the way for Holocaust denial legislation, because cultivating the memory of the Shoah was not on the agenda of the communist rulers, whose anti-racist diatribes were directed above all against "American imperialism," viewed as the stronghold of the most aggressive and reactionary bourgeoisie groups that had earlier brought fascism to power. Holocaust denial laws in Eastern Europe were motivated by those countries' desire to join the European Union, rather than by their own legislative tradition. However, the tradition of anti-fascist and anti-racist legislation has also had some impact on the approaches toward criminalizing the past in post-communist Eastern Europe, in that it provided a model for de-communization laws, which have created a legal framework for adopting typically Eastern European memory laws that criminalize the denial of both Nazi and communist crimes. While studying current Eastern European legislation about the past, one often gets the impression that, as Dan Stone puts it, "anti-fascism is only employed [there] insofar as it does not impinge on the anti-communist narrative."[72]

De-communization Laws

The fall of communism was accompanied by the first wave of Eastern European laws concerning historical memory, but the memory in question was primarily that of communism rather than of fascism, although in many cases both legacies were approached jointly. That legislation, which

---

[72] Stone, *The Holocaust, Fascism, and Memory,* p. 178.

is commonly viewed as a set of de-communization laws, dealt with issues as varied as state symbols, holidays, and memorial days, rehabilitation of the victims of political repressions, investigation and prosecution of communist crimes, the opening of archives, lustration, restitution of property confiscated under the communist rule to its former owners, and so on. In Latvia and Estonia, citizenship laws that refused full citizenship to population groups most closely associated with the Soviet occupation were among the most important tools of de-communization. Several countries also banned, or attempted to ban, communist parties along with their symbols and ideology. Various aspects of that blanket agenda were highlighted depending on the country, the time period, and the government in place at the time. The memorial component of most of those acts was quite significant, and considerations associated with symbolic politics often were the main reasons for their adoption.[73]

The de-communization laws were the products of fierce struggles, since powerful political forces were seeking to sabotage the democratization process in the Eastern European countries. Unsurprisingly, many democratic leaders, such as Tadeusz Mazowiecki in Poland, Václav Havel in Czechoslovakia, and Boris Yeltsin in Russia (all differences between them notwithstanding), warned about the dangers of a "witch-hunt" and encouraged drawing "a thick line under the past"[74] in order to obtain the broadest possible support for market reforms. And even those de-communization laws that had been passed were often poorly implemented and proved ineffective. However, their adoption was an important aspect of the symbolic revolution that followed the collapse of the Eastern bloc.

---

[73] The de-communization process and transitional justice in post-communist countries is a well-researched topic. See Tismaneanu, *Fantasies of Salvation*, pp. 111–140; *Transitional Justice: How Emerging Democracies Reckon with Former Regimes*, ed. Neil Kritz (Washington, DC: United States Institute for Peace Press, 1995), vols. 1–3; *Transitional Justice in Eastern Europe and the Former Soviet Union: Reckoning with the Communist Past*, ed. Lavinia Stan (London, New York: Routledge, 2009); Monika Nalepa, *Skeletons in the Closet: Transitional Justice in Post-Communist Europe* (Cambridge: Cambridge University Press, 2010); Vesselin Popovski and Mónica Serrano, eds., *After Oppression: Transitional Justice in Latin America and Eastern Europe* (Tokyo: United Nations University Press, 2012); Olivera Simić and Zala Volčič, eds., *Transitional Justice and Civil Society in the Balkans* (New York: Springer, 2013); Lavinia Stan and Nadya Nedelsky, eds., *Encyclopedia of Transitional Justice* (Cambridge: Cambridge University Press, 2013), vols. 1–3; Lavinia Stan and Nadya Nedelsky, eds., *Post-Communist Transitional Justice: Lessons from Twenty-Five Years of Experience* (Cambridge: Cambridge University Press, 2015).

[74] Timothy Garton Ash, "Trials, Purges and History Lessons: Treating a Difficult Past in Post-Communist Europe," in *Memory and Power in Post-War Europe*, p. 267; Ewa Ochman, *Post-Communist Poland - Contested Pasts and Future Identities* (Abingdon: Routledge, 2013), pp. 17–18; Dovile Budryte, "Lithuania," in *Encyclopedia of Transitional Justice*, vol. 2, pp. 286–293.

All post-communist constitutions proclaimed their respective countries to be democracies based on the rule of law and respect for human rights, banned incitement to hatred, and prohibited political parties that sought to overthrow their constitutional order. In the context of the time, those statements obviously implied a condemnation of communism, although most of the constitutions did not do so explicitly. There were notable exceptions, however. Thus, the Polish Constitution of 1997 provided that

> Political parties and other organizations whose programs are based upon totalitarian methods and the modes of activity of Nazism, fascism, and communism, as well as those whose programs or activities sanction racial or national hatred... shall be forbidden.[75]

Parts of the Hungarian Basic Law of 2011, especially as amended in March 2013, read almost like a declarative memory law. This constitution, which was adopted on the initiative of Viktor Orbán's nationalist Fidesz party when it took power in 2010, was Hungary's first since 1949, which may partly explain why it dealt with the communist past at such length.[76] The document characterizes the communist regime as "a tyrannical rule" that resulted in the country's "moral decay" and implicitly declares it unlawful by refusing to recognize the Constitution of 1949, which had been imposed as a result of "foreign occupation." The beginning of the occupation is dated in the document to March 19, 1944, when German troops invaded Hungary, and no distinction is made between Nazi and communist rule. Article U, which was appended to the Basic Law in March 2013, declares the Hungarian Socialist Workers' Party a criminal organization and provides that its leaders will be held responsible, "without statute of limitations," for "a) maintaining and directing an oppressive regime, violating the law and betraying the nation; b) thwarting with Soviet military assistance the democratic attempt built on a multi-party system in the years after World War II;... [and] h) suppressing with bloodshed, in cooperation with Soviet occupying forces, the Revolution and War of Independence which broke out on 23 October 1956" (the full list of offenses is far too long to quote here). And so, in order "for the State to preserve the memory of the communist dictatorship," the Constitution (!) provides that a Committee of National Memory be established with the goal of assessing the responsibility of various organizations and individuals

---

[75] Konstytucja Rzeczypospolitej Polskiej z dnia 2 kwietnia 1997 r., Article 13.
[76] The Fundamental Law of Hungary of April 25, 2011, Preamble ("National Avowal").

for the crimes in question. Such regulations obviously refer to the memory of the communist rule, rather than to that of the Nazi occupation.

No other aspect of de-communization has been as widely discussed as the unsealing of the secret police archives and the "purification" of the state organs from its spies (also known as "lustration"). Most of those laws had a clear commemorative agenda. The Czechoslovak Lustration Act of October 1991 banned members of the political police and its secret agents as well as Communist Party officials and employees of "the People's Militia" from governmental, judiciary, military, and other similar positions (Czechoslovakia – and since the 1993 split, the Czech Republic – has been a leader of the de-communization process).[77] In December of the same year, the Federal Republic of Germany passed the Stasi Records Act, which was one of the first steps of the most systematic lustration conducted in post-communist Eastern Europe.[78] In Hungary, several lustration proposals were turned down by the parliament before a lustration law was finally adopted in 1994, which gave citizens only a limited access to their secret files.[79] In Poland, six different lustration bills were submitted to the parliament in 1992, but none was passed, because the left-wing coalition, whose influence was rapidly growing in the country on the eve of its coming to power in 1993, was not supportive of the idea. It was not until 1997 that, in preparation for the next elections, the left-wing coalition initiated a broad legislative reform that included a tentative lustration act (as well as the first Eastern European law to criminalize certain statements about the past, which was adopted in 1998).[80] In Romania, the State Security Files Access Act was passed in 1999, after several years of

[77] Law No. 451/1991 of October 4, 1991 "[Zákon] kterým se stanoví některé další předpoklady pro výkon některých funkcí ve státních orgánech a organizacích České a Slovenské Federativní Republiky, České republiky a Slovenské republiky" [[Law] Determining Some Further Prerequisites for Certain Positions in State Bodies and Organizations of the Czech and Slovak Federative Republic, the Czech Republic, and the Slovak Republic].The law was originally set to expire in five years, but after the division of Czechoslovakia it was extended several times in the Czech Republic and forgotten in the Slovak Republic, where the old communist elites were almost undisturbed and remained in power. See Nadya Nedelsky, "Slovak Republic," in *Encyclopedia of Transitional Justice*, vol. 2, pp. 433–439; Roman David, "The Czech Republic," in *Encyclopedia of Transitional Justice*, vol. 2, pp. 131–137.
[78] Act regarding the Records of the State Security Service of the Former German Democratic Republic (Stasi Records Act) of December 20, 1991.
[79] Law No. 23/1994 of March 9, 1994 "On Background Checks to Be Conducted on Individuals Holding Certain Important Positions," in *Transitional Justice: How Emerging Democracies Reckon with Former Regimes*, vol. 3, pp. 418–425. The Constitutional Court found some provisions of the law unconstitutional and considerably restricted its sphere of application.
[80] Law No. 443 of April 11, 1997 "O ujawnieniu pracy lub służby w organach bezpieczeństwa państwa lub współpracy z nimi w latach 1944–1990 osób pełniących funkcje publiczne" [On Disclosing the Work or Service in the Organs of State Security or Cooperation with Them in the

passionate debate.[81] The Bulgarian parliament initially decided (in 1991) not to open secret police files to citizens,[82] but several later acts (including a 2006 law) gave citizens limited access to their files and established a procedure for "announcing the affiliation of Bulgarian citizens" with the security services of communist times.[83] Slovakia, which, in contrast to the Czech Republic, largely discontinued the de-communization process after the split of the two countries and developed a nationalistic politics of memory that glorified the wartime pro-Nazi leader Father Tiso, returned to the democratization agenda on the turn of the 2000s and passed a lustration law (2002) and a Holocaust denial act (2001).

Most countries created special institutions charged with investigating secret police files, such as the Stasi Records Agency in Germany (1991), the Office for the Investigation and Documentation of the Crimes of Communism in the Czech Republic (1995, transformed into the Institute for the Study of Totalitarian Regimes in 2007, which remained focused on the communist period), the Nation's Memory Institute in Slovakia (2002), the History Office in Hungary (1996, transformed into the Historical Archives of Hungarian State Security in 2003), the Institute of National Remembrance in Poland (1998),[84] and the National Council for the Study of Securitate Archives in Romania (1999).[85] In the Baltic countries, whose KGB archives were either destroyed or transferred to Moscow before the collapse of the USSR, museums rather than archives emerged as the main institutions responsible for the official politics of memory. Those museums have characteristic names: the Latvian Museum of Occupation and the Estonian Museum of Occupations opened, respectively, in 1993 and 2003 and dealing with both the communist and the Nazi rule, and Lithuania's

---

Years 1944–1990 by Persons Fulfilling Public Functions]; Monika Nalepa, "Poland," in *Encyclopedia of Transitional Justice*, vol. 2, pp. 383–391.

[81] Law No. 183 of December 7, 1999 "[Legea] privind accesul la propriul dosar si deconspirarea securitatii ca politie politica" [[Law] Concerning Access to [the Citizen's] Own Security File and Disclosure of the [Nature] of the Security Service as a Political Police].

[82] Momchil Metodiev, "Bulgaria," in *Encyclopedia of Transitional Justice*, vol. 2, pp. 73–79.

[83] Law No. 109 of December 19, 2006 "[Zakon] za dostup i raskrivane na dokumentite i za obyavyavane na prinadlezhnost' na bulgarski grazhdanu kum d'rzhavna sigurnost i razuznavatelnite sluzhbi na bulgarskata Narodna Armiya" [[Law] Regarding the Access to and Disclosure of Documents and the Announcement of the Affiliation of Bulgarian Citizens with the State Security Service and the Intelligence Services of the Bulgarian National Army].

[84] In Polish (as in other Slavic languages) the same word – "*narod*" – means both "people" and "nation" (much like the German *Volk*), so that "pamięć narodowa" means both "national memory" and "the people's memory."

[85] Georges Mink, "Institutions of National Memory in Post-Communist Europe: From Transitional Justice to Political Uses of Biographies (1989–2010)," in *History, Memory and Politics in Central and Eastern Europe*, pp. 155–170.

Museum of Genocide Victims (now the Genocide and Resistance Research Center, commonly known as the KGB Museum) opened in 1992. The term "genocide" here, as in most other post-communist countries, refers to both the Nazi and the Soviet repressions.

The language of the de-communization laws leaves no doubt as to the historical assessment of the communist regimes. Some of them use the concept of communist crimes,[86] viewed as crimes against humanity similar to Nazi crimes, and/or the notion of genocide. Thus, in 1995, Albania passed a lustration act commonly known as the Genocide Law, which unambiguously categorized political repressions of the communist period as crimes against humanity or genocide.[87] Some countries also adopted declarative memory laws that contained quite detailed characterizations of the communist period of their history, such as, for example, Czech laws of 1993 and 2011. The 1993 Act on the Illegality of the Communist Regime and on Resistance to It was perhaps Eastern European law's most straight-forward declaration of the illegitimacy of a communist regime and the criminality of a communist party (much as the Nazi Party had been assessed by the Nuremberg Tribunal).[88] The 2011 law On the Participants in Anti-Communist Opposition and Resistance further developed some norms of the 1993 law, confirmed the status of members of the anti-communist resistance as war veterans, defined their rights and privileges, and reiterated the interpretation of the communist regime as "the time of non-freedom."[89] In May 2000, Bulgaria also passed a law on the criminal nature of the communist regime.[90] This law itemized a roster of communist misdeeds, from the illegal seizure of power in collusion with a foreign country to violations of human rights, political persecutions, moral decay, and so on.

[86] The term "Stalinist crimes," which predominated in the late 1980s, implied a more ambiguous attitude to communism, but soon the collocation of choice across the entire region became "communist crimes."

[87] Law No. 8001 of 22 September 1995 "On Genocide and Crimes against Humanity Committed in Albania during Communist Rule for Political, Ideological or Religious Motives (the Genocide Law)," available (in fragments) in English in *Building Democracy: The OMRI [Open Media Research Institute] Annual Survey of Eastern Europe and the Former Soviet Union, 1995* (New York: M.E. Sharpe, 1996) p. 149–150; Robert C. Austin and Jonathan Ellison, "Albania," in *Transitional Justice in Eastern Europe and the Former Soviet Union*, pp. 184–186.

[88] Law No. 198/1993 of July 9, 1993 "O protiprávnosti komunistického režimu a o odporu proti němu," available in English in *Transitional Justice: How Emerging Democracies Reckon with Former Regimes*, vol. 3, pp. 366–368.

[89] Law No. 262/2011 of July 20, 2011 "O účastnících odboje a odporu proti komunismu" [On the Participants in Anti-Communist Opposition and Resistance].

[90] Law No. 37 of May 5, 2000 "[Zakon] za obyavyavane na komunisticheskiya rezhim v Bulgariya za prestupen" [[Law] on Declaring the Criminal Nature of the Communist Regime in Bulgaria].

The preamble of the Slovak lustration act of 2002, which is also known as the Nation's Memory Act, is an interesting case of post-communist political rhetoric, since it lists several reasons for creating the aforementioned Nation's Memory Institute, including "the duty to prosecute crimes against peace and humanity, and crimes of war." Another reason given is "the duty of our State to rectify the wrongdoings to all those who suffered damage on behalf of the State, which violated human rights and its own laws." This is certainly an allusion to the notion of state repentance, which is an important foundation of the democratic politics of memory. Still another reason evoked in the act refers to "the patriotic traditions of the Slovak Nation in fighting occupants, fascism, and communism," which rather looks to be an attempt to shift the blame for past injustices to others and to wreathe the Slovak people in the aura of a patriotic resistance myth. This expression is a word-for-word borrowing from the 1998 Polish law that created the Institute of National Remembrance, which was the first Eastern European memory law per se (we will return to it later). The following description of the functions of the Slovak Nation's Memory Institute also reproduces the corresponding passage (Article 1) of the Polish law:

> Recording, collecting, disclosing, publishing, managing and using documents of the security authorities of the German Third Reich and of the Union of Soviet Socialist Republics, as well as the security authorities of the State, which were created and collected in the period from April 18, 1939 to December 31, 1989... regarding crimes committed against persons of Slovak nationality or Slovak citizens of other nationalities, i.e. 1. Nazi crimes, 2. communist crimes, 3. other crimes, which include crimes against peace, crimes against humanity, and war crimes.[91]

However, as we will see, those borrowings notwithstanding, statements about the past were criminalized in Slovakia in a way that differed considerably from the Polish approach.

Several de-communization laws contained provisions penalizing the use of communist and Nazi symbols, participation in communist or fascist parties and groups, and the spreading of their propaganda materials. Some laws suspended the statute of limitations for certain crimes committed by

---

[91] Law 553/2002 of August 19, 2002 "[Zákon] o sprístupnení dokumentov o činnosti bezpečnostných zložiek štátu 1939 - 1989 a o založení Ústavu pamäti národa a o doplnení niektorých zákonov (zákon o pamäti národa)" [[Law] on Disclosure of Documents Regarding the Activity of State Security Authorities in the Period 1939–1989 and On Founding the Nation's Memory Institute (Nation's Memory Act)], available in English at www.upn.gov.sk/data/pdf/553_2002_en.pdf.

state officials during the communist period.[92] In December 1991, the parliament of the Czech and Slovak Republic amended the above-quoted Article 260 of the Penal Code to forbid not only "fascist and other similar movements" but also "movements that demonstrably aim at suppressing the rights and freedoms of citizens or preach national, racial, class or religious hatred (such as, for example, fascism or communism)."[93] De-communization here clearly presents as a continuation of denazification. However, the Constitutional Court invalidated Article 260's reference to fascism and communism in response to criticism suggesting that by referring to those movements, the legislators were endorsing the notion of collective guilt (but the reference to class hatred was not removed from the law, thus implicitly upholding the ban on communism). In 1993, Hungary forbade the dissemination and public use of "the symbols of despotism," including "a swastika, an SS-badge, an arrow-cross, a sickle and hammer, or a five-pointed red star," which became a misdemeanor punishable with a "criminal fine." In 2000, the Constitutional Court declined a petition against this article on the grounds that "the [Hungarian] constitution is not value-neutral" and that those symbols "offend the dignity of the community." The new Penal Code of 2012 retained this norm as Article 335, which was once again brought before the Constitutional Court and invalidated in February 2013 because of its ambiguous language, but by April, the parliament had adopted it again in a slightly different wording.[94] Subsequent to the adoption of its Constitution of April 1997, Poland passed a new Penal Code in June of the same year, whose Article 256 provided that

> Whoever publicly promotes a fascist or other totalitarian system of state or incites hatred based on national, ethnic, race or religious differences or for reason of lack of any religious denomination shall be subject to a fine, the penalty of restriction of liberty or the penalty of deprivation of liberty for up to 2 years.[95]

---

[92] E.g., the Hungarian law of November 4, 1991, which soon thereafter (in March 1992) was invalidated by the Constitutional Court, and a narrower bill that was passed in 1993. See Csilla Kiss, "Hungary," in *Encyclopedia of Transitional Justice*, vol. 2, pp. 230–236. See also the Slovak Nation's Memory Act of 2002, quoted earlier, which amended Article 67 of the Penal Code by cancelling statuary limitations for crimes that "for political reasons" had not been prosecuted under communist rule.

[93] Law 557/1991 Sb. of December 11, 1991 "[Zákon] kterým se mění a doplňuje trestní zákon" [[Law] that Makes Changes and Additions to the Criminal Code].

[94] András Koltay, "Hate Speech and the Protection of Communities in the Hungarian Legal System: A Short Overview," Social Science Research Network, January 8, 2013: http://papers.ssrn.com/sol3/papers.cfm?abstract_id=2197914; Act C of July 13, 2012 "On the Criminal Code," Article 335.

[95] Ustawa z dnia 6 czerwca 1997 – Kodeks karny, available in English at /www.imolin.org/doc/amlid/Poland_Penal_Code1.pdf.

In November 2009, Poland amended its Penal Code by introducing Article 256.2, which prohibited the production and dissemination of "objects that bear fascist, communist, or other totalitarian symbols." But in July 2011, the Constitutional Tribunal invalidated this provision as an infringement on the freedom of expression.[96]At the turn of the 2010s, similar laws banning communist symbols were also passed in some other countries.[97]

Criminalizing the Past in Eastern Europe

The de-communization laws, including those that ban Nazi and communist symbols and propaganda, raised the idea of criminalizing certain statements about the past. Since 1996, and especially since 2003, the European Union has officially endorsed the notion of Holocaust denial laws and has encouraged its potential and new members to criminalize negationism. However, in light of their own legislative evolution, it comes as no surprise that some Eastern European countries were tempted to expand the prohibition of Holocaust negationism to a ban on the denial of communist crimes. International documents such as the Prague Declaration of 2008, which called for treating those crimes as similar to Nazi crimes, referred to a recent, but already well-established, Eastern European legislative tradition. Although the EU has not supported the proposal to criminalize denial of communist crimes, it has officially and unambiguously condemned them on several occasions, and some Eastern European countries took that as an incentive for banning their denial. As a result, two main categories of laws criminalizing the past have been passed in Eastern Europe: those that reproduce the Western model of Holocaust denial laws and those that also ban the denial of communist crimes.

Poland was the first Eastern European country to adopt a memory law per se in 1998, in the aftermath of the legislative reform of 1997 that had made communist and fascist propaganda a criminal offense. The law of 1998 created the Institute of National Remembrance – Commission for the Prosecution of Crimes against the Polish Nation.[98] As discussed

---

[96] Agata Fijalkowski, "The Criminalisation of Symbols of the Past: Expression, Law and Memory," *International Journal of Law in Context* 10/03 (2014), pp. 295–314.

[97] E.g., Estonia, Lithuania, Latvia, Moldova, Ukraine.

[98] On the origins of the Polish Institute, see Paweł Machcewicz, "Poland's Way of Coming to Terms with the Legacy of Communism": www.eurhistxx.de/spip.php%3Farticle40&lang=en.html, and Dariusz Stola, "Poland's Institute of National Remembrance: A Ministry of Memory?" in *The*

earlier, that commission had been founded in 1945 during the run-up to the Nuremberg trials and had its mandate expanded after the fall of communism to include the investigation of communist crimes. The Institute of National Remembrance has inherited both those functions, which is why the Polish secret service archives were transferred to it. Between 2005 and 2010, under Polish president Lech Kaczyński, the Institute of National Remembrance was an important policy tool in presidential hands (in 2007, it was made responsible for updating and publishing the lists of Polish citizens who had collaborated with the secret services).

Article 55 of the 1998 Act stipulates that "Anyone who publicly and contrary to the facts denies crimes referred to in art. 1, point 1 shall be subject to a fine or the penalty of imprisonment of up to 3 years." Article 1.1 had listed the following crimes:

> a) Crimes perpetrated against persons of Polish nationality and Polish citizens of other ethnicity, nationalities between 1 September 1939 and 31 December 1989:
>
> - the Nazi crimes,
> - the communist crimes,
> - other crimes against peace, humanity or war crimes, perpetrated on persons of Polish nationality or Polish citizens of other nationalities between September 1, 1939 until July 31, 1990,
>
> b) Other politically motivated reprisals, instigated by the officers of the Polish law enforcement agencies or the judiciary or persons acting on their order.[99]

Obviously, the law views both Nazi and communist crimes as belonging to the category of crimes against humanity. However, misdeeds committed by the law enforcement bodies of communist Poland are not subsumed under that notion; moreover, those misdeeds are conceived as committed by individual functionaries rather than by the Polish state or the Polish

---

Convolutions of Historical Politics, eds. Alexei Miller and Maria Lipman (Budapest: Central European University Press, 2012), pp. 45–58.

[99] Law No. 155 of December 18, 1998 "O Instytucie Pamięci Narodowej – Komisji Ścigania Zbrodni przeciwko Narodowi Polskiemu" [On the Institute of National Remembrance – Commission for the Prosecution of Crimes against the Polish Nation], available in English at https://ipn.gov.pl/en/about-the-institute/documents/institute-documents/the-act-on-the-institute-of-national-remembrance. See also *Legislating for Equality*, p. 354, and Robert Traba, "Polskiye spory ob istoriyi v XX veke" [Polish Debates over History in the Twenty-First Century], *Pro et Contra*, May–August 2009, pp. 43–64. The word "nationality" is used in the law with respect to ethnicity rather than to citizenship, as is common in Slavic languages.

United Workers' Party.[100] But if crimes perpetrated by Polish communists were different from communist crimes, which crimes does the latter expression denote? The only possible answer is crimes committed by the USSR. In other words, the lawmakers have done their best to minimize the Polish state's responsibility for the communist terror "against the Polish nation." It is clearly not by chance that the law emphasizes the concept of crimes *against the Polish nation*.[101] The law tacitly prohibits Holocaust denial, because the extermination of the Jews is covered by the notion of "crimes perpetrated... against Polish citizens of other ethnicity [than ethnic Poles]," but this phrase, as well as the formula "crimes against the Polish nation," is certainly not the most unequivocal way of referring to the Shoah; it continues, rather, the Soviet tradition of "dissolving" the Holocaust into other Nazi crimes. The communist regime is implicitly viewed in the law as an occupation, which simplifies the historical reality and calls into question the need for the Polish state to repent for the repressions of the communist period. The fact that such important things are said here between the lines probably explains the ambiguity of the law with regard to the question of exactly which crimes can no longer be denied (a typical feature of several Eastern European memory laws). The reference to the Charter of the Nuremberg Tribunal that had been used in the Gayssot Act would not have been of any help to the Polish lawmakers, and they have not found any equivalent formula to serve their purpose.

When the Polish memory law was adopted, Brussels was just about to endorse the notion of criminalizing negationism and Poland was not yet an EU member. The 1998 law was a product of the Eastern European de-communization process (which was to some extent, and especially in Poland, modeled on the prosecution of Nazi crimes) rather than a case of the European trend toward combating racism and xenophobia and com-memorating the Holocaust. Poland has created a paradigm of criminalizing the denial of both Nazi and communist crimes, with an emphasis on the latter, which was substantially different from the Gayssot Act model and the

---

[100] In 2008, Polish Constitutional Tribunal invalidated, on procedural grounds, the new article (132a) of the Criminal Code that penalized insults to the Polish nation "by making accusations of participation in communist or Nazi crimes or responsibility for them." See Uladzislau Belavusau, "Historical Revisionism in Comparative Perspective: Law, Politics, and Surrogate Mourning," European University Institute, Department of Law, Working Paper Law 2013/12, p. 18: http://papers.ssrn.com/sol3/papers.cfm?abstract_id=2368955. A similar bill ("On Changing the Statute of the Institute of National Remembrance") introduced in the Polish parliament in August 2016 was still under consideration at the time of writing. See http://www.sejm.gov.pl/sejm8.nsf/druk.xsp?nr=993.

[101] The term was even incorporated into the name of the commission whose original postwar name had been the Central Commission for the Investigation of German Crimes in Poland, which thus became the Central Commission for the Prosecution of Crimes against the Polish Nation.

emerging European Holocaust denial legislation. In the years that followed, Eastern European countries were able to choose between those two models while passing their memory laws. However, the Polish law had also had its predecessors. On the one hand, the 1985 German statute had already criminalized, although in a somewhat indirect way, the denial of crimes committed by Nazism or by "another violent and arbitrary dominance," in an attempt to "normalize" German history. But all such references disappeared from later Western legislation, as the Holocaust-and-heritage memory regime acquired its classical forms after the fall of communism. On the other hand, several Russian bills of 1995–1997 had tried, albeit unsuccessfully, to criminalize the denial of Stalinist crimes (see Chapter 5).

There was no rigid correlation between prohibition of negationism and accession to the EU, although the prospect of "joining Europe" has undoubtedly influenced history politics in many Eastern European countries. However, while some of them penalized Holocaust denial far in advance of their accession to the EU, others did so only upon accession. And several party states still have no memory laws per se on their books.

The Czech Republic was the second Eastern European country to pass an actual memory law, and in that, predictably, it followed the Polish rather than the French model. Indeed, as mentioned earlier, the Czech Republic had, from the turn of the 1990s, been among the leaders of the de-communization process, and the groundwork for the new law that prohibited the denial of both Nazi and communist crimes in October 2000 had been laid by its previous legislation (e.g., the 1993 Act on the Illegality of the Communist Regime). The new law supplemented the Penal Code with Article 261A, which stated:

> A person who publicly denies, questions, approves, or seeks to justify Nazi or communist genocide or other crimes against humanity as committed of Nazis or communists will be punished by deprivation of liberty of from 6 months to 3 years.[102]

---

[102] Law No. 405 of October 25, 2000 "[Zákon] kterým se mění zákon č. 140/1961, trestní zákon, ve znění pozdějších předpisů" [[Law] Making Changes to Law No. 140/1961, the Penal Code, as Amended by Subsequent Regulations], Article 6. The law also modified, in Article 5, the wording of Article 261 of the Penal Code, which now banned public expressions of "sympathy" toward movements promoting national, racial, class, or religious hatred, rather than toward fascism and other similar movements, as the initial text of 1961 had worded it. It is often claimed in the literature that articles 260, 261, and 261A were parts of a 2001 Law against Support and Dissemination of Movements Oppressing Human Rights and Freedoms. See *Legislating for Equality*, p. 117; Jacqueline Lechtholz-Zey, "The Laws Banning Holocaust Denial": www .genocidepreventionnow.org/portals/0/docs/holocaust_denial_updated_2.8.pdf; and William M. Downs, *Political Extremism in Democracies: Combating Intolerance* (New York: Palgrave Macmillan, 2012), p. 38. In fact, those articles were parts of the Penal Code, and "Support and

As in the Polish law, there is here no definition of the precise category of offenses the law is criminalizing. This norm (along with articles 260 and 261) was maintained in the new Czech Penal Code of 2009, although in a slightly different form. The same punishment applies now to any person "who publicly denies, questions, approves, or seeks to justify the Nazi, communist, or other genocide or Nazi, communist, or other crimes against humanity, or war crimes, or crimes against peace."[103] The new formulation reflects the influence of the 2008 EU Framework Decision, which also referred to the Nuremberg classification of Nazi crimes, but it has not solved the problem of clarifying exactly what the law forbids. The scope of the law has been expanded to include denial of "other genocides," which also corresponds to the recent European trend. But notwithstanding the Europeanization of the official Czech commemorative agenda, the emphasis on communist crimes has not disappeared from the law.

Slovakia criminalized Holocaust denial soon after the Czech Republic but in a different way. The Slovak Penal Code included the same Articles 260 and 261 that respectively prohibited participating in and expressing sympathies with movements that seek to suppress human rights and freedoms. With the formation of Mikuláš Dzurinda's democratic government in 1998, the Slovak politics of memory took a pro-Western turn that contrasted with the nationalistic rhetoric dominant under Vladimír Mečiar.[104] In November 2001, the Slovak parliament reformulated Article 261 of the Penal Code as follows:

> A person who publicly expresses sympathy with fascism or another similar movement mentioned in Article 260 [which banned "movement[s] that manifestly seek to suppress human rights and freedoms or preach national, racial, class or religious hatred"] or publicly denies, questions, approves, or seeks to justify the crimes of fascism or another similar movement mentioned in Article 260 will be punished by deprivation of liberty of from 6 months to 3 years.[105]

Dissemination of Movements Oppressing Human Rights and Freedoms" was the name of the Penal Code's Article 260.

[103] Zákon 40/2009 ze dne 8. ledna 2009: trestní zákoník, Article 405. Articles 260 and 261 of the 1961 code became, respectively, Articles 403 and 404 of the new code, which also contains norms criminalizing genocide and incitement to hatred (Articles 400 and 356).

[104] Cohen, *Politics Without a Past*; Eyal, "Identity and Trauma"; Blutinger, "An Inconvenient Past"; and Nadya Nedelsky, "From Velvet Revolution to Velvet Justice: The Case of Slovakia," in *After Oppression*, pp. 390–417.

[105] Law No. 485/2001 of November 8, 2001 "[Zákon] ktorým sa mení zákon č. 140/1961 Trestný zákon v znení neskorších predpisov' [[Law] Making Changes to Law No. 140/1961 Penal Code, as Amended]. The version of the Slovak Penal Code as amended by this law is available at www.slov-lex.sk/pravne-predpisy/SK/ZZ/1961/140/20050701.html.

There is no explicit reference here to communist crimes, for post-communist Slovak elites were much less interested in de-communization than their Polish and Czech counterparts, although formulations such as "class hatred" (inherited from the Czechoslovak law of 1991) could potentially be used to subsume communism under the category of "other similar" regimes. But the explicit ban on the denial of fascist crimes meant a lot in Slovakia, given the country's support for Nazism during World War II and the celebration of Father Tiso's memory in the 1990s.

As in the Czech Republic, this norm was maintained in modified form in the new Slovak Penal Code adopted in 2005. During the debates over the new code, the parliament rejected the proposal to invalidate the 2001 law so as not to impinge on freedom of expression;[106] instead, it significantly changed the wording of the relevant article (now Article 424A):

> Any person who publicly (a) incites to violence or hatred against a group of persons or an individual because of their affiliation to any race, nation, nationality, skin color, ethnic group, family origin, or religion, if they constitute a pretext for the incitement on the aforementioned grounds, or (b) defames such group or individual or threatens them by vindicating an offense that is deemed to be genocide, a crime against humanity or a war crime under articles 6, 7 and 8 of the Rome Statute of the International Criminal Court, or an offense that is deemed to be a crime against peace, a war crime or a crime against humanity under Article 6 of the Statute of the International Military Tribunal annexed to the Agreement of 8 August 1945 for the Prosecution and Punishment of the Major War Criminals of the European Axis, if such crime was committed against such group of persons or individuals, or if a perpetrator or abettor of such a criminal act was convicted by a final and conclusive judgment rendered by an international court, unless it was rendered null and void in lawful proceedings, publicly denies or grossly derogates such offense, if committed against such person or individual, shall be liable to a term of imprisonment of one to three years.[107]

Denial of crimes against humanity is, in fact, seen here as an insult to descendants of the oppressed group, just as it was viewed in Germany until the 1980s, which is atypical of other post-Gayssot Act legislation. For the rest, the language of the article is far more in line with the most recent European recommendations, including the 2008 Framework Decision

---

[106] See "Slovakia Keeps Law against Holocaust Denial," *Associated Press*, February 9, 2005.

[107] Zákon č. 300/2005 z 20. mája 2005 Trestný zákon, available in English at www.legislationline.org/documents/id/16895. The aggravating circumstance of "specific motivation" could increase the penalty to up to five years.

(which had at the time not been adopted, having been under discussion in
the European Parliament since 2001). To be sure, the denial of any
properly established crime against humanity falls within the scope of the
article, but it is formulated in such a way as to make us think, first and
foremost, of Nazi crimes (although Slovak legislation, especially since the
2002 lustration act, is well familiar with the concept of communist
crimes): it refers to the Nuremberg Tribunal and in addition considers
negationism a crime of a racist nature (which is not the most widespread
understanding of communist crimes).

Most interestingly, and unlike the rest of Eastern Europe, the Slovak
code also refers to the verdicts of international courts (including the
Nuremberg Tribunal) that established the fact of concrete crimes against
humanity and convicted the perpetrators. This approach, obviously suggested by the Gayssot Act, shows the legislators' interest in clarifying the
facts whose denial was now prohibited. The code also maintained the ban
on "supporting and promoting groups aiming to suppress fundamental
rights and freedoms" (Article 421), the incitement of hatred (Article 424),
and the defamation of nation, race, and belief (Article 423). An important
innovation, however, consisted in the ban on using "flags, badges, uniforms or slogans" with the intent to demonstrate "sympathy" toward
groups or movements that use violence or the threat of violence and
"aim to suppress citizens' fundamental rights and freedoms" (Article
422). Here, again, the lawmakers chose the most general wording to avoid
direct references to communist symbols and prevent accusations that they
failed to ban them. Slovak legislation, as we see, follows the Gayssot Act
model rather than that of the 1998 Polish law.

Romanian memory law first came into being as a government emergency ordinance of March 2002 (the Romanian Constitution gives the
government the ability to make laws under exceptional circumstances). It
was adopted as part of the country's hurried preparation for entry into
NATO, which was to be approved at NATO's Prague Summit in November 2002.[108] The outcome of that summit was, however, in doubt due to
the situation in Romania, which included growing anti-Semitism, Holocaust negationism, and the cult of Marshal Antonescu, who was being
honored by monuments that were going up all across Romania. The

[108] Gabriel Andreescu, *Right-Wing Extremism in Romania* (Cluj-Napoca: *Fundaţia* CRDE, 2003),
pp. 99–116; Nasty Vladoiu, "Emergency Ordinance No. 31/2002 Prohibiting Organizations and
Symbols of Fascist, Racist or Xenophobic Character and Promoting the Cult of Persons Guilty of
Crimes against Peace and Humanity Approved by Law No. 107/2006 – 'The Legal Damage,'"
Criminal Law Review 2/1 (2012), pp. 1–9.

ordinance introduced penalties of up to five years' imprisonment for the dissemination and public exhibition of fascist symbols (Articles 3 and 4) as well as the promotion of fascist, racist, and xenophobic ideology, and the cult of historical figures who had perpetrated crimes against humanity (Article 5). With regard to negationism, Article 6 stated: "Public disavowal or denial of the Holocaust, or of the effects thereof, is punishable with imprisonment between 6 months and 6 years and the loss of certain rights."[109]

The ordinance was approved by the parliament with some modifications in April 2006 and then again amended in July. The April 2006 Act reduced maximal penalties for promoting fascist ideology and the cult of fascist leaders to three years, and introduced definitions of such notions as the Holocaust, fascist symbols, and persons guilty of crimes against peace and humanity (characteristically, only those who had been "convicted by final judgment of a Romanian or foreign court of law" could be included in the latter category). The Holocaust was defined here as "the systematic State-sponsored persecution and annihilation of European Jews by Nazi Germany, its allies and collaborators in the period 1933–1945." (The Romanian involvement in the Shoah clearly falls under this definition.) Further, the law now forbade "Public disavowal of the Holocaust, or of the effects thereof."[110] The July 2006 Act supplemented the ordinance with a ban on any "systematic apologia" of fascist and xenophobic ideas (Article 5). As for Article 6, the new law maintained the same punishment for the offense of negationism, which was now formulated as follows: "Public disavowal, contestation, approbation or justification, by whatsoever means, of the Holocaust, genocide, or a crime against humanity."[111] This

---

[109] Emergency Ordinance No. 31/2002 of March 13, 2002: "[Ordonanţa de urgenţă] privind interzicerea organizaţiilor şi simbolurilor cu caracter fascist, rasist sau xenofob şi a promovării cultului persoanelor vinovate de săvârşirea unor infracţiuni contra păcii şi omenirii" [[Emergency Ordinance] Prohibiting Organizations and Symbols with Fascist, Racist or Xenophobic Character and the Promotion of the Cult of Persons Guilty of Crimes against Peace and Humanity], available in English at www.hsph.harvard.edu/population/aids/romania.aids.pdf.

[110] Law No. 107/2006 of April 27, 2006 "[Legea] pentru aprobarea Ordonanţei de urgenţă a Guvernului nr. 31/2002 privind interzicerea organizaţiilor şi simbolurilor cu caracter fascist, rasist sau xenofob şi a promovării cultului persoanelor vinovate de săvârşirea unor infracţiuni contra păcii şi omenirii" [[Law] Approving the Government Emergency Ordinance No. 31/2002 Prohibiting Organizations and Symbols with Fascist, Racist or Xenophobic Character and the Promotion of the Cult of Persons Guilty of Crimes against Peace and Humanity]. The law also mentions the deportations and annihilation of the Roma people.

[111] Law No. 278/2006 of July 4, 2006 "[Legea] pentru modificarea şi completarea Codului penal, precum şi pentru modificarea şi completarea altor legi" [[Law] on Modifying and Completing the Penal Code and on Modifying and Completing Other Laws].

reformulation was obviously suggested by the pan-European tendency to expand the scope of Holocaust denial legislation to other genocides.

However, all those norms were poorly implemented and could not stop the growing Holocaust denial, despite the constantly accumulating evidence that made it impossible to deny the involvement of the Romanian state and a part of the population in the extermination of the Jews (which Romanians had seen since communist times as a strictly German crime for which Romania could in no way be held responsible).[112] The 2015 memory law reformulated the ban on Holocaust denial, introducing a new section to Article 6 that reads:

> The public negation, questioning, approbation, justification, or obvious minimalization by any means, of a genocide, a crime against humanity, or a war crime, as defined in international law, in the Statute of the International Criminal Court and in the Charter of the International Military Tribunal established by the London Agreement of August 8, 1945, and recognized as such by the final judgment of the International Criminal Court, the International Military Tribunal established by the London Agreement of August 8, 1945, the International Criminal Tribunal for the Former Yugoslavia, the International Criminal Tribunal for Rwanda, or any other international criminal tribunal established by relevant international bodies and whose competence is recognized by the Romanian State, or of their effects is punishable with incarceration of from 6 months to 3 years or a fine.[113]

One notes here the influence of the 2005 Slovak law, with its dependence on EU terminology and on the logic of anti-fascism and anti-racism rather than de-communization, as well as its tendency to expand the scope of the criminalization of denial and to apply formal legal criteria in defining the object of prohibition. The judgments of international courts, including the Nuremberg Tribunal, are seen here as documents that have established the ultimate historical truth.

Slovenia, whose successful democratization in the 1990s had resulted in the triumph of a "forgive and forget" approach and in a failure of

---

[112] Ed Maxfield, "Romania," in *Encyclopedia of Transitional Justice*, vol. 2, pp. 398–404.
[113] Law No. 217/2015 of July 23, 2015 "[Legea] pentru modificarea și completarea Ordonanței de urgență a Guvernului nr. 31/2002 privind interzicerea organizațiilor și simbolurilor cu caracter fascist, rasist sau xenofob și a promovării cultului persoanelor vinovate de săvârșirea unor infracțiuni contra păcii și omenirii" [[Law] on Modifying and Completing the Government Emergency Ordinance No. 31/2002 Prohibiting Organizations and Symbols with Fascist, Racist or Xenophobic Character and the Promotion of the Cult of Persons Guilty of Crimes against Peace and Humanity]; Adam Taylor, "Why Romania had to ban Holocaust denial twice," *Washington Post*, July 27, 2015.

lustration,[114] took a minimalist stand on the regulation of historical memory by law, merely implementing the EU recommendations while, in 2004, amending its Penal Code, by adding to the list of racist offenses punishable by a prison term of up to two years, the words "[whoever] denies, diminishes the significance of, approves of or advocates genocide."[115] This provision was retained in a modified form in the new code of 2008:

> The same sentence [imprisonment of up to two years] shall be imposed on a person who publicly disseminates ideas on the supremacy of one race over another, or provides aid in any manner for racist activity or denies, diminishes the significance of, approves, disregards, makes fun of, or advocates genocide, holocaust, crimes against humanity, war crime, aggression, or other criminal offences against humanity.[116]

Like Slovenia, Macedonia amended its Penal Code in March 2004, clearly in response to the Council of Europe's 2003 Additional Protocol on Cybercrime:

> 1. One that will publicly negate, [grossly] minimize, approve or justify the crimes stipulated in the articles 403 through 407 [genocide, crimes against humanity, war crimes], through an information system, shall be sentenced [to] imprisonment of one to five years.

> 2. If the negation, minimizing, approval or the justification is performed with intention to [incite] hate, discrimination or violence against a person or a group of persons due to their national, ethnic or racial origins or religion, the perpetrator, shall be sentenced [to] imprisonment of at least four years.[117]

Characteristically, in Slovenia and Macedonia (which were both parts of the former Yugoslavia) there seems to be little interest in prohibiting the denial of communist crimes, although there had been no shortage of such crimes in Yugoslav history. But the communists' coming to power there had been an outcome of their predominant role in the wartime partisan movement rather than of the Soviet occupation, and Yugoslavia remained an independent country rather than a Soviet satellite throughout the entire communist period. Consequently, shifting the blame for communist

---

[114] Tamara Kotar, "Slovenia," in *Encyclopedia of Transitional Justice*, vol. 2, pp. 439–445; Kotar, "Slovenia," in *Transitional Justice in Eastern Europe and the Former Soviet Union*, pp. 200–220.

[115] Kazenski zakonik z dne 17. junija 2004, Article 300: Stirring up Hatred, Strife or Intolerance based on Violation of the Principle of Equality; ECRI Third Report on Slovenia, 2006, p. 9.

[116] Kazenski zakonik z dne 4. junija 2008, Article 297.2; *Legislating for Equality*, p. 425.

[117] Republic of Macedonia. Criminal Code of 1996, Article 407-a: Approving or justifying of a genocide, crimes against humanity or military crimes; *Legislation for Equality*, p. 288; ECRI Third Report on "the Former Yugoslav Republic of Macedonia," 2004, p. 11.

crimes to Soviet occupiers was not an option there. Additionally, in the late communist period Slovenian elites were much less implicated in political repressions than those of most other socialist countries, which was an important premise for the democratic reforms of the 1990s.

After the adoption of the Slovenian and Macedonian acts in 2004, there was a pause in the development of legislation criminalizing statements about the past in Eastern Europe. The next group of such laws was not passed, mostly under the influence of the 2008 Framework Decision, until 2008–2011 (with several more bills adopted in 2014 and 2015).

Between 2004 and 2008, the situation with the politics of memory in Eastern Europe changed dramatically and for many reasons, including the general rise of far-right parties in Europe as well as the ambiguous effects of the entry of several Eastern European countries into the EU in 2004.[118] Most importantly, prior to 2004, Putin's neo-imperial ambitions were not yet as obvious as they later became. An important change in Russian politics, including the politics of memory, occurred in 2004, with Putin's reelection to a second term as president, the consolidation of his personal power, the Kremlin's increasing intervention in the domestic politics of Eastern European countries (Ukraine above all), and the beginning of the propaganda campaign leading up to the seventieth anniversary of the victory over Nazism. In 2005, with Lech Kaczyński's election as Polish president and Viktor Yushchenko's coming to power in Ukraine, the politics of memory agenda came to the forefront in those countries as well.[119] By the middle of the 2000s, memory wars were flaring up all across Eastern Europe, and Russia's disputes over the past with Ukraine, Poland, and the Baltic countries were proving central to the rapidly deteriorating international climate in the region. The Ukraine crisis of 2014 further degraded the situation.

For all these reasons, attitudes toward memory laws as an instrument of the politics of memory have undergone significant changes. In the late 1990s and early 2000s, memory laws that did not specifically criminalize the denial of communist crimes (the Slovak, Romanian, Slovenian, and Macedonian laws) had prevailed in Eastern Europe over those that did (the Polish and Czech laws), which was no longer the case in 2008–2015. In addition, the memory laws of 1998–2004 were adopted mostly in those

---

[118] Ochman, *Post-Communist Poland*, pp. 1–2.
[119] On 2005 as a turning point, see Michal Kopeček, "In Search of 'National Memory': The Politics of History, Nostalgia and the Historiography of Communism in the Czech Republic and Eastern Europe," in *Past in Making: Historical Revisionism in Central Europe after 1989* (Budapest: Central European University Press, 2008), p. 85.

Eastern European countries that (with the exception of Poland) did not border Russia and consequently had fewer reasons to fear it. By contrast, there are more of Russia's neighbors among the countries that have passed memory laws since 2008 (Latvia, Lithuania, and Ukraine). Notwithstanding the failure to include the ban on the denial of communist crimes in the 2008 Framework Decision, most of the Eastern European countries that passed such laws in 2008–2015 adopted the Polish model (Lithuania, Hungary, Latvia, and Ukraine) rather than the French (Albania, Bulgaria, Montenegro). Hungary and Latvia, for their part, initially passed EU-style bills but later switched to the Polish paradigm.

The Albanian law of 2008 was still reminiscent of the earlier legislations, since it was passed in response to the 2003 Additional Protocol to the Convention on Cybercrime, and that country was in any event too remote from Russia to seriously worry about any possible unfriendly actions, not to mention that during the communist period Albania, like Yugoslavia, had remained largely independent from Moscow. In November 2008, the Albanian Penal Code was amended to include Article 74a, "Computer dissemination of materials in favor of genocide or crimes against humanity," which provided:

> Offering in public or deliberately disseminating to the public through computer systems materials that deny, minimize significantly, approve of or justify acts that are genocide or crimes against humanity are punishable by three to six years of imprisonment.[120]

This is of course a standard EU-inspired law. Latvia's first official move to criminalize certain statements about the past also followed the EU recommendations. In May 2009, Latvia amended its Penal Code by introducing the following article:

> For a person who commits public glorification of genocide, crime against humanity, crime against peace or war crime or public denial or acquittal of implemented genocide, crime against humanity, crime against peace or war crime – the applicable punishment is deprivation of liberty for a term of not exceeding five years.[121]

---

[120] This article was introduced into the Penal Code by Law No. 10023 of November 27, 2008 "On Some Amendments and Changes on Law No. 7895, dated 27.1.1995, 'Penal Code of Republic of Albania.'" See also Law No. 7895 of 27 January 1995, Criminal Code of the Republic of Albania as of October 13, 2009, Article 74a; ECRI Report on Albania (fourth monitoring cycle), 2009/2010, p. 14.

[121] The Criminal Code of the Republic of Latvia of 1998 as amended of 2013, Article 74.1: Acquittal of Genocide, Crime against Humanity, amended on May 23, 2009 and on December 13, 2012; *Legislating for Equality*, p. 252, and ECRI Report on Latvia (fourth monitoring cycle), 2011, p. 12.

There is no attempt here to reflect the complexity of the country's historical experience (e.g., the painful memories of Soviet crimes and largely suppressed memories of the German occupation, including the Latvians' own participation in both the Holocaust and the Soviet terror). However, in May 2014, in the midst of the Ukrainian crisis, Latvia modified this provision and maintained the same punishment for

> [P]ublic glorification of genocide, crime against humanity, crime against peace or war crime or glorification, denial, acquittal or gross trivialisation of committed genocide, crime against humanity, crime against peace or war crime, including genocide, crime against humanity, crime against peace or war crime committed by the USSR or Nazi Germany against the Republic of Latvia and its inhabitants.[122]

The communist crimes listed here ahead of those committed by the Nazis are clearly viewed as offenses perpetrated by an external force (the USSR) against Latvia, without any mention of the country's responsibility for the involvement of some of its citizens in those repressions. This interpretation of history is typical of an influential segment of public opinion in the Baltic countries (and, more broadly, in Eastern Europe), while the unusually straightforward way in which it is expressed in the 2014 Latvian law arguably relates to the exceptionally tense political context created by the Russian aggression against Ukraine and the Kremlin's threats against Russia's other neighbors.

Similarly to Latvia, Hungary initially introduced (in January 2010, under a socialist government) a memory law that specifically criminalized Holocaust denial. But in contrast to the initial Latvian law, which mechanically reproduced the EU model, the first Hungarian law developed the traditional German understanding of denial as a denigration of the victims of the Holocaust:

> Those who publicly hurt the dignity of a victim of the Holocaust by denying or questioning the Holocaust itself, or claim it insignificant, infringe the law and can be punished by prison sentence of up to three years.[123]

---

[122] The Criminal Code of the Republic of Latvia of 1998, as amended of 2015, Article 74.1 amended on May 15, 2014, available in English at www.vvc.gov.lv/export/sites/default/docs/.../The_Criminal_Law.doc.L.

[123] Hungarian Criminal Code, Article 269-C, quoted by Talia Na'amat, "Holocaust Denial as a Form of Hate Speech – New Developments": http://ec.europa.eu/.../holocaust_denial_as_a_form_of_hate_speech241011; Veronika Gulyas, "Hungary's Parliament Votes Holocaust Denial to Be against Law," *Wall Street Journal,* February 25, 2010.

In June 2010, shortly after Viktor Orbán's government came to power in May, this law was amended to include the denial of both Nazi and communist offenses:

> A person, who denies or questions the occurrence or belittles the significance of the genocides and other grave crimes against humanity committed by the National Socialist or Communist regimes, shall be liable to punishment for a felony offence by imprisonment for up to three years.[124]

The brevity of the law makes it more of a propaganda tool than anything else, but its message is still clear, especially given that it was an amendment to a law adopted just a few months earlier. For Orbán, a nationalist conservative and a partisan of limiting democratic freedoms who was in addition seeking to compromise his socialist opponents, antifascism without anti-communism was not an acceptable position.

Article 370–2 of Montenegro's Penal Code as amended in April 2010 provides that

> The sentence referred to in paragraph 1 of this article [imprisonment of six months to five years] shall also be imposed on anyone who publicly approves, renounces the existence or significantly reduces the gravity of criminal offences of genocide, crimes against humanity and war crimes committed against a group or member of a group based on race, skin colour, religion, origin, national or ethnic affiliation, in the manner which can lead to violence or cause hatred against a group of persons or a member of such group, if those criminal offences have been determined by a final and enforceable judgment of a court in Montenegro or of the International Criminal Tribunal.[125]

This statute is also a typical EU-style memory law. In contrast, the amendment to the Lithuanian Criminal Code passed in June 2010 followed the updated (in light of more recent European legislation) Polish model by stipulating that:

> A person who publicly condones the crimes of genocide or other crimes against humanity or war crimes recognized under legal acts of the Republic of Lithuania or the European Union or effective judgments passed by courts of the Republic of Lithuania or international courts, denies or grossly

---

[124] Act LVI of June 2010, section 7. See *Legislating for Equality*, p. 210, and ECRI Conclusions on the Implementation of the Recommendations in Respect of Hungary Subject to Interim Follow-Up, 2011, p. 5. This norm in a slightly modified form (the words "or attempts to justify such crimes" have been added to the text) was upheld by the new Penal Code of 2012. See Act C of July 13, 2012, On the Criminal Code, Article 333.

[125] Article 108 of the Law Amending the Criminal Code of April 2010; ECRI Report on Montenegro (fourth monitoring cycle), 2011, p. 12.

trivialises them, where this is accomplished in a manner which is threatening, abusive or insulting or which disturbs the public order, also a person who publicly condones the aggression perpetrated by the USSR or Nazi Germany against the Republic of Lithuania, the crimes of genocide or other crimes against humanity or war crimes committed by the USSR or Nazi Germany in the territory of the Republic of Lithuania or against the inhabitants of the Republic of Lithuania or other grave or serious crimes committed during 1990–1991 against the Republic of Lithuania by the persons perpetrating or participating in perpetration of the aggression against the Republic of Lithuania or grave crimes against the inhabitants of the Republic of Lithuania, denies or grossly trivialises them, where this is accomplished in a manner which is threatening, abusive or insulting or which disturbs the public order, shall be punished by a fine or by restriction of liberty or by arrest or by a custodial sentence for a term of up to two years.[126]

The reference to the EU legislation and the verdicts of international courts as well as the clause that denial constitutes an offense only if it is done in a threatening manner are important indications of the lawmakers' desire to meet Brussels' expectations. But beyond the technicalities, the Lithuanian enactment is an extreme example of the tendency to use memory laws to promote national narratives and shift the blame for crimes against humanity to others, namely, Nazi Germany and especially the USSR. It is not by chance that Soviet crimes are here put first and Nazi offenses second (a model that was later reproduced by the 2014 Latvian law). Most importantly, the law speaks of the USSR's aggression against Lithuania and makes it illegal to deny that the Soviet period in Lithuanian history was an occupation. It specifically prohibits the denial of the "official" Lithuanian version of circumstances related to the disintegration of the USSR, including the events in Vilnius during January 1991 (the failed attempt to suppress the Lithuanian movement for national liberation by force). And, of course, the law gives protection to a narrative that leaves no room to question the Lithuanians' own responsibility for crimes perpetrated "within the territory of the Republic of Lithuania or against the inhabitants of the Republic of Lithuania." This is a clear case of "deflective negationism" with regard to both Nazi and communist crimes.

---

[126] Law No. VIII-1968 of September 26, 2000, on the Approval and Entry into Force of the Criminal Code, consolidated version valid as of 1 April 2016, Article 170.2; ECRI Report on Lithuania (fourth monitoring cycle), 2011, p. 15; Justinas Žilinskas, "Introduction of 'Crime of Denial' in the Lithuanian Criminal Law and First Instances of its Application," *Jurisprudencja/Jurispridence* 19 (2012), pp. 315–329.

Finally, in April 2011, Bulgaria amended its Penal Code to comply with the 2008 Framework Decision:

> Whosoever in any way justifies, denies, or grossly downplays crimes against peace and humankind thus risking the infliction of violence upon or the incitement of hatred against individuals or groups of people united by race, color, religion, descent, or national or ethnic origin will be punished by deprivation of liberty for from one to five years.[127]

This is, of course, just another EU-style statute similar to those adopted in Slovakia, Romania, Slovenia, Albania, and Montenegro and clearly differs from the bans on denial of both Nazi and communist crimes passed in the Czech Republic, Hungary, Latvia, Lithuania, and Poland.

Let us now compare Eastern and Western European prohibitions of statements about the past. As in the West, few Eastern European laws use the term "Holocaust."[128] Much more typical are references to Nazi (or sometimes fascist) crimes,[129] which are often understood in the region primarily as crimes against ethnic groups other than the Jews. Finally, as in the West, several laws penalize denial of any genocide and/or crime against humanity.[130] References to war crimes are somewhat more typical of Eastern than of Western European statutes: they are mentioned in the laws passed in eight out of twelve countries in the east of the continent (excluding Russia)[131] compared with six out of fourteen countries to the west. Even more tellingly, the denial of crimes against peace is outlawed in five Eastern European countries[132] and in only two Western countries (Portugal and Malta), which is arguably due to the persisting Soviet tradition of viewing the unleashing of the war, not the Holocaust, as the Nazis' main crime.

---

[127] Nakazatelen kodeks ot 1 May 1968, Article 419a.

[128] The 2002 Romanian law, the 2008 Slovenian law, and the January 2010 version of the Hungarian law.

[129] The 1998 Polish law, the 2000 and 2009 versions of the Czech law, the 2001 and 2005 versions of the Slovak law, the June 2010 version of the Hungarian law, the 2010 Lithuanian law, the 2014 Latvian law, and the 2015 Romanian law, as well as the 2014 Ukrainian and Russian laws that we will consider in the chapters that follow.

[130] The 2004 Macedonian law, the 2004 and 2008 versions of the Slovenian laws, the 2005 Slovak law, the 2008 Albanian law, the 2009 Latvian law, the 2010 Lithuanian and Montenegrin laws, and the 2015 Romanian law.

[131] The 2004 Macedonian law, the 2005 Slovak law, the 2008 Slovenian law, the 2009 Czech law, the 2009 and 2014 versions of the Latvian law, the 2010 Lithuanian and Montenegrin laws, and the 2015 Romanian law.

[132] The 1998 Polish law, the 2005 Slovak law, the 2009 Czech law, the 2009 and 2014 versions of the Latvian law, and the 2011 Bulgarian law.

However, the most important difference between Western and Eastern European bans on statements about the past consists in two other formulae that appear in several Eastern European laws but nowhere in the West. On the one hand, the 1998 Polish, the 2010 Lithuanian, and the 2014 Latvian acts outlaw the denial of crimes perpetrated against the inhabitants and/or on the territory of those countries, which certainly implies a strong tendency toward self-victimization. On the other hand, as mentioned earlier, Poland, the Czech Republic, Hungary, Lithuania, and Latvia have also criminalized the denial of communist crimes, and those bans, while to some extent understandable, are nevertheless typically formulated in such a way as to shift the blame for both Nazi and communist crimes to others and to sanitize their own national narratives. Reproducing the European Union's paradigm of criminalizing negationism viewed as a manifestation of racism and xenophobia seems especially typical of those countries that are, although for somewhat different reasons, "ambivalent" (to use Troebst's classification) with regard to their communist past and do not have serious memory conflicts with Russia. In contrast, the Polish model of criminalizing the denial of both Nazi and communist crimes prevails in those countries that have stronger historical records of anti-communist resistance and are today typically embroiled in memory wars with Russia. I believe that the following chapter, which considers Ukrainian memory law projects, also supports this conclusion.

Eastern European legislators have been even less interested (and successful) than their Western colleagues in defining exactly which crimes have to be considered definitely established and therefore cannot be problematized. The 2005 Slovak law pays unusual attention to this question by referring, as some Western enactments also do, to the definition of crimes against humanity in the Charter of the Nuremberg Tribunal and in the Rome Statute, as well as to individual convictions rendered by international jurisdictions (although these are, as we know, rather unconvincing solutions). The 2015 Romanian law refers to the same definitions but also to the judgments (not individual sentences) of international jurisdictions, including the Nuremberg Tribunal whose entire Judgment the act explicitly endorses. The endorsement of this document is fundamental for Putin's history politics but quite exceptional for legislative acts outside Russia. In fact, only the 2003 Additional Protocol and the 2010 Montenegrin law also refer to the Nuremberg Judgment, which may be the worst solution for defining what exactly a law penalizes, because it implies that every single claim of this complex and in many respects problematic document is historically accurate (we will return to this question in Chapter 6).

CHAPTER 4

Memory Laws in Ukraine

There are several reasons for paying special attention here to Ukraine, one of them being the importance of the Ukraine crisis and the need to consider it from the politics-of-memory angle, as those politics had a role to play in laying its groundwork. Also, over the past decade, Ukrainian legislators have been exceptionally prolific drafters of bills related to historical memory, which provide a valuable source for an investigation of the roots of the current crisis. The study of those bills invites an unexpected conclusion, in that the vocabulary of most Russian and some Ukrainian memory law projects and, more broadly, the language of Putin's current politics of memory were initially developed by a group of pro-Russian Ukrainian politicians and Russian nationalists actively involved in Ukraine's internal affairs, which is yet another confirmation of Ukraine's centrality to Eastern European politics.

History Politics

In the Kremlin's view, Ukraine is the key to the former Soviet empire, which largely explains Putin's opposition to Kiev's Association Agreement with the EU in 2013 and his subsequent policy with regard to the Maidan Revolution of Dignity and the attempts of the new Ukrainian leadership to foster the country's integration with the West. "The struggle for Ukraine" has been high on Putin's agenda from the beginning of his rule, but especially since 2004, when Russia forcefully intervened in Ukraine's domestic politics and gave its full support to Viktor Yanukovych during the presidential elections in the fall of that year. To consolidate pro-Russian forces there, especially after Yanukovych's failure, the Kremlin used the theory of "two Ukraines," which presented Ukraine as a profoundly divided society (indeed, a failed state), the main divide being that between the country's Russian-speaking East and Ukrainian-speaking West.

In April 2008, Putin was reported to have angrily protested, at a NATO summit in Bucharest, against NATO's potential alliance with Ukraine: "Ukraine is not even a state. What is Ukraine? Part of its territories is Eastern Europe, but the greater part is a gift from us."[1] That statement – addressed to George W. Bush – could be interpreted as a warning that Russia would not "let Ukraine go." The notion that it is an artificial geopolitical construction with no authentic tradition of "statehood," and whose very existence is due to a series of benevolent acts performed by Russian tsars and Soviet rulers, is reminiscent of the ways in which Stalin's government justified the Soviet invasion of Poland after the Soviet–Nazi Pact of August 1939. Indeed, in October 1939, speaking to the Supreme Soviet on the unification of Western Ukraine and Western Belorussia with the Soviet Union, Vyacheslav Molotov, the head of the Soviet government, said: "One blow from the German army and another from the Soviet army put an end to this ugly product of Versailles [meaning an independent Poland, which was even younger in 1939 than independent Ukraine was in 2014]."[2] What both Poland and Ukraine were ostensibly lacking was the character of an organic entity, a nation with its own uninterrupted tradition of "statehood."[3]

However, it was not enough just to convince Ukrainians that they were a profoundly divided nation (for all that "two Ukraines" had been a widely used rhetorical figure in Ukrainian political discourse well before it was appropriated by Russian propagandists). The goal was, rather, to impose a black-and-white interpretation of that divide, which would prevent Ukrainians from developing a democratic and pluralistic society, the notion that informed the project of an independent Ukraine after the collapse of the USSR.

The politics of memory is the main instrument that Putin's government has used to divide Ukraine and render it politically dependent on Moscow. That politics, and in particular the cult of the Great Patriotic War, has become central to the ideology of Putin's regime for many reasons that we will discuss in Chapter 6. With regard to Ukraine, though, the cult was

---

[1] Olga Allenova, Yelena Geda, Vladimir Novikov, "Blok NATO razoshelsya na blokpakety" [The NATO Bloc Split into Blocking Shares], April 7, 2008: www.kommersant.ru/doc/877224.
[2] Quoted in Jeane J. Kirkpatrick, *Legitimacy and Force* (New Brunswick, N.J.: Transactions books, 1988), vol. 1, p. 49.
[3] There seems to be an interesting parallel here with Hitler's understanding of *Staatlichkeit* as a quality atypical of racially inferior peoples, which is in part the rationale behind the extermination of the "stateless" Jews, as Timothy Snyder has recently suggested. See his *Black Earth: The Holocaust as History and Warning* (New York: Tim Duggan Books, 2015), p. 117.

used to demonize all "anti-Russian" forces in that country, from liberal nationalists to far-right groups, by presenting them as "Nazi allies." Putin's "battle for Ukraine" could thus be viewed as a continuation of Russia's struggle against Nazi Germany, in which all "good [meaning pro-Russian] Ukrainians" should support Moscow against the "neo-fascist" West and its Ukrainian "accomplices."[4]

The task of compelling Ukrainians to interiorize this vision of Russia's politics was facilitated by the fact that Ukraine (alongside Belorussia) had been one of the most Russified Soviet republics (with the exception of Western Ukraine, which was annexed by Stalin after the Molotov-Ribbentrop Pact of 1939 and remained a stronghold of Ukrainian nationalism). In the 1960s and 1970s, the formation of Soviet identity (as opposed to Russian, Ukrainian, Armenian, and other identities) was at a quite advanced stage, so that many (and in Ukraine arguably most) Soviet subjects saw no contradiction in being simultaneously Soviet and Russian (Ukrainian, Tatar, Armenian, etc.),[5] even if, on the eve of perestroika, the incipient decomposition of the Soviet system was rapidly making "everything Soviet" ever less attractive to the empire's inhabitants. Unsurprisingly, most Ukrainians were therefore personally attached to the symbols of Soviet community, and the cult of World War II was deeply rooted in Ukrainian culture of the Soviet period. The demonization of anti-Soviet Ukrainian partisans was an important aspect of the Soviet war myth, although (or, rather, because) official Soviet propaganda did not, in the name of "the peoples' friendship," emphasize the Ukrainians' massive support of the nationalist guerrillas. The revival of the Soviet cult of the war in Ukraine in the 2000s required only the reactivation of that "shared knowledge" that most Ukrainians (and Russians) had acquired long ago.[6] That is why the inroads made by Putin's "propaganda state" in Russian-speaking parts of Ukraine were quite comparable to its success in Russia.[7]

[4] On the use of the notion of fascism with regard to the Ukrainian movement for independence, see Taras Kuzio, "Soviet and Russian anti-(Ukrainian) Nationalism and Re-Stalinization," *Communist and Post-Communist Studies* 49/1 (2016), pp. 87–99.
[5] In which the emphasis on being Soviet versus, say, Ukrainian was strongly context-dependent. See Ronald Grigor Suny, "The Contradictions of Identity: Being Soviet and National in the USSR and after," in *Soviet and Post-Soviet Identities*, eds. Mark Bassin and Catriona Kelly (Cambridge: Cambridge University Press, 2012), pp. 17–36.
[6] Serhy Yekelchyk, *Stalin's Empire of Memory: Russian-Ukrainian Relations in the Soviet Historical Imagination* (Toronto: University of Toronto Press, 2004).
[7] By the end of the 2000s, three-quarters of Ukrainians considered Victory Day a major holiday, while the number of those who admired Stalin was approximately equal to the number of his critics. See Volodymyr V. Kravchenko, "Ukraine Faces Its Soviet Past: History versus Policy versus Memory," in *Mass Dictatorship and Memory as Ever Present Past*, eds. Jie-Hyun Lim, Barbara Walker, and Peter

Ukraine is, to be sure, a country whose unusually complex (even by Eastern European standards) ethno-linguistic composition and inherited historical divides make the goal of nation-building particularly challenging. Finding historical symbols to express a common Ukrainian identity that would be shared by all the country's regions and all cultural, religious, ethnic, and linguistic groups was (and still is) no easy task. Of course, all leaders of independent Ukraine had seen the danger of the polarization of society and, at least before 2004, had tried not to provoke internal confrontations by promoting either of the competing historical narratives, be it the Soviet/Russian imperial mythology or the Ukrainian national romance that presented the country's trajectory as its perennial struggle for independence and whitewashed the history of the Ukrainian nationalist movement.

Keeping those narratives in balance was relatively easy in the 1990s and early 2000s. First, after the fall of communism, all ideologies, including historical grievances (that had been efficiently used to question the legitimacy of the communist rule in the late 1980s) came to be seen, throughout the former Soviet empire, as less important than pragmatic policies aimed at building a better future. Second, Russia's democratic leadership was at that time far more interested in promoting (both internationally and domestically) a shared vision of the dark Soviet past than in advancing the patriotic war myth. Memories of the common struggle waged by Russian democrats and national liberals in the former Soviet republics against the communist regime were too fresh, and in addition, Russia was too weak to pursue a great power politics. Third, Ukrainian nationalism was still in the early stage of its revival, and its prospects did not look particularly bright.[8]

In the 1990s, Ukraine did not witness dramatic internal confrontations similar to those that shook Russia, for its communist elites had adopted moderately nationalist slogans and remained in control of the country. Pursuing above all the goal of nation-building, they did not foster radical market reforms and refrained from applying "shock therapy"; the absence of the latter caused economic stagnation but also helped avoid the polarization of political forces.[9] In Yeltsin's Russia, liberal economists (such as

Lambert (New York: Palgrave Macmillan, 2014), p. 108. In Russia, Stalin's admirers outnumbered his critics by approximately one-third at that time.
[8] Thus, writing in 1997, Andrew Wilson underlined "the weakness of the Ukrainian national movement" and characterized Ukrainian nationalism as a "minority faith," which he explained by the absence of a "'natural' ethno-cultural unity in Ukraine." See his *Ukrainian Nationalism in the 1990s: A Minority Faith* (Cambridge: Cambridge University Press, 1997), pp. 1, 92, 113, 195, 196.
[9] Serhy Yekelchyk, *Ukraine: Birth of a Modern Nation* (Oxford: Oxford University Press, 2007), pp. 191–216.

Yegor Gaidar and Anatoliy Chubais) did at times determine the government's economic policy, while their Ukrainian counterparts were far less influential. Russian nationalists nostalgically claimed that Crimea was a Russian land, but those statements were generally perceived as irrelevant demagogy. President Yeltsin, for his part, opted for a "civilized divorce" with Ukraine, in which he was supported by Russian democrats and the international community. The Budapest memorandum of 1994, by which Russia guaranteed the frontiers of independent Ukraine in return for Ukraine giving up its nuclear arsenal, and the 1997 Partition Treaty that divided the Soviet Black Sea Fleet between Russia and Ukraine were the main stages of this divorce.[10] In that context, even the "historyless" Ukrainian elites could rule the country without becoming bogged down in major ideological battles between partisans of liberal democracy, communists, and nationalists.

The first Ukrainian presidents, Leonid Kravchuk (1991–1994) and Leonid Kuchma (1994–2005), were respectively a former secretary for ideology of the Central Committee of the Communist Party of Ukraine and a former director of one of the leading Ukrainian machine-building enterprises, and neither had been involved in any dissident movement, whether democratic or nationalist. Their politics of memory was extremely cautious and "multi-vector," which drew severe criticism from all sides, but especially from Ukrainian liberals, who complained about the failed decommunization that according to them was as badly needed in Ukraine as it was in Poland, the Czech Republic, or the Baltic countries. Depending on their audience at the time, both Kravchuk and (for most of his term as president) Kuchma might emphasize the need for a democratic transition, praise Ukraine's newly acquired independence, or toy with nostalgia for Soviet times.[11] Above all, both tried not to overemphasize the importance of historical grievances. During their tenure, Ukraine presented as a typical case of "politics without a past," as described by Shari J. Cohen.[12]

Things began changing at the turn of the 2000s, when, on the one hand, Ukrainian nationalism, and especially radical nationalism, emerged as a much stronger movement than it had been in the 1990s, and on the

[10] Serhii Plokhy, *The Gates of Europe: A History of Ukraine* (New York: Basic Books, 2015), pp. 325–328.
[11] Andrey Portnov, *Uprazhneniya s istoriyey po-ukrainski* [Ukrainian Exercises with History] (Moscow: OGI, Polit.ru, Memorial, 2010).
[12] Although Cohen focuses on Slovakia, she stresses that Ukraine was a similar case. See her *Politics without a Past: The Absence of History in Post-Communist Nationalism* (Durham, N.C.: Duke University Press, 1999), p. 180.

other, Russia's neo-imperial restoration resulted in the radicalization of pro-Russian forces (including Russian nationalists) in Eastern Ukraine. In 2004 (to quote Ukrainian historian Andrey Portnov), "on the eve of the presidential elections there occurred a radical turn in [Kuchma's] symbolic politics, as evidenced by the Soviet-style military parade with Vladimir Putin in attendance, which was held on October 28, 2004 to celebrate the [sixtieth] anniversary of the liberation of Ukraine [from the Germans in 1944]."[13] Pro-Russian political forces in Ukraine were obviously aligning themselves on the platform of the Soviet/Russian cult of the war, which in 2004 and 2005, in preparation to the sixtieth anniversary of the victory over Nazism, was rapidly emerging as the foundation of the new Russian ideology.

After the Orange Revolution, which brought Viktor Yushchenko, Yanukovych's main rival, to power in January 2005, Moscow made (as Portnov shows) the theory of two Ukraines the basis of its Ukrainian policy and began successfully promoting it in Eastern Ukraine. As a result, the relatively peaceful ideological climate of the 1990s and early 2000s in Ukraine gave way to increasingly fierce conflicts over the interpretation of the past between pro-Russian forces (Yanukovych's Party of the Regions and the communists) energetically supported by Russian media (which were very popular among Russian-speaking Ukrainians) and Ukrainian nationalists and national democrats. Russian nationalists such as Konstantin Zatulin, deputy chair of the State Duma Committee on the Affairs of the Community of Independent States, were among the architects of the Russian propaganda campaign in Ukraine during and after the 2004 elections.

Upon coming to power, Yushchenko made an attempt to pursue a compromise in politics of memory but soon thereafter gave his full support to the narrative of the Ukrainian struggle for independence (and in the years that followed, an alliance with nationalists became increasingly important to him as his popularity and moderate allies gradually slipped away).[14] In particular, he spared no effort in celebrating

---

[13] Portnov, *Uprazhneniya s istoriyey*, pp. 68, 29–31, 40–42. Cf. Georgiy Kasianov who suggests that Putin became involved in the Ukrainian politics of memory only "around 2005–2006." See Kasianov "How a War for the Past Becomes a War in the Present," *Kritika: Explorations in Russian and Eurasian History* 16/1 (2015), p. 153.

[14] Some historians claim that Yushchenko's history politics split Ukrainian society and triggered memory wars in Ukraine. See Georgiy Kasyanov, *Danse macabre: Golod 1932–1933 rokiv u polititsi, masoviy svidomosti ta istoriografii, 1980-ti – pochatok 2000-kh* [Danse Macabre: The 1932–1933 Famine in [Ukrainian] Politics, Mass Consciousness, and Historiography in the 1980s – Early 2000s] (Kiev: Nash Chas, 2010); Kasyanov, "Revisiting the Great Famine of

the memory of Ivan Mazepa (the hetman of Ukraine who had revolted against the tsar and had supported King Charles XII of Sweden during his invasion of Russia in 1708–1709) and promoting the cults of the wartime Ukrainian nationalists Stepan Bandera, the leader of the Organization of Ukrainian Nationalists (OUN), and Roman Shukhevych, the head of the Ukrainian Insurgent Army (UPA). In 2007 and 2010, he even awarded the title of Hero of Ukraine to Shukhevych and Bandera, although both had collaborated at length with the Nazis during the war (those decrees, used by pro-Russian opinion makers to present Yushchenko as a "fascist," were invalidated under Viktor Yanukovych in 2010).[15] The upshot of all this, as we will see, is that attempts to develop the memory of the Holocaust in Ukraine have been among the least successful in Eastern Europe to date.[16]

Central to Yushchenko's politics of memory was his attempt to create a national consensus around the memory of the Holodomor, a man-made famine in 1932–1933 that cost about three million Ukrainian lives (and another three million in Kazakhstan and the North Caucasus). Yushchenko arguably hoped that, in contrast to the divisive memories of the

1932–1933: Politics of Memory and Public Consciousness (Ukraine after 1991)," in *Past in the Making: Historical Revisionism in Central Europe after 1989*, ed. Michal Kopeček (Budapest: Central European University Press, 2008), pp. 197–215; and Serhii Plokhy, *The Gates of Europe*, p. 335. I, rather, see this politics as an exaggerated and ill-advised (although to some extent understandable) reaction to Russia's unceremonious attempts to intervene in Ukrainian domestic politics and there promote a Soviet-style cult of the war in order to split Ukrainian society. Of course, Yushchenko's reaction to those attempts also contributed to further conflicts. However, as Portnov shows, Yushchenko tried not to side exclusively with the nationalists but instead to find consensual symbols, and my analysis of his memory law drafts confirms this conclusion. See Portnov, *Uprazhneniya s istoriyey*, pp. 79–84.

[15] David R. Marples, *Heroes and Villains: Creating National History in Contemporary Ukraine* (Budapest: Central European University Press, 2007), pp. 79–166; Andre Liebich and Oksana Myshlovska, "Bandera: Memorialization and Commemoration," *Nationalities Papers* 42/5 (2014), pp. 750–770; Ivan Katchanovski, "Terrorists or National Heroes? Politics and Perceptions of the OUN and the UPA in Ukraine," *Communist and Post-Communist Studies* 48/2–3 (2015), pp. 217–228.

[16] Omer Bartov, *Erased: Vanishing Traces of Jewish Galicia in Present-Day Ukraine* (Princeton, N.J.: Princeton University Press, 2007), pp. 201–211; Aleksandr Burakovskiy, "Holocaust Remembrance in Ukraine: Memorialization of the Jewish Tragedy at Babi Yar," *Nationalities Papers* 39/3 (2011), pp. 371–389; John-Paul Himka, "Debates in Ukraine over Nationalist Involvement in the Holocaust, 2004–2008," *Nationalities Papers* 39/3 (2011), pp. 353–370; Himka, "The Reception of the Holocaust in Postcommunist Ukraine," in *Bringing the Dark Past to Light: The Reception of the Holocaust in Postcommunist Europe*, eds. Himka and Joanna Beata Michlic (Lincoln: University of Nebraska Press, 2013), pp. 626–661; Sarah Fainberg, "Memory at the Margins: The Shoah in Ukraine (1991–2011)," in *History, Memory and Politics in Central and Eastern Europe: Memory Games*, eds. Georges Mink and Laure Neumayer (Basingstoke: Palgrave Macmillan, 2013), pp. 86–102.

war,[17] the memory of the Holodomor had the potential to become a foundation for a common Ukrainian identity, especially since the Moscow communists, a force alien to Ukraine, could be billed as the only perpetrators of that crime.[18] Given that the memory of the Holodomor was relatively recent in Ukraine, the idea was that it could help overcome traditional divides in the perceptions of the past, especially because the famine had taken place in Central and Eastern Ukraine (Western Ukraine would not be annexed by the USSR until 1939). The task of garnering the support for a narrative centered on the Holodomor on behalf of the Eastern, predominantly Russian-speaking, part of Ukraine seemed quite achievable. And if successfully implemented, it would be a far better starting point for developing a new Ukrainian national narrative than the much more problematic memories of the OUN and UPA, the organizations that had been involved in the Holocaust and other crimes against humanity (including the Volhynia massacre of Poles in 1943). Yushchenko's politics of memory thus consisted in securing the radical nationalists' loyalty by celebrating the cults of Bandera and Shukhevych and winning the support of national liberals and Eastern Ukrainians by raising the Holodomor to the rank of Ukraine's main historical symbol. He could also anticipate receiving international endorsement for the memory of the Holodomor that had some aspects of genocide and was perfectly suited to the goal of victimizing the past for Ukraine's benefit.

During the communist period, the memory of the Holodomor (and other repressions that had accompanied the collectivization) was largely suppressed by the regime, although some of its elements would certainly have survived in family stories. Subsequent events, and above all the war (during which all of Ukraine was occupied by Germany and then reconquered by the Soviets), had largely erased the tragedy of collectivization from people's memory, which is hardly surprising since families that preserved the memory of repressions ran a considerable risk. As Amir

[17] Tatiana Zhurzhenko, "From the 'Reunification of the Ukrainian Lands' to 'Soviet Occupation': The Molotov-Ribbentrop Pact in the Ukrainian Political Memory," in *The Use and Abuse of Memory: Interpreting World War II in Contemporary European Politics*, eds. Christian Karner and Bram Mertens (New Brunswick, N.J.: Transaction Publishers, 2013), pp. 229–248.
[18] On the memory of the Holodomor, see (in addition to works quoted in note 14) Mykola Riabchuk, "Holodomor: The Politics of Memory and Political Infighting in Contemporary Ukraine," *Harriman Review* 16/2 (2008), pp. 3–9; Marples, *Heroes and Villains*, pp. 35–78. On both the morally and the historically problematic aspects of Yushchenko's promotion of the Holodomor as Ukraine's main historical symbol while silencing the history of the Ukrainians' participation in the Holocaust, see John-Paul Himka, "Interventions: Challenging the Myths of Twentieth-Century Ukrainian History," *The Convolutions of Historical Politics*, eds. Alexei Miller and Maria Lipman (Budapest: Central European University Press, 2012), pp. 211–238.

Weiner has shown, postwar social identities in Ukraine were determined above all by the wartime experience, which according to him became the foundation of postwar Soviet identity.[19] The memory of the Holodomor did survive in the Ukrainian diaspora, but not to the same extent as the memory of the West Ukrainian anti-Soviet guerrillas had. It was not, in fact, until the 1980s that the memory of the Holodomor reemerged there, Robert Conquest's famous book *The Harvest of Sorrow* (1986) having played a crucial role in that resurgence. In a sense, the memory of the Holodomor was a typical case of artificially constructed memory, with all the advantages and disadvantages that that entailed.

However, Ukrainian communists and pro-Russian politicians were by no means interested in creating a shared Ukrainian identity expressed through anti-Russian symbols. They sought to downplay the place of the Holodomor (and Stalin's repressions in general) in Ukrainian history and to present it as just one of the many historical tragedies that accompanied the modernization of the Soviet economy. The Kremlin did not go along with Yushchenko either, since to accuse Russia of genocide was to put it on an equal footing with Nazi Germany and thus critically undermine the Russian war myth. In 2009, Russia's puppet president Dmitriy Medvedev even wrote a letter to Viktor Yushchenko in which he formulated his understanding of the Ukrainian famine. He claimed that the Holodomor had been a crime perpetrated by the communist regime against the peoples of the USSR (Russians as well as Ukrainians) rather than a genocide of the Ukrainian people committed by Russia.[20] Yushchenko, of course, was not impressed by Medvedev's arguments.

In 2006, Yushchenko launched an extensive campaign to have the Holodomor recognized as genocide, both domestically and internationally. In October 2008, the European Parliament adopted a resolution that recognized it as a crime against humanity but not explicitly as genocide.[21] Several countries (mostly those with an active Ukrainian diaspora, such as Canada, or that clash with Russia over the interpretation of the past, as many Eastern European countries do) have formally recognized the Holodomor as genocide or at least as a crime against humanity.

---

[19] Amir Weiner, *Making Sense of War: The Second World War and the Fate of the Bolshevik Revolution* (Princeton, N.J.: Princeton University Press, 2001).

[20] D.A. Medvedev, Poslaniye Prezidentu Ukrainy V.A. Yushchenko [Letter to the President of Ukraine V.A. Yushchenko], October 14, 2008.

[21] European Parliament Resolution of 23 October 2008 on the Commemoration of the Holodomor, the Ukraine Artificial Famine (1932–1933).

The increasing glorification of wartime nationalist leaders and the first successes of the ultra-nationalist Svoboda ("Liberty") Party in Western Ukraine's regional election in 2006 caused some moderate Ukrainian politicians to worry about arising fascist danger. One of those moderates was Oleksandr Feldman, a multi-millionaire from Kharkov (the center of the Russian-speaking Eastern Ukraine), a leading Jewish activist, and Rada deputy from the Yulia Tymoshenko Bloc, the centrist party that had been Yushchenko's main ally during and after the Orange Revolution (in 2011, Feldman joined the Party of the Regions because of his disapproval of Tymoshenko's nationalist turn). He was also the founder of Oleksandr Feldman Foundation, which energetically supported the Soviet/Russian cult of the war, in particular by taking care of military graves and war memorials. He vigorously endorsed the criminalization of fascist propaganda and the rallying of forces all across Europe to counter the rise of far-right movements that he saw as a pan-European trend.

With this goal in mind, Feldman approached Boris Spiegel, a Russian oligarch and pro-Kremlin politician who had recently been elected president of the World Congress of Russian Jewry. Born in Ukraine, Spiegel had an extensive business and political network there, especially in circles close to Yanukovych. He threw his support behind Feldman's initiatives, including plans for a huge international anti-fascist conference to be held in the fall of 2009 in Kiev.[22] That conference (moved to Berlin due to the swine flu pandemic) gave birth to a new international human rights movement, World without Nazism, which was formally founded at the following conference, held in Kiev in June 2010, with Spiegel as its chairman. Enjoying powerful backing from the Russian Ministry of Foreign Affairs, that movement has since become one of the key actors in the Eastern European politics of memory. It brings together heterogeneous political forces, from moderate politicians concerned about the rise of anti-Semitism and neo-fascism (such as Feldman and, to some extent, Spiegel himself) to pro-Russian Ukrainian radicals (such as Vadim Kolesnichenko) and Russian nationalists (such as Modest Kolerov), all of whom have been authors of Ukrainian and Russian memory law projects. The World without Nazism milieu gave rise to the new

---

[22] Shimon Briman and Mikhail Fal'kov, "Provokatsiya Kremlya ili bor'ba s geroizatsiyey fashizma: Yekhat' li izrail'skim politikam v Kiev?" [A Kremlin Provocation or a Struggle against the Heroization of Fascism: Should Israeli Politicians Go to Kiev?], *Izrus*, October 8, 2009, and "Opyt velikogo pogroma: Istoriki Kholokosta – 'antiukrainskaya sila'?" [The Experience of the Great Pogrom: Are Historians of the Holocaust an "Anti-Ukrainian Force"?], *Izrus*, November 11, 2009.

conceptual vocabulary used in the Russian and Ukrainian memory laws that defended the Soviet/Russian war myth, two of whose central concepts are the rehabilitation of Nazism and the heroization of Nazi criminals and their accomplices.

Thus the internal Ukrainian debate about the past became interwoven with the Russian-Ukrainian memory war. We will return to the Russian part of the story in Chapter 6 and will focus here on the Ukrainian memory law proposals, which were a privileged weapon in the Ukrainian battles over history.

Legislation about the Past

In contrast to Russia and most Eastern European countries, there were few attempts in Ukraine to legislate on the issues of the past in the 1990s, which comes as no surprise given how circumspect Kravchuk's and Kuchma's politics of memory was. The laws passed during that period were modest in their ambitions, sometimes continuing the Soviet legislative tradition rather than launching a new one. Like other Eastern European countries, Ukraine adopted (even before the fall of the USSR) a law that established procedures for rehabilitating those victims of the communist terror, whose sentences had not been set aside during Khrushchev's rehabilitation campaign of the late 1950s and early 1960s. Many had been members of the anti-Soviet resistance. The 1991 Rehabilitation Act was still very tentative in their regard: only those who had not collaborated with the Nazis and had not been found guilty of war crimes would be entitled to rehabilitation.[23] In October 1993, the Rada passed a bill on veterans' rights that protected the interests of powerful veterans' lobbies and was in many respects similar to a Russian law on veterans of January 1995; both acts, of course, had commemorative implications and promoted the cult of World War II.[24] In 2000, in preparation for the fifty-fifth anniversary of the victory over Nazism, Ukraine adopted a law on the commemoration of the Great Patriotic War, which was modeled after the Russian law of 1995 that had been passed to celebrate the fiftieth anniversary of that victory; the Ukrainian bill even reproduced verbatim some of its predecessor's provisions (e.g., regarding the protection of military

---

[23] Law No. 962-XII of April 17, 1991 "Pro reabiliatsiyu zhertv politichnikh repressiv na Ukraini" [On Rehabilitation of Victims of Political Repressions in Ukraine].

[24] Law No. 3551-XII of October 22, 1993 "Pro status veteraniv viyni, garantii ikh sotsial'nogo zakhistu" [On the Status of War Veterans and on Guaranteeing Their Social Protection].

graves).[25] In contrast to its Russian prototype, though, the Ukrainian law did not declare the struggle against fascism to be the duty of the government, thus avoiding a topic that could potentially lead to a confrontation between various segments of the population. But at the very same time, Ukraine also passed a law granting privileges to the victims of Nazi repressions. Nothing comparable has ever been adopted in Russia, because of its far more "heroic" memory of the war.[26]

At the turn of the 2000s, several memory laws were presented to the Rada, proposing that "fighters for Ukraine's independence" be fully rehabilitated and communist ideology (or, alternatively, the propaganda of fascism) be banned. This signaled the gradual radicalization of the Ukrainian politics of memory.[27] It was not until the Orange Revolution, however, that a new period in the history of Ukrainian memory laws actually began.

The first comprehensive memory law project was introduced into the parliament by Oleh Tyahnibok, the new leader of the Svoboda Party, in 2005. He proposed to ban communist party, symbols, and ideology (although without introducing criminal liability for violations) and to recognize the anti-communist resistance as a struggle for Ukraine's independence. His other suggestions comprised lustration (including "a radical toponymic lustration"), the dismantling of Soviet memorials, the opening of the KGB archives, and the creation of an Institute of National Memory that, similarly to its counterpart in Poland, would be responsible for studying those archives. Tyahnibok's draft, in fact, contained a program of the memory politics that Ukrainian nationalists (and, in a softer form, national liberals) have been trying to implement from the early 2000s all the way to the present.[28] Every one of those norms were included in the "de-communization laws" of April 2015. In 2005, however, the Rada refused to consider Tyahnibok's bill because (its lawyers claimed) it contradicted the constitutional principle of political pluralism.[29]

---

[25] Law No. 1684-III of April 20, 2000 "Pro Uvichnennya Peremogi u Velikiy Vitchiznyaniy viyni 1941–1945 rokiv" [On Perpetuating (the memory of) the Victory in the Great Patriotic War of 1941–1945].

[26] Law No. 1584-III of March 23, 2000 "Pro zhertvi natsistskikh peresliduvan" [On Victims of the Nazi Persecutions].

[27] See bills No. 4189 of May 10, 2001, No. 1154 of June 4, 2002, and No. 1250 of June 20, 2002.

[28] Draft Law No. 8364 of November 1, 2005 "Pro zaboronu komunistichnoy ideologii v Ukraini" [On Prohibiting Communist Ideology in Ukraine].

[29] In 2013, Tyahnibok presented the Rada with almost the same bill (No. 3530 of November 4, 2013).

In 2006, Yushchenko brought to the parliament a draft law that recognized the Holodomor as a genocide of the Ukrainian people and introduced administrative liability for its denial (earlier in the same year, the president had created the Institute of National Memory; although his history politics had largely been inspired by the Polish example, the secret service archives were not transferred to the new institute, as they had been to its Polish counterpart). The Ukrainian parliament accepted the first part of the president's proposal but refused to introduce any penalties for alternative interpretations of the Holodomor. The law reads:

> The Holodomor of 1932–1933 in Ukraine was a genocide of the Ukrainian people.
>
> Public denial of the Holodomor of 1932–1933 in Ukraine is considered desecration of the memory of millions of victims of the Holodomor, an insult to, and humiliation of, the dignity of the Ukrainian people, and is unlawful.[30]

In 2007, Yushchenko proposed a new bill, this time criminalizing "denial of the Holodomor... as a genocide of the Ukrainian people and of the Holocaust as a genocide of the Jewish people."[31] Once again the parliament rejected the bill as a violation of freedom of expression (let me mention parenthetically that the Rada's legal advisers were remarkably consistent in rejecting the criminalization of the past).[32] In the years that followed, the Rada withheld support from several other drafts amending the 2006 Act: the Party of the Regions was proposing to call the Holodomor merely a "tragedy" of the Ukrainian people,[33] while the supporters of Yushchenko and Tymoshenko were pushing for its denial to be criminalized.[34] Symptomatically, a recurrent argument in favor of prohibiting

---

[30] Draft Law No. 2470 of November 2, 2006 "Pro Golodomor 1932–1933 rokiv v Ukraini" [On the Holodomor of 1932–1933 in Ukraine]; Law No. 376-V of November 28, 2006 "Pro Golodomor 1932–1933 rokiv v Ukraini" [On the Holodomor of 1932–1933 in Ukraine]; Kasyanov, *Danse macabre*, pp. 56–69, and Portnov, *Uprazhneniya s istoriyey*, pp. 84–88.

[31] Draft Law No. 1143 of December 7, 2007 "Pro vnesennya zmin do Kriminal'nogo ta Kriminal'nogo-protsessual'nogo kodeksiv Ukraini (shchodo vstanovlennya vidpovidal'nosti za publischne zaperechennya Golodomoru 1932–1933 rokiv v Ukraini" [On Introducing Changes to the Criminal Code and the Code of Criminal Procedure of Ukraine (Regarding the Introduction of Liability for the Public Denial of the Holodomor of 1932–1933 in Ukraine)].

[32] The Rada lawyers' reviews of submitted bills can be found on the parliament's website at the same addresses as the drafts themselves.

[33] See bills No. 6427 of May 26, 2010, and No. 6427–2 of June 16, 2010.

[34] See bills No. 1427 of January 24, 2008; No. 6427–1 of June 9, 2010 (which characterized the Holodomor as "a genocide of the Ukrainian people and a crime against the Ukrainian people [perpetrated by] the All-Union Communist Party (of Bolsheviks) and its filial, the Communist Party of Bolsheviks of Ukraine"); No. 7443 of December 9, 2010; and No. 3165 of September 3,

negationism, as formulated in explanatory notes attached to the bills, was that freedom of speech in a democratic society is not absolute and cannot be used to undermine democracy, which is the main principle that the partisans of militant democracy use in promoting the notion of memory laws.

Following the president's example, various political forces in Ukraine attempted to provide their historical narratives with legal protection, introducing some ninety memory law projects (in the broad sense) into the Rada between 2006 and 2015. The 2008 Prague declaration, the EU Framework Decision, and the spreading of memory laws across Eastern Europe had a powerful impact on Ukrainian history politics. Russia's example was another important influence on the proliferation of those bills: since 2007, and especially 2008, the notion of criminalizing "historical revisionism" with regard to World War II had been rapidly gaining popularity in Moscow.

The wave of memory law drafts in Ukraine reached its acme in 2008–2012, on the eve and in the aftermath of the presidential elections of January 2010 that brought Yanukovych to power, in a win that was largely attributable to a general disappointment with Yushchenko's failure to undertake efficient economic reforms. The years 2008 and 2009 also witnessed a heated confrontation between Russia and its Western neighbors over the interpretation of the past.[35] Upon his coming to power, which coincided with the "reset" in Russo-American relationships and consequently with a lull in the Eastern European memory wars, Yanukovych had tried, if not to return to the "multi-vector" history politics, at least to downplay the political importance of memory issues. However, pro-Russian radicals and communists were in no hurry to make their peace with the "zapadentsy" ("Westerners," a common – and unfriendly –

2013. See also a bill submitted in 2008 by Gennadiy Moscal, a senior official then close to Yushchenko, who proposed to criminalize the use of fascist symbols and "the justification [not "denial"] in Ukraine of genocide, the Holodomor, the Holocaust, deportations, political repressions and crimes against peace and humankind," with the goal of creating an instrument for the prosecution of both far-right and far-left activists. See Draft Law No. 1325 of January 1, 2008 "Pro vnesennya zmin do deyakikh zakonodavchikh aktiv Ukraini (shchodo posilennya vidpovidal'nosti za proyavi ekstremizmu, ksenofobii, antisemitiszmu, rasovoy i religioznoy neterpimosti" [On Introducing Changes to Certain Legislative Acts of Ukraine (Regarding an Increase in the Liability for Manifestations of Extremism, Xenophobia, Anti-Semitism, and Racial and Religious Intolerance)]. The main concept that Moscal used in describing those offenses was that of extremism. See also his bill No. 5276 of October 26, 2009, from which the mention of both the Holocaust and the Holodomor has disappeared and which proposed merely the prohibition of extremist activities.

[35] See Chapter 6.

epithet for Western Ukrainians in the east of the country).[36] It was not until 2013 that memory law projects began to be seen as an overused political weapon, especially given the politicians' obvious failure to find historical symbols that would be accepted by most Ukrainians.[37]

A detailed discussion of all those bills is out of the question here, not least because an overwhelming majority was rejected by the parliament as underdeveloped (indeed, while reading those drafts, one can hardly escape the impression that their authors saw them mostly as a means of self-promotion). A characteristic feature of those legislative battles consisted in the fact that many bills formed a sort of chain: often, the same author re-introduced, with almost no revision, a bill that had already been rejected by the parliament; and when one party presented its bills, other parties typically responded with alternative drafts. I will therefore limit myself here to a brief summary of the main categories of bills proposed.[38]

Most bills submitted by communists and pro-Russian radicals from the Party of the Regions criminalized fascist propaganda, the "rehabilitation of Nazism," and the desecration of military graves and war memorials. In January 2009, Vadim Kolesnichenko, an MP from the Party of the Regions, presented his bill "On Banning the Rehabilitation and Heroiza-tion of Fascist Collaborationists in 1933–1945," which was rejected by the parliament because of its imprecise language.[39] (Much later, in January 2014, Kolesnichenko would reportedly sponsor the "dictatorship laws" adopted by the Rada to halt the escalation of democratic protests against Yanukovych's regime.) Kolesnichenko's bill of January 2009 was the first-ever instance (to my knowledge) in which the expression "rehabilitation and heroization" of Nazi criminals was used in a memory law draft. (Since December 2008, Russian nationalists Zatulin and Kolerov had also been working on a bill of their own, in which they used a similar formula, but their draft was not ready until April 2009.) The penalty foreseen by the Kolesnichenko bill was deprivation of liberty for up to fifteen years (which the Rada experts assessed as disproportionate, because Ukrainian law provided such lengthy punishments only for intentional actions resulting

---

[36] Georgiy Kasianov, "The 'Nationalization' of History in Ukraine," in *The Convolutions of Historical Politics*, p. 164.

[37] To my knowledge, fifteen bills relating to historical memory were presented to the Rada in 2008, sixteen in 2009, thirteen in 2010, twelve in 2011, eleven in 2012, and seven in 2013.

[38] For more details, see my "Ustawy memorialne w Rosji i na Ukrainie: krzyżujące się historie" [Memory Laws in Russia and Ukraine: Intersecting Stories], *Rocznik Instytutu Europy Środkowo-Wschodniej* 13/2 (2015), pp. 167–216.

[39] Draft Law No. 3612 of 15 January 2009 "Pro zaboronu reabilitatsii ta geroizatsii fashistskikh kollaboratsionistiv 1933–1945 rokakh."

in death). Later, in September 2011, Kolesnichenko proposed prohibiting the use of fascist symbols and the dissemination of fascist materials in a bill that was, at least in part, a verbatim reproduction of the 2002 Russian law against extremism.[40] In May 2013, he came up with a new version of his 2009 draft; this time, the bill forbade the rehabilitation of persons and organizations that had fought against the anti-Hitler coalition, and the maximum penalty was reduced to eight years' incarceration. In other words, the accent had shifted from siding with the Nazis to battling Russia, which corresponded to the spirit of the Russian war myth.[41] The reference to the anti-Hitler coalition was probably borrowed from the Russian project of 2009 (the first draft of Irina Yarovaya's bill),[42] whose third version was about to be presented to the Duma, also in May 2013. The proximity in time and similarity in content between Kolesnichenko's drafts and the Russian memory law projects suggests that there had been some coordination of effort.

The same is true of the bills presented by Petro Simonenko, the leader of Ukrainian communists, who (alone or with colleagues) presented the Rada with no less than eight memory bills that prohibited the rehabilitation of Nazism and the desecration of Soviet soldiers' graves. The first appeared in July 2009, just two months after the first draft of the Yarovaya bill was presented, and the similarity between the two is striking: Simonenko proposed criminalizing "the public denial of facts established by the Judgment of the International Military Tribunal... with the goal of rehabilitating Nazism, Nazi criminals and their accomplices,"[43] while Yarovaya's intention was to prohibit the "distortion of the Judgment of the Nuremberg Tribunal... with the aim of fully or partially rehabilitating Nazism and Nazi criminals."[44] When the Duma did not support the Russian bill because of the "reset" of Russo-American relations, Simonenko came up (in March 2010) with a new draft, which did not refer to

---

[40] For example, the expression "publicly displaying Nazi attributes or symbols or attributes or symbols that are confusingly similar to Nazi attributes or symbols" is used in both documents. See Draft Law No. 9156 of September 15, 2011 "Pro protidiyu ekstremizmu" [On Counteracting Extremism]. For the 2002 Russian law, see Chapter 5.

[41] Draft Law No. 2950 of May 8, 2013 "Pro zaboronu reabilitatsii ta geroizatsii osib i organizatsiy, shcho borolisya proti antigitlerovskoy koalitsii" [On Prohibiting the Rehabilitation and Heroization of Persons and Organizations That Fought against the Anti-Hitler Coalition].

[42] See Chapter 6.

[43] Draft Law No. 4745 of July 1, 2009 "Pro vnesennya zmin do deyakikh kodeksiv Ukraini (shchodo vidpovidal'nosti za publichne viroku Mizhnarodnogo viys'kovogo tribunalu u m. Nyurnberg)" [On Introducing Changes to Some Codes of Ukraine (Regarding Liability for Publicly Denying the Judgment of the International Military Tribunal in the City of Nuremberg)].

[44] See Chapter 6.

the Nuremberg Judgment (a seemingly "European" strategy that had failed even in Russia) but, using more familiar terms, simply prohibited the propaganda of fascism.[45] The third version (co-authored with communist deputy Ihor Bevz) was presented by Simonenko in February 2011 and synthesized the approaches of 2009 and 2010. The bill banned

> The propaganda or public glorification of Nazism and fascism, denial or justification of crimes against humanity perpetrated during the Second World War, including crimes committed by the Waffen-SS and those who fought against the anti-Hitler coalition and collaborated with the Nazi movement and fascist occupiers, as well as incitement to, and practical actions aimed at, the propaganda of neo-Nazism, neo-fascism, and an aggressive nationalist ideology.[46]

The proposed punishment was up to two years' deprivation of liberty. Here too, the reference to the anti-Hitler coalition was probably borrowed from the Russian bill. Somewhat later, in 2012, when Putin's policy took a radical conservative turn in response to protests against the rigged elections of December 2011, Simonenko and Bevz submitted two more versions of the same bill, which, like the initial 2009 draft, focused now on the denial of Nazi crimes (the last one was passed as part of the "dictatorship legislation" in January 2014).[47]

Similar bills promoting the Soviet/Russian war myth were presented by two members of the Party of the Regions – Oleh Tsarev, a future leader of Donbass separatists, and Yuriy Miroshnichenko, who after the 2010 presidential elections became Yanukovych's representative in the Rada. Both proposals aimed at prohibiting fascist ideology, and Tsarev's bill also penalized the rehabilitation of Ukrainian organizations that had collaborated with Nazism (the draft provided a list that included both the OUN and the UPA).[48]

---

[45] Draft Law No. 4745 of March 11, 2010 "Pro zaboronu propagandi fashizmu ta natsizmu v Ukraini" [On prohibiting propaganda of Fascism and Nazism in Ukraine].

[46] Draft Law No. 8149 of February 22, 2011 "Pro vnesennya zmin do deyakikh kodeksiv Ukraini (shchodo vidpovidal'nosti za propagandu natsizmu i fashizmu)" [On Introducing Changes to Some Codes of Ukraine (Regarding the Liability for Public Denial or Justification of Crimes of Nazism and Fascism)].

[47] Draft Law No. 10050 of February 15, 2012 "Pro vnesennya zmin do Kriminal'nogo kodeksu Ukraini shchodo vidpovidal'nosti za publichne zaperechennya chi vipravdannya zlochinstv fashizmu" [On Introducing Changes to the Criminal Code of Ukraine Regarding Liability for the Public Denial or Justification of the Crimes of Fascism]; see also a later version of this draft (No. 11150 of September 3, 2012).

[48] Bills No. 5247 of October 20, 2009 "Pro osnovy zapobigannya ta protidii propaganda natsizmu i fashizmu v Ukraini" [On Principles of the Prevention, and Counteraction of the Propaganda of Nazism and Fascism in Ukraine] and No. 5247-1 of November 12, 2009 "Pro zaboronu

Another batch of communist-sponsored bills were intended to amend Article 297 of the Penal Code on the desecration of graves. The first was brought to the Rada in April 2009, a month after it had adopted a similar law proposed by a group of centrist deputies that had increased the maximum punishment for such desecration from three to five years, if that desecration was an act of hooliganism or had been committed against a mass military burial known as a "bed of honor" or against a grave where unknown soldiers were interred.[49] The communists, however, wanted to make the connection to the Russian war myth even more explicit, by penalizing "the desecration of the memory of the Soviet soldier-liberators,"[50] while some representatives of nationalist and liberal parties preferred to increase penalties for acts of vandalism aimed at inciting racial, national, or religious hatred (which would allow for the protection of Jewish cemeteries as well as the graves of the victims of the Holodomor or of Ukraine's independence fighters).[51] When the 2009 communist project was turned down by the Rada, Simonenko and his colleagues submitted another three similar drafts, the last of which was passed in January 2014.[52]

Of course, nationalists and national liberals also had their projects, which typically included bills proposing full rehabilitation for participants in the struggle for Ukraine's independence, prohibition of desecration of their graves, and a ban on communist ideology and symbols. Often those

propagandi fashizmu ta natsizmu v Ukraini" [On Prohibiting Propaganda of Fascism and Nazism in Ukraine].

[49] Draft Law No. 2160 of March 4, 2008 "Pro vnesennya zmin do deyakikh zakonodavchikh aktiv Ukraini shchodo posilennya vidpovidal'nosti za nadrugu nad mogiloyu ta inshimi mistsyzmi pokhovannya" [On Introducing Changes to Certain Legislative Acts of Ukraine Regarding an Increase in Liability for the Desecration of Graves and Other Burial Places]. The bill was adopted on March 19, 2009 as Law No. 1166-VI.

[50] Draft Law No. 4362 of April 14, 2009 "Pro vnesennya zmin do statti 297 Kriminal'nogo kodeksu Ukraini (shchodo posilennya kriminal'noy vidpovidal'nosti za nadrugu nad pamyatyu radyans'kikh voiniv-vizvoliteliv" [On Introducing Changes to Article 297 of the Criminal Code of Ukraine (Regarding an Increase in Criminal Liability for the Desecration of the Memory of the Soviet Soldier-Liberators)].

[51] Draft Law No. 4076 of February 18, 2009 "Pro vnesennya zmin do Kriminal'nogo kodeksu Ukraini shchodo vidpovidal'nosti za nadrugu nad mogiloyu abo znishchennya, ruynuvannya chi poshkodzhennya pam'yatok-ob'yektiv kul'turnoy spadshchini z motiviv natsional'noy, rasovoy chi religioznoy nenavisti abo vorozhnechi" [On Introducing Changes to the Criminal Code of Ukraine Regarding Liability for the Desecration of Graves or Destruction, Demolition, or Damaging of Memorials and Objects of Cultural Heritage out of National, Racial, or Religious Hatred or Hostility].

[52] Bills No. 8150 of February 22, 2011; No. 10077 of February 17, 2012 (both drafts were submitted to coincide with the celebration of February 23, which was an old Soviet holiday – Soviet Army Day); and No. 11167 of September 4, 2012.

projects were no more than responses to pro-Russian initiatives. Thus, Vyacheslav Kirilenko authored and co-authored several bills criminalizing communist ideology and acts of vandalism against the graves of independence fighters, all of which were introduced into the Rada shortly after Simonenko's aforementioned projects. Kirilenko was the leader of the For Ukraine! Party and a long-standing partner of the future Ukrainian Prime Minister, Arseniy Yatsenyuk (in 2014, Kirilenko became Vice-Prime Minister and Minister of Culture in Yatsenyuk's government). In February 2011, he proposed punishing "the propaganda of totalitarian ideologies and practices of communism, Nazism, and fascism" (in that order)[53] with exactly the same penalties (up to two years) envisaged by Simonenko's bill on the propaganda of fascism that had appeared a week earlier. And when in 2012 Simonenko proposed criminalizing the denial of Nazi crimes rather than the advocacy of fascist ideology, Kirilenko responded with two drafts that banned "the public denial or approval of the crimes of Nazism and Stalinism" and "the public denial of the Holodomor as a genocide of the Ukrainian people and of the Holocaust as a genocide of the Jewish people" (the latter proposal drew directly from Yushchenko's 2007 draft).[54] Criminalizing both denials at the same time implied that communist crimes were tantamount to Nazi crimes, and could also preempt accusations of anti-Semitism that could potentially be leveled against Ukrainian nationalists. With regard to the desecration of graves, Kirilenko proposed the same increase in punishment as Simonenko but applied it only to acts of vandalism against the graves of "participants in the national liberation struggle for Ukraine's freedom and independence,... victims of repressions of the totalitarian communist regime, and victims of the genocide of 1932–1933."[55]

53 Draft Law 8149–1 of February 28, 2011 "Pro vnesennya zmin do deyakikh kodeksiv Ukraini (shchodo vidpovidal'nosti za propagandu totalitarnoy ideologii ta praktiki komunismu, natsizmu, fashizmu)" [On Introducing Changes to Some Codes of Ukraine (Regarding the Liability for the Propaganda of the Totalitarian Ideology and Practice of Communism, Nazism, and Fascism)].

54 Draft Law No. 11150–1 of September 14, 2012 "Pro vnesennya zmin do Kriminal'nogo kodeksu Ukraini shchodo vstanovlennya kriminal'noy vidpovidal'nosti za publichne zaperechennya chi vipravdannya zlochinstv natsizma ta stalinizmu" [On Introducing Changes to the Criminal Code of Ukraine Regarding the Introduction of Criminal Liability for Public Denial or Justification of Crimes of Nazism and Stalinism]. See also Kirilenko's bill No. 2729 of April 4, 2013, where the same article criminalizing denial of communist and Nazi crimes was inserted into the Penal Code after the article on genocide, rather than after the article on the propaganda of war (as had been the case in 2012), which served to emphasize that communist and Nazi crimes had been equally racist and that the Holodomor, like the Holocaust, had been a genocide.

55 Draft Law No. 8150–1 of February 28, 2011 "Pro vnesennya zmin do statti 297 Kriminal'nogo kodeksu Ukraini (shchodo posilennya kriminal'noy vidpovidal'nosti za nadrugu nad mogilami uchastnikiv borot'by za svobodu y nezalyezhnist' Ukraini, zhertv repressiy ta genotsidu)" [On

Other anti-communist drafts included two projects submitted by a group of deputies from Yushchenko's Our Ukraine bloc, who in 2009 proposed one bill on lustration and another prohibiting communist ideology and symbols (although without penalizing their use).[56] The explanatory note gives the following rationale for the latter law:

> In the history of the twentieth century, the Jewish people has successfully performed its mission by securing international condemnation of Nazi ideology; today the hour has come for the Ukrainian people to secure international condemnation of communist ideology as criminal and founded on hatred toward humanity.[57]

The category of bills aimed at protecting the memory of "the fighters for Ukraine's independence" was not, however, limited to the aforementioned projects that banned the desecration of their graves. Several drafts proposed granting full rehabilitation to members of OUN, UPA, and other Ukrainian nationalist organizations, and recognizing them as "a party to World War II," alongside Nazi Germany and the USSR (rather than as traitors, terrorists, or Nazi collaborators, as they are customarily viewed in Russia). According to the authors of those bills (who were all members of either the Yushchenko or the Tymoshenko bloc), the nationalist guerillas' activities were a national liberation movement "against the German-fascist occupiers and Stalin's totalitarian regime."[58] Those laws were largely declarative in nature, and their practical ambition went no further than conferring the status of war veterans on former members of the UPA. The explanatory note to one of those drafts claimed that

> All of Europe has long ago effected a reconciliation between soldiers who fought on either side of the frontline on the eve of and during the Second

Introducing Changes to Article 297 of the Criminal Code of Ukraine (Regarding an Increase in Criminal Liability for the Desecration of Graves of Participants in the Struggle for Freedom and Independence of Ukraine and of Victims of Repressions and Genocide)]. See also Kirilenko's bills No. 10249 of March 22, 2012 and No. 11167-1 of September 14, 2012. Their titles were modified to ensure that the words "repressions and genocide" referred specifically to "repressions of the totalitarian communist regime and the genocide of 1932–1933" [the Holodomor].

[56] Draft Law No. 5389 of December 1, 2009 "Pro Lyustratsiyu" [On Lustration]; Draft Law No. 5382 of November 26, 2009 "Pro zaboronu komunistichnoy ideologiyi ta likvidatsiyu simvoliv totalitarnogo ta komunistichnogo rezhimiv" [On Prohibiting Communist Ideology and Liquidating Symbols of Totalitarian and Communist Regimes].

[57] Explanatory Note to Draft Law No. 5382 of November 26, 2009.

[58] Draft Law No. 1404 of January 30, 2008 "Pro viznannya Ogranizatsii Ukrains'kikh Natsionalistiv i Ukrains'koy Povstans'koy Armii voyuyuchoyu storonoyu u Drugiy svitoviy viyni" [On Recognizing the Organization of Ukrainian Nationalists and the Ukrainian Insurgent Army as a Party to the Second World War]: See also Draft Law No. 4180 of March 10, 2009, which reproduced the title and some passages of the 2008 draft almost verbatim.

World War. [The Baltic countries] have even ventured to recognize the presence of Soviet troops on their territories as an occupation. And only Ukraine is still afraid to recognize soldiers of the UPA as a party to the war. All of them, soldiers of the UPA and the Red Army [the Soviet army], fought for Ukraine, although viewing it from different viewpoints.[59]

The rhetoric of national reconciliation is applied very inconsistently in this draft, for recognizing that the Red Army fought "for Ukraine" is hardly compatible with the assessment of its victory in the Baltic countries as an occupation. To pro-Russian Ukrainian activists, those bills, aimed as they were at rehabilitating nationalist guerrillas, were highly reminiscent of the rehabilitation and heroization of "Nazi allies."

As we see, the Ukrainian war of laws reflected vehement political disagreements about the past.[60] There were, however, more moderate drafts too. Thus, Oleksandr Feldman proposed several bills imposing administrative liability for Nazi propaganda, and the Rada rejected them all on the grounds that the existing anti-racist norms already provided criminal liability for comparable offenses.[61]

Some projects sought to provide benefits for the victims of Soviet repressions, including the Crimean Tatars[62] and those Ukrainians who

[59] Explanatory Note to Draft Law No. 5373 of November 23, 2009 "Pro viznannya borot'by Ukrains'koy Povstans'koy Armii natsional'no-vizvol'noyu borot'boyu za vidnovlennya Ukrains'koy nezalyozhnoy derzhavi, viznannya Ukrains'koy Povstans'koy Armii voyuyuchoyu storonoyu u Drugiy svitoviy viyni. . . ." [On Recognizing the Struggle of the Ukrainian Insurgent Army as a National-Liberation Struggle for the Restoration of the Ukrainian Independent State, Recognizing the Ukrainian Insurgent Army as a Party to the Second World War. . .]. See also Draft Law 5373–1 of November 27, 2009.

[60] Law No. 3298-VI of April 21, 2011 (submitted as Draft Law No. 4355 of April 14, 2009) provides another example of that. This document, clearly inspired by the 2007 Russian law "On the Banner of Victory," amended the 2000 legislation on perpetuating the memory of the victory over Nazism and specified the rules for using the red Soviet flag during the Victory Day celebrations. In response to a wave of protests, especially in Western Ukraine, the Constitutional Court (Decision No. 6 – rp/ 2011 of June 16, 2011) invalidated its most debatable article (according to which, during those celebrations, "the Banner of Victory" had to be displayed along with the flag of Ukraine) on the ground that the Ukrainian constitution does not consider the Banner of Victory a Ukrainian state symbol.

[61] Draft Law 2024 of February 8, 2008 "Pro vnesennya zmin do deyakikh zakonodavchikh aktiv Ukraini (shchodo vidpovidal'nosti za publichne skhvalennya i propaganda idey natsizmu ta inshikh diskriminatsiynikh ideologiy)" [On Introducing Changes to Certain Legislative Acts of Ukraine (Regarding the Liability for Public Glorification and Propaganda of the Ideas of Nazism and Other Discriminatory Ideologies)]. Feldman withdrew his first draft, which proposed to criminalize those offenses when committed by group action, shortly after submitting it, and limited himself in his following proposals to imposing only administrative liability (see bills No. 2024 of April 17, 2008, and No. 1395–1 of January 23, 2008).

[62] See Draft Law No. 3142 of September 11, 2008, submitted by Prime Minister Yulia Tymoshenko on behalf of the government, "Pro vidnovlennya prav osob, deportovanikh za natsional'noyu oznakoyu" [On Restoring the Rights of Persons Deported on the Basis of Their National Origin]

had been deported from Poland after World War II[63] (which shows that the memory conflict with Poland was still ongoing). Other laws concerned issues of toponymy. Thus, the communists were proposing a ban on renaming cities or streets whose current names honored war heroes and the like.[64] Finally, a draft law submitted in February 2011 by deputies from the Our Ukraine party prohibited the erection of monuments to Stalin and other Soviet leaders responsible for the Holodomor.[65]

In November 2013, Yanukovych decided to postpone signing the Association Agreement with the EU and instead to follow Russia's urging and join the Eurasian Customs Union, which triggered an acute political crisis that led to the fall of his regime in February 2014.[66] On January 16, Yanukovych's partisans in the Rada illegally (in violation of parliamentary procedures) passed a series of "dictatorship laws," most of which were modeled after recent Russian enactments adopted upon Putin's return in the Kremlin in 2012 to strengthen his authoritarian regime. Two of those anti-democratic laws dealt with historical memory, and both had been authored by Simonenko, although Vadim Kolesnichenko, who had reportedly played a crucial role in the events of January 16, had also had comparable projects of his own. The fact that Simonenko's bills prevailed shows that the Party of the Regions was seeking to ensure the communists' support of what was, to all intents and purposes, a coup. The first of the two memory laws introduced Article 436.1 into the Penal Code, to provide a penalty of up to two years' incarceration for

> The public denial or justification of fascist crimes against humanity perpetrated during the Second World War, including crimes committed by the Waffen-SS and its subordinate structures, and those who fought against the anti-Hitler coalition and collaborated with the fascist occupiers, as well as the propaganda of neo-Nazi ideology and the fabrication

and the bill authored by Mustafa Dzhemilev, Chairman of the Mejlis of the Crimean Tatar People, No. 5515 of February 24, 2010, under the same title.
[63] Four such bills were proposed with minor changes by Mikhailo Kosiv from Yulia Tymoshenko's party. See Draft Laws No. 1398 of January 28, 2008; No. 4783 of July 8, 2009; No. 7152 of September 21, 2010; and No. 8692 of June 16, 2011. All were rejected by the Rada.
[64] Draft Law No. 1040 of December 12, 2012, resubmitted with minor changes as Draft Law No. 2180a on May 30, 2013.
[65] Draft Law No. 8115 of February 16, 2001.
[66] Andrew Wilson, *Ukraine Crisis: What It Means for the West* (New Haven, Conn.: Yale University Press, 2014).

and/or dissemination of materials that justify the crimes of the fascists and their accomplices.[67]

Here we can clearly see the influence of both the 2009 Russian draft and the Ukrainian communists' particular concerns about the Waffen-SS and its subordinate structures (such as the Waffen-SS's volunteer Galicia Division or the Nachtigall Battalion, which had consisted, to varying degrees, of Ukrainians). However, the reference to the anti-Hitler coalition is used here only to ban the rehabilitation of OUN and UPA, not to outlaw criticism of Stalinism, which is why the Simonenko Act is closer to the Western European model than to the Russian one. The second memory law of January 16 added to Article 297 of the Penal Code a paragraph increasing the punishment for desecration of graves to a maximum of five years if those acts were committed against military cemeteries and war memorials "erected in the memory of those who struggled against Nazism during the Second World War – Soviet soldier-liberators, participants in the partisan and underground resistance movements, and victims of Nazi persecutions, as well as internationalist warriors and peacekeepers." Penalties for the same deeds committed by a group were increased to up to seven years.[68] The list of categories of protected graves (including those of "victims of Nazi persecution") was based on the 1993 law on veterans, and the expression "internationalist warriors" referred to participants in the Afghanistan war and other similar Soviet operations.

On January 28, the dictatorship laws were repealed under pressure from public opinion at home and abroad.[69] On the same day, however, the Rada once again passed both memory bills,[70] which shows that the coalition of liberals and nationalists was prepared to make concessions in symbolic politics so as not to alienate any potential ally against Yanukovych. Both laws remained in effect (although they were never applied) until April 2015, when the new Ukrainian government decided that it had

[67] Law No. 729-VII of January 16, 2014 "Pro vnesennya zmini do Kriminal'nogo kodeksu Ukraini shchodo vidpovidal'nosti za zaperechennya chi vidpravdannya zlochiniv fashizmu" [On Introducing Changes to the Criminal Code of Ukraine Regarding Liability for the Denial or Justification of the Crimes of Fascism].
[68] Law No. 728-VII of January 16, 2014 "Pro vnesennya zmini do statti 297 Kriminal'nogo kodeksu Ukraini shchodo vidpovidal'nosti za oskvernennya abo ruynuvannya pamyatnikiv, sporudzhenikh v pamyat' tikh, khto borovsya proti natsizmu v roki Drugoy svitovoy viyni..." [On Introducing a Change to Article 297 of the Criminal Code of Ukraine Regarding Liability for the Desecration and Destruction of Memorials Erected to Honor Those Who Struggled against Nazism During World War II...].
[69] Law 732-VII of January 28, 2014.
[70] Both laws (Nos. 735-VII and 734-VII) were passed in exactly the same form and under the same names.

become strong enough to give the force of law to its own historical narrative. The Russian annexation of Crimea in 2014 and the war in Donbass had, in fact, considerably weakened pro-Kremlin forces in Ukraine and undermined the appeal of the Russian war myth.

Plans for new legislation regarding the past began to emerge as of the fall of 2014, when deputies from the Svoboda Party submitted a bill that reproduced the 2007 Yushchenko bill, which criminalized denial of the Holocaust and the Holodomor.[71] The authors, however, retracted the project just a few days later. Soon thereafter, the government took the initiative, and in April 2015, Prime Minister Yatsenyuk presented to the Rada three de-communization bills prepared by the Ukrainian Institute of National Memory (explanatory notes to them were signed by the Institute's director Volodymyr Viatrovych), which the government had tapped to become the main instrument of its de-communization policy (under Yanukovych, the Institute had been transformed into a research institution).

The Institute had drawn up three carefully interrelated drafts that represented a compromise between the narrative of the struggle for Ukraine's independence and a modified version of the Soviet/Russian war myth. Those bills dealt respectively with the opening of the secret services archives, the memory of the victory over fascism, and the legal status of participants in the national liberation movement. The first draft resembled similar laws that had been adopted long ago in most post-communist countries. The second, which was to replace the 2000 law on the commemoration of the victory, attempted to incorporate the memory of the war into the new Ukrainian national narrative by purifying it of its imperial Soviet overtones. Finally, the third, and most important, bill was intended to give legal protection to the Ukrainian narrative, the main theme of which was to be the country's century-long struggle for independence, as is also typical of most Eastern European national romances.

At exactly the same time, two other bills were introduced into the parliament by representatives of Oleh Lyashko's Radical Party, which had emerged in 2014 as Ukraine's most influential ultra-nationalist party. One was submitted by Yuriy Shukhevych, son of UPA leader Roman Shukhevych, which gave his proposal special clout in the eyes of Ukrainian nationalists (Yuriy Shukhevych, who had spent most of his life in Soviet camps, had been one of the most visible Ukrainian dissidents). This bill

---

[71] Draft Law No. 5202 of November 24, 2014.

was an alternative to the government's analogous project. The second, "On Condemnation of Communist and National Socialist (Nazi) Regimes in Ukraine and on a Ban on the Dissemination of their Symbols," was submitted by a group of deputies that included, along with a number of Radical Party members, several representatives of other centrist and nationalist parties, from the Petro Poroshenko bloc to Svoboda; Lyashko's name headed the list of authors.

In Spring 2015, the Radical Party was still a member of the ruling coalition, and the centrists (the Poroshenko and Yatsenyuk parties) could not ignore its position. For that reason a compromise was achieved to submit four bills for the Rada's consideration: two drafts from the government's original package (on the archives and on the victory over fascism) and the Lyashko and Shukhevych projects. This package of decommunization bills proved significantly more radical than the government's initial proposal.

The four bills had an easy passage through the Rada on April 9, 2015, but drew sharp criticism, both domestically and internationally. Thus, a group of highly reputed (mostly American and European) specialists in Ukrainian history wrote a letter to President Poroshenko asking him not to sign the bills into law, given that they contravened freedom of speech and imposed a problematic conception of history. The letter resembled the aforementioned petitions submitted by French and American historians against memory laws (as well as the petitions signed by Russian historians against the 2009 Russian bill). Characteristically, it called on Poroshenko not to follow Putin's example of politicizing history and to return to the Ukrainian tradition of tolerance with regard to varying historical narratives. However, the President, although not without hesitation, approved the bills.[72]

The law on the archives is perhaps the least problematic, for it simply states that Soviet archives (including the security files) must be declassified and moved to the Institute of National Memory for safekeeping and study.[73] The law on the victory over fascism differs significantly from its

---

[72] Soon after this, a group of deputies from the Opposition Bloc presented a bill to repeal the Lyashko Act for the sake of freedom of speech. At the time of writing, that project was still under consideration in the Rada. See Draft Law 2905 of May 19, 2015.

[73] Law No. 316-VIII of April 9, 2015 "Pro dostup do arkhiviv repressivnykh organiv komunistichnogo totalitarnogo rezhimu 1917–1991 rokiv" [On Access to the Archives of Repressive Bodies of the Communist Totalitarian Regime of 1917–1991]. However, as John-Paul Himka notes, the law concerns only the Soviet security archives and says nothing about those containing materials on the Ukrainian police under the German occupation. See Himka

counterpart of 2000, even while reproducing some of the latter's passages (especially on war memorials and military graves) almost without change. But the name of the event is changed in the new law, which speaks of World War II rather than the Great Patriotic War (following countless suggestions made in preceding years to ban the Soviet name for the war). The Rada recognizes (the law states) "the world-historical significance of the victory over Nazism," which is a quotation from the 2000 Act, but with the omission of the words "of the Soviet Union" following the word "victory," which changes everything: a "victory over Nazism" can be glossed as the liberation of Ukraine, whereas a "victory of the Soviet Union" would mean its occupation. The law also holds that "the Second World War began as a result of an agreement between the national socialist... regime in Germany and the communist totalitarian regime in the USSR" (Preamble). Unquestionably, retaining the name of the Great Patriotic War would scarcely be compatible with accusing the USSR of having unleashed that war. The law also mentions crimes against humanity perpetrated by both regimes against Ukrainians but not the participation of Ukrainians themselves in some of those crimes (which, as we know, is typical of Eastern European political rhetoric).

The key difference between the laws of 2000 and 2015 consists in the fact that the latter holds that "war veterans, members of the Ukrainian independence movement, and victims of Nazism" are equally entitled to respect of their memory. The emphasis has obviously shifted here from the heroic myth of soldier-liberators to the memory of the victims, and fallen soldiers on both sides – the Soviet army and the anti-Soviet resistance – are now considered victims rather than heroes. This explains the main practical innovation introduced by the law: "With the goal of honoring the memory of all victims of the Second World War... a Day of Remembrance and Reconciliation is established in Ukraine, to be celebrated annually on May 8" (Article 1.2). However, May 9 has also been kept as "a State holiday – the Day of the Victory over Nazism" (Article 1.3). The lawmakers have manifestly attempted to leave room for all memories of the war, from which the less established tradition of commemorating the anti-Soviet resistance could only profit.[74]

"Legislating Historical Truth: Ukraine's Laws of April 9, 2015," April 21, 2015: http://net.abimperio.net/node/3442.

[74] Law No. 315-VIII of April 9, 2015 "Pro uvichnennya peremogi nad natsizmom u Drugiy svitoviy viyni 1939–1945 rokiv" [On Commemorating the Victory over Nazism in World War II of 1939–1945].

The Shukhevych Act – as well as the parallel Yatsenyuk project – continues two themes of previous memory law drafts, namely, the rehabilitation of those involved in the struggle for Ukraine's independence (including the OUN and the UPA) and a ban on the desecration of their graves. Both projects go far beyond previous proposals: they explicitly assess the struggle for independence as the main aspect of Ukrainian history. The government's project refers here to the 1973 UN declaration on the legitimacy of national liberation movements and underlines, in the spirit of the 1991 Rehabilitation Act, that a struggle for independence is legitimate to the extent that "its goals, forms, and methods do not contradict the UN Charter, the Universal Declaration of Human Rights, and other international legal acts" (Preamble). The clear implication of this is that those Ukrainian nationalists who had committed acts of genocide or war crimes were not eligible for rehabilitation. One finds no similar provisions in the Shukhevych Act, which rehabilitates members of the OUN and UPA without reservation and was, not surprisingly, received very negatively in Poland, since both organizations had been involved in the 1943 massacre of the Polish population in Volhynia.

Both the Shukhevych Act and the government's project focus on the ways in which the Ukrainian state must perpetuate the memory of the struggle for independence (by supporting research and teaching, creating commemorative museums, and so on). Yatsenyuk's bill mentioned liability for encroaching upon the rights and interests of fighters for independence (Article 7.1), which presumably entailed banning discrimination against them, but it introduced no new penalties for those offenses. In contrast, the Shukhevych Act bans any criticism of the independence movement and specifically "lack of respect" toward its participants and "public denial of the lawfulness of the struggle for Ukraine's independence in the twentieth century" (Article 6.1). The law states that such denial "is recognized as an outrage toward the memory of fighters for Ukraine's freedom in the twentieth century and as a disparagement of the Ukrainian people, and is unlawful" (Article 6.2). However, the law has introduced no special sanctions for those acts (as some Western laws, including the 2005 Mekachera Act, have also avoided doing).[75]

---

[75] Law No. 314-VIII of April 9, 2015 "Pro pravovoy status ta vshanuvannya pamyati bortsiv za nezalezhnist' Ukraini u XX stolitti" [On the Legal Status and Honoring the Memory of the Fighters for Ukraine's Independence in the Twentieth Century]. See also the government's project No. 2538 of April 3, 2015. The only difference between its title and that of the adopted law is that the government uses the less emotionally charged expression "participants in the struggle for

Finally, the Lyashko Act develops the tradition of anti-communist projects as represented in particular by the Tyahnibok and Kirilenko bills. The law recognizes both communist and fascist regimes as criminal enterprises guilty of pursuing a "policy of state terror," with no attempt to differentiate between them (or between Stalinism and the late Soviet period). The law bans "the public denial of the criminal character" of the communist and Nazi regimes as well as the use of communist and Nazi symbols, offenses that can result in the deregistration of any political parties or media outlets that commit them (Articles 1.2, 2, 3.1). The law also prescribes a "symbolic lustration" (to use Tyahnibok's expression), the demolition of Soviet monuments (which inaugurated the *Leninopad*, literally "Lenin's fall," a mass destruction of Lenin's statues), and changes in communist toponymy. The Lyashko Act also introduced criminal liability (incarceration for up to five years and up to ten years under aggravating circumstances) for "producing, disseminating, and publicly using the symbols of communist and national-socialist totalitarian regimes" (Article 7.2).[76] However, in contrast to the Simonenko Act of January 2014, none of these de-communization laws explicitly introduced a ban on statements about the past (although the Shukhevych Act does declare certain statements illegal, as the 2006 law on the Holodomor also did).

The adoption of the de-communization laws was not the end of the legislation on the issues of the past in Ukraine. In February 2016, a group of deputies introduced in the parliament a project proposing to criminalize "public denial of the Holodomor... as genocide of the Ukrainian people, of the Holocaust as genocide of the Jewish people, and of the deportations of the Crimean Tatars in 1944 as genocide of the Crimean Tatar people."[77] This is obviously the old Yushchenko project, with the deportations of the Crimean Tatars now included alongside the Holocaust and the Holodomor. The memory of the 1944 deportations has become a hot

---

independence" instead of "fighters for independence," which reflects the more moderate character of the government's project.

[76] Law No. 317-VIII of April 9, 2015 "Pro zasuzhdennya komunistichnogo ta natsional-sotsialistichnogo (natsists'kogo) rezhimov v Ukraini ta zaboronu propagandi ikhn'oy simvoliki" [On Condemning the Communist and National Socialist (Nazi) Totalitarian Regimes in Ukraine and Prohibiting Propaganda of Their Symbols].

[77] Draft Law No. 4120 of February 19, 2016 "Pro vnesennya zmin do deyakikh zakonodavchikh aktiv Ukraini (shchodo kiminal'noy vidpovidal'nosti za zaperechennya Golodomoru, Golokostu, genotsidu krims'kotatars'kogo narodu" [On Introducing Changes to Certain Legislative Acts of Ukraine (Regarding Criminal Liability for Denial of the Holodomor, the Holocaust, and the Deportations of the People of Crimean Tatars)].

political issue as a result of the Russian annexation of Crimea and the new wave of repressions against Crimean Tatars. Unsurprisingly, two main leaders of the Mejlis, Mustafa Dzhemilev and Refat Chubarov, were among the bill's authors along with politicians as different as Oleksandr Feldman (who has left the Party of the Regions to become an independent deputy), Oleh Lyashko (whose Radical Party has left the governing coalition), members of the Poroshenko bloc and of Yatsenyuk's People's Front (which apparently initiated the proposal), the influential Lviv-based Samopomoshch (literally Self-Defense) party, and even a deputy (Borislav Bereza) with close ties to the Right Sector (a far-right movement that played an important role in the Revolution of Dignity). But despite broad support, the bill was still bogged down in the Rada at the time of writing. I was privately informed that the Institute of National Memory is currently preparing a new version of the de-communization laws.

The 2015 Ukrainian de-communization laws have contributed to the launching of new initiatives to legislate on the issues of the past in Eastern Europe, including the Polish De-communization Act of April 2016 that prohibits – in the spirit of the Lyashko Act – "the propagation of communism or any other totalitarian system through the names of public buildings, structures and facilities," an anti-communist turn in Polish politics having been prepared by the coming to power of Jarosław Kaczyński's Law and Justice party in October 2015.[78] This party also began a new round in the Polish-Ukrainian memory war, largely focused on the 1943 Volhynia massacre, which the Polish parliament officially recognized as a genocide in July 2016.[79]

The Ukrainian case clearly demonstrates the interconnection between de-communization policy and the emergence of the specifically Eastern European type of memory laws that focus on the legacy of communism rather than of fascism and on the protection of national narratives rather than state repentance and co-responsibility for crimes against humanity.

---

[78] Law No. 744 of April 1, 2016 "O zakazie propagowania komunizmu lub innego ustroju totalitarnego przez nazwy budowli, obiektów i urządzeń użyteczności publicznej" [On the Prohibition of Propagation of Communism or Any Other Totalitarian System through the Names of All Public Buildings, Structures and Facilities].

[79] Andrii Portnov, "Clash of Victimhoods: The Volhynia Massacre in Polish and Ukrainian Memory," November 16, 2016: www.opendemocracy.net/od-russia/andrii-portnov/clash-of-victimhood-1943-volhynian-massacre-in-polish-and-ukrainian-culture. A recent Polish bill adds "crimes of Ukrainian nationalists" to the roster of crimes whose denial is banned by the 1998 memory law. See Draft Law of August 11, 2016, "O zmianie ustawy o Instytucie Pamięci Narodowej. . ." ["On Changing the Statute of the Institute of National Remembrance. . ."]: http://www.sejm.gov.pl/sejm8.nsf/druk.xsp?nr=993.

Ukraine happened to be the main battlefield between the Russian war myth and the memories of communist crimes: nowhere else (with the exception of Russia itself) has Putin's propaganda been as persistent in promoting the cult of the war as in Ukraine (although the Kremlin also pursued a similar policy with regard to Russian minorities in the Baltic countries and, more broadly, across the entire post-communist space). Ukraine's internal debates over the legacy of the USSR have become inseparable from the Russian-Ukrainian memory war. Of course, the emphasis on the legacy of communism in Eastern Europe cannot be entirely attributed to the formation of Putin's authoritarian regime, because this emphasis has been salient in the region's politics of memory ever since the time of perestroika. However, Putin's neo-imperial rhetoric did play a key role in exacerbating the international tensions in the region, among all else by abetting the rise of self-victimizing national narratives. In Chapter 6, we will see that aggressive nationalism has informed the development of Russia's own historical memory since Putin's coming to power in 2000. But despite their intense conflicts with Putin's government over the interpretation of the past, some Eastern European countries have also developed a manipulative politics of history that is not altogether different from the Russian paradigm.

CHAPTER 5

Memory Laws in Yeltsin's Russia

The Russian memory law adopted in May 2014 was a direct outcome of the Ukrainian crisis and, in a broader sense, of Putin's politics of memory, which was crucial to his project of neo-imperial reconstruction. The main goal of this politics was to promote the cult of the Russian state, whose primary incarnation rests in the celebration of the heroic memory of World War II.

From the early 2000s on, the revival of the war mythology under Putin was taken by many Eastern European countries as a sign of Russia's renewed imperial ambitions: that mythology did indeed embrace the spirit of the Yalta System. The groundwork of the Russian annexation of Crimea and the war in Donbass was evidently laid by the memory wars that in the 2000s and 2010s have opposed Russia to its Eastern European neighbors, including in particular such countries as Ukraine, Poland, Lithuania, Latvia, and Estonia. The myth of the war has provided an explanatory framework within which the Russian state and people present as an unbreakable unity, while all anti-Russian forces are categorized as "Nazi allies" or the equivalent. The memory law of 2014 therefore had a twofold goal: to mobilize support for the regime within the country and to legitimize Russia's aggression against Ukraine by presenting it as a continuation of the Great Patriotic War.

Yet the first attempts to pass a memory law in Russia were made long before Putin's coming to power, in the context of Boris Yeltsin's democratic reforms and his struggle against the communist and nationalist opposition. This chapter, which continues the discussion of Russian historical memory begun in Chapter 3, examines the memory law projects of the 1990s and their role in the battles over the past between Russian democrats, communists, and nationalists.

History Politics

Post-Soviet historical memory has always been strongly politicized, largely due to the legacy of the communist regime, whose legitimacy was based on the Soviet conception of history.[1] Unsurprisingly, though, history provided another venue for the delegitimization of the Soviet system, with the perestroika period (1985–1991) in particular witnessing a radical reassessment of the communist past.[2]

Initially, the critique of communism was focused largely on Stalin's repressions. Further, a concept of totalitarianism that assimilated Soviet communism to fascism provided a privileged instrument for the denunciation of Stalinism. On a question about Stalinism and fascism, 64 percent of respondents to a sociological survey conducted in Leningrad in May 1990 professed to see no difference between the two regimes, while 18 percent held that there was only a superficial resemblance (but a resemblance nevertheless) between them.[3] According to the same survey, Stalin's approval rating in Leningrad was as low as 9 percent, while 56 percent evaluated his role in Soviet history negatively. Significantly, 35 percent refused to give a clear assessment of Stalin. Arguably, some of them did not dare to openly express a leaning toward him even in the context of a sociological interview, due to the "democratic censorship" exercised by the dominant anti-Stalinist discourse. Leningrad was, of course, the most Western-oriented Russian city, but surveys conducted in other regions have also shown a general disillusionment with the results of the "Soviet experiment."[4]

[1] On the role of history for Soviet ideology, see David Brandenberger, *National Bolshevism: Stalinist Mass Culture and the Formation of Modern Russian National Identity, 1931–1956* (Cambridge, Mass.: Harvard University Press, 2002); Evgeny Dobrenko, *Stalinist Cinema and the Production of History: Museum of the Revolution* (Edinburgh: Edinburgh University Press and Yale University Press, 2008); Kevin F.M. Platt, *Terror and Greatness: Ivan and Peter as Russian Myths* (Ithaca, N.Y.: Cornell University Press, 2011); and Serhy Yekelchyk, *Stalin's Empire of Memory: Russian-Ukrainian Relations in the Soviet Historical Imagination* (Toronto: University of Toronto Press, 2004).

[2] Robert W. Davies, *Soviet History in the Gorbachev Revolution* (London: Palgrave Macmillan, 1989); Davies, *Soviet History in the Yeltsin Era* (Basingstoke: Macmillan, 1997); Nanci Adler, *Victims of Soviet Terror: The Story of the Memorial Movement* (Westport, Conn.: Praeger Publishers, 1993); Kathleen E. Smith, *Remembering Stalin's Victims: Popular Memory and the End of the USSR* (Ithaca, N.Y.: Cornell University Press, 1996); Smith, *Mythmaking in the New Russia: Politics and Memory during the Yeltsin Era* (Ithaca, N.Y.: Cornell University Press, 2002); Thomas Sherlock, *Historical Narratives in the Soviet Union and Post-Soviet Russia: Destroying the Settled Past, Creating an Uncertain Future* (New York: Palgrave Macmillan, 2007).

[3] The survey was conducted by Dina Khapaeva and the author in Leningrad in May 1990 (representative city sample of 1,700). See Khapaeva and Koposov, "Les demi-dieux de la mythologie soviétique," *Annales: Economies, Sociétés, Civilisations* 47/5–6 (1992), pp. 963–987; Koposov, "Pierre le Grand et Staline: Retour sur le panthéon historique en Russie," in *Histoire et mémoire dans l'espace postsoviétique: Le passé qui encombre*, eds. Wladimir Berelowitch and Korine Amacher (Paris: L'Harmattan, Université de Genève, 2013), pp. 33–62; and Koposov, *Pamyat' strogogo rezhima: Istoriya i politika v Rossii* [Strict-Security Memory: History and Politics in Russia] (Moscow: Novoye literaturnoye obozreniye, 2011), chapter 3.

[4] Yu.A. Levada, ed., *Sovetskiy prostoy chelovek: Opyt sotsial'nogo portreta na rubezhe 90-kh* [The Simple Soviet Man: An Experiment in Social Portraiture at the Turn of the 1990s] (Moscow: Mirovoy okean, 1993).

By the end of perestroika, all elements of the Soviet conception of history, from the theory of class struggle to the myth of the economic superiority of communism over capitalism, had been discarded. In light of the liberal master narrative, the Soviet period presented as a tragic detour from the "high road" of history. Most Russians thought that their country had to "reenter humankind," create a market economy, become a democracy, and abandon the messianic ambition of leading other peoples to communism. They also thought that Russia had to repudiate its claims to a "special path of historical development," a notion that had been cherished by nineteenth-century Slavophiles and twentieth-century theorists of Eurasianism alike. The idea of Russia's singularity was also part of the Soviet conception of history, which was based on both Marxist universalism and Russian nationalism.

Nothing was as typical of the late-Soviet historical consciousness as the idealization of the West (which was also characteristic of other countries of the Eastern bloc). By the end of the 1980s, the West came to be commonly perceived in Russia as an incarnation of moral and aesthetic perfection, economic efficiency, and political freedom.[5] This image, with its roots in the tradition of the nineteenth-century Russian Westernizers, legitimized Yeltsin's democratic reforms, which were expected to make Russia similar to the West or, in the language of the time, to transform it into "a normal country." The aforementioned survey of May 1990 in Leningrad also produced an unexpected but significant result, in that Peter the Great, the founder of the Russian Empire in the early eighteenth century, was ranked first among favorably viewed historical figures. Since then, Peter has become the unquestionable leader of Russian ratings, his image symbolizing, above all, the policy of Russian Westernization and modernization. Vladimir Lenin, the founder of the Soviet state, was ranked in fifth place (although as recently as 1989 he had been the most popular historical figure in Russia). And, amazingly, the second, third, and forth places were taken by three American presidents, Franklin Roosevelt, Abraham Lincoln, and George Washington, which demonstrates the powerful pro-Western sympathies of many respondents.[6]

---

[5] On the ideal image of the West, see Dina Khapaeva, "L'Occident dans l'imaginaire russe," *Social Sciences Information* 33/1 (1994), pp. 553–569; Khapaeva, "As the Whole Civilized World," *Social Sciences Information*, 34/4 (1995), pp. 687–704; and Khapaeva, "L'Occident sera demain," *Annales: Histoire, Sciences Sociales* 50/6 (1995), pp. 1259–1270.

[6] Roosevelt, of course, symbolized the New Deal and efficient reform policies; but the positive feelings toward him were also due to his reputation as the Soviet Union's most reliable ally during the war. Lincoln betokened the abolition of slavery and was seen as the American "tsar-liberator," a

When the USSR collapsed in 1991, history lost some of its appeal.[7] After the fall of communism, no further proofs of the liberal master narrative seemed to be needed. By the end of 1991, the choice in favor of the market economy had been made, and the democrats who now had power in Russia were preoccupied by urgently needed economic reforms. In their eyes, the explorations of the Stalinist past had played their role in discrediting the Soviet system but had since outlived their usefulness. National history would be of no help in planning market reforms. It was the future, not the past, economy, not history, and the West, not Russia that in the early 1990s interested most post-Soviet citizens, including the country's democratic leadership. In addition, "disturbing the remains" of the Soviet system seemed hazardous, in that it could engender doubt regarding the applicability of Western models to Russia or result in the kind of witch hunt that Yeltsin wanted to avoid at all costs. Indeed, the democrats had only limited support in the country and could not allow themselves to alienate potential allies from among the old communist *nomenklatura* who were now eager to become capitalist entrepreneurs.

As the liberal master narrative was triumphing in Russia, the "crisis of the future" was occurring in the West. As we know, the communist world had also lived through its own crisis of the future in the 1980s, but that had been the crisis of a communist future. The hope was that an alternative, capitalist future now lay before the former socialist countries. It was not until most Russians realized that building capitalism and living under it was much harder than they had expected that Russia entered into "an age of diminishing expectations." Changes in the country's socio-psychological climate began shortly after the launching of the market reforms in 1992 and took several years to complete.

By 1993, one could discern clear signs of nostalgia for the Soviet past in Russia, and that nostalgia only intensified in the years that followed. Nevertheless, until the end of the decade the liberal master narrative remained attractive to a considerable proportion of the population (especially the younger generation and the well-educated). Characteristically, in the midst of a deep economic and political crisis, most Russians supported Yeltsin in the presidential elections of 1996. By that time, Yeltsin's popularity had waned, and the only motivation for voting for him lay in

counterpart of Russian tsar Alexander II who had liberated Russian serfs in 1861. And Washington's popularity was a pure expression of the "Americomania" typical of the late 1980s.

[7] Arfon Rees, "Managing the History of the Past in the Former Communist States," in *A European Memory? Contested Histories and Politics of Remembrance*, eds. Małgorzata Pakier and Bo Stråth (New York: Berghahn Books, 2010), pp. 222–224.

the liberal master narrative, which for many Russians remained a more reliable basis on which to explain the country's present, past, and future than communist or nationalist interpretations of history. Yeltsin's advisors had been successful in building his campaign around the idea that the only alternative to Yeltsin's reforms, no matter how painful they may be, was a return to the communist system, and most Russians did not welcome such a prospect. They continued to believe that their country was living through a transition from communism to capitalism and that the latter, once in place, would inevitably improve their living conditions. In 1996, of course, those feelings were very different from the market idealism of the early 1990s; they had, rather, an aspect of gloomy fatalism. Nevertheless, in 1996, the liberal master narrative had yet to be replaced by an alternative philosophy of history.

An alternative narrative was gradually emerging in the works of Russian nationalists such as Aleksandr Dugin, Aleksandr Panarin, and Igor Froyanov. Inspired by the ideas of the nineteenth-century Slavophiles and the proponents of the Eurasian theories of the interwar period, those authors developed a notion of Slavic-Orthodox civilization that differs fundamentally from its Western counterpart. They hold that Russia, with its collectivism and high spiritual values, presents a challenge to the individualistic and utilitarian West, which therefore hates, fears, and tries to "contain" Russia within the narrowest possible limits.[8] Although those theories were slowly gaining popularity in the 1990s, most Russians tended to perceive them as too radical, if not frankly fascist, and indeed some of their authors, Dugin above all, did not hide their sympathy toward fascism. They had little political support and limited access to television coverage, which was controlled by the "oligarchs" who did not usually support extreme

---

[8] Aleksandr Dugin, *Osnovy geopolitiki: Geopoliticheskoye budushchee Rossii* [The Foundations of Geopolitics: The Geopolitical Future of Russia] (Moscow: Arktogeya, 1997); Dugin, *Absolyutnaya Rodina* [The Absolute Motherland] (Moscow: Arktogeya, 1999); Aleksandr Panarin, *Pravoslavnaya tsivilizatsiya v global'nom mire* [Orthodox Civilization in a Globalized World] (Moscow: Algoritm, 2002); Igor Froyanov, *Pogruzheniye v bezdnu* [Plunging into the Abyss] (Saint Petersburg: Izdatel'stvo Sankt-Peterburgskogo universiteta, 1999). On Russian nationalism and the far-right movement, see Yitzhak M. Brudny, *Reinventing Russia: Russian Nationalism and the Soviet State, 1953–1991* (Cambridge, Mass.: Harvard University Press, 1998); Nikolay Mitrokhin, *Russkaya partiya: Dvizheniye russkikh natsionalistov v SSSR, 1953–1985* [The Russian Party: The Russian Nationalist Movement in the USSR, 1953–1985] (Moscow: Novoye Literaturnoye Obozreniye, 2003); Marlène Laruelle, *Russian Eurasianism: An Ideology of Empire* (Washington, DC: Woodrow Wilson Press, Johns Hopkins University Press, 2008); Laruelle, *In the Name of the Nation: Nationalism and Politics in Contemporary Russia* (New York: Palgrave Macmillan, 2009); Stephen Shenfield, *Russian Fascism: Traditions, Tendencies, Movements* (Armonk, N.Y.: M.E. Sharpe, 2001); Andreas Umland, ed., *The Nature of Russian "Neo-Eurasianism": Approaches to Aleksandr Dugin's Post-Soviet Movement of Radical Anti-Americanism* (Armonk, N.Y.: M. E. Sharpe, 2009).

nationalists. Several leaders of the opposition (e.g., Gennadiy Seleznyov, the communist chairman of the State Duma in 1996–2003) showed some interest in Dugin's ideas but could not risk going along with his program.

One of the paradoxes of the anti-Yeltsin opposition lay in the fact that its ideology was largely nationalistic, while its main organizational force was the Communist Party of the Russian Federation (CPRF), which controlled one-third of the seats in the Duma and had a strong network in the regions. The leading nationalist party, the Liberal Democratic Party of Russia (LDPR), was a vocal critic of liberalism, democracy, and the West but in practice tended to compromise with the government. There were also numerous minor far-right groups that were not represented in the parliament.

Although the CPRF claimed to be the successor of the Communist Party of the Soviet Union, its ideology had little to do with communism. It was, rather, a populist and nationalist party. The post-Soviet communists largely repudiated the principles of socialist revolution, laws of history, "proletarian internationalism," and "scientific atheism." Instead, they broached the issue of Russia's non-Western path of historical development and began putting out feelers to the Orthodox Church. But they could not fully endorse the far-right Eurasian theories, for this would mean an open break with Marxism. Nourished in the traditions of Soviet anti-fascism, most of them viewed the far-right groups as an inescapable but undesirable ally. Under these circumstances, theories of a Slavic-Orthodox or Eurasian civilization fell short in replacing the liberal master narrative as the dominant philosophy of history.[9]

Growing anti-Western feelings strongly impacted the evolution of Russian historical consciousness. In the early 1990s, Yeltsin's foreign policy was largely pro-Western, not least because the country was dependent on Western expertise and financial help in reforming its economy. From the mid-1990s, developing relationships with non-Western partners became a priority of the new Foreign Minister, Evgeniy Primakov. But mid-decade also witnessed Russia's successful integration into the system of partnerships with the West. In February 1996, Russia joined the Council of

---

[9] On the "nationalization" of the Communist Party's political agenda, see Marlène Laruelle, *In the Name of the Nation*, pp. 87–95, and Luke March, *The Communist Party in Post-Soviet Russia* (Manchester: Manchester University Press, 2002). March speaks of the CPRF's "move from Marxist-Leninist orthodoxy toward a form of national bolshevism" or an "ideology of statehood" based on the idea of Russian "civilization" (p. 67). He overestimates the role of "residual Marxism-Leninism" in the party's ideology but rightly emphasizes the "loss of historical optimism" and "revolutionary fervor" as typifying present-day communists (pp. 53–55).

Europe. The NATO-Russia Founding Act was signed in May 1997. In June 1997, the "Group of Seven" added Boris Yeltsin, which marked its transformation into a G8. It was not until the Kosovo crisis of 1999 that a more profound anti-Western turn began taking shape in Russian foreign policy.

In other words, the situation with historical memory in Yeltsin's Russia was uncertain and contradictory. On the one hand, it was characterized by a growing nostalgia for Soviet times, increasing anti-Western sentiments, and the rise of nationalism. On the other hand, the liberal master narrative, which was gradually losing credibility, remained the government's official position and continued to enjoy some popular support. But no political force was able to offer an alternative vision of history that most Russians were ready to embrace. And all of this could only contribute to the decreasing interest in the past.

The memory of Stalin's repressions was the first victim of this will to forget (or, rather, not to remember) that became typical of the 1990s. By 1994, the dictator's popularity had grown considerably. In the late 1980s, many respondents had refrained from evaluating his role in Soviet history, but now the proportion of non-responses, as well as that of critical assessments, began to decrease, while the proportion of positive sentiments increased. From 1994 on, Stalin was usually ranked in the third or fourth (and occasionally even the second) place in the ratings of popularity of historical figures. However, Peter the Great, the symbol of Russia's opening toward the West, remained the unrivaled champion of those rankings. By the end of the 1990s, Catherine II, an emblematic figure of eighteenth-century enlightened absolutism, rose to second place, after Peter but before Stalin. Leonid Brezhnev also emerged as a popular historical figure. He symbolized the last decades of the USSR's existence, which in the 1990s many Russian saw as a "lost paradise." As for foreign historical figures, they gradually disappeared from the top of the ratings in the course of the 1990s.[10]

The collapse of the USSR was accompanied by a "symbolic revolution," when "historical names" were returned to the cities (beginning with Leningrad renamed Saint Petersburg in the aftermath of the August putsch of 1991), streets, factories, and the like that under the Soviets had been

---

[10] Aleksey Levinson, "Massovyie predstavleniya ob 'istoricheskikh lichnostyiakh'" [Collective Representations of "Historical Figures"], *Odissey 1996: Chelovek v istorii* (Moscow: 1996), pp. 252–267, and Levinson, "Arkhiv i prostota: replika neistorika" [Archive and Simplicity: A Comment by a Non-Historian], *Novoye literaturnoye obozreniye* 74 (2005), pp. 34–46.

renamed for communist leaders. But soon after 1991, the symbolic revolution began to slow down. As a result of this unfinished revolution, a mélange of Western, Soviet, and pre-revolutionary Russian symbols came to inform the everyday life of post-Soviet citizens. Confusion about the meaning of history was both a cause and an outcome of this situation, while the growing indifference with which these symbols were perceived often masked a hidden predilection for the Soviet symbolism. An equivocal stance on the Soviet legacy was a dominant feature of the cultural and political climate of the 1990s.

Yeltsin's government had insufficient political and financial resources to conduct a sustained and efficient "history politics." It was unable in particular to win the "CPSU Trial" of 1992, when a group of communist leaders petitioned the Constitutional Court to review Yeltsin's decrees of 1991, which had dissolved the Communist Party. The Court's decision reflected an unstable power balance between the president and the opposition. The former CPSU was declared unconstitutional insofar as it had substituted itself for the state and had used public funding and property, but communist ideology and symbols were not outlawed and a few months later, a new Communist Party came into being.[11]

Part of the problem was that in the stormy years that witnessed the beginning of the market reforms, the past was the last thing on the government's agenda. The young liberal economists who were in charge of those reforms (Yegor Gaidar and his team) do not seem to have appreciated the importance of history politics. To them, it was at best a form of propaganda, which was as much a thing of the past as communism. Instead, they addressed the population using the language of an economic theory that few people understood. It was not until the prospect of losing the presidential elections of 1996 loomed that Yeltsin and other democratic leaders (primarily Anatoliy Chubais) radically changed their take on the issue. Yeltsin's presidential campaign of 1996 contributed to the rise of populist politics in Russia, with its use of diverse, and even mutually exclusive, languages to win the support of various "target groups." The new art of politics became known in Russia as "political technologies."

A manipulative politics of memory was an essential part of the new political art. Nationalistic ideas would subsequently begin to penetrate the ideology of Russian liberals, but under Yeltsin, that politics did not, and could hardly have been expected to, develop beyond its initial stage. Soon

[11] Smith, *Mythmaking in the New Russia*, pp. 11–29.

after the elections, Yeltsin publicly announced that the country needed a "national idea"[12] and invited politicians and intellectuals to invent one. But they failed, largely because ironic distancing was the population's prevailing response to the attempts of an unpopular government to galvanize its image. Indeed, in the eyes of the public opinion, Yeltsin's politics was too closely associated with the liberal master narrative. Without radically changing direction (which was not their intention), adding some nationalistic motifs to their liberal narrative was the best that the president and his team could do.

The development of a kind of cultural patriotism was Yeltsin's main instrument for achieving this goal. In this respect, his strategy was similar to the politics of national heritage being pursued by his friend Helmut Kohl and other Western leaders.[13] Already in the 1980s, and even more so in the 1990s, the period of the Russian Empire (1721–1917) came to be commonly perceived in Russia as the most glorious time in its national history. As we know, Peter the Great (since 1990) and Catherine II (since the end of the decade) were the two most popular historical figures in Russia, both being perceived less as powerful rulers (and certainly not as cruel despots) than as enlightened monarchs, modernizers, and Westernizers. Yeltsin's politics of memory assiduously highlighted the country's cultural attainments, especially of the eighteenth and nineteenth centuries, which many Russians considered at least comparable to those of the West.[14] In particular, the government threw its support behind a cult of the great poet Alexander Pushkin, the founder of modern Russian literature, one of the country's greatest achievements in the eyes of many Russians. The celebration of Pushkin's bicentenary in 1999 was a high point of Yeltsin's politics of memory. But a lack of resources prevented the government from developing a large-scale politics of national heritage, involving such costly undertakings as the restoration of historical monuments, the creation of museums, and so on. Cultural tourism, which is one of the main sources of funding for the heritage industry in the West, was underdeveloped in Russia, partly because of the inadequate infrastructure and partly because wealthy Russians preferred traveling abroad. And so Yeltsin's politics of cultural patriotism failed to provide Russians with a

---

[12] *Ibid.*, pp. 158–172; Laruelle, *In the Name of the Nation*, pp. 122–124. [13] See Chapter 2.

[14] Fifty-five and 58 percent of the respondents of the Leningrad survey of May 1990 believed that, in the eighteenth and nineteenth centuries, respectively, Russian culture was on a par with or superior to the culture of the West. In a similar survey in 2007, 68 percent of respondents answered similarly. See Koposov, *Pamyat' strogogo rezhima*, p. 177.

positive national identity. Putin continued this work in the 2000s using quite different means in pursuit of quite different political goals.

As we will see in the next chapter, Putin used the Soviet cult of the Great Patriotic War to build a national consensus, in a radical break with Yeltsin's politics of cultural patriotism. The myth of the war was formed in the 1960s, although many of its themes harken back to Stalin's wartime propaganda.[15] Characteristically, between 1948 and 1965, May 9 (the USSR's Victory Day) remained an ordinary working day.

Under Stalin, the memory of war was still fresh and painful. It was difficult to celebrate the victory without reopening wounds and, even worse, without praising the army generals who won the war and could potentially challenge Stalin's leadership. Under Nikita Khrushchev, Stalin's successor, the war myth was sidelined, because Stalin's image as a great state leader was integral to it. In 1956, the same Twentieth Party Congress that began dismantling the Stalin cult declared that a Third World War was no longer unavoidable, thanks to the USSR's achievements, the formation of the "socialist camp," and the crisis of the colonial system. A reduction in defense spending was therefore an important aspect of destalinization. Of course, praising the army generals and cutting their funding were two very different strategies. In addition, the Khrushchev years (1953–1964) witnessed rapid economic development, which inspired optimistic expectations. The new program of the CPSU, adopted in 1961, promised "full communism" by 1980. A project of the future, not the glory of the past, was central to Khrushchev's history politics.

Brezhnev's situation was different. He did not intend to continue dismantling the Stalin cult but was not prepared to endorse the dictator's full rehabilitation either. The cult of the war was a way to bring Stalin back without justifying his repressions, which most of the Party leaders of the new generation would never risk doing, not least because the repressions had devastated the ranks of the Party elite. The war was already sufficiently remote in time to facilitate adjusting its image to propaganda needs, and Stalin's redoubtable generals were all either retired or deceased. The army and the military-industrial complex had become Brezhnev's key allies, and the war memory was instrumental in legitimizing the increases in the defense budget. The plan to build communism by 1980 had clearly failed, and this created the need for a glorious past to compensate for the country's uncertain future. The myth of the war enabled all those goals

---

[15] Nina Tumarkin, *The Living and the Dead: The Rise and Fall of the Cult of WWII in Russia* (New York: Basic Books, 1994).

to be achieved and could in addition only be welcomed by the populace, because the war had been a fundamental aspect of its collective experience. In the late 1960s and 1970s, the cult of the war became firmly established in Russia (although its institutionalization was not without problems).[16] The less promising the economic prospects of the USSR were, the more official propaganda had to rely on the cult of the war.

Unsurprisingly, at the end of the 1980s, the war myth shared the fate of all other aspects of Soviet ideology, even as one of its least compromised components. At the dawn of the 1990s, the heroic image of the war created by Brezhnev's propaganda came under heavy attack. Its critics emphasized not only the war's disastrous start, its meaningless casualties, and the cruelty of Stalin's generals but also the USSR's ambiguous role in the outbreak of war, the massive collaboration of Soviet citizens with the Nazis, the war crimes perpetrated by the Red Army, and the Soviet occupation of Eastern Europe in the aftermath of the war.

The collapse of the Soviet empire was accompanied by vehement conflicts over the interpretation of the war between the newly emerging independent states and the Soviet communist leadership. The revolt of the subject peoples against the Kremlin was largely rooted in counter-memories of the war that the communist regimes in Eastern Europe had not succeeded in eradicating, and the truth about the war became one of the most powerful tools used in the delegitimization of communism. Under pressure from Russian democrats and the national movements in the Soviet republics and Russia's former satellites, the Kremlin was forced to acknowledge the USSR's complicity in unleashing the war and its responsibility for certain war crimes.

In December 1989, the Congress of People's Deputies of the Soviet Union passed a resolution "On the Political and Juridical Appraisal of the Soviet-German Non-Aggression Treaty of 1939," which represented Russia's first official acknowledgment of the "secret protocols" of the Molotov-Ribbentrop Pact. The parliament condemned those protocols, which had divided Eastern Europe "into Soviet and German 'spheres of influence'" (however, it also conceded that the treaty itself "had not contradicted the norms of international law and the practice of agreements between states that had been in use for the arrangements of this kind").[17]

---

[16] Mark Edele, *Soviet Veterans of the Second World War: A Popular Movement in an Authoritarian Society, 1941–1991* (Oxford: Oxford University Press, 2008).

[17] Resolution of the Congress of People's Deputies of the USSR of December 24, 1989 "O politicheskoy i pravovoy otsenke sovetsko-germanskogo dogovora o nenapadenii ot 1939 goda," *Pravda*, December 28, 1989.

In April 1990, Gorbachev had acknowledged Soviet responsibility for Katyn, and in October 1992, Yeltsin transmitted to the Polish government the documents relating to the massacre, including the Politburo decision to execute the Polish prisoners of war.[18] In their turn, in the course of the 1990s, historians found strong though mostly indirect evidence suggesting that Stalin had been planning to invade Germany in July 1941. These new interpretations of the war became widely known outside the narrow circle of specialists. Viktor Suvorov's *Icebreaker: Who Started the Second World War?* (1990) and his other bestsellers accusing Stalin of unleashing the war were widely read in Russia,[19] which resulted in the heroic image of the war being seriously undermined. Symptomatically, Nina Tumarkin, a student of the "cult" of the war, was describing in the early 1990s its "rise and [more importantly] fall."[20] Although subsequent events have shown this diagnosis to be premature, the war myth was clearly not doing as well in the 1990s as it once had. Nevertheless, as Lisa A. Kirschenbaum puts it, "the myth of the people's war... outlived the state that sponsored it."[21]

Not everyone in the country shared the new interpretations of the war, including the veterans' associations that held a prominent place in Gorbachev's concept of civil society. The growing communist and nationalist opposition also continued promoting the cult of the war, an aspect of the

[18] I.S. Yazhborovskaya, A.Yu. Yablokov, V.S. Parsadanova, *Katynskiy sindrom v sovetsko-pol'skikh i rossiysko-pol'skikh otnosheniyakh* [The Katyn Syndrome in Soviet-Polish and Russian-Polish Relationships], [2001], 2nd ed., (Moscow: ROSSPEN, 2009); George Sanford, *Katyn and the Soviet Massacre of 1940: Truth, Justice and Memory* (Abingdon: Routledge, 2005), pp. 196–200.

[19] Viktor Suvorov, *Icebreaker: Who Started the Second World War?* (London: Hamish Hamilton, 1990); Yu.N. Afanasyev, ed., *Drugaya voyna: 1939–1945* [A Different War: 1939–1945] (Moscow: Izdatel'stvo Rossiyskogo gosudarstvennogo gumanitarnogo universiteta, 1996); Mikhail Mel'tyukhov, *Upushchennyi shans Stalina: Sovetskiy Soyuz i bor'ba za Yevropu, 1939–1941* [Stalin's Lost Chance: The Soviet Union and the Struggle for Europe, 1939–1941] (Moscow: Veche, 2000); Mark Solonin, *22 Iyunya, ili Kogda nachalas' Velikaya Otechestvennaya voina* [June 22, or When Did the Great Patriotic War Begin?] (Moscow: Yauza/Eksmo, 2004); V.A. Nevezhin and G.A. Bordyugov, eds., *Gotovil li Stalin nastupatel'nuyu voinu protiv Gitlera? Nezaplanirovannaya diskussiya: Sbornik materialov* [Was Stalin Preparing an Offensive War against Hitler? An Unplanned Discussion: Sourcebook] (Moscow: AIRO-XX, 1995); and Teddy J. Uldricks, "The Icebreaker Controversy: Did Stalin Plan to Attack Hitler?" *The Slavic Review* 53/3 (1999), pp. 626–643. The Russian revisionism was to some extent similar to the more recent American criticism of "the good war" concept, although with one important difference: Suvorov's and Solonin's assessment of the USSR as an aggressor did not entail any rehabilitation of Nazism. As for Mel'tyukhov, he was criticizing Stalin not for his aggressive intentions but for having failed to destroy Germany by a preemptive attack, conquering all of Europe in the process. On American revisionism, see Gavriel D. Rosenfeld, *Hi Hitler! How the Nazi Past Is Being Normalized in Contemporary Culture* (Cambridge: Cambridge University Press, 2015), pp. 48–72.

[20] Tumarkin, *The Living and the Dead;* Tumarkin, "The Great Patriotic War as Myth and Memory," *European Review* 11/4 (2003), pp. 595–611.

[21] Lisa A. Kirschenbaum, *The Legacy of the Siege of Leningrad, 1941–1995: Myth, Memories, and Monuments* (Cambridge: Cambridge University Press, 2009), p. 4.

Soviet legacy that was equally dear to both groups. And although many Russian democrats shared new conceptions of the war, Yeltsin could not risk alienating supporters of the traditional war myth by founding his history politics on those new interpretations. On the contrary, he tried to find a middle ground between the supporters and the critics of the war myth. And his way of doing that was to emphasize the tragic aspects of the war and the mistakes of the Soviet government while praising the heroism of the ordinary people. (This position was reflected in the legislation on veterans and other bills that we will consider later in this chapter.) In May 1995, Yeltsin organized a magnificent celebration of the fiftieth anniversary of the victory over Nazi Germany. For the first time since the dissolution of the USSR a Soviet-style military parade was staged in Moscow with the participation of both war veterans and regular military units.

Those festivities were of course an attempt to boost the morale of the army against the backdrop of the First Chechen War, which began in December 1994 and proved much more challenging than the Russian leadership and military command had expected. However, during his second term as president, Yeltsin took care not to invigorate the cult of the war, even as he searched for a new "national idea." While trying not to relinquish the memory of the war to the communist and nationalist opposition, Yeltsin was still far from making it the cornerstone of his own history politics. The cult of the war remained incomparably less important to him than it had been to his predecessors and would be to his successor.

As we know, the Russian myth of the war did not include the Holocaust. During the Soviet period, in fact, that concept was almost unknown. Nazi crimes were of course a key element in the Soviet narrative of the war, but their victims were identified as civilians, not Jews. Silence on the Holocaust typified Soviet history politics until the end of the 1980s, when, with the fall of communism, it at last came to be recognized as a major crime against humanity, in Russia as in Eastern Europe at large. This recognition was linked to the formation of an anti-fascist movement, which emerged in response to the growing far-right danger in Russia. In 1992, the Russian Research and Educational Holocaust Center was founded in Moscow, opening offices in several other Russian cities in the years that followed. In 1997, the Interregional Holocaust Foundation was created under the leadership of Alla Gerber, a co-organizer of the Moscow Anti-Fascist Center.[22] These organizations enjoyed the support of the

[22] Ilya Altman and Claudio Ingerflom, "Le Kremlin et l'holocauste, 1933–2001," in Général Petrenko, *Avant et après Auschwitz, suivi de* Ilya Altman and Claudio Ingerflom, *Le Kremlin et*

Russian government and Moscow City Hall. But all efforts notwithstanding, the memory of the Holocaust failed to become an integral part of the Russian national memory. Yeltsin's government and Russian liberals were unable to develop a Western-style democratic culture of memory, of which Holocaust remembrance would be a pillar.

To sum up: Yeltsin remained committed to the liberal master narrative, which in the 1990s was gradually losing, but had not completely lost, its attractiveness to Russian citizens. His politics of memory was episodic and lacked resources. To the extent that it existed, however, it was somewhat similar to that of most Western governments of his time. Yeltsin tried to develop a cultural patriotism comparable to the cult of national heritage as well as a memory of the Holocaust that had not existed in Russia in the Soviet period. In both respects, his politics of memory was largely unsuccessful. An alternative version of history politics was gradually emerging among Russian nationalists, but until the 2000s this politics enjoyed only limited political support. The complexities of this situation found their reflection in the legislation on the issues of the past and the memory law projects of the 1990s.

Legislation about the Past

The first proposals to criminalize certain statements about the past were brought to the Russian parliament in 1995. The groundwork for those initiatives, which were inspired by the French Gayssot Act, had been laid by the political debates and legal developments of the previous years. At the turn of the 1990s, the legislative bodies of the USSR and Russia[23] passed several bills and adopted numerous declarations that expressed their

---

l'holocauste, 1933–2001 (Paris: Flammarion, 2002), pp. 217–281; Klas-Göran Karlsson, "The Reception of the Holocaust in Russia: Silence, Conspiracy, and Glimpses of Light," in *Bringing the Dark Past to Light: The Reception of the Holocaust in Postcommunist Europe*, eds. John-Paul Himka and Joanna Beata Michlic (Lincoln: University of Nebraska Press, 2013), pp. 487–514; Tarik Cyril Amar, "A Disturbed Silence: Discourse on the Holocaust in the Soviet West as an Anti-Site of Memory," in *The Holocaust in the East: Local Perpetrators and Soviet Responses*, eds. Michael David-Fox, Peter Holquist, and Alexander M. Martin (Pittsburgh, Pa.: University of Pittsburgh Press, 2014), pp. 158–184; and Maria Ferretti, "The Shoah and the Gulag in Russian Memory," in *Clashes in European Memory: The Case of Communist Repression and the Holocaust*, eds. Muriel Blaive, Christian Gerbel and Thomas Lindenberger (Innsbruck: Studien Verlag, 2011), pp. 23–36.

[23] Before the constitutional reform of December 1988, the highest legislative body in the USSR was Supreme Soviet of the Soviet Union. In 1989, a new highest body – the Congress of People's Deputies of the Soviet Union, which elected the Supreme Soviet to carry out its functions when it was not in session – was introduced. Similar changes were made to the legislative organs of Soviet republics including Russia (the Russian Soviet Federal Socialist Republic before December 25, 1991, the Russian Federation since then).

official positions on a number of historical issues but did not criminalize "erroneous" opinions about them. Those bills were particularly important because battles over the past were at that time an essential aspect of Russian politics. The crisis of the Soviet system of ideological control and the emergence of a pluralistic society was prompting various political forces to look for alternative ways of protecting the "values" embedded in their conceptions of the national past. Memory laws appeared promising as a solution to this problem.

Under the Soviet regime, there were no specific laws banning any statements about the past that contradicted the official version of history, although "falsifications of history" could be punished on the basis of the Penal Code's articles forbidding anti-Soviet propaganda. In the late Soviet period, political repressions were, to be sure, most often limited to much less severe punishments than imprisonment (dismissal from one's job or expulsion from the Communist Party, which spelled the end of any meaningful career).[24] These relatively lenient measures were, however, enough to sustain the tradition of self-censorship that had been deeply rooted in Soviet academia and among the population in general since the Great Purges of the 1930s.

There were also no special provisions prohibiting Nazi symbols and ideology. But the Penal Code offered a spectrum of possibilities for punishing their dissemination. Fascist symbols could be considered manifestations of either anti-Soviet propaganda (Article 70) or propaganda of war that was forbidden by Article 71. In addition, Article 74 criminalized "propaganda and agitation aimed at incitement to racial or national hatred" as well as discrimination with regard to race or nationality. This article was similar to the anti-discriminatory articles that in the 1960s and 1970s were introduced into the penal codes of most European countries.[25]

Some of the laws and official declarations on the issues of the past that were adopted by the parliaments of the USSR and the Russian Federation at the turn of the 1990s articulated new democratic approaches to national history similar to Eastern European de-communization laws, while others

[24] Thus, in 1967, Alexander Nekrich was expelled from the party and later forced to emigrate because of his book *June 22, 1941*, which severely criticized Stalin for having failed to prepare the Soviet Union for the war (Aleksandr Nekrich, *1941, 22 iyunya* [Moscow: Nauka, 1965]). See also the appendices to the second Russian edition of that book (Moscow: Pamyatniki istoricheskoy mysli, 1995).
[25] The punishment for these offences was deprivation of liberty for up to five (Articles 70 and 74) or eight (Article 71) years. Aggravating circumstances could increase the punishment for anti-Soviet propaganda to a maximum of ten years.

were reminiscent of Soviet times. During this period, the political initiative usually lay with the democrats; the communists and nationalists developed their politics of memory largely in response to the democrats' proposals.

In November 1989, the Supreme Soviet of the USSR declared Stalin's deportations of the repressed peoples "illegal and criminal."[26] A month later, the Congress of People's Deputies of the USSR condemned the "secret protocols" of the Molotov-Ribbentrop non-aggression pact of August 23, 1939. And under the leadership of Boris Yeltsin, the Supreme Soviet of Russia enacted several laws dealing with the legacy of Stalinism. The law "On the Rehabilitation of the Repressed Peoples" of April 26, 1991, characterized Stalin's deportations of entire peoples as acts of genocide (Article 2). This, obviously, was among the first of the "new-style" (that is, genocide-focused) declarative memory laws.[27] The law "On the Rehabilitation of Victims of Political Repressions" of October 18, 1991, condemned Stalinism as a "totalitarian state," defined the notion of political repressions, and established procedures for rehabilitating victims.[28] As we know, similar bills were passed all across the former Soviet empire.

This law was drafted with the active participation of Memorial, a newly formed society that was to become an important agent in Russian history politics during the 1990s and 2000s.[29] Memorial was formally established in January 1989 at a conference of about 250 regional organizations involved in collecting information on, and perpetuating the memory of, the victims of the communist terror. But the movement that gave birth to the society had begun as early as 1987. It was, in fact, one of the first outcomes of Gorbachev's politics of public openness (*glasnost*). From the outset, the society's agenda included the publication of memory books containing the names of, and information about, victims of repression. In the decades that followed, Memorial supported the publication of hundreds of research monographs and regional memory books. It has also

---

[26] Declaration of the Supreme Soviet of the USSR of November 14, 1989 "O priznanii nezakonnymi i prestupnymi repressivnykh aktov protiv narodov, podvergshikhsya nasil'stvennomu pereseleniyu, i obespecheniyi ikh prav" [On Declaring the Repression of Forcibly Resettled Peoples Illegal and Criminal, and on Guaranteeing Their Rights].

[27] Law of the RSFSR No. 1107-I of April 26, 1991 "O reabilitatsii repressirovannykh narodov."

[28] Law of the RSFSR No. 1761-I of October 18, 1991 "O reabilitatsii zhertv politicheskikh repressiy"; Cathy A. Frierson, *Russia's Law 'On Rehabilitation of Victims of Political Repression': 1991–2011, An Enduring Artifact of Transitional Justice*, Working Paper, National Council for Eurasian and East European Research, February 28, 2014: www.ucis.pitt.edu/nceeer/2014_827-13h_Frierson_1.pdf.

[29] Adler, *Victims of Soviet Terror*; Smith, *Remembering Stalin's Victims*, pp. 78–130.

created an electronic database comprising the names of several million victims. However, the society's grand design to create a memorial complex to the victims of repression in Moscow has not succeeded, although numerous more modest local monuments have been erected throughout the country.

Memorial enjoyed some support from the higher echelons of the Soviet hierarchy (above all, from Aleksandr Yakovlev, Politburo member and Gorbachev's closest collaborator). But other forces in the Party leadership opted for an alternative politics of memory. They proposed using some of Memorial's approaches to foster the Soviet cult of the war rather than the memory of the Great Terror, and both Gorbachev and Yakovlev were supportive of those initiatives.

In January 1989, just a few days before Memorial's organizing conference, the Central Committee of the Communist Party had resolved to create an All-Union Memory Book that was to include names of all members of the military, the secret services, and the partisan movement who had participated in the war.[30] This book was to consist of regional books to be published by local war veterans' associations in collaboration with "search parties," which were groups of volunteers involved in the hunt for and burial of the remains of fallen soldiers as well as the care of military graves.[31]

The search movement with which Party conservatives tried to offset the efforts of the Memorial society had actually emerged at the turn of the 1960s. Initially, it was a volunteer movement, although supported by the Komsomol leadership, the Ministry of Defense, and the veterans' organizations. But the veterans' movement itself was poorly institutionalized at that time. In the 1950s and 1960s, the memory of the war, focusing as it did on casualties and the people's sufferings, had an aspect of countermemory in that it highlighted the government's indifference toward veterans and the unburied remains of its soldiers. In contrast to the official self-congratulatory narrative of the war, this counter-memory resembled to some extent the memory of the repressions. This situation changed in the

---

[30] O Vsesoyuznoy Knige Pamyati [On the All-Union Memory Book], *Izvestiya TsK KPSS* 2 (1989), pp. 37–39.

[31] More recently, in November 2006, the very name of Memorial was "borrowed" by the Ministry of Defense for its new project, an electronic data base ("OBD Memorial") containing the names of fallen soldiers and modeled after Memorial's own database. At the time of writing, OBD Memorial ranks higher on Russian Google than the original Memorial society. See Obobshchennyi bank dannykh "Memorial" [The "Memorial" Aggregated Database]: www.obd-memorial.ru/html/index .html.

1970s with the growing institutionalization of the cult of the war. Both the veterans' organizations and the search movement became more fully endorsed by the Communist Party and bureaucratized.[32] The veterans' organizations transformed into lobbyist networks consisting of retired members of the Soviet elites, and the search movement degenerated in a routine exercise in "patriotic education."

The project of the All-Union Memory Book was originated by the All-Union Committee of Veterans of War and Labor. That committee was established in September 1986, replacing the Committee of War Veterans (1956), on the initiative of Gorbachev, who saw veterans' organizations as "an institutionalized pillar of the [Soviet] political system" and "one of the 'strata' into which Soviet society was divided."[33] Naturally, Gorbachev was eager to win the veterans' support. Much like Aleksandr Yakovlev, himself a war veteran, Gorbachev saw the rehabilitation of victims of repression and the burial of soldiers' remains as two aspects of the same humanistic approach to the country's tragic past. But notwithstanding their partial intersection, the memory of the war and that of the repressions had very different political implications. Cultivating the veterans' memories of suffering, which merged with the smug official narrative of victory, was one way of marginalizing the memory of the Terror.

The All-Union Committee of Veterans, renamed All-Russian Societal Organization of Veterans of War, Labor, and Law Enforcement Agencies (ARSOV) in November 1991, played an important role in legislative initiatives related to the memory of the war. In February 1991, Gorbachev, in his capacity of President of the USSR, signed the decree "On Additional Measures for Perpetuating the Memory of the Soviet Citizens Who Died Defending the Country in the Pre-War Years and the Period of the Great Patriotic War, and Also of Those Who Have Fulfilled Their International Duty" (the latter term being a euphemism for the War in Afghanistan).[34] Gorbachev's decree quoted the veterans' discontent with the "indifference" of the "state organs" with respect to military graves as an important reason for improving the situation.

---

[32] Edele, *Soviet Veterans of the Second World War;* Natalia Danilova, "Veterans' Policy in Russia: A Puzzle of Creation," *The Journal of Power Institutions in Post-Soviet Societies* [Online] 6/7 (2007): http://pipss.revues.org/873; Danilova, "The Development of an Exclusive Veteran's Policy: The Case of Russia," *Armed Forces and Society* 36/5 (2009), pp. 890–916.

[33] Edele, *Soviet Veterans of the Second World War*, pp. 181–183.

[34] Decree of the President of the USSR of February 8, 1991 "O dopolnitelnykh merakh po uvekovecheniyu pamyati sovetskikh grazhdan, pogibshikh pri zashchite Rodiny v predvoyennyie gody i v period Velikoy Otechestvennoy voiny, a takzhe ispolnyavshikh internatsional'nyi dolg."

Later in the 1990s, the veterans' organizations became an important ally of the communist and nationalist opposition to Yeltsin's regime. From 1991 to 2009, ARSOV was chaired by Mikhail Trunov, a member of the CPRF Central Committee and formerly the first secretary of the CPSU regional organization in Belgorod. The veterans' organizations were, in fact, active in restoring the myth of the war that was to become one of the opposition's main ideological weapons. In January 1993, on the veterans' initiative, Yeltsin signed a law "On Perpetuating the Memory of Those Who Perished in Defending the Fatherland," which defined the responsibilities of local authorities relative to the protection and maintenance of military burial sites and the activities of the search parties.[35] The law provided that, alongside the memory of individual soldiers, the memory of the "associations, units, and institutions that distinguished themselves in the defense of the fatherland" was also to be perpetuated. The law did not specify which particular institutions it referred to, but the term "veterans" unambiguously included former employees of the law enforcement agencies such as the Ministry of the Interior and the KGB. In other words, the law was defending, albeit indirectly, the memory of the institutions that had been the instruments of Stalin's repressions. Although Yeltsin had reorganized the KGB after the August Putsch of 1991, he was in no position to furnish its "veterans" with fewer privileges than those afforded to former members of the military. That would certainly propel the secret services into the arms of the opposition.

In the years that followed, the reorganized Communist Party gave its full support to the activities of the veterans' organizations, including their legislative initiatives. Those initiatives traditionally dealt with issues regarding the search movement and the rights of veterans. But some also came in response to the rise of Russian fascism after 1993. Russian democrats too proposed legislative measures to counter the danger from the far right.

The first far-right organizations emerged in Russia during perestroika, often with the informal support of the KGB. The most influential of these organizations was Dmitriy Vasilyev's *Pamyat'* ("Memory") Society. The far-right movement had been devastated and disordered by the collapse of the communist regime but had regained some of its influence by 1993, forming paramilitary organizations, such as Aleksandr Barkashov's Russian National Unity, which openly declared themselves in sympathy with

[35] Law No. 4292–1 of January 14, 1993 "Ob uvekovechenii pamyati pogibshikh pri zashchite Otechestva."

fascism. Many far-right "combatants" supported the Supreme Soviet of the Russian Federation during the anti-Yeltsin insurgency of October 1993. The success of Vladimir Zhirinovskiy and his ultra-nationalist Liberal Democratic Party in the parliamentary elections of December 1993 was another sign of the mounting fascist danger. The rise of the far-right movement was obviously a reaction to severe economic hardships, which had generated disappointment with democracy and the West.

By 1994, the fascist danger was one of the most hotly debated topics in the Russian media. Several anti-fascist organizations, including the Moscow Anti-Fascist Center, launched a discussion of legislative ways of countering it. The new Constitution adopted in December 1993 banned organizations based on the ideas of "social, national, racial, or religious" inequality and prohibited the promotion of those ideas.[36] Several laws (on mass media, on public associations, etc.) adopted in the 1990s reiterated the same norms. The old Soviet Penal Code, which remained in use until 1996, criminalized incitement to hatred and other offences of a racist nature. Its Article 74 would have served well to punish neo-Nazi activities had it ever been practically implemented by the courts. But Russian prosecutors and judges, most of whom were quite conservative in their political outlook, were in no hurry to use that article against neo-fascists. They claimed that its wording was too general for it to be an effective weapon against racism and xenophobia. Democratic politicians then proposed new laws specifically targeted against manifestations of neo-fascism.

The initiative for that legislation came from Alla Gerber and Evgeniy Proshechkin. In March 1994, Proshechkin, the president of the Moscow Anti-Fascist Center and a deputy of the Moscow City Duma, wrote to Yeltsin regarding an anti-fascist law. Yeltsin was quick to support the idea. Gerber was a journalist and organizer of the Moscow Anti-Fascist Center. Elected to the State Duma as a deputy from Yegor Gaidar's Russia's Choice party in December 1993, she was instrumental in promoting the anti-fascist agenda in the parliament. In February 1995, she organized parliamentary hearings under the rubric of "On the Prevention of Manifestations of the Fascist Danger in the Russian Federation," which introduced Russian political circles to the notion of memory law.

But the Russian communists, unwilling to cede the anti-fascism "territory" to democrats, continued to insist, as they had during the Soviet period, that the Communist Party had been the major anti-fascist force and had made a decisive contribution to the victory over Nazism.

---

[36] The Constitution of the Russian Federation, Articles 13.5 and 29.2.

However, in the 1990s, the CPRF was becoming increasingly nationalist. Reluctant to alienate the far-right combatants who had been the main paramilitary force behind the communist-supported insurgency of October 1993, many communist leaders began making openly xenophobic and anti-Semitic statements,[37] which explains why communists were often labeled "fascists." Democrats typically viewed the fascist danger as both "red" and "brown," meaning that it emanated from both the communist and ultra-nationalist camps. And the communists and nationalists, in turn, stigmatized the democrats as fascists, accused them of betraying Russia's national interests, and called the market reforms "the genocide of the Russian people." However, the prevailing understanding of the fascist danger was closer to its interpretation by the democrats.

In December 1994, on the initiative of the veterans' lobby supported by the CPRF, the Russian parliament passed a law "On Veterans" (signed by Yeltsin in January 1995).[38] This piece of legislation created several categories of veterans: veterans of World War II; veterans of other "military combats" including the war in Afghanistan; veterans of other military services, including the Ministry of the Interior and the KGB; veterans of state service; and veterans of labor. It also defined the privileges extended to each of these categories, with the war veterans being the most highly preferred. Focusing as it did on entitlements, the law was only indirectly linked to historical memory. But it clearly demonstrated the political importance of the veterans' lobby.

The reader will remember that in 1995, during the First Chechen War, the fiftieth anniversary of the victory over Nazi Germany was celebrated with much pomp and ceremony. Meanwhile, the January 1995 law "On Veterans" launched a legislative campaign that was timed to coincide with this anniversary. In March 1995, Yeltsin signed a law "On Days of Military Glory and Memorial Days in Russia,"[39] which established the celebration of some fifteen "days of military glory" every year, ordering this to include the commemoration of the Soviet victories during World War II as well as victories won by pre-revolutionary Russian rulers and generals.

Ten days later, Yeltsin signed a decree titled "On Measures Designed to Ensure the Coordinated Action of Bodies of State Power in the Struggle against Manifestations of Fascism and Other Forms of Political Extremism

---

[37] March, *The Communist Party in Post-Soviet Russia*, pp. 111–114.
[38] Federal Law No. 5-FZ of January 12, 1995 "O veteranakh."
[39] Federal Law No. 32-FZ of March 13, 1995 "O dnyakh voinskoy slavy i pamyatnykh datakh Rossii."

in the Russian Federation."⁴⁰ This document opens with a disturbing picture of the revival of fascist ideology in Russia and the law enforcement system's inability to prevent it. It goes on to refer to veterans who are insulted by manifestations of fascism. Yeltsin then instructed his administration to join the Ministry of the Interior and the Ministry of Justice in drafting a law criminalizing manifestations of fascism. This decree clearly shows that, in the context of the First Chechen War, supporting anti-fascist initiatives, expanding veterans' privileges, and promoting Russian military glory were seen as aspects of a single propaganda campaign.

That campaign culminated in May 1995, with the adoption of the law "On Perpetuating [the Memory of] the Victory of the Soviet People in the Great Patriotic War of 1941–1945." This law provided the rules for celebrating Victory Day, maintaining war memorials, and so on. However, Article 6 introduced, for the first time in the history of Russian legislation, special provisions against fascist ideology and symbols:

> A resolute struggle against any manifestations of fascism represents a major aspect of the state politics of the Russian Federation with respect to perpetuating [the memory of] the victory of the Soviet People in the Great Patriotic War. The Russian Federation has assumed an obligation to make every effort to prevent the establishment and operation of fascist organizations and movements on its territory.
>
> In the Russian Federation it shall be forbidden to use Nazi symbols in any form, as an affront to the multiethnic nature of Russian people and the memory of the victims of the Great Patriotic War.⁴¹

The choice of the word "victims" (instead of "veterans") demonstrated the authors' intention to victimize the tragic past rather than to further develop the traditional Soviet heroic narrative. Nonetheless, the law did not introduce criminal penalties for violating the ban on Nazi symbols and ideology. Yeltsin did not want to jeopardize this law by including a provision that could create controversy in the parliament, intending instead to draw up a separate law criminalizing manifestations of fascism.

---

⁴⁰ Decree of the President of the RF No. 310 of March 23, 1995 "O merakh po obespecheniyu soglasovannykh deystviy organov gosudarstvennoy vlasti v bor'be s proyavleniyami fashizma i inykh form politicheskogo ekstremizma v Rossiyskoy Federatsii."
⁴¹ Federal Law No. 80-FZ of May 19, 1995 "Ob uvekovechenii Pobedy sovetskogo naroda v Velikoy Otechestvennoy voyne 1941–1945 godov." The English translation is quoted from www.mhg.ru/english/1FF846B. On the same day, Yeltsin signed a law "On Public Associations" that also prohibited organizations whose aim was to incite social, national or racial hatred and whose name and symbols "insult national or religious feelings." See Federal Law No. 82-FZ of May 19, 1995 "Ob obshchestvennykh obyedineniyakh," Articles 16, 23, and 24.

The bill in question was introduced into the parliament in June 1995.[42] The president proposed to add two new articles (74.2 and 74.3) to the Penal Code prohibiting both "the propaganda of fascism" and public associations using "the theory and practices of fascism as the basis for their activities and [pursuing] as their goal the creation of a totalitarian state."[43] Yeltsin also proposed to modify Article 229, "Desecration of Graves," to specifically criminalize the desecration of military graves and monuments "dedicated to the struggle against fascism or to victims of fascism" with fascist symbols. Finally, he proposed to add to the administrative code an article prohibiting fascist symbols. Yeltsin's initiative further developed the tradition of legislation on veterans, the search movement, and the burial of fallen soldiers. But it also promoted the new democratic agenda of counteracting the rise of the far-right movement. This draft penalizing both fascist propaganda and desecration of military graves set up a paradigm that in the 2000s would be reproduced in the significantly different political context of several Ukrainian draft laws (including the dictatorship laws of January 2014). In Ukraine, this combination would signify the endorsement of the Soviet war myth; in contrast, in the Russian context of the 1990s it looked much more like a compromise between different memories.

Unsurprisingly, the president's project sank without trace in the parliament, although his proposals regarding the desecration of graves and the display of fascist symbols later found their way, respectively, into the new Penal Code of 1996 (in force since 1997) and the new administrative code (in force since 2002). Yeltsin did not push his project, partly because he preferred the initiative for anti-fascist legislation to come from "below,"[44] and because several other relevant proposals were in fact introduced into the Duma at about the same time.

Several bills were initiated in particular by Evgeniy Proshechkin who, as a deputy of the Moscow City Duma, was responsible for coordinating its anti-extremist policy. During his term (1993–1997), the capital's parliament was an important source of memory law initiatives. In addition to several drafts of federal laws submitted to the State Duma, the Moscow

---

[42] The following discussion is based upon A.M. Verkhovskiy, *Politika gosudarstva po otnosheniyu k natsional-radikal'nym obyedineniyam, 1991–2002* [Government Policies towards Radical Nationalist Groups] [2002] (Moscow: Tsentr "Sova," 2013), pp. 84–129 (an abridged English translation is available at www.mhg.ru/english/1FF6905). The electronic archives of the State Duma are incomplete for the mid-1990s, but some bills that interest us here were initiated by the Moscow City Duma and are available on its website.

[43] A.M. Verkhovskiy, *Politika gosudarstva*, p. 85.

[44] Proshechkin received this information from Yeltsin's political advisor, Georgiy Satarov (http://site .mgd.mos.ru/ru/956/page/proshechkin-evgeniy-viktorovich/).

Duma adopted, in 1997, a law "On Administrative Liability for Manufacturing, Disseminating, and Displaying Nazi Symbols [in Moscow]" (similar laws were also adopted in Moscow Region in 1999 and in St. Petersburg in 2000).[45]

In his first draft of 1995, Proshechkin proposed an indirect ban on neofascist ideology. The bill listed several criteria on whose basis an organization could be declared extremist. Alongside "public calls for the establishment of a dictatorship," "setting up military units," and "conducting propaganda of war," these criteria included

> [The use of] symbols historically associated with the national-socialist regime of Germany and fascist regime of Italy, [including the] swastika in any of its modifications;
>
> Public approval of national-socialist, fascist or any other totalitarian regimes; denial of the crimes committed by such regimes; and justifying their leaders and politics.[46]

In addition to this draft, Proshechkin submitted another bill that amended the Penal Code by introducing penalties for organizing or actively participating in an extremist organization,[47] his goal being to outlaw organizations such as Russian National Unity rather than to proscribe undesirable statements about the past.

An important difference between Proshechkin's proposal and its Western prototypes consisted in the mention of "other totalitarian regimes." This was, of course, a way to criminalize justification of Stalinism and the denial of communist crimes, which explains why the communist-dominated parliament took a dim view of the draft. The State Duma rejected two successive versions of both bills.[48]

---

[45] Moscow City Law No. 1 of January 15, 1997 "Ob administrativnoy otvetstvennosti za izgotovleniye, rasprostraneniye i demonstratsiyu natsistkoy simvoliki."

[46] Moscow City Duma Decision No. 38 of May 24, 1995, "O zakonodatel'noy initsiative Moskovskoy Gorodskoy Dumy o proekte federal'nogo zakona 'O zapreshcheniyi deyatel'nosti ekstremistskikh obshchestvennykh ob'edineniy v Rossii' i o proekte federal'nogo zakona 'O vneseniyi izmeneniy i dopolneniy v Ugolovnyi kodeks Rossiyskoy Federatsiyi' [On the Legislative Initiative of the Moscow State Duma with Respect to the Federal Law Draft "On the Banning of Activities of Extremist Public Associations in Russia" and to the Federal Law Draft "On Introducing Changes and Additions to the Penal Code of the Russian Federation"]; Verkhovskiy, Politika gosudarstva, p. 89, and Aleksandr Verkhovskiy, Anatoliy Papp, and Vladimir Pribylovskiy, Politicheskiy ekstremizm v Rossii [Political Extremism in Russia] (Moscow: Panorama, 1996), pp. 82–83.

[47] Imprisonment of up to five or three years, respectively.

[48] The second versions of both bills were introduced in the parliament by Decision No. 7 of the Moscow City Duma of January 17, 1996, under the same titles as the drafts of May 1995. See Draft Laws Nos. 96037631–2 of February 8, 1996, and 96900657–2 of February 8, 1996.

In May 1996, as the anti-communist propaganda campaign hit a peak on the eve of the presidential elections, the Moscow City Duma presented another draft modeled after European memory laws. This time, the bill proposed to outlaw the justification of Nazi crimes rather than proscribing extremist organizations. More specifically, Proshechkin and his colleagues suggested an amendment to the Penal Code (Article 74.1) that provided up to four years' incarceration for

> Public justification, approval, glorification or denial and gross diminishing of the crimes of national-socialist, fascist and other regimes that had been involved in acts of genocide, war crimes, crimes against peace and humanity, as well as public glorification and attempts to justify the leaders of such regimes that have been called criminal by the decisions of international tribunals.[49]

The punishment could be increased to up to five years if the offenses were committed through the mass media and up to seven years if they were "committed repeatedly, by an organized group or an official using his official position."

The language of the draft, including the reference to the decisions of international tribunals, reveals the influence of the Gayssot Act. The classification of Nazi crimes ("war crimes, crimes against peace and humanity") is taken from the Charter of the Nuremberg Tribunal. The fact that Article 74.1 was to follow Article 74, "Infringement of National and Racial Equality," shows that Nazi crimes were understood as offenses of a racist nature, which was also typical of the European legislation.

The bill was so formulated as to give no firm impression that denial of Stalin's crimes fell within its scope. Indeed, Stalinism had not been condemned as criminal by any international tribunal, so that the second part of the article could not possibly apply to its "glorification." But the first part, prohibiting approval of any "regime that had been involved in acts of genocide, war crimes, or crimes against peace and humanity," makes no reference to any international tribunals, so that it was possible to claim that the bill also outlawed pro-Stalinist statements. In any event, the communist and nationalist majority in the parliament refused to consider this project under the pretext that, since a new penal code was in the making, modifications to the old one would be pointless. However,

---

[49] Draft Law No. 96027807-2 of June 11, 1996 "O vneseniyi izmemeniya v Ugolovnyi kodeks Rossiyskoy Federatsiyi" [On Introducing a Change to the Penal Code of the Russian Federation]; Moscow City Duma Decision No. 49 of May 29, 1996; and Verkhovskiy, *Politika gosudarstva*, p. 94.

the new code, which was adopted in June 1996, contained nothing that criminalized fascist propaganda or denial of Nazi crimes.

In that code, Article 282, "Incitement to National, Racial, or Religious Enmity," replaced Article 74 of the 1960 code. It reads:

> Actions aimed at the incitement of national, racial, or religious enmity, abasement of human dignity, and also propaganda of the exceptionality, superiority, or inferiority of individuals by reason of their attitude to religion, national, or racial affiliation, if these acts have been committed in public or with the use of mass media, shall be punishable by a fine... or by deprivation of liberty for a term of two to four years.[50]

The scope of this article is narrower than that of Article 74 of the 1960 code, which also criminalized discrimination with regard to race or nationality. In the code of 1996, those offenses are forbidden by Article 136, "Violation of the Equality of Human and Civil Rights and Freedoms."

Proshechkin was not discouraged by the parliament's refusal to consider his bill. In May 1997, he proposed adding the same article (now Article 282.1) to the new Penal Code. However, the reference to "other [criminal] regimes" was now included into the name of the bill.[51] But in October, that draft too was turned down by the parliament, on the grounds that those offenses were already punishable under Article 282. Also in October, the Moscow City Duma initiated a new bill, introducing Article 282.2, "On Criminal Liability for the Use of Nazi Symbols, in any form, in the Russian Federation,"[52] which was no more successful than its predecessors. Soon after that, in December 1997, Proshechkin failed in his bid for reelection, and the Moscow City Duma ceased being an important center

[50] Or up to 5 years under aggravating circumstances. See The Criminal Code of the Russian Federation of June 13, 1996.
[51] Draft Law No. 97700740-2 of May 13, 1997 "O vneseniyi izmeneniy v Ugolovnyi kodeks Rossiyskoy Federatsiyi (po voprosu ustanovleniya ugolovnoy otvetstvennosti za opravdaniye prestupleniy national-sotsialisticheskogo, fashistskogo i inykh rezhimov)" [On Introducing Changes to the Penal Code of the Russian Federation (Regarding the Introduction of Criminal Liability for the Justification of Crimes of the National-Socialist, Fascist, and Other Regimes)]; Moscow City Duma Decision No. 13 of February 19, 1997, and Verkhovskiy, *Politika gosudarstva*, p. 95.
[52] Draft Law No. 97075221 of October 10, 1997 "O vneseniyi dopolneniya v Ugolovnyi kodeks Rossiyskoy Federatsiyi (ob ugolovnoy otvetstvennosti za ispol'zovaniye natsistskoy simvoliki)" [On Introducing an Addition to the Penal Code of the Russian Federation (Regarding Criminal Liability for the Use of Nazi Symbols)]; Verkhovskiy, *Politika gosudarstva*, p. 96. The same proposal was resubmitted, as Draft Law No. 97077104-2, on November 10, 1997. Also in October, Proshechkin proposed to modify the 1995 law "On Public Associations" by prohibiting associations whose activities involved the denial and justification of fascist crimes and the promotion of Nazi symbols. See Moscow City Duma Decision No. 72 of October 15, 1997, and Verkhovskiy, *Politika gosudarstva*, p. 97.

of anti-fascist legislative initiatives. Yet before Proshechkin's departure, the Moscow Duma succeeded including an anti-fascist article into the new administrative code (drafted in 1997, adopted in 2001, and enacted in 2002). That article (Article 20.3) introduced administrative penalties for "displaying fascist attributes and symbolism for the purposes of popularization of such attributes and symbolism."[53]

Let us now return to the summer of 1995. The main alternative to the Moscow City Duma's first effort was a bill submitted by Viktor Zorkaltsev, MP and a communist representative at the 1992 "CPSU Trial." But, unlike Proshechkin's drafts, Zorkaltsev's bill did not criminalize fascist ideology and the use of fascist symbols; instead, the justification of fascism was categorized an administrative offense punishable with a fine. According to Aleksandr Verkhovskiy, this bill "was aimed at creating an instrument of soft pressure on radical nationalists, while at the same time providing protection to moderate nationalists."[54] The draft also introduced administrative liability for officials who have "wrongfully" accused "citizens or legal entities" of being fascists. The bill defined fascism as the "ideology and practice" of domination of some nations and races over the other, without mentioning such features as political repression, the denial of democracy, or a leader cult. Those omissions were clearly intentional: Zorkaltsev was being careful not to give democrats an opening to use his bill against neo-Stalinists. The law also prohibited "propaganda of fascism" and "the distribution in public places of materials rehabilitating the fascist leaders, clearing them of the blame for genocide and other crimes against peace, humankind and humanity."[55]

The parliament's Legal Department supported the project but suggested that some important modifications be made to it. First, the Duma lawyers advised introducing criminal rather than administrative liability for the offenses envisaged in the draft, given that similar crimes of a racist nature were considered criminal offenses by Article 74 of the Penal Code. The Legal Department also suggested rephrasing the bill in the following way:

---

[53] In its current version, Article 20.3 reads: "1. Displaying fascist attributes and symbolism for the purpose of popularizing such attributes and symbolism shall entail the imposition of an administrative fine in the amount of five hundred to one thousand rubles, accompanied by confiscation of the fascist attributes and symbols, or administrative arrest for a term of up to fifteen days accompanied by confiscation of the fascist attributes and symbols." See Kodeks Rossiyskoy Federatsii ob administrativnykh pravonarusheniyakh ot 30.12.2001 [Code of Administrative Offences of the Russian Federation of December 20, 2001]. A partial English translation (www.wipo.int/edocs/lexdocs/laws/en/ru/ru073en.pdf) is quoted here with necessary revisions.

[54] Verkhovskiy, *Politika gosudarstva*, p. 100.   [55] *Ibid.*, p. 99.

Public distribution of materials rehabilitating Nazi (fascist) war criminals, exonerating them from the responsibility for the crimes committed against peace, war crimes and crimes against humanity as defined in Article 6 of the Charter of the International Military Tribunal, which is an integral part of the Agreement between the governments of the Union of the Soviet Socialist Republics, United States of America and the United Kingdom of Great Britain and Northern Ireland and the Interim Government of the French Republic on the legal prosecution and punishment of the principal war criminals of the European countries of the Axis, signed in London on August 8, 1945, and as defined in Article 1 of the Convention of November 26, 1968 "On the Non-Applicability of Time Limitations for War Crimes and Crimes against Humanity," shall be prohibited.[56]

This modification was clearly inspired by the Gayssot Act, which also refers to the definition of Nazi crimes in the Charter of the Nuremberg Tribunal. But the lawyers' suggestions were ignored by Zorkaltsev. In any event, his project, along with Proshechkin's, was turned down by the State Duma in July 1995. In July 1996, Zorkaltsev came up with a slightly rephrased version of his bill (in which the typology of Nazi crimes was modified in accordance with the Nuremberg Charter).[57] But that project was also rejected, in March 1997, because neither the democrats nor the nationalists were fully satisfied with it: for the former, it was not sufficiently radical, while the latter found it dangerous. In April 1999, Zorkaltsev proposed the third version of the same bill, which now contained a better definition of fascism seen as both a manifestation of racism and an anti-democratic system.[58] But the upcoming regime change made the project untimely, and it was buried in the Duma.

The government produced several other anti-fascist legal initiatives in the late 1990s. In August 1998, shortly before its fall, the government of Sergey Kiriyenko introduced into the parliament a bill titled "On the Banning of Nazi Symbols and Literature,"[59] which resembled both the Moscow law of January 1997 and Proshechkin's draft of October 1997. Interestingly, this draft privileged the concept of Nazism over that of fascism, in a tendency that was to prevail in the 2000s.

The government's main goal was to provide a workable definition of the notions of "Nazi symbols and literature." By "Nazi literature" the bill

---

[56] *Ibid.*, pp. 101–102.
[57] Draft Law No. 96700070-2 of February 12, 1996 "O zapreshchenii propagandy fashizma v Rossiyskoy Federatsii" [On the Banning of Fascist Propaganda in the Russian Federation].
[58] Draft Law No. 99041517-2 of April 4, 1999.
[59] Draft Law No. 98067778-2 of August 10, 1998 "O zapreshchenii natsistskoy simvoliki i literatury."

means not only the writings of Nazi and fascist leaders but also "other publications justifying national and racial inequality or the practice of committing war and other crimes of Nazism that had been condemned by the Nuremberg International Military Tribunal." The bill then expands this concept to include publications "calling for the genocide of ethnic groups or violent actions against their individual members" (Article 2). The ban concerns not pro-Nazi statements as such but the manufacturing and display of their material vehicles. This makes the Kiriyenko bill similar to several European acts, including the German law of 1960, which criminalized the dissemination of pro-Nazi literature.

The government's project did not introduce any penalties for the actions it prohibited, stating only that these offenses were punishable "in accordance with applicable law" (Article 4). Most likely, "applicable law" is none other than Article 282 of the Penal Code.

The Russian financial default of August 1998 and the fall of the Kiriyenko government destroyed his bill's chances. In June 1999, Sergey Stepashin's short-lived government included similar provisions in its broader anti-extremist bill, which defined the responsibility of various public institutions in the fight against political extremism. This law did not introduce any new sanctions either, and referred only to existing legislation. Its focus was on counteracting extremist organizations in their role of a potential fomenter of violence – an unsurprising emphasis on the eve of the Second Chechen War, which began in August 1999 but was already foreseeable in June. It was probably no coincidence that the bill on extremism came from a government led by a former Minister of the Interior (who had also headed Federal Security Service). This tradition of limiting democratic freedoms under color of the fight against extremism was to be continued by Putin.

The new government's bill viewed fascism – or, rather, the incitement to national or racial hatred – as an aspect of extremism:

> Political extremism is activity... aimed at changing by force the consti-
> tutional order of the Russian Federation, forcible seizure or retention of
> power, violation of the sovereignty and territorial integrity of the Russian
> Federation, organization of illegal armed groups, and incitement to
> national, racial, or religious hatred, as well as public calls for the use of
> illegal actions for political purposes.[60]

---

[60] Draft Law No. 99058804–2 of June 8, 1999 "O protivodeystvii politicheskomu ekstremizmu" [On Counteracting Political Extremism], Article 3.

The Stepashin government fell shortly after submitting the bill. The outbreak of the Second Chechen War and Putin's rise to power changed the political situation in the country, rendering many draft laws obsolete.

The law on extremism, which was proposed by the new administration and adopted in July 2002, was expected to solve all the problems that the anti-fascist drafts of the 1990s had failed to face. With some notable changes, it developed the approach outlined in Stepashin's project of 1999. Significantly, the concept of political extremism here gave place to that of extremism tout court. The reason was obvious: the authorities planned to use the law less against Russian nationalists than against various Islamic (and in particular Chechen) groups, which is made clear by the bill's description of extremist organizations as "public or religious associations." The law lists a spectrum of measures to be taken not only against extremist organizations but also against media publishers of extremist materials (provisions that would later become a key instrument of censorship). Although this enactment associated extremism first and foremost with terrorism and the seizure of political power by force, racism and nationalism were still important. It mentioned in particular the following criteria for "extremist activities":

> [I]ncitation of social, racial, nationalistic or religious animosity; debasement of national dignity;... propaganda of exclusivity, advocating either superiority or inferiority of citizens on the basis of religion, social, racial, national, religious or linguistic affiliation;... propaganda and public demonstration of Nazi paraphernalia or symbolism. (Articles 1.1, 1.2)[61]

The law explicitly addresses issues of historical memory when giving the following definition of the notion of "extremist materials":

> Extremist materials [are] documents... encouraging extremist activity, either supporting or justifying the necessity for carrying out such activity, including works of the leaders of the National-Socialist Workers Party of Germany, the Fascist Party of Italy, publications supporting or justifying national and (or) racial supremacy, either supporting or justifying the practice of committing... crimes directed at the complete or partial destruction of any social, national, ethic, racial, or religious group. (Article 1.3)

---

[61] Federal Law No. 114/FZ of July 25, 2002 "O protivodeystvii ekstremistskoy deyatel'nosti" [On Countering Extremist Activity], Articles 1.1, 1.2. The English translation is quoted from http://host.uniroma3.it/progetti/cedir/cedir/Lex-doc/Ru_Ext-2002.pdf. See also Andrei Richter, "One Step Beyond Hate Speech: Post-Soviet Regulation of 'Extremist' and 'Terrorist' Speech in the Media," in *The Content and Context of Hate Speech: Rethinking Regulation and Responses*, eds. Michael Herz and Peter Molnar (Cambridge: Cambridge University Press, 2012), pp. 290–305.

Characteristically, it avoids privileging either the concept of fascism or that of Nazism, subsuming both under the generic concept of "extremism." It did not provide new criminal or administrative penalties for the aforementioned offenses, but it did simplify the procedures to be used in shutting down public associations and mass media outlets found guilty of extremist activities. The parliament, now under Putin's control, adopted the new law two months after its submission. About the same time, in July 2002, the new administrative code came into force, making the use of fascist symbols an administrative offense nationwide.

The adoption of the anti-extremist bill and the new administrative code closed the 1990s' cycle of anti-fascist legislation. Fascist activities, including the dissemination of fascist literature and the demonstration of fascist symbols, became an administrative offense and a criterion for considering an organization extremist, which could entail its closure and result in criminal charges being brought against its leaders. In a sense, it was a worthy end to the efforts of the democratic politicians who in the 1990s called for the outlawing of fascist ideology. But this legislation's true goal was to counter religious and political dissent rather than to combat neo-fascism.[62]

Although the legislation of the 1990s and early 2000s contained some aspects of memory laws, several proposals for criminalizing statements about the past, including Holocaust denial, were unsuccessful. Those democratic initiatives, although basically inspired by the Gayssot Act, also sought to penalize the denial of communist crimes. But those bills failed to pass, mostly because the communist and nationalist opposition perceived them as a potential hazard. It is worth noting that, in contrast to most Eastern European countries, the Russian democrats' memory law drafts, including proposals aimed at counteracting neo-Stalinist interpretations of Soviet history, developed the tradition of anti-fascist legislation rather than that of de-communization which can be explained by both the exceptional status of anti-fascism in Soviet/Russian political rhetoric and the failure of Boris Yeltsin's regime to pursue systematic de-communization of the country. No doubt, this failure also explains the turn that the Russian politics of the past took under Yeltsin's successor. A new period in the history of Russian legislation on the issues of the past began in the late 2000s, when memory laws became an instrument of a politics of memory that promoted Putin's myth of the war.

---

[62] In fact, the regime proved reluctant to take on the far-right organizations until the end of the 2000s. See Aleksandr Verkhovskiy, "Natsisty i kuratory" [The Nazis and Their Curators]: www.sova-center.ru/racism-xenophobia/publications/2011/05/d21684/.

CHAPTER 6

Memory Laws in Putin's Russia

The Politics of History under Putin

Putin's coming to power on December 31, 1999, marked the beginning of Russia's "derailment from democracy," a process in which a nationalistic politics of memory played an important role. This politics has, in part, continued a tendency already noticeable under Yeltsin, in particular his search for a "national idea" that reflected Russian public opinion's conservative and anti-Western shift in the late 1990s. Yeltsin's politics of memory, however, consisted largely in rejecting the communist past and praising eighteenth- and nineteenth-century Russian culture. By contrast, Putin's government chose to partially rehabilitate the Soviet period, which had to be purified of its specifically communist aspects and incorporated into the longue durée of the history of the Russian state. Yeltsin's "soft" cultural patriotism resembled that which Western governments had sought to develop through a politics of cultural heritage. Putin's government, on the other hand, has chosen the idea of the state as its key ideological reference.[1]

The nostalgia for the Soviet past was reinforced by the beginning of Russia's economic recovery in the mid-1990s and by the rise in oil prices and the economic growth of the 2000s. As the deprivations of the Yeltsin period gave way to relatively prosperous years under Putin, Russian society gradually became less critical of its Soviet roots. Russians were infatuated with the supposedly heroic aspects of their history and did not care to think about its tragic side, even though they knew all about that

---

[1] On Putin's politics of memory, see Catherine Merridale, "Redesigning History in Contemporary Russia," *Journal of Contemporary History* 38/1 (2003), pp. 13–28; Nanci Adler, "The Future of the Soviet Past Remains Unpredictable: The Resurrection of Stalinist Symbols Amidst the Exhumation of Mass Graves," *Europe-Asia Studies* 57/8 (2005), pp. 1093–1119; Dina Khapaeva, "Historical Memory in Post-Soviet Gothic Society," *Social Research* 76/1 (2009), pp. 359–394; Thomas Sherlock, "Confronting the Stalinist Past: The Politics of Memory in Russia," *Washington Quarterly* 34/2 (2011), pp. 93–109.

tragedy.[2] And the "new regime" was not lax in exploiting and reinforcing that state of mind.

As is typically the case in countries rich in natural resources, Putin's government chose a conservative model of development, which relied almost completely on the economic infrastructure inherited from Soviet times. It was a choice that entailed an increasingly elevated level of state control over the economy.[3] Notwithstanding the rhetoric of modernization, Putin's Russia presents as a past-dependent rather than a future-oriented society, in both economic and cultural terms. But that being so, the regime's obsession with historical memory was inevitable. Living on the "heritage" of the USSR, including its oil and gas industry, and defending the national past against its "denigrators" are merely two aspects of the same strategy.[4] The Soviet legacy has come to be seen as the foundation of national cohesion, prosperity, and greatness. The past, which had been rejected and all but forgotten during the period of market reforms, when the nation placed great hopes on the future, made a robust return in the 2000s, when it came to inform Russian politics and cultural life. And the legacy of the Russian/Soviet empire was central to this reemergence of the past.[5]

---

[2] Thus, the respondents of a sociological survey (St. Petersburg, May–June 2007) give the following estimates of the number of victims of Stalin's terror: 34 percent believe the number of victims to be between 10 and 30 million, 17 percent between 1 and 10 million, and 14 percent between 30 and 50 million. Parallel surveys conducted in Kazan' (capital of the autonomous republic of Tatarstan) and Ulyanovsk (a Volga region city) give very similar results. (The question was formulated in intentionally vague terms to try to elicit the respondent's spontaneous evaluations of the scale of the repressions.) Respectively, 70, 61, and 56 percent of the respondents in these cities stated that the repressions were "totally unjustified." See my *Pamyat' strogogo rezhima: Istoriya i politika v Rossii* [Strict Security Memory: History and Politics in Russia] (Moscow: Novoye literaturnoye obozreniye, 2011), pp. 168–180.

[3] M. Steven Fish, *Democracy Derailed in Russia: The Failure of Open Politics* (Cambridge: Cambridge University Press, 2005); Anders Åslund, *How Capitalism Was Built: The Transformation of Central and Eastern Europe, Russia, and Central Asia* (Cambridge: Cambridge University Press, 2007); and Åslund, *Russia's Capitalist Revolution: Why Market Reform Succeeded and Democracy Failed* (Washington, DC: Peterson Institute for International Economics, 2007).

[4] David M. Kotz and Fred Weir, *Russia's Path from Gorbachev to Putin: The Demise of the Soviet System and the New Russia* (London: Routledge, 2007); Richard Sakwa, *Putin: Russia's Choice*, 2nd ed. (Abingdon: Routledge, 2008); Sakwa, *Putin Redux: Power and Contradiction in Contemporary Russia* (London, New York: Routledge, 2014); Marcel H. Van Herpen, *Putinism: The Slow Rise of a Radical Right Regime in Russia* (Basingstoke: Palgrave Macmillan, 2013); and Karen Dawisha, *Putin's Kleptocracy: Who Owns Russia?* (New York: Simon and Schuster 2014). On Russia's "conservative modernization" and the past viewed as a "natural resource," see Ilya Kalinin, "Nostalgic Modernization: The Soviet Past as a 'Historical Horizon,'" *Slavonica* 17/2 (2011), pp. 156–167, and Kalinin, "Boyi za istoriyu: Proshloye kak ogranichennyi resurs" [Battles over History: The Past as a Limited Resource], *Neprikosnovennyi zapas* 78 (2011), pp. 330–339. Cf. Miguel Vázquez Liñán, "Modernization and Historical Memory in Russia: Two Sides of the Same Coin," *Problems of Post-Communism* 59/6 (2012), pp. 15–26.

[5] Writing in 2009, Jeffrey Mankoff maintained that "Russia still confronts the burdens of history in a way few large states do." He refers here to Russia's past, which he views as powerfully determining the country's choices in the present. See his *Russian Foreign Policy: The Return of Great Power Politics*,

Relative prosperity largely explains the self-congratulatory mood typical of Russian society in the 2000s. Reveling in their newly acquired wealth, the elites as well as the middle class were eager to align themselves with the state, which became the main source of funding due to its control over the country's natural resources and the rise of oil prices. The idea of the state was central to the "conception of self" that typified Russian bureaucrats, who tellingly called themselves "the sovereign's men" (*slugi gosudarevy*), but was even more characteristic of the secret services, whose representatives formed the core of the new president's team. As for the underprivileged classes, their involvement in the cult of the state was attributable to the tradition of paternalism that imbued Russian political culture in both the pre-revolutionary and the Soviet periods.[6]

One might expect the cult of the state to be alien to the group of liberal economists who had formed the core of Yeltsin's team and became important partners in the coalition of political and social forces that gave their support to Putin's regime. However, many of those liberals were recently engaged in a fierce jockeying for power with the "oligarchs" who had tried to control the government in the late 1990s.[7] As a result, a strong state that could overcome the resistance of interest groups ("redistribution coalitions," in the liberal idiom) and implement their program of reforms became one of the liberals' main watchwords. Under such circumstances, an ideology that emphasized the beneficial role of the state in Russian history was well positioned for popularity.

At the beginning of Putin's rule, it was not clear exactly how the ideal state should look and which historical symbols might best represent it. The program of restoring the country's "dignity" vis-à-vis the West was one of the key elements on which Putin's popularity was built. However, in order

2nd ed. (Lanham, Md.: Rowman and Littlefield, 2012), p. 2. For a similar position emphasizing the historically inevitable character of Russia's "imperial choice," see Walter Laqueur, *Putinism: Russia and Its Future with the West* (New York: Thomas Dunne Books, 2015), pp. 3–4. While I am totally in agreement with the notion of the exceptionally important role of history, including the imperial legacy, for present-day Russian politics, I would see those "imperial dreams" as a strategy consciously chosen to legitimize Putin's authoritarianism, rather than as its cause, although I do not deny that there are some elements of determinism here. Cf. Viatcheslav Morozov, *Rossiya i drugiye: Identichnost' i granitsy politicheskogo soobshchestva* [Russia and the Others: Identity and the Limits of a Political Community] (Moscow: Novoye Literaturnoye Obozreniye, 2009) and Morozov, *Russia's Postcolonial Identity: A Subaltern Empire in a Eurocentric World* (Houndmills: Palgrave Macmillan, 2015).

[6] Tamara Kondratieva, *Gouverner et nourrir: Du pouvoir en Russie (XVIe–XXe siècles)* (Paris: Les Belles Lettres, 2002).

[7] David E. Hoffman, *The Oligarchs: Wealth and Power in the New Russia* (Oxford: Public Affairs, 2002).

for Russia to play the part of "a great power" and become an "equal partner" of the West, Putin had to continue its integration in the system of international institutions and alliances.[8] Russia was not strong enough, militarily or economically, to make its voice heard without some skillful maneuvering to compensate for a lack of resources. And that is why the regime could go neither too fast nor too far in rehabilitating the Soviet past and re-Stalinizing its domestic and foreign policy. Despite a powerful nationalist movement that was ready to give full support to a radical nationalist turn in Russian politics, the government could not openly idealize Russian autocracy and the Orthodox Church. A considerable portion of the country's population, including the "liberal" faction of the ruling coalition, remained attached to at least some elements of the liberal master narrative, even though most liberals could accept the use of nationalist slogans to disarm the communist-nationalist opposition. Unsurprisingly, in the first years of Putin's rule, his politics of memory was cautiously pursued. The search for symbols of the strong state was carefully conducted within limits compatible with the claim that Russia's firm intention was to follow the path of democracy.

In 2006, Vladislav Surkov, the Kremlin's chief ideologist, formulated the concept of "sovereign democracy," which remained a quasi-official self-description of Putin's Russia until Medvedev's election as president in 2008. This concept was, however, remarkably ambivalent on the issue of the ideal Russian state,[9] unequivocally categorizing Russia as a democratic

[8] Marlène Laruelle, *In the Name of the Nation: Nationalism and Politics in Contemporary Russia* (New York: Palgrave Macmillan, 2009), pp. 200–203. Writing in 2009, Laruelle may well have overestimated the "Europeanness of Russian nationalism." She maintains that for the Kremlin, nationalism was an instrument of the country's westernization. In light of the events of 2012–2014, one would say, rather, that the "Europeanization of ideological references" was just a way of rendering Russian nationalism more respectable in the eyes of the West (and of the liberal segment of the country's population). The history of the memory law clearly shows that Russian attempts to imitate European legislation on the issues of the past had no other function. This said, Russian nationalism has always been influenced by Western nationalism. The influence of European, and more specifically German, far-right thinkers was obvious in the Eurasian theories of Russian "near-fascists" during the interwar period. Finally, in Russia and everywhere in Europe, the reconstruction of far-right parties and movements in the late twentieth century was crucially dependent on the emerging international neo-fascist networks. See Andrea Mammone, *Transnational Neofascism in France and Italy* (New York: Cambridge University Press, 2015); Thomas Parland, *The Extreme Nationalist Threat in Russia: The Growing Influence of Western Rightist Ideas* (London: RoutledgeCurzon, 2006).

[9] This concept, which was widely used in 2006–2008 (including by Putin), was abandoned after 2008: the new president, Dmitriy Medvedev, considered it to be based on a *contradictio in terminis*, which it certainly was. See Vladislav Surkov, "Natsionalisatsiya budushchego" [The Nationalization of the Future], *Ekspert* 43 (537), November 20, 2006; Dmitriy Medvedev, "Dlya protsvetaniya vsekh nado uchityvat' interesy kazhdogo" [To Ensure the Prosperity of Us All, We Need to Take Everyone's

country but also describing it as differing from other democracies and resolutely rejecting their right to "dictate their rules" to it. However, Surkov had nothing to say about the rules that Russia was to follow, except that they had to be its own.

It is therefore no wonder that the ideal image of the Russian state remained diffuse in the official propaganda. Symbols borrowed from the history of the Russian empire, the USSR, and occasionally even the West were commingled in the repository of the official rhetoric, and the propagandists could pick and choose depending on the context and their target audience.

Some symbol combinations that they produced reflected the absence of a clear system of historical coordinates within which they were to operate. Thus, in 2007, the authors of the most important government-sponsored textbook of Soviet history (the "Filippov textbook") gave a positive assessment of Stalin's role in Soviet history. Without denying the dictator's responsibility for the repressions, they presented him at least as an "efficient manager."[10] This formula immediately became subject of passionate debates between Stalin's admirers and his critics. The word "manager" had come to be widely used in Russia in the period of market reforms and with regard to Western-style business practices. When applied to Stalin, however, this expression "extracts" the dictator from national history and invites the reader to assess him instead by the standards of transnational corporations. This becomes particularly obvious if one takes into account the theory of modernization that in the textbook serves to explain the course of Soviet history. The technical aspects of the country's industrialization are presented as much more fundamental than social conflicts, political repressions, or messianic communist ambitions. The singularity of the communist experience is almost entirely banished from Filippov's

Interests into Account], *Ekspert* 28 (522), July 24, 2006; and Ya.A. Plyais, "Suverennaya demokratiya – novyi kontsept partii vlasti" [Sovereign Democracy: A New Concept of the Party in Power], *Vlast'* 4 (2008), pp. 24–32.

[10] A.V. Filippov, *Noveyshaya istoriya Rossii, 1945–2006: Kniga dlya uchitelya* [The Modern History of Russia, 1945–2006: A Teacher's Handbook] (Moscow: Prosveshcheniye, 2007); A.A. Danilov, A.I. Utkin, and A.V. Filippov, eds., *Istoriya Rossii, 1945–2008: Uchebnik* [The History of Russia, 1945–2008: A Textbook] (Moscow: Prosveshcheniye, 2008). The formula "efficient manager" dates back to the proposal for a Russian history textbook submitted by the same group of historians and published on the website of the same publishing house. See "O Kontseptsii kursa 'Istoriya Rossii, 1900–1945'" [On a Conception for a Course 'Russian History, 1900–1945']: www .prosv.ru/umk/io/info.aspx?ob_no=15378. See also David Brandenberger, "Promotion of a Usable Past: Official Efforts to Rewrite Russo-Soviet History, 2000–2014," in *Remembrance, History, and Justice: Coming to Terms with Traumatic Past in Democratic Societies*, eds. Vladimir Tismaneanu and Bogdan C. Iacob (Budapest: Central European University Press, 2015), pp. 191–212.

textbook, where Soviet history is normalized and thus deprived of its national specificity. The bottom line of this "political philosophy" would have to be the abstract notion of a strong state that a variety of symbols might evoke. "Sovereign democracy" was therefore an empty signifier or a proper name – and therefore neither more nor less than a synonym for Russia itself.

Here we encounter an important theoretical problem: as already mentioned, the current politics of memory and identity in Russia and elsewhere often privilege concepts that are logically closer to proper names than to general names.[11] The invention of "sovereign democracy" reflects the eagerness of Putin's team to find a "more proper" name than the generic "democracy" to refer to Russia. Of course, as with most historical concepts, "democracy" is not a purely abstract concept either, for alongside its general meaning it also references a specific part of the world, namely, the West. The concept of "sovereign democracy" was coined precisely to distinguish Russia from the West within the loose category of democratic countries, and the way in which it makes that distinction is worth noting. Compare this concept to "the first country of socialism," a notion that under the communist regime was widely used to denote the USSR. Both expressions subsume Russia under a generic name while also indicating its *differentia specifica*. Nevertheless, each term's logical status differs greatly from the other's. Being the first country of socialism means leading humankind on a shared journey to a happy future. The abstract (or general) component of this concept is rather strong. In contrast, being a sovereign democracy means simply being independent and, by implication, different from other democracies without specifying where exactly that difference lies. This latter concept is therefore much more of a proper than a general name, since the collocation "sovereign democracy" refers directly to Russia and is consequently its "rigid designator."[12] Later in this chapter, we will encounter other examples showing the predilection of Russian ideologists for concepts expressed by more proper names. A style of thinking that systematically relies on such concepts can be said to follow the logic of proper names.

Let us now return to Putin's politics of memory. Until the radical conservative turn of 2012, this politics retained a kind of flexibility typically justified by the notion of "political technology" that became

---

[11] See Introduction and Chapter 1.
[12] On proper names as "rigid designators," see Saul A. Kripke, *Naming and Necessity* (Oxford: Blackwell, 1980).

popular after the presidential elections of 1996. According to this concept, fragments of diverse ideologies could legitimately be used to secure electoral support. The concept of political technology was explicitly opposed to that of ideology, which came to be seen as having nothing to do with how politics actually works.

The rise of historical memory provided political technologists with new concepts and materials. In Russia more than anywhere else, the notion of ideology was closely associated with that of history, for the communist ideology was profoundly historicist. The collapse of the communist experiment engendered a profound mistrust of all philosophies of history. And after its precarious triumph in the late 1980s, the liberal master narrative was, in its turn, discredited by the difficulties attendant on the market reforms. Fragmented, manipulative, and emotionally charged memories thus came to be seen as an ideal alternative to those outdated "master narratives." Memory, the thinking goes, is personal and hence reliable, while history only claims to be objective. These are the same motifs that many Western advocates of the "memory turn" were discussing in works that were not exactly unknown in Russia. After the collapse of the traditional ideologies, according to Gleb Pavlovskiy (who was then one of the leading political technologists in the service of Vladimir Putin), "the politics of history will become the standard of politics as such."[13]

The fascination with memory became paradigmatic of Putin's political propagandists. Thus, most "new style" (pro-Putin) history textbooks of the mid- and late 2000s include assignments in which students are asked to interview their grandparents on the events of Soviet history. By that time, the state's control over the mass media was sufficiently systematic for the textbooks' authors to be sure that most of those grandparents would share "correct memories" with their grandchildren.[14] Writing in 2007, the authors of the Filippov textbook quoted the results of a sociological survey of 2006 in which 47 percent of respondents had given a positive evaluation of Stalin and 29 percent had given a negative one, the implication being that historians should take their bearings from "national memory."[15] As the authors of the textbook remind their critics, historians can be wrong

[13] Gleb Pavlovskiy, "Plokho s pamyatyu – Plokho s politikoy" [Bad with Memory – Bad with Politics], *Russkiy zhurnal*, December 9, 2008.

[14] N.D. Potapova, Shkol'nye uchebniki o noveyshey istorii Rossii: Poetika i politika: Analiticheskiy otchet fondu D. i K. Makarturov, 2008 [School Textbooks on Recent Russian History: Poetics and Politics: Analytical Report for the D. and C. McArthur Foundation, 2008], the author's archive.

[15] Filippov, *Noveyshaya istoriya Rossii*, p. 93.

but the people cannot.[16] Historians – they who have lied for so long following the fluctuations of the "party line" – must now temper their pretentions. But Filippov and his co-authors cannot seriously have lost sight of the way in which social memory is created by various "agents of memory" (including political technologists). Playing the card of memory against history was a natural expedient after the "archival revolution" of the 1990s, which resulted in Stalin's repressions becoming one of the best-known pages of Russian history.[17] A more emotional and more easily controllable "people's memory" thus came to be seen as an important counterbalance to the historians' archival discoveries. The Belgian historians' invocation, in 2006, of "the duty of history and knowledge" versus the duty of memory is perhaps even more justified here than it is in Western Europe.[18]

However, one should not overestimate the flexibility of Putin's politics of history. As time passed, the regime developed, if not a firm conception of history, then at least a relatively coherent vision of national memory.

Yeltsin's government had never been strong enough to have a sustained politics of memory, not to mention that it drew its legitimacy above all from its project of the future. By contrast, the consolidation of power under Putin allowed for the creation of a systematic politics of the past forcefully promoted by the state-controlled media. The 2000s saw an "archival counter-revolution" when the opening of the Soviet archives slowed and some archival collections were even closed again. That decade also witnessed the government's attempts to meddle with the content of school textbooks (which it had virtually ignored under Yeltsin) and the creation of an entire industry of television documentaries and historical dramas intended to stuff the Russian imagination with a diet rich in the great deeds of Soviet history.[19] The trivialization of Stalin's Terror and the

---

[16] See the polemical exchange between Filippov and Danilov, on the one hand, and Dina Khapaeva, on the other: Aleksandr Filippov and Aleksandr Danilov, "Ratsional'nyi podkhod" [A Rational Approach], *Nezavisimaya gazeta*, August 17, 2008; Dina Khapaeva, "Zaryad pozitiva" [Let's Be Positive], *Novaya gazeta*, December 4, 2008.

[17] Alter Litvin and John Keep, *Stalinism: Russian and Western Views on the Turn of the Millennium* (London: Routledge, 2005); Catriona Kelly, "What Was Soviet Studies and What Came Next?" *The Journal of Modern History* 85/1 (2013), pp. 109–149.

[18] See Chapter 2.

[19] Marietta Chudakova, "V zashchitu dvoinykh standartov" [In Defense of Double Standards], *Novoye literaturnoye obozreniye* 74 (2005), pp. 203–261 (see also other materials of this issue); Vera Kaplan, "The Vicissitudes of Socialism in Russian History Textbooks," *History and Memory* 21/2 (2009), pp. 83–109; Dmitry Shlapentokh, "Russian History and the Ideology of Putin's Regime Through the Window of Contemporary Russian Movies," *Russian History* 36/2 (2009), pp. 278–301.

glorification of the state and its agencies (especially the army and secret services) became important themes of this "televised history."[20]

Putin's conception of national memory has emerged in a process of trial and error in which the president's personal pronouncements about the past have provided important benchmarks. Beginning in his first years in office, Putin several times allowed himself to express a much more positive evaluation of Stalin than could ever have been articulated by a state official under Yeltsin,[21] which was taken as a sign of encouragement by numerous Stalinists eager to rehabilitate the dictator, so that the early 2000s saw a rise in pro-Stalin propaganda.[22] However, by 2003 or 2004, it became clear that there were limits to Stalin's possible rehabilitation, not to mention that, if successful, that rehabilitation would be apt to undermine Russia's image as a democratic country. The image of Stalin was proving too problematic to be chosen as the key historical symbol of post-Soviet Russia.

Sociological surveys of the 2000s show a fairly stable proportion of Stalin advocates and adversaries in the Russian population. As the reader may remember, Stalin's popularity reached its lowest point during perestroika but was growing considerably by the mid-1990s. Since then, he has often been ranked second or third in the national "popularity contest"

---

[20] Julie Fedor, *Russia and the Cult of State Security: The Chekist Tradition, from Lenin to Putin* (London: Routledge, 2011).

[21] As a rule, Putin has avoided discussing Stalin's role in history, and in the few exceptional instances, his assessment of the dictator has been fairly ambiguous. He has condemned Stalin's repressions while underlining certain "positive" aspects of his legacy. Thus, in January 2002, speaking to Polish journalists during a visit to Poland, Putin called Stalin a dictator but added that his name had been closely associated with the victory in World War II. In May 2005, in an interview given to the German daily *Bild* (during his visit to Germany on the eve of the sixtieth anniversary of the victory over Nazi Germany), Putin said: "I can't understand you equating Stalin and Hitler. It goes without saying that Stalin was a tyrant. . . .. But he wasn't a Nazi." He also took the opportunity to add that Hitler, not Stalin, had been responsible for the war. In the same interview, he refused to categorize the Soviet invasion of the Baltic countries as an occupation. See "Putin nazval Stalina diktatorom i sravnil ego s Tamerlanom" [Putin called Stalin a Dictator and Compared Him to Tamerlane]: http://lenta .ru/russia/2002/01/15/stalin/ and "Putin Calls Josef Stalin a Tyrant," *Free Republic*, May 5, 2005: www.freerepublic.com/focus/f-news/1397412/posts. Characteristically, both interviews were given to foreign journalists. In recent years, Putin has become more outspoken, praising Stalin for his leadership during the war and the industrialization of the country. See Dmitry Solovyov "Putin Calls for Balanced Assessment of Stalin," Reuters, December 3, 2009: www.reuters.com/article/2009/ 12/03/idUSGEE5B21J6; Gleb Bryanski, "Putin Calls for Stalin-Style 'Leap Forward,'" Reuters, Aug 31, 2012: www.reuters.com/article/2012/08/31/us-russia-putin-stalin-idUSBRE87U16420120831; and "Putin: Bez Stalina my ne pobedili by v voine" [Putin: Without Stalin We Would Not Have Won the War], August 29, 2014: http://ok-inform.ru/vlast-i-zakon/politika/19904-putin-bez-stalina-my-by-ne-pobedili-v-vojne.html.

[22] Merridale, "Redesigning History in Contemporary Russia"; Adler, "The Future of the Soviet Past Remains Unpredictable."

among historical figures. But this rise of positive feelings toward him was due mostly to changes in the prevailing political discourse. Early in the 1990s, democratic opinion-makers were dominating the scene in Russia, and many respondents did not dare openly express their affinities for Stalin, not even in the context of a sociological interview. (The proportion of non-responses about Stalin at that time was normally about 35 percent.) But in the late 1990s and the 2000s, such respondents began to give positive evaluations of Stalin instead of declining to respond. That said, while the proportion of respondents who supported Stalin increased considerably during the 1990s and early 2000s, there was a significantly more modest decrease in the percentage of his critics.

Russian public opinion remains profoundly and irreparably divided on the issue of Stalinism. In various surveys from the 2000s, about half of the respondents give a positive evaluation of his role in Russian history, while about one-third assess him negatively.[23] However, this proportion almost reverses for respondents who are younger than 45, have a higher level of education, or live in big cities, and neither Putin's cautious statements nor the efforts of overt Stalinists could change this "vote" in any meaningful way.[24] A different symbol was therefore needed to express the idea of the strong state and to unite rather than to split public opinion.

The Cult of the War

The circumstances described here explain why the regime's ideologists turned their attention to the memory of World War II. Already Putin's early years had witnessed a growing interest in the theme of Russia's military glory. The sixtieth anniversary of the victory over Nazism, celebrated with great fanfare in 2005, marked the emergence of a systematic politics of history based upon the cult of the war (the propaganda campaign in preparation for the celebration began in 2004). The image of Stalin was, to be sure, an important aspect of the memory of the war. But this memory is much broader than that, since it has a Stalinist version

---

[23] See the results of the Levada Center survey: "Rossiyane o roli Stalina v istorii" [Russians on Stalin's Role in History], March 4, 2013: www.levada.ru/04-03-2013/rossiyane-o-roli-stalina-v-istorii-initsiative-vozvrashcheniya-volgogradu-nazvaniya-stali. See also my *Pamyat' strogogo rezhima*, pp. 168–180.

[24] Koposov, *Pamyat' strogogo rezhima*, pp. 174–177. Since 2014, the popularity of Stalin has increased somewhat in the context of the Ukraine crisis and the militarization of Russian public opinion. See Dina Khapaeva, "Triumphant Memory of the Perpetrators: Putin's Politics of Re-Stalinization," *Communist and Post-Communist Studies* 49/1 (2016), pp. 61–73.

("We won the war thanks to Stalin") and an anti-Stalinist one ("We won in spite of Stalin's mistakes and repressions"). The cult of the war could therefore accommodate Stalinists and anti-Stalinists alike.

Sociological surveys show that belief in the cult of the war is shared by an overwhelming majority of Russians. Usually, 70 to 80 percent of respondents agree that the victory over Nazi Germany (which in Russia is almost entirely attributed to the Soviet Army) was the most important event in the history of the twentieth century and that Victory Day is an even more important holiday than New Year's Day.[25] Under Soviet rule, the 1917 Bolshevik revolution was considered the founding event of the Soviet state; in the 1990s, Yeltsin's government had tried to transform the abortive communist putsch of August 1991 into the new Russia's "myth of origins" but failed in this because many Russians viewed, and still view, the dismantling of the USSR in December 1991 as the beginning of a period of national humiliation and misery. And so the cult of the Great Patriotic War emerged in the 2000s as the foundation myth of a post-Soviet Russia that was determined to establish a continuity with the "glorious pages" of Soviet history.

The cult of the war is deeply rooted in the Russian historical memory. Putin's regime did not have to create it afresh but only to readapt it to the new political conditions. An advantage of the revived cult was that it could leverage an enormous Soviet infrastructure of museums, associations of veterans, movies, and other institutions to create a widely shared ideological consensus.

Putin's myth of the war differs from Brezhnev's in two main respects. First, Putin's version has been purified of its communist component, as is also the case with all other aspects of the Soviet past. According to the official Soviet version of the war, the USSR's victory had been due to the "advantages of socialism" and the "leading role of the Communist Party." This reading is unacceptable to Putin's regime, the legitimacy of which has been largely built on its anti-communist claims of the early 2000s. Russian, not Soviet, patriotism and leadership of the state, not the Party, are now the myth's dominant themes.

---

[25] Lev Gudkov, "'Pamyat' o voine' i massovaya identichnost' rossiyan" ["The Memory of War" and the Russians' Mass Identity] *Pamyat' o voine 60 let spustya: Germaniya, Rossiya, Yevropa* [The Memory of the War 60 Years On: Germany, Russia, Europe], a special issue of *Neprikosnovennyi zapas* Nos. 2–3 (2005), pp. 46–58; and Boris Dubin, "'Krovavaya' voina i 'velikaya' pobeda" [The "Bloody" War and the "Great" Victory], *Otechestvennyie zapiski* 5 (2004): http://magazines .russ.ru/oz/2004/5/2004_5_5.html; O.Yu. Malinova, *Aktual'noye proshloye: Simvolicheskaya politika vlastvuyushchey elity i dilemmy rossiyskoy identichnosti* [The Topical Past: The Symbolic Politics of the Ruling Elites and Dilemmas of Russian Identity] (Moscow: Politicheskaya entsiklopediya, 2015), pp. 88–127.

Second, Putin's myth of the war is far more inclusive than the late-Soviet myth. Critical publications and movies of the 1980s and 1990s have so profoundly changed the image of the war that it has become difficult to maintain the silence about the atrocities committed by the Soviet army and secret services as well as the hardships of ordinary people. (Soviet authors had tried not to overemphasize those aspects of the war while still acknowledging the people's sufferings.) In the 2000s, the image of the war has become more realistic and therefore more tragic. It reflects a broader spectrum of wartime experiences, which only makes it more efficient as a propaganda tool.[26] However, its role in identity politics remains essentially the same. Today, it excludes certain accusations against the USSR as assiduously as it did under the Soviet regime, even though those accusations (such as the USSR's complicity in causing the war or the war crimes committed by the Soviet army) have been largely confirmed by recent historiography, both Russian and foreign.[27]

The idea that the state and its people are one lies at the heart of this cult. It obviously functions to obliterate the memory of communist repressions, the violence visited by the state on its own people. It paints the Russian people as victims not of the Stalinist Terror but of foreign aggression. As Dina Khapaeva puts it:

> The war myth was constructed... to rename and suppress the memory of the irrational, unjustifiable sufferings of the victims of the Soviet system.... The most important function of the war myth (which it has successfully fulfilled into the present day) is to assure [Russians] that the Gulag remains just a minor episode in a heroic Soviet history.[28]

Another important advantage of the myth of the war is that it has a strong mobilizing potential. It revitalizes Stalin's black-and-white formula of whoever is against communism (now Russia) is for fascism.[29] As we have seen, anti-fascism is one of the key aspects of the USSR's political legacy, and within its framework, fascism is understood as a profoundly anti-Russian force that is absolutely alien to Russia's political tradition. The myth of the war therefore implicitly denies the possibility of a fascist

---

[26] It was hardly a coincidence that, parallel to the formation of Putin's war myth, a change in prevailing attitudes toward the past occurred among the Russian population, when an emotional personal attachment to historical symbols (above all, of the war) began replacing the ironic distancing typical of the 1990s. See Serguei Oushakine, "Remembering in Public: On the Affective Management of History," *Ab Imperio* 1 (2013), pp. 269–302.

[27] See Chapter 5.   [28] Khapaeva, "Historical Memory in Post-Soviet Gothic Society," p. 367.

[29] François Furet, *The Passing of an Illusion: The Idea of Communism in the Twentieth Century* (Chicago, Ill.: The University of Chicago Press, 1999), pp. 209–314.

movement in Russia. Characteristically, though, the Holocaust is not part of this myth of the war; Russians, not Jews, are seen as Hitler's main victims.

The myth also has a strong international dimension. It praises the USSR/Russia as the champion of peace and the world's savior from fascism. It seeks to persuade citizens that the only goal of the Soviet Union's foreign policy was the pursuit of peace. The USSR's ambiguous role in provoking World War II is ignored, and the Soviet occupation of Eastern Europe is praised as its liberation. The myth implies that Russia's decisive part in the victory over Nazi Germany gives it a right to universal recognition – and to those parts of Eastern Europe that Stalin occupied with the consent of his Western Allies.

The Russian myth of the war is not specifically anti-Western, although it draws heavily on xenophobic and anti-Western feelings. It holds that the USSR and its Western allies were struggling for common humanistic values.[30] Participation in the joint struggle against fascism, however, is routinely used to whitewash Russia's own misdeeds. The myth even sanctions Russia's rapprochement with the West, while making it contingent on the latter's recognition of the Yalta System. It looks toward an alliance with the great powers, ruling out Eastern Europe, which is seen as Russia's legitimate sphere of influence. In other words, it denies subjectivity to the Eastern European countries and invites the West to do the same, as the latter had to all intents and purposes done in 1945. For the supporters of this myth, that would mean acknowledging Russia's status as a great power. But should the West reject the Yalta System, the Russian myth can just as easily become anti-Western.[31]

---

[30] Speaking at a PACE (Parliamentary Assembly of Council of Europe) session in April 2010, Russian Foreign Minister Sergey Lavrov said: "This is our common victory – the victory of those values that make us human": http://assembly.coe.int/Main.asp?link=/Documents/Records/2010/E/1004 291000E.htm.

[31] Many researchers justly underline the role played by status considerations and resentment toward the West in Russia's foreign policy from the formation of the Russian empire to the present, and the myth of the war somewhat supports this claim. See Andrei P. Tsygankov, *Russia and the West from Alexander to Putin: Honor in International Relations* (Cambridge: Cambridge University Press, 2012); Olga Malinova, "Obsession with Status and Ressentiment: Historical Backgrounds of the Russian Discursive Identity Construction," *Communist and Post-Communist Studies* 47/3–4 (2014), pp. 291–303 (and other materials in this same issue); Morozov, *Russia's Postcolonial Identity*; Anne L. Clunan, *Social Construction of Russia's Resurgence: Aspirations, Identity, and Security Interests* (Baltimore, Md.: The Johns Hopkins University Press, 2009). However, it would be a simplification to see Putin's emphasis on the Yalta System as essentially symbolic: rather, it serves to legitimize some very practical political goals, including the Russian ruling groups' willingness to establish their domination, by any means, in the countries of the former Soviet bloc. It would be equally misleading to view Putin's Russia as just another Western country that only wants some

The myth of the war has become central to Putin's politics of memory. It has marginalized other memories, including that of the Russian empire (notwithstanding Peter the Great's enduring popularity), which increasingly often appears, in the writings of Russian nationalists, as a reservoir of traditional values and a predecessor to the Soviet empire, rather than as the birthplace of Russia's modern Western-oriented culture.

The 1990s witnessed a rise in Russian nationalism that has continued under Putin. Influential nationalist ideologists such as Alexander Dugin developed a conception of Russian history built on the idea of the country's perennial struggle against the West's corruption and aggression in the name of Orthodox values and national traditions.[32] Some endorsed the notion of Eurasian civilization that was most famously developed in the 1920s and 1930s by a group of Russian conservative émigrés. Many nationalists also took a very dim view of the Bolshevik period, which they saw as an ascendency of rootless internationalism that according to them had been closer to liberalism than to traditional Russian values. If there was one single episode of the Soviet period that nationalists could embrace as their historical symbol, it was the Great Patriotic War, which was also the source of a popular cult among communists.

In the 2000s, nationalist ideologists became far more politically influential than ever before, and some began working for the government. In particular, Alexander Dugin is reportedly quite close to Putin.[33] Much of the philosophy of history that underlies Putin's politics of memory has been borrowed from those nationalists who, in the best traditions of conspiracy theories, argue that the West is essentially anti-Russian because it is afraid of Russia's spiritual values. This has become one of the key themes of the cult of the war.

A typical example of the nationalist interpretation of the war is provided by the book *For What and with Whom Did We Fight?* published in 2005 by Nataliya Narochnitskaya, a Duma Deputy from 2003 to 2007 and later the director of the Russian Institute of Democracy and Cooperation in

---

recognition from its partners: the Putinists clearly seek to undermine Western democratic values, which they see as a threat to their power within the country.

[32] See Chapter 5.

[33] Anton Barbashin and Hannah Thoburn, "Putin's Brain: Alexander Dugin and the Philosophy Behind Putin's Invasion of Crimea," *Foreign Affairs*, March 31, 2014; Vincent Jauvert, "Le Raspoutine de Poutine," *Le Nouvel observateur*, April 30, 2014; Andreas Umland, "Alexander Dugin and Moscow's New Right-Radical Intellectual Circles at the Start of Putin's Third Presidential Term 2012–2013: The Anti-Orange Committee, the Izborsk Club and the Florian Geyer Club in Their Political Context," *Europolity: Continuity and Change in European Governance* 10/2 (2016), pp. 7–31.

Paris (founded to promote Putin's cultural politics in Europe). The book professes to explain the meaning of the war, which, according to the author, has been misrepresented by Russia's enemies, whose aggressive politics of memory continue the West's century-long crusade against Holy Russia. Narochnitskaya remains true to the Orthodox tradition of viewing the Soviet regime as ungodly. She protests against imputing all Soviet crimes to Stalin alone, arguing that Lenin, the founder of the regime, was at least as guilty as his successor. She sees the Bolshevik terror as an outcome of atheism and cosmopolitism, and therefore intimately linked to political radicalism.

However, Stalin, whom Narochnitskaya condemns as a communist leader, is portrayed in her book much more positively as a national leader. In order to downplay the memory of his repressions, Narochnitskaya contrasts the state that, according to her, is essentially imperfect with the Fatherland as a metaphysical concept. She believes this concept to be a key element of "the Christian and especially the Orthodox consciousness."[34] That is why the idea of the Fatherland, a corollary of the notion of God, has nothing in common with a cult of the state. This notion she holds to be alien to the "secular consciousness," whether communist or liberal. Narochnitskaya's concept of a metaphysical Fatherland resembles Dugin's notion of an absolute Motherland. Upon closer inspection, however, this "Fatherland" loses its metaphysical aura.

For Narochnitskaya, the "metaphysical Russia" actually has physical borders, which she sees as sacred by dint of having been established by such emblematic figures of the national pantheon as Peter I and Catherine II. Stalin is praised for having reestablished them, thus incorporating the Yalta System into the concept of the metaphysical Fatherland. Narochnitskaya's Fatherland is, in fact, nothing other than the Soviet empire. Although the borders of the USSR never actually coincided with those of the Eastern bloc, Narochnitskaya, from her metaphysical eminence, overlooks this "detail." And she ends by extending her aegis over the reputation of the USSR, however imperfect it may have been, because otherwise she might encounter difficulties in justifying the physical borders of her metaphysical Russia:

> The idea that the USSR was as criminal a state as Hitler's Reich, with which it fought, serves to change the meaning of the war [sic!] and legitimize a revision of the outcomes of Yalta and Potsdam.[35]

[34] Narochnitskaya, *Za chto i s kem my voyevali?* (Moscow: Minuvsheye, 2005), pp. 8–10.
[35] *Ibid.*, p. 17.

This interpretation of the war as the crucial juncture in the struggle of a metaphysical Russia against a metaphysical West has strongly influenced the official cult of the war, as we will see later in this chapter.

The choice to make war rather than culture the symbol of national identity provides the key to understanding Putin's foreign policy, which is aimed primarily at mobilizing political support within the country. In particular, it explains the origins of the memory wars in Eastern Europe. In contradistinction to the relatively peaceful 1990s, the 2000s witnessed a series of bitter memory conflicts between Russia and its Eastern European neighbors. The Russian government has always claimed to be the victim of aggression in these cases, which corresponds to its familiar image of the "defender of peace." But the question of responsibility for the memory wars in the region is far more complex than the Kremlin would have us believe.

It is hard to say if, in embracing the cult of the war in the early 2000s, Putin's government, preoccupied as it was with consolidating its domestic support, foresaw the reaction of the Eastern European countries. That reaction was more than predictable, though, since those countries' historical experience has left them convinced that Russia is a potential (if at times not an actual) threat. Poland, Ukraine, and the Baltic countries were ahead of Russia in creating an institutional infrastructure for a "politics of memory" (such as the Institutes of National Memory or memory laws).[36] But this was the result, rather than the cause, of their disputes with Russia. Putin's politics of memory was perceived in the region as a confirmation of the worst expectations about Russia's "real" attitudes toward its neighbors.

In light of the Russian myth, however, most Eastern European memories of the war appear profoundly distorted. Any criticism of the USSR on the grounds of the Nazi-Soviet Pact of August 1939 or of its liberation of Eastern Europe from the yoke of Nazism only to replace it with that of another totalitarian regime came to be perceived by Russia as an affront to its national dignity. Yet these events are of fundamental importance to Eastern European memories. The same is true of the crimes committed by the communist regimes in the region. The Kremlin can accept that the Soviet and local communists must bear equal responsibility for them but it is not prepared to consider them a result of the *Russian* occupation of these countries. Blame may therefore be placed on communism but never on Russia.

[36] See Chapter 3.

Moscow is even less prepared to accept the idea that communist crimes should be treated "in the same way as Nazi crimes were assessed by the Nuremberg Tribunal," to quote the formulation in the 2008 Prague Declaration. Highly popular in Eastern Europe, this idea undermines the Russian myth of the war and calls into question the foreign policy that this myth informs. Indeed, if the Great Patriotic War was nothing but a struggle between two equally criminal regimes, it makes little sense to take pride in the victory of one side over the other. That is why the concept of totalitarianism is so persistently rejected by the Russian government and the officially sponsored history textbooks.[37]

The official Russian interpretation of the East European memory wars envisions them as an element of the US-led Western crusade against Russia, inspired by the aim of "substituting the results of the Cold War for those of the Second World War." The interpretation of the war that found expression in the Judgment of the Nuremberg Tribunal, which for obvious reasons did not, and could not, consider "communist crimes," is viewed by the Russian government as *the* historical truth. All attempts to call into question Russia's role in the war are declared "historical revision-ism," which, from the Kremlin's vantage, relates in no way to other peoples' legitimate grievances but only to the West's unscrupulous and futile attempts to prevent Russia's rising from its knees after the collapse of the Soviet Union. Russia's case is, furthermore, presented as an example of the West's unfair treatment of all independent political forces. This interpretation was well articulated in the 2008 *Foreign Policy Concept of the Russian Federation*:

> The reaction to the prospect of loss by the historic West of its monopoly in global processes finds its expression, in particular, in the continued political and psychological policy of "containing" Russia, including the use of a selective approach to history, for those purposes, first of all as regards the World War Two and the postwar period.

Historical revisionism is considered here as an aspect of a geopolitical struggle in which Russia takes the side of a multi-polar world that is expected to replace the outdated US hegemony. Confronted with attempts to revise the past, the Russian Federation expresses its intention

---

[37] Sovmestnoye zayavleniye Gosdumy i Soveta Federatsii po povodu rezolyutsii OBSE [Joint Declaration of the State Duma and the Council of the Federation Regarding the OSCE Resolution], July 7, 2009: http://vz.ru/information/2009/7/7/304857.html; *Istoriya Rossii, 1945–2008: Uchebnik*, p. 5.

To firmly counter manifestations of neofascism, any forms of racial discrimination, aggressive nationalism, anti-Semitism and xenophobia,
attempts to rewrite the history, use it for instigating confrontation and
revanchism in the world politics, and revise the outcome of the World War
Two.[38]

Historical revisionism therefore appears here as a manifestation of neo-
fascism, racism, and even anti-Semitism.

This document was published in July 2008, just as the work on a new
memory law project was about to begin. A year later, similar ideas were
formulated by Russian Foreign Minister Sergey Lavrov in his article "The
65th Anniversary of the Great Victory," which is one of the key official
texts that formulate the Russian government's position on this issue.[39]

For Lavrov, the revision of "the outcomes of World War II, enshrined
in the UN Charter and other international legal instruments," undermines
international order and confronts "European security... with serious
problems." The responsibility for those problems lies entirely with the
anti-Russian forces that the minister sees as all but predominant in the
West. Using less exotic language than the Russian nationalists, he nevertheless claims that Russia's "very existence... seems to be a source of
'nervousness' among [some Western] leaders." Lavrov attributes most of
the tragic mistakes that the West has committed over the course of the
twentieth century to its "'reflex' reaction to the Soviet Union, subordin-
ating sensible analysis and practical politics to ideological dogma." This
"'reflex' reaction" was responsible for the "irrational and self-destructive...
policy of European cabinets from Versailles to the end of the Phony War."
"The same tendency was observed in postwar developments," Lavrov adds,
pointing out that it also underlies some countries' current "desire to draw
new dividing lines on our continent" (in place of those established at
Yalta). The historical litigation between Russia and the West, of which the
West's groundless and unjustified "nervousness" is the only cause, is very
nearly presented here as a drama of global proportions, which is exactly
how Russian nationalists see it.

Lavrov avoids defining the ideology that explains the West's "neurotic"
policy regarding Russia. Propagandists of the Soviet period called this
ideology anti-communism, but Lavrov cannot subscribe to that: he

---

[38] The Foreign Policy Concept of the Russian Federation: http://archive.kremlin.ru/eng/text/docs/
2008/07/204750.shtml.
[39] Lavrov, "65-letiye velikoy pobedy," *Diplomaticheskiy Yezhegodnik* [Diplomatic Yearbook], 2009.
A translation into English is available at www.sri-lanka.mid.ru/victory-e-06.html.

manifestly intends to say that the West has for centuries been predisposed to an anti-Russian ideology.

Lavrov's diatribes against this hostile ideology, even if the reader is left to wonder about its precise nature, are meaningful indeed. What else, if not ideology (whose time, as Lavrov repeats again and again, has passed), could be the motive force of international politics? The answer is clear: national geopolitical interests. Whatever a country's ideology might be, geopolitics is what really counts. And in the world of geopolitics, all interests are equally legitimate. This position ultimately normalizes authoritarian regimes as subjects of international politics and is, unsurprisingly, also embraced by Western supporters of Putin's regime.[40]

Lavrov's position on the origins of World War II is somewhat ambiguous. On the one hand, fascism was "a mortal threat hanging over mankind," which implies that it was responsible for the war. But on the other hand, "the Second World War revealed the invalidity of the policy of all European states, regardless of the nature of governance." In other words, democratic countries were also to some extent guilty. So far, this looks like a reasonable position. Lavrov even accepts that the USSR bore some responsibility for the war: he praises the Russian government for having officially denounced (in 1989) the Molotov-Ribbentrop Pact of August 23, 1939. However, his next step is to downplay the role of that pact: "Had there been no Munich, there would not have been much else that followed it." Putting "an equal sign between August 23 and September 1, 1939" is to him "the height of historical revisionism." In signing the pact with Hitler, "the Soviet Union... acted in line with the usual diplomacy for that time," while Munich was the war's starting point. (Russian nationalists believe today that the German occupation of Czechoslovakia, not the invasion of Poland, marked the beginning of World War II.[41])

To disclaim the USSR's responsibility for the war, Lavrov substitutes the question of the long-term historical causes of World War II for that of the immediate responsibility for unleashing it. Stalin's USSR and Hitler's Germany both appear as products of "a crisis of European society, whose traditional foundations had been destroyed by the many revolutions in Europe." Lavrov continues: "The fallacious Versailles system, to which Soviet Russia bore no relation, by the universal acknowledgement of historians made the next war inevitable." In other words, the same

---

[40] See my "Back to Yalta? Stephen Cohen and the Ukrainian Crisis," *Eurozine*, September 3, 2014.

[41] Modest Kolerov, "Za nami narod!" [The People Are behind Us!], July 13, 2009: http://zaxid.net/news/showNews.do?za_nami_narod__modest_kolerov&objectId=1081725.

"winner-takes-all" approach that Lavrov imputes to his own "Western partners" brought Hitler to power. . . and then there was Munich. Indeed, the reader may begin to doubt if the USSR really needed to apologize for the Molotov-Ribbentrop Pact at all.

The West's responsibility for the war is therefore comparable to that of Hitler's Germany. But it is also responsible for the Cold War and even for the Soviet occupation of Eastern Europe, not because it agreed to concede the region to Stalin but because it forced the USSR to respond to the Western countries' aggressive policies. "It is cynical and blasphemous to compare with the Nazi occupation, the events of the postwar period in Central and Eastern Europe, although they also involved tragedies," Lavrov claims. The Soviet system, whatever its sins, is in no way comparable to Nazism. Had the West not begun the Cold War, Lavrov speculates, "this would have encouraged the same Stalin to undertake moderate policies in Europe, but this chance – not only for Europe but also the Soviet Union itself – was missed." In other words, Stalinism could have become more moderate after the war, but the West had prevented this from happening.

But there is more. As I have shown, Lavrov pays lip service to anti-fascist rhetoric, while at the same time implying that the contrast between Nazi Germany and its Western adversaries was not absolute. Not only was the West largely responsible for the war, but it was also much less democratic than one might have thought: "In most countries [there existed] authoritarian or semi-authoritarian regimes" in the interwar period. One could add that far-right movements existed in democratic countries too; the fascist danger was serious indeed. But Lavrov avoids mentioning which countries were authoritarian and which were democratic. Instead, he states:

> Fascism – in varying degrees – was the most common response to the contradictions of European society, which World War I had failed to resolve. The way out of the crisis was found through militarizing the economy and international relations, which became a key factor in unleashing World War II.

Lavrov does not mention that some countries (and not minor ones, either) have struggled successfully against the fascist danger at home and abroad and that those countries have become the leaders of the postwar West. For him, on the contrary, the West as a whole was palpably fascist, and this was the main reason for the war. Soviet propagandists also insisted that fascism, as well as the two world wars, were an outcome of the crisis of capitalism. Lavrov does not want to blame capitalism and praise communism, however; instead, he praises Russia and blames modernity, revolutions, and the West.

Yet this is still not all. In Lavrov's article, fascism appears as a property not only of the interwar period but also of the present-day West. He castigates "the right-wing radical tendencies in the modern political life of those countries" that are attempting "to rehabilitate the fascist regimes and make heroes of the Nazis and SS men" while "claiming to be a part of the democratic community." He is, no doubt, referring here to the Baltic countries and Ukraine, Russia's prime adversaries in its memory wars. But he is also implying that more important political players support a historical revisionism that aims "at discrediting the policy of the Soviet Union before, during and after the Second World War." A diplomat to the last, he does not say who these players are. But the Foreign Policy Concept has already provided the answer: it is the historic West. Speaking of the "winner-take-all" approach that, according to him, underlies the politics of historical revisionism, Lavrov makes it clear that the latter is in fact supported by the US. In other words, fascism is as inherent to the West as are the anti-Russian "reflexes." Western "democracy" is therefore but a latent form of fascism. (This was also a communist claim.) In light of this "philosophy," it is hardly surprising that all pro-Western forces in Ukraine and elsewhere are unambiguously identified in Russia as "Nazi allies."

Lavrov describes the present-day revisionism as something unprecedented:

> Yet even during the Cold War no one ever tried to equate the Nazi regime with Stalin's dictatorship. It never occurred to anyone to compare the Nazi threat, which implied enslaving and destroying whole peoples, and the policy of the Soviet Union.

He is pretending never to have heard of the concept of totalitarianism. This part of his argument is, rather, intended to show how deeply the "truth of the war" has been forgotten. He reminds his readers of the facts that demonstrate Russia's role in the victory over fascism, but then promptly quits the terrain of history to engage in an almost metaphysical discussion of Russia's "historic mission of saving Europe from. . . its own folly." Before rescuing Europe from Hitler, Russia had saved it from Napoleon. To his credit, Lavrov does not mention the Tartar invasion of the thirteenth century from which, as many Russians believe, their country also saved the West. But he does call upon the West to stop rewriting history and to "recognize the grandeur and superiority of the peoples of the Soviet Union" (read: Russia).

Lavrov's article is a typical example of the Putin regime's historical propaganda, with all its inconsistencies and factual manipulations, and the metaphysical opposition it establishes between peaceful, anti-fascist Russia and the aggressive, pro-fascist West. It shows the background thinking behind the projects of memory laws that appeared in 2009.

The First Drafts (2009)

The new bills were completely different in spirit from the drafts of the 1990s (though some of them used language borrowed from those drafts). Indeed, by 2009, the cult of the war had become the foundational myth of Putin's Russia and intense memory conflicts had set Russia at odds with Ukraine, Poland, and the Baltic countries. These new bills reflected the centrality of that cult to the "new Russian ideology."

Their prehistory dates back to the Russian-Estonian conflict of 2007 that followed the removal of the bronze memorial to Soviet soldiers from the center of Tallinn and its relocation to a war cemetery. Russian public opinion reacted violently to this, all the more so because pictures of parades of Estonian veterans of the SS had for some time been receiving broad coverage on Russian television. In the midst of the conflict, a few days prior to May 9 (Victory Day), the Russian parliament passed a law titled "On the Banner of Victory," which regulated the ways in which the red flag that had been raised on the Reichstag building in Berlin in May 1945 was to be preserved and used in public ceremonies.[42] One result of the 2007 conflict was to popularize the notion of introducing new legislation that would "ban insults to the significance of [Russia's] great Victory,"[43] the criminalization of Holocaust denial in the West being routinely invoked as a precedent for that. The 2008 war with Georgia and the subsequent confrontation with the West, as well as the adoption of the 2008 Prague Declaration, contributed yet further to the radicalization of the Kremlin's politics of memory.

The new memory law proposals were preceded by a propaganda campaign, one element of which was Gleb Pavlovskiy's previously mentioned article "Bad with Memory – Bad with Politics,"[44] which was published in December 2008, shortly after the Russian police raid on the Memorial

---

[42] Federal Law No. 68-FZ of May 7, 2008 "O Znameni Pobedy."
[43] Nataliya Narochnitskaya, "Komu vygoden peresmotr itogov Vtoroy mirovoy?" [Who Is Interested in Revising the Outcomes of the Second World War?], May 8, 2007: www.rian.ru/online/20070508/65130644.html.
[44] Pavlovskiy, "Plokho s pamyatyu – Plokho s politikoy."

Society's offices in St. Petersburg (which, not surprisingly, coincided with the opening of an international conference on Stalinism organized by Memorial).[45] And that was approximately when a group of Russian nationalists led by Konstantin Zatulin reportedly began working on their memory law project.

Pavlovskiy claims that, in contrast to its neighbors, Russia does not have any politics of memory, because the Memorial society had proved incapable of "proposing to society a non-partisan critical research program for studying the Soviet civilizational (not only totalitarian!) legacy." Pavlovskiy does not explain why Memorial, an association of former political prisoners and historians of the communist terror, was supposed to go so far beyond its program goals. But he claims that due to Memorial, "Soviet civilization has been reduced to a chain of crimes." Worse than that, Russian society "has lost its sovereignty in working through its past." Pavlovskiy has not a word to say about the rehabilitation of the Soviet past that began in the 1990s and enjoyed the support of Putin's government in the 2000s. According to him, in the present-day world anti-Russian "official memories" become the political ideologies of Russia's neighbors. The absence of a politics of memory transforms Russia into a "defenseless and secure screen for [the display of other countries'] defamatory projections and aggressive phobias." The need to adopt a memory law to counter such "projections" would be the logical conclusion to draw from this analysis.

Konstantin Zatulin was deputy chairman of the Duma Committee on the Affairs of the Commonwealth of Independent States. Although a member of the ruling United Russia party, he never belonged to its "inner circle" but he was close to Moscow Mayor Yuriy Luzhkov, Putin's competitor in the struggle for power in 1999, who was famous for his nationalist pronouncements. An extreme nationalist, Zatulin was active in organizing pro-Russian movements in "near abroad" countries including Ukraine, especially during its Orange Revolution of 2004. On many occasions, he called (as did Luzhkov) for Crimea's reunification with Russia, which resulted in him being repeatedly denied entry into Ukraine. His working group consisted of nationalist activists, including Modest Kolerov, a leading theorist of Russian nationalism, who was many times declared persona non grata in Georgia, Lithuania, Latvia, and Estonia.

---

[45] Jonathan Brent, "Postmodern Stalinism: Revisionist Histories Help Revive His Reputation in Russia," *Chronicle of Higher Education*, September 21, 2009.

In February 2009, Sergey Shoygu, minister for Civil Defense and a leader of United Russia, declared at a veterans' reunion that a law was to be drafted to combat historical revisionism pertaining to the Great Patriotic War. Shortly afterwards, United Russia announced that a law designed to punish anyone who denied the decisive role of the Soviet people in the victory over Nazi Germany was in preparation. The media, however, was reporting rumors that the ruling party was not unanimously in favor of this law.[46] It seems that a backstage struggle was taking place between groups advocating at least two different approaches to the problem. The first approach was developed by the Zatulin group, the second by the leadership of United Russia.

On April 20, 2009, Zatulin published a draft titled "On Countermeasures against the Rehabilitation of Nazism, Nazi Criminals and Their Accomplices in the Newly Independent States on the Territory of the Former USSR."[47] The bill was posted on the website of the Regnum News Agency, whose editor-in-chief happened to be Modest Kolerov. The next day, it was discussed at a Duma meeting hosted by Zatulin. This lengthy document proposed a series of definitions (of the notions of Nazism, Nazi criminals, etc.) and practical steps to combat "the rehabilitation of Nazism." In a ranking of the bill's goals, however, "the struggle against Nazism in all its manifestations" appears only in fourth place, after such goals as "countering attempts to revise the Judgment of the Nuremberg Tribunal" and "countering the rehabilitation of Nazism, Nazi criminals and their accomplices" (Article 1). In other words, the draft was specifically conceived as a memory law. Let me remind the reader that the notion of "rehabilitation of Nazism" was first used in a Ukrainian draft of January 2009.

In the spirit of Pavlovskiy's article, Zatulin and Kolerov presented their project as a response to "the rehabilitation of Nazism in the newly independent states." The authors define those who are guilty of this crime as "partisans of Nazism" (Article 3.5), thus presenting their own efforts as a continuation of the Great Patriotic War.

---

[46] Isabelle de Keghel, "Na puti k 'predskazuyemomu' proshlomu? Kommentariy k sozdaniyu Komissii po protivodeystviyu popytkam falsifikatsii istorii v Rossii" [On the Path toward a "Predictable" Past? Comments on the Establishment of the Presidential Commission to Counter Attempts to Harm Russia's Interests by Falsifying History], *Ab Imperio* 3 (2009), pp. 365–387; Pavel Polyan, "Po kom probil Tsar-Kolokol? [For Whom Did the Tsar-Bell Toll?]," *Ab Imperio* 3 (2009), pp. 388–401; and Brandenberger, "Promotion of a Usable Past," pp. 200–205.

[47] Draft Law "O protivodeystvii reabilitatsii v novykh nezavisimykh gosudarstvakh na territorii byvshego Soyuza SSR natsizma, natsistskikh prestupnikov i ikh posobnikov," April 20, 2009: www.regnum.ru/news/1153517.html.

In contrast to the projects of the 1990s, the draft uses the term "Nazism" rather than "fascism." Its definition of Nazism, in Article 3.1, reads as follows:

> Nazism (National Socialism) is a totalitarian ideology and its application in practice by Hitler's Germany, its allies and accomplices from 1933 through 1945, [and is] associated with totalitarian terrorist methods of [executing] power, the official gradation of all nations according to the degree of their [racial] value, the propaganda of superiority of some nations over others, accompanied by war crimes, crimes against humanity, and genocide, which were recognized as such by the International Military Tribunal in Nuremberg.

Compare this definition of Nazism with the definitions of fascism in the projects of the 1990s (I quote here the most detailed of these definitions, given by communist deputy Zorkaltsev in 1999):

> Fascism refers to an ideology and practice proclaiming the superiority and exceptionality of a nation or a race and aiming at incitement of national intolerance, justification of discrimination against members of other nations, denial of democracy, establishment of a leader's cult, introduction of violence and terror for the suppression of political rivals and other forms of dissent, and the justification of war as a means of solving problems between nations.[48]

The difference is considerable indeed. Zatulin mentions neither the denial of democracy nor a leader cult, although they were both character-istic of Nazism (Zorkaltsev too had not mentioned them in his 1995 bill). One might suppose that these were not, in his view, such bad things. Even more important, though, was the very idea of privileging the concept of Nazism over fascism. Throughout the Soviet period, the term "fascism" was far more commonly employed than "Nazism," which was considered a species of the genus called fascism. The communist-led movement of "progressive humankind" was therefore described as working against fas-cism in general, not against Nazism in particular, and was labeled "anti-fascist" rather than "anti-Nazi" (a concept that scarcely existed at all).

Zorkaltsev's 1999 definition of fascism differed significantly from Soviet characterizations. Without denying that fascism was a form of racism, Soviet theorists emphasized its "class essence" and defined it as "a terrorist dictatorship, headed by the most reactionary forces of monopoly capital and implemented for the purpose of preserving the capitalist system"

---

[48] Draft Law No. 99041517–2 of April 19, 1999 "O zapreshchenii propagandy fashizma v Rossiyskoy Federatsii" [On the Prohibition of the Propaganda of Fascism in the Russian Federation], Article 1.

during "the general crisis of capitalism."[49] From this point of view, the fascists' anti-communist ideas were far more important than their racist convictions.

This understanding of fascism became outdated in the 1990s. On the one hand, in Russia as elsewhere, few people now believed that capitalism had adopted fascism as its one remaining hope. Nationalism and racism came to be seen as far more dominant and destructive elements of fascism. On the other hand, post-Soviet communists had abandoned most of their Marxist legacy and became national-populists. In their eyes, the idea of class struggle had lost its ideological centrality.

However, both the Soviet and the Zorkaltsev definitions of fascism envision it as a general concept. Zorkaltsev's definition points to a potentially infinite number of hypostases that might be subsumed under it, without reference to the phenomenon's spatial and temporal coordinates. The Soviet definition, while specifying a particular point in history (a crisis of capitalism resulting from socialist revolutions), also uses broadly applicable terms. Indeed, Soviet propaganda tended to portray fascism as a generic property of contemporary "bourgeois" society. By contrast, Zatulin's definition specifically refers to Nazi Germany. But this does not mean that the draft condones the rehabilitation of Italian fascism; it mentions Germany's allies as partisans of Nazism and specifies that they too are not to be rehabilitated. This definition therefore abandons the notion of fascism and expands that of Nazism. The category of Russia's enemies is formed around a prototypical Nazi Germany to which "less good examples" (allies, accomplices, and partisans of Nazism, from Mussolini's Italy to the present-day US) are associated by a sort of "family resemblance" (in accordance with the aforementioned theory of prototypical categorization).

This is another interesting case that begs to be examined from the viewpoint of historical semantics. We have already seen how the logic of proper names informed the concept of sovereign democracy. The same approach is directly relevant in understanding the meanings of "fascism" and "Nazism" as they are currently used in Russia. The fact that the term "Nazism" is capitalized in English suggests that it is a "more proper" name than "fascism," even though, to some extent, it can also be considered a general name and can be defined in general terms that refer to its main properties. In its turn, the concept of fascism, although expressed by a

---

[49] A.A. Galkin, "Fascism," in *The Great Soviet Encyclopedia:* http://greatsovietencyclopedia.wikia.com/wiki/Fascism.

"more common" name, also comprises a reference to a historically concrete phenomenon that is limited in space and time (notwithstanding some definitions that do not include such a reference). But fascism is certainly a "more general" concept than Nazism.

Why, though, does the Zatulin draft (as well as almost all other memory laws of the Putin period to date) prefer "Nazism" over "fascism"? Andreas Umland speaks of the "rapid disintegration" of the concept of fascism in Russia during the 1990s as a result of the "multiplication of [its] meaning."[50] Fascism had, in fact, become too debatable a concept to be safely used in law. Its meaning could be easily expanded to include, say, the far-right movements in Russia, and it was actually understood in that sense by some authors of the memory law projects of the 1990s. "Nazism," by contrast, has a narrower meaning, in that it refers unambiguously to Nazi Germany. By choosing the more historically concrete concept of Nazism as a basis for their memory laws, Russian legislators hoped to safeguard the myth of the war and keep it within the framework of the familiar opposition between two concrete entities, Russia and Nazi Germany, thus distracting attention from Russia's own tradition of fascism, which powerfully informs the Russian nationalist movement and, as some researchers suggest, the current Russian regime.[51] Assimilating all unfriendly forces to the paradigmatic enemy allows exploitation of the "us" versus "them" dichotomy without the need for risky questions as to who *we* are and who *they* are. Stepping up the level of generality would, in fact, lead first to the concept of fascism and then to the theory of totalitarianism.

Using proper rather than general names helps maintain a level of concrete thought that confines one to the realm of myth.[52] An alternative strategy would be to create a more general concept of enemy by abstracting common properties shared by all unfriendly forces. Yet this would entail a complex operation involving extensive analysis that undermines the direct emotional appeal (and apparent clarity) of the "us" versus "them" dichotomy. Proper names are much more at home in the domain of memory than general concepts: what the memory law projects of the late 2000s sought to ban were historically concrete statements rather than general political claims. The form of historical thought that underlies

[50] Andreas Umland, "Concepts of Fascism in Contemporary Russia and the West," *Political Studies Review* 3 (2005), p. 36.
[51] Alexander J. Motyl, "Putin's Russia as a Fascist Political System," *Communist and Post-Communist Studies* 49/1 (2016), pp. 25–36.
[52] Claude Lévi-Strauss, *The Savage Mind* (Chicago, Ill.: The University of Chicago Press, 1966), chapter 1: "The Science of the Concrete."

Zatulin's memory law project (and other more recent Russian drafts) thus relies heavily on the logic of proper names: "Nazi Germany" is the logical name for the paradigmatic enemy of a "sovereign democracy." More generally, the present-day rise of memory and identity politics seems to work to the advantage of both this logic and its associated political mythologies.

But let us continue our close reading of the bill. Its title makes clear that the authors' key considerations pertained to Russia's relations with the newly independent states. One of the bill's most striking aspects is how narrowly it focuses on the problems of the "near-abroad" (the former Soviet republics, excluding Russia). Thus, it defines as "accomplices of Nazism" only those individuals who served in "organizations or institutions of the National-Socialist regime in Germany or collaborated with the occupational administration on the territory of the USSR within the borders of June 22, 1941" (Article 3). Apparently, the French, Dutch, and other Western collaborators who had not been employed by German organizations and institutions were not considered Nazi accomplices. The draft clearly distinguishes between the former Soviet republics whose historical memory it professes to regulate and the rest of the world. The rehabilitation of Nazism outside the former Soviet space was excluded from its scope, as if its authors were unaware of the existence of far-right parties in Western Europe or simply felt that Russia bore no responsibility for what was happening there. This creates the impression that a *corpus mysticum* of the USSR persisted in the lawmakers' imagination. By showing that they respected the "sovereignty" of Western European countries, Russian nationalists were inviting them, in turn, to respect Russia's sovereignty, including its right to control its former satellites. They proposed to reestablish an "anti-Hitler coalition of memory" as a part of a renewed Yalta System. Finally, there is strong fellow-feeling between Russia's nationalists and many of their Western counterparts. Western European far-right movements also cultivate the idea of the national state and speak out against European integration and the model of a US-dominated world. These nationalisms often present as Russia's allies, while the Eastern European national movements tend to oppose the Putin regime.

As for punishment, the bill follows the standard model of Russian laws on extremism, political parties, and the mass media. It establishes a procedure that envisions the court-ordered closure of those organizations and media outlets that, despite formal warnings, continue activities aimed at the rehabilitation of Nazism. The bill also specifies a range of actions to be taken against the newly independent states, should they be found culpable, ranging from economic sanctions to the outright severing of diplomatic relations (Article 20). As for private individuals, whether citizens of Russia or of the newly independent states, they were declared responsible under the criminal and administrative codes and the law against extremism (Article 21.3). But the Penal Code (unlike its administrative counterpart) contained no article prohibiting the rehabilitation of Nazism, except for Article 282, which criminalized incitement to racial hatred. It is improbable that the authors of the draft had this article in mind, however, as that would entail classifying the rehabilitation of Nazism as a crime of racism, which was certainly not their take on the issue. It seems more likely that they expected the Penal Code to be modified in due course, to ban certain statements about the past.

The most important innovation foreseen by the bill was the creation of a Civil Tribunal (or Civil Committee) that would oversee the preservation of national memory, monitor instances of "the rehabilitation of Nazism," and introduce programs for combating it. One third of the members of this tribunal were to be chosen by the President, one third by the Duma, and one third by the Civic Chamber. The tribunal was, in particular, to decide whether a given action or statement "contained elements of the rehabilitation of Nazism" (Article 13.1). Although the tribunal was to have only a deliberative vote, the state agencies were to consider its recommendations in the presence of its members (articles 13.3, 13.4). Zatulin and his co-authors probably expected to become members of that tribunal.

However, United Russia chose not to endorse this bill. The authorities most definitely disliked the idea of a political body that would not be entirely under their control and could include radical nationalists whom they did not want to benefit from the position of leaders of a patriotic campaign. The United Russia leadership decided instead to submit its own project, which Kolerov characterized as a purely "bureaucratic" move. He accused the party apparatchiks of unwillingness to take the danger of Nazism seriously.[53]

The two projects can, however, be seen as two sides of a single coin. First, both declared that counteracting attempts to "revise the Judgment of the Nuremberg Tribunal" was their major goal. Second, there are verbatim

---

[53] Kolerov, "Za nami narod!" Some journalists interpreted the existence of the two projects as a sign of the competition between "pragmatics" and "radicals" within United Russia. See Svetlana Samoylova, "Ushcherb istorii" [A Detriment to History], May 25, 2009: www.politcom.ru/8205 .html.

parallels between them, which suggests that they had common roots[54] and that there had presumably been consultations between the groups of lawmakers. Third, as has been already noted, the Zatulin project's establishment of responsibility for the rehabilitation of Nazism assumed that a corresponding amendment would be inserted into the Penal Code, and the United Russia bill proposed to do exactly that.

Arguably, the initial plan was to adopt two laws: a long law containing definitions of all relevant concepts and modeled after the law against extremism, and a short law modifying the Penal Code (a memory law per se). An indirect argument in favor of this hypothesis is that three years later, a group of Federation Council members adopted the same strategy, proposing two memory laws: a longer one that resembled Zatulin's draft and a short bill that amended the Penal Code. And in 1995, Proshechkin also submitted two different bills to define the meaning of "fascist symbols" and prohibit their use. In 2009, however, United Russia's bill clearly stole the thunder of Zatulin's proposal, which ended up interred in the Presidential Administration archives.[55] However, both components of what may well have been the initial plan were ultimately realized, albeit not in their original form.

The United Russia bill was presented to the Duma on May 6, 2009. The next day, President Dmitriy Medvedev asserted, in a video published on his blog in advance of Victory Day, that falsifications of Russian history were growing increasingly aggressive and had to be confronted. "We will allow no one to cast doubt on the achievements of our people," he said.[56] His speech was followed up by a decree signed on May 15, establishing "a commission reporting to the President to counter attempts to falsify history to the detriment of Russia's interests."[57]

The functions of the commission looked suspiciously like those assigned by Zatulin's bill to the "civil tribunal," although its makeup was different. The members were to be appointed by the President alone and were to

---

[54] Thus, one finds in both laws the same formula: "The Judgment of the Nuremberg Tribunal and the judgments of national courts or tribunals based on the Judgment of the Nuremberg Tribunal."

[55] O rabote deputata Gosudarstvennoy Dumy Rossii K.F. Zatulina v 2009 godu [On the Work of K.F. Zatulin, Deputy of the State Duma of Russia, in 2009]: www.zatulin.ru/index.php?section=news&id=430.

[56] Dmitriy Medvedev, "O Velikoy Otechestvennoy voyne, istoricheskoy istine i o nashey pamyati [On the Great Patriotic War, Historical Truth, and Our Memory], May 7, 2009: http://blog.da-medvedev.ru/post/11/transcript.

[57] Decree of the President of the Russian Federation No. 549 of May 15, 2009 "O Komissii pri Prezidente Rossiyskoy Federatsii po protivodeystviyu popytkam falsifikatsii istorii v ushcherb interesam Rossii" [On the Commission Reporting to the President of the Russian Federation to Counter Attempts to Falsify History to the Detriment of Russia's Interests].

offer their opinions on the politics of historical memory and on cases of falsification of history; there were twenty-eight in all, with Sergey Naryshkin, chief of the Presidential Administration, in the chair. The commission included only three historians (directors of the Academy of Sciences' historical research institutes and of the National Archives). Other members included the deputy ministers of Foreign Affairs, Defense, Education, and Culture, as well as members of the secret services and of some parliamentary committees. Zatulin and Narochnitskaya were also invited to join. The commission held several meetings and supported the publication of several leaflets before it was abolished by Medvedev's decree in February 2012, shortly before his term as president ended.

Let us now consider the United Russia project. It carried the signatures of the highest party officials including Duma President Boris Gryzlov, his deputy Vyacheslav Volodin, and the chairs of the Duma committees for veterans' affairs and for legislation. The draft law reads as follows:

> Distortion of the Judgment of the Nuremberg Tribunal, or of the judgments of national courts or tribunals based on the Judgment of the Nuremberg Tribunal, with the aim of fully or partially rehabilitating Nazism and Nazi criminals; declarations that actions of countries participating in the anti-Hitler coalition were criminal, and also the public approval and denial of Nazi crimes against peace and the security of humanity shall be punishable by a fine... or up to three years' imprisonment.[58]

The same infringements committed by persons in official positions or through the mass media, would, it was proposed, be punishable by imprisonment for up to five years.

The draft was clearly inspired by France's Gayssot Act and the Framework Decision of 2008. The bill's most original feature, however, is its protection of the memory of the member states of the anti-Hitler coalition. It could be used to vindicate any political action or act of war, from the Molotov-Ribbentrop Pact of 1939 to the atomic bombing of Hiroshima and Nagasaki, as if its authors wanted to send a signal to Russia's wartime allies in the West that they also had the reputations of those former confederates at heart.

The United Russia bill, like the Zatulin draft, is specifically directed against the rehabilitation of Nazism. It also views distortion of the Judgment of the Nuremberg Tribunal as central to any such rehabilitation and

---

[58] Draft Law No. 197582–5 of May 6, 2009 "O vnesenii izmeneniya v Ugolovnyi kodeks Rossiyskoi Federatsii" [On a Change to the Penal Code of Russian Federation].

considers those engaged in it as partisans and allies of Nazism. The bill's explanatory note explicitly equates the "near-abroad" countries' anti-Russian history politics with Nazism:

> The states that treat actions undertaken by the member states of the anti-Hitler coalition during World War Two as antagonistic and hostile to themselves declare themselves allies of Nazism.[59]

The bill was received positively by the Supreme Court and included in the Duma schedule so that it could be passed before the legislature's summer break. However, this did not happen, although the propaganda campaign exploiting the myth of the war retained its momentum throughout the summer months, in advance of the seventieth anniversary of the outbreak of World War II. In response to the Organization for Security and Cooperation in Europe's Vilnius Declaration of July 3, 2009, which stressed the importance of studying totalitarian regimes and commemorating their victims, the two chambers of the Russian parliament issued a joint declaration against equating fascism and communism, while Sergey Mironov, president of the Federation Council, published an article heatedly condemning "falsifications of history" and urging that they be criminalized.[60] Why, then, was the law not adopted?

Several factors played a role in this failure. Public opinion on the bill, and especially on the presidential commission, was mixed, largely because the commission consisted mostly of bureaucrats. According to a survey, 60 percent of Russians supported the idea of a law against the falsification of history, which is hardly surprising in view of the myth of the war, but 26 percent were opposed.[61] Further, there was no certainty that the proposed draft (not just the underlying concept of the bill) would have garnered similar support. Democratic politicians and NGOs severely

---

[59] Explanatory note to Draft Law No. 197582–5 of May 6, 2009.

[60] The OSCE declaration voices "deep concern at the glorification of the totalitarian regimes, including the holding of public demonstrations glorifying the Nazi or Stalinist past." See Divided Europe Reunited: Promoting Human Rights and Civil Liberties in the OSCE Region in the 21st Century, Vilnius Declaration of the OSCE Parliamentary Assembly, July 3, 2009; Sovmestnoye zayavleniye Gosdumy i Soveta Federatsii po povodu resolyutsii OBSE [Joint Declaration of the State Duma and the Federation Council Regarding the OSCE Resolution], July 7, 2009; Sergey Mironov, "Prigovor istorii obzhalovaniyu ne podlezhit" [The Verdict of History is Not Subject to Appeal], *Rossiyskaya gazeta*, July 17, 2009.

[61] The survey was conducted by VTsIOM (the Russian Public Opinion Research Center) on April 18–19, 2009. See "VTsIOM: Rossiyane schitayut prestupleniyem otritsaniye pobedy SSSR v VOV [VTsIOM: Russians Consider Denial of the Victory of the USSR in the Great Patriotic War To Be a Crime]": http://top.rbc.ru/society/07/05/2009/299676.shtml.

criticized both initiatives as manifestations of censorship. Several group petitions calling for the decree and the draft to be withdrawn were published.[62]

Historians, meanwhile, were divided. Some of them expressed their hope that the creation of the presidential commission would result in the archives finally being opened, while most objected because they saw the commission and the law as impinging upon the freedom of research. Some even declared that, in order to combat the law, they would create an association similar to the French *Liberté pour l'histoire* (which they never did). These protests were supported by international public opinion, including professional historians' organizations. The American Historical Association sent an open letter to President Medvedev, shortly thereafter, receiving support in this from the American Association for the Advancement of Slavic Studies. The letter reads, in part:

> The Council of the American Historical Association believes that it can never be in the public interest to forbid study of or publication about any historical topic or to forbid the publication of particular historical theses.[63]

The letter emphasizes that the Association takes the same position regarding any memory laws in any country. Likewise, in their letter to President Medvedev, a group of Italian historians characterized the creation of the presidential commission and the project of the law as an attempt "to impose a 'State truth'" and "a serious injury to the interests of the international scientific community."[64]

These protests may have had some influence on the outcome of the bill. In any event, the Russian government itself rejected the draft on the grounds that its wording was imprecise:

> The bill is problematic because it contains statements such as "the declaration that actions of countries which were participants in the anti-Hitler coalition were criminal": it is not clear what range of actions or period of time that provision covers.[65]

---

[62] E.g., Appeal to the Citizens of Russia, the President, and the State Duma, May 27, 2009: www.lph-asso.fr/index.php?option=com_content&view=article&id=77%3Aappel-aux-citoyens-de-russie-a-son-president-et-a-la-douma&catid=31%3Adossier-russie&Itemid=78&lang=en.

[63] American Historical Association Letter to Russian President Dmitrii Medvedev, June 17, 2009, the author's archive.

[64] Petition of Italian historians for the freedom of historical research in Russia, December 11, 2009: www.lph-asso.fr/index.php?option=com_content&view=article&id=128%3Apetition-des-historiens-italiens-pour-la-liberte-de-la-recherche-historique-en-russie&catid=31%3Adossier-russie&Itemid=78&lang=en.

[65] Official Response to Draft Law No. 197582–5 of May 6, 2009, July 29, 2009.

The Draft of 2010: Why Nuremberg?

Neither the public protests nor the government's negative response can in itself explain the failure of the United Russia bill. After Barack Obama's July 2009 meeting with President Medvedev in Moscow, a distinct change took place in Russian foreign policy, as the government began to modify its rhetoric in line with its new rapprochement with the West. Indeed, Medvedev on several occasions condemned Stalin's repressions in a language that was typical of the 1990s rather than the 2000s. Speaking on October 30 (the official Day of Remembrance of the Victims of Political Repressions in Russia), he said: "Nothing can be valued above human life, and there is no excuse for repressions."[66] As for Putin (then Prime Minister), he was busy spearheading the improvement of relations with Poland, one of Russia's main opponents in conflicts over the interpretation of the past. On August 31, he published an article in *Gazeta Wyborca* in which he recommended "turning the page" on the past, forgiving historical offenses, and developing friendly relationships in the future.[67] In April 2010, Putin and Polish Prime Minister Donald Tusk went together to Katyn in connection with the seventieth anniversary of the massacre of the Polish prisoners of war, and knelt before their tomb. The next day, Andrzej Wajda's movie *Katyn* was shown on Russian television. A few months later, in November 2010, the Russian parliament formally acknowledged Soviet responsibility for the Katyn massacre.[68] Although its declaration was highly ambiguous (trivializing Katyn in comparison with Stalin's other crimes, with the implication that it was a relatively minor episode and that the real victims of twentieth-century atrocities were Russians), it did explicitly call the USSR "a totalitarian state." It is hard to overestimate the distance that separated the November 2010 declaration from the July 2009 declaration, which had claimed that "accusing the USSR of war crimes [would be] nothing other than a revision of the spirit and the letter of the Nuremberg agreements"[69] (by which the

---

[66] Ellen Barry, "Don't Gloss over Stalin's Crimes, Medvedev Says," *New York Times*, October 31, 2009.

[67] Putin, "Karty historii – powód do wzajemnych pretensji czy podstawa pojednania i partnerstwa?" [Pages of History – Reason for Mutual Complaints or Grounds for Reconciliation and Partnership?], *Gazeta Wyborca*, August 31, 2009.

[68] Declaration of the State Duma of December 3, 2010 "O Katynskoy tragedii i yeyo zhertvakh" [On the Katyn Tragedy and Its Victims].

[69] Joint Declaration of the State Duma and the Federation Council Regarding the OSCE Resolution. Interestingly, this joint declaration contains verbatim quotations from the explanatory note to United Russia's memory law project.

parliament must have meant the London Agreement instituting the Nuremberg Tribunal).

Under these circumstances, United Russia's strategy was to make their bill resemble Western European memory laws as closely as possible. On April 16, 2010, a new draft was submitted to the Duma by the same group of deputies. However, this bill, although revised in light of the earlier criticisms from the government, was not much clearer: its authors limited themselves to a vague reference to the Judgment of the Nuremberg Tribunal and prohibited "the denial or approval of Nazi crimes against the peace and security of humankind, as established by the Judgment of the Nuremberg Tribunal."[70] We will consider this project in some detail, because it enables an appreciation of the broader problems associated with referencing the Nuremburg Trials in a law.

As we know, European memory laws typically penalize the denial of Nazi crimes against humanity *as defined* by the London Agreement of August 1945. The Russian project, by contrast, proposed to criminalize the denial of Nazi crimes that had been *established* by the Judgment of the Nuremberg Tribunal. Does this solve the problem of making clear what exactly the bill renders illegal?

The Nuremberg Judgment is a long and complex document[71] that is unfamiliar to an overwhelming majority in Russia (and arguably in other countries too). Ignorance of the law is generally no excuse, but does that rule extend to this Judgment? Does a citizen of the Russian Federation (or any other state) have the right to be ignorant of precisely which Nazi crimes have been "established by the Nuremberg Tribunal"? And if he does, how can he be punished for denying those crimes?

In addition, the Judgment is awkwardly referenced in the bill. How does the wording of the bill relate to the Nuremberg classification of Nazi crimes, including crimes against peace, war crimes, and crimes against humanity? Are "crimes against the peace and security of humankind" the equivalent of crimes against peace or of crimes against humanity? If the former, the law did not mandate any punishment for Holocaust denial, among all else. Furthermore, Nazi war crimes are not even mentioned in the bill, which would normally mean that their denial would not be

[70] Draft Law No 197582–5 of April 16, 2010 (a new redaction) "O vnesenii izmeneniy v Ugolovnyi kodeks Rossiyskoi Federatsii i v stat'yu 151 Ugolovno-protsessual'nogo kodeksa Rossiyskoy Federatsii" [On Changes to the Penal Code of the Russian Federation and to Article 151 of the Code of Criminal Procedure of the Russian Federation].
[71] I use here the materials of the Nuremberg Trials published by the Avalon Project: http://avalon.law.yale.edu/subject_menus/imt.asp.

considered a criminal offense. Curiously, the Duma's legal office had already identified the problematic wording of the first version of the bill and alerted its authors;[72] they disregarded that warning entirely.

Presumably, the goal of the Russian lawmakers was to justify the Soviet Union's policies in response to the three main charges leveled at its actions before, during, and after World War II: its involvement in the outbreak of war, war crimes committed by the Red Army, and the establishment of puppet regimes in the "people's democracies" of Eastern Europe. The earlier United Russia variant proposed outlawing "declarations that actions of countries participating in the anti-Hitler coalition were criminal," which gave legal protection to the Red Army's conquest of Eastern Europe. But that is precisely the wording that the government found too vague, so the authors of the new bill simply discarded it. The second version of the draft defended the reputation of the Soviet Union on only one point: the outbreak of the war.

Yet even here the Nuremberg Judgment is of little relevance. It could only have been used to identify beyond a doubt who was responsible for the outbreak of war if none of the claims presented at the Tribunal had been subsequently subject to revision. Absent that, it is nowhere specified how and by whom the claims that remain valid are to be distinguished from those that do not. In fact, various claims have been revised by the Russian authorities themselves.

Let us take the examples of the Munich Agreement and the Molotov-Ribbentrop Pact. The Nuremberg Judgment says nothing about the desire of the governments of France and Britain at Munich to direct Germany's aggression toward the Soviet Union, nor does it speak to the role of the Nazi-Soviet pact in starting the war. The secret protocol under which Hitler and Stalin divided up Eastern Europe is not even mentioned in the Judgment, although it was discussed at length during the trials. There is nothing surprising about that: the Allies did not create the Tribunal in order to confess their own iniquities, and the Tribunal, as a compromise struck between them, was not always in a position to determine the truth about the past. Consequently, there is no obligation to accept all of its findings without question today. But to differentiate between them all would require a vast corpus of historical and legal interpretation.

In 1989, the secret Molotov-Ribbentrop Protocol was officially condemned by the Russian parliament. Referring to that decision, Foreign Minister Sergey Lavrov had called on Western governments to officially

---

[72] Conclusion on the Draft Law No. 197582–5 of May 6, 2009, May 10, 2009.

censure the errors committed by the West, including the Munich Agreement, in the same way:

> The Russian parliament in due time acknowledged the mistake made by the Soviet Union, by denouncing the Molotov-Ribbentrop Pact. And we are entitled to expect the other countries that struck a deal with the Nazis to do so as well. . ... The West, like Soviet Russia, was not infallible.[73]

The bill's authors probably did not realize that the decision of the Russian parliament to which Lavrov refers is a revision of the Nuremberg Judgment, and that the minister was calling for more such revisions, especially since, a few months later, they themselves would vote in favor of the aforementioned declaration acknowledging the Soviet Union's responsibility for the Katyn massacre, which Gorbachev and Yeltsin had earlier recognized as a Soviet crime.[74] As for the Nuremberg Tribunal, it had been somewhat equivocal on this important issue. Under pressure from the USSR, it had initially accused the Nazis of the massacre, but the Judgment itself did not mention the tragedy at all. Conclusive eyewitness accounts of Soviet responsibility for the massacre had been presented during the trials, but the Tribunal ultimately chose not to enter any ruling concerning it. But it also did not repudiate the original accusation.[75] Are we then to conclude that the Tribunal formally determined that the Germans were responsible for that crime, as the Communist Party of the Russian Federation continues to believe? The CPRF energetically protested the Duma's declaration of November 2010, accusing the parliament of historical revisionism and the rehabilitation of Nazism.[76] Was the new law to apply to those Russian state officials who denied that Katyn had been a Nazi crime?

This case also reveals a broader problem. The relevant paragraph of the Judgment opens with the following statement:

[73] Lavrov, "65-letiye velikoy pobedy."
[74] I.S. Yazhborovskaya, A.Yu. Yablokov, and V.S. Parsadanova, *Katynskiy sindrom v sovetsko-pol'skikh i rossiysko-pol'skikh otnosheniyakh* [The Katyn Syndrome in Soviet-Polish and Russian-Polish Relationships] (Moscow: ROSSPEN, 2009).
[75] Annette Wieviorka, *Le procès de Nuremberg* (Paris: Liana Levi, 2009), p. 83; Alexandra Viatteau, "Comment a été traité la question de Katyn à Nuremberg," in *Les procès de Nuremberg et de Tokyo*, ed. Annette Wieviorka (Waterloo: André Versaille, 2010), pp. 145–157. On the ambiguous position of the Western Allies with regard to Katyn, see George Sanford, *Katyn and the Soviet Massacre of 1940: Truth, Justice and Memory* (New York: Routledge, 2005), pp. 1–3, 157–193.
[76] Declaration of the Presidium of the Central Committee of the Communist Party of the Russian Federation "O nedopustimosti peresmotra itogov Nyurnbergskogo protsessa v otnoshenii Katynskogo dela" [On the Inadmissibility of Revising the Outcomes of the Nuremberg Trials with Respect to the Katyn Case], December 26, 2010: http://kprf.ru/party_live/85039.html.

> An enormous amount of detailed proof of war crimes was laid before the court. It is not possible to examine it properly in this judgment, so the Tribunal will dwell on it in the most general terms.

The most important Nazi crimes had been included in the Indictment, but only some of them were listed in the Judgment. Should the other charges then be regarded as unproven? Of course not, as is made clear by the quotation. But can we correctly say that all the crimes enumerated in the Indictment but not mentioned in the Judgment were established? Who should decide, and how and on what basis should it be decided, if a specific accusation had been proven?

For all these reasons, the documents of the Nuremberg Tribunal are historical sources that are extremely hard to interpret and would not stand up well in a court of law. In order to be absolutely clear about the historical claims they were seeking to outlaw, the lawmakers ought to have proposed unambiguous wording with blanket legal applicability. They signally failed to do that. While the example of European legislators is also not ideal, as we have seen, their approach may still seem preferable: to refer to the London Agreement *only* for its *definition* of Nazi crimes.

Why did the authors of the bill decide to seek cover behind the Nuremberg Judgment? Most likely they imagined that, should this law be used in court, it would be interpreted by politically loyal experts and judges. The episode does, to be sure, demonstrate the low quality of legislative work being done in Russia and its subordination to the considerations of political propaganda. It could also be that, in the context of the more friendly relations with the West, the authors of the bill did not expect it to pass and viewed it as the window-dressing needed to save face after the government's negative response to the first draft. In any event, the bill would languish in the Duma's archives until the political crisis of 2011–2012 made the authorities circle back to this idea.

Putinism Mark II

The political crisis of 2011–2012 and the rise of the protest movement against Putin's regime reinforced the authoritarian and nationalistic tendencies of its development. The crisis also marked the end of the relative rapprochement with the West in 2009–2011. In 2014, the war in Ukraine further exacerbated Russia's face-off with the West.

The protests provoked by massive fraud during the December 2011 legislative elections were a sign of a profound crisis of confidence in Russian politics, which found expression in the educated middle class's growing discontent with corruption, restrictions of democratic freedoms, and the monopolization of power by a narrow group of politicians and "oligarchs." The economic crisis of 2008, limited as its direct impact on Russian society had been, had shown the precarious character of the Putin "stabilization." It had also demonstrated the vulnerability of the middle class that was almost completely excluded from politics and was therefore unable to defend its interests.

In March 2011, the Center for Strategic Research Foundation (CSR), a think tank with close ties to the Russian government, published a report that predicted the crisis that was to break in December of the same year:

> The period of political stability in Russia is coming to an end.... Crisis phenomena are mounting rapidly in the social and political spheres in Russia.... If confidence in the authorities continues to fall over the next 10–15 months a full-scale political crisis in Russia is a distinct possibility.[77]

The authors of the report, sociologists Mikhail Dmitriyev and Sergey Belanovskiy,[78] had based their remarkably accurate forecasts on an analysis of the new concerns voiced by respondents during focus group interviews:

> The operational characteristic of the new trend that arose in recent months is the statement... that "the people are regarded as a herd." ... Over the past decade respondents said that while the state of affairs left much to be desired there was a new stability and there were signs of improvement. At present... the prevailing opinion is that everything in the country is bad, the economy is stagnating and the petrodollars are pocketed by the ruling elite.

Dmitriyev and Belanovskiy went on to predict the following scenario:

> In the context of diminishing confidence in the authorities... mass disapproval of the authorities will turn a critical attitude to the authorities into a behavioural norm.... The conformist majority will rally ever more actively around opposition centers of influence. Such a shift will take place not only among the grassroots but within the party [United Russia] and state apparatus.

This scenario is reminiscent of the breakdown of the Soviet regime, an analogy that, although not spelled out in the report, would have been quite

---

[77] Sergey Belanovskiy and Mikhail Dmitriyev, *Politicheskiy krizis v Rossii i vozmozhnyie mekhanizmy ego razvitiya*, March 30, 2011. I quote here from the abridged English version of the report: *Political Crisis in Russia and How It May Develop*: http://csis.org/files/attachments/110330_CSR_Political_ Crisis_in_Russia.pdf.

[78] Dmitriyev, former Deputy Minister of Economic Development (2000–2004), was director of the CSR in 2011 (he lost that position in January 2014). Belanovskiy is the CSR's leading sociologist.

clear to both the authors and their audience. To prevent collapse, they called for immediate measures to be taken, including a transition "towards a more competitive political model." They urged the country leadership to accept as a fact "the growing political consciousness of the middle class in big cities" and to "create a party that expresses [its] interests." In other words, they were advocating a political compromise with the democratic opposition within the framework of a "controlled democracy."

While the protest movement was drawing the authorities' attention to alarmist predictions, the Kremlin's actual reaction to the crisis was not in line with the sociologists' recommendations. In the spring of 2012, the regime embraced the politics of radical cultural conservatism, a move that is virtually incomprehensible unless one takes into consideration the memories of the Soviet collapse – memories that are quite fresh for Putin's generation in general and for the professional group he belongs to (the secret services) in particular.

The protest movement in Moscow found expression in a series of rallies, each involving up to 100,000 people. Some of them resulted in clashes with police, most notably on Bolotnaya Square in Moscow in May 2012, by which time many observers were speaking of "the end of the Putin consensus."[79] Indeed, slogans such as "people are treated as a herd" allowed all social groups to express their dissatisfaction with the regime's policies.

From the spring of 2012, Putin (reelected president in March 2012) and his advisors abandoned their previous efforts to balance economic liberalism and neo-imperial reconstruction, in order to ensure the support of nationalists, conservatives, and pro-Western liberals. That could, however, only be achieved at the cost of ideological incoherence involving a compromise between the liberal master narrative and the "nationalization of the past." The new Presidential Administration, with Vyacheslav Volodin (a co-author of the 2009 United Russia bill) now serving as the Kremlin's chief ideologist, feared that in the current crisis, such maneuvering risked eroding the regime's cultural foundations. The authorities therefore resolved to consolidate the support of the conservative majority and to isolate the democratic minority, whose influence was rapidly growing countrywide.

The regime's response to the democratic movement consisted, first of all, in repressions, from the Pussy Riot case to the Bolotnaya affair (the trial

---

[79] Ben Judah and Andrew Wilson, "The End of the Putin Consensus," European Council of Foreign Relation, Policy memo: www.files.ethz.ch/isn/173630/Putin_final.pdf.

of those who had clashed with police on Bolotnaya Square). In 2012–2013, the Russian parliament hurriedly passed several repressive laws that limited democratic freedoms (especially freedom of expression and the right to assemble); instituted censorship of the Internet (which had been the main instrument of political mobilization during the crisis of 2011–2012); expanded the powers of law enforcement agencies; obliged NGOs that had international funding to accept the legal status of "foreign agents," etc. These laws were introduced mostly on the initiative of the government and United Russia, but they were enthusiastically supported by the "systemic opposition" (formally oppositional parties in the parliament that support Putin's regime).

The politics of radical cultural conservatism (or the "new traditionalism," as Richard Sakwa calls it),[80] which was another way of undercutting the vanguard of the grassroots protest movement, has become the hallmark of Putinism Mark II. In order to politically isolate the "creative class" (the motive force of the protest movement), the regime attempted to broaden the gap between the two Russias, the liberal and the traditionalist.

The Medvedev years (2008–2011) had witnessed the government's persistent but futile attempts to embark on a policy of modernization in Russian society. The modernization program was formulated in September 2009 in Medvedev's seminal article "Go, Russia!"[81] However, as Sakwa notes, "Medvedev was unable to forge a genuine coalition for modernization"[82] partly due to the fact that Putin remained in control of "the apparat" (the state apparatus). Modernization, furthermore, necessarily entailed an anti-corruption policy that would encroach on the apparat's interests. In addition, the crisis of 2008 had resulted in a far less favorable economic landscape. The government had to face the reality that, given the quality of Russian public institutions, no further economic growth comparable to the recovery of 2000–2008 was likely in the foreseeable future.

[80] Sakwa, *Putin Redux*, pp. 190–221; Gulnaz Sharafutdinova, "The Pussy Riot Affair and Putin's Démarche from Sovereign Democracy to Sovereign Morality," *Nationalities Papers* 42/4 (2014), pp. 615–621; and Marlene Laruelle, "The Izborsky Club, or the New Conservative Avant-Garde in Russia," *The Russian Review* 75/4 (2016), pp. 626–644. Viatcheslav Morozov (*Russia's Postcolonial Identity*, p. 111) views Putin's "paleotraditionalism" mostly as a negation of Western hegemony, which I think is a simplification: we cannot ignore the Putin regime's proven incapacity to pursue an efficient modernization agenda or the dynamics of the country's domestic policy, including the apparat's struggle for self-preservation, although Russia's traditional complex of inferiority with regard to the West has certainly also had a role to play.

[81] Medvedev, "Go, Russia!" (September 10, 2009): http://eng.kremlin.ru/news/298; Sakwa, *Putin Redux*, pp. 38–60, 83; and Sakwa, *The Crisis of Russian Democracy: The Dual State, Factionalism and the Medvedev Succession* (Cambridge: Cambridge University Press, 2011), pp. 347–348.

[82] Sakwa, *Putin Redux*, p. 43.

But even when faced with the prospect of recession, the corrupt regime had little to offer in terms of social and economic policies. Radical cultural conservatism and an aggressive foreign policy were its last resort.

The program of cultural conservatism includes: a quest for stability and hostility to change, especially revolutions; an emphasis on traditional values and an alliance with the Orthodox Church; revival of a Soviet-style anti-intellectualism; and a crusade against "deviant behavior" (including "non-traditional" sexual behavior). Nationalism and hatred for the West, portrayed as inherently immoral and anti-Russian, form the common denominator of all these tendencies.

The Russian media, which are almost totally controlled by the regime, were working hard to make their audiences feel that they were living in a fortress under siege. And all of this was compounded by the mythology of "color revolutions" (such as the 2003 Rose Revolution in Georgia and the 2004 Orange Revolution in Ukraine), which are viewed by the Kremlin as a result of the West's subversive anti-Russian policies.

Many Russians are receptive to such propaganda. The Russian media present the democratic opposition as a handful of street (and Internet) hooligans who hate their country, insult national symbols, and act as a "fifth column." It is, further, suggested that liberals differ little from fascists, as do their "masters abroad" (the Soviet tradition of portraying the capitalist West, including the United States, as quintessentially fascist is alive and well in Russia). And all of this comes together to revitalize the cult of World War II: never in recent history have the denouncers of "Nazi allies" been as vocal in Russia as they are today, resulting in a nationalist hysteria that is also accompanied by determined attempts to rehabilitate Stalin, including in particular the erection of his statues all across the Russian Federation.[83]

To create a legal foundation for the politics of cultural conservatism, the Russian parliament passed several bills, including laws criminalizing "insults to religious sentiments" and prohibiting "the denial of traditional family values" (or "the propaganda of homosexuality") among children.[84]

---

[83] Khapaeva, "Triumphant Memory of the Perpetrators."

[84] Putin signed both laws on June 29, 2013. The first introduced criminal liability for "actions that express obvious disrespect to society and are committed to insulting the religious sentiments of believers." The punishment was up to one year's imprisonment or a fine. See Federal Law No. 136-FZ of June 29, 2013 "O vnesenii izmeneniy v stat'yu 148 Ugolovnogo kodeksa Rossiyskoy Federatsii i otdel'nyie zakonodatel'nyie akty Rossiyskoy Federatsii v tselyakh protivodeystviya oskorbleniyu religioznykh ubezhdeniy i chuvstv grazhdan" [On Changes to Article 148 of the Criminal Code of the Russian Federation and to Certain Legislative Acts of the Russian Federation with the Purpose of Countering Insults to Religious Convictions and Sentiments of Citizens].

These laws are formulated in intentionally broad terms, with some politicians even going so far as to suggest that laws be passed to prevent offenses against patriotic sentiments and publications detrimental to Russia's prestige. A law criminalizing counter-memories of the war was a logical continuation of this policy.

Putinism Mark II found its most characteristic expression in the aggression against Ukraine. Rational factors, such as economic interests or security considerations, cannot fully explain Russia's obsession with Ukraine, which is, in fact, largely rooted in Putin's cultural politics, and above all in the politics of historical memory, anti-Western rhetoric, and "besieged fortress" fantasies. In a sense, the annexation of Crimea is an expression of cultural conservatism, with its premodern land hunger and predilection for tangible symbols of power.

Putin's politics of memory has created a lens through which the only analog to the contemporary Ukrainian movement for national liberation is the *Banderivtsy* (Ukrainian nationalists, followers of Stepan Bandera) of World War II, who were traditionally depicted in Russia as Nazi collaborators. Characteristically, a recent Russian bill equated the symbols of the Bandera movement to Nazi symbols, making their public display an offense under the law on extremism and the administrative code.[85] The politics of memory that was based on the cult of the war had managed to produce a worldview within which new acts of war could be justified (in the same way as in the West the "good war" consensus has been used to legitimize military interventions in the 1990s and 2000s). It has also created a language of political mobilization against the external enemy, which the regime needed in order to marginalize the in-country opposition.

The second law introduced administrative fines for disseminating any information that could be interpreted as approving homosexuality. See Federal Law No. 135-FZ of June 29, 2013 "O vnesenii izmeneniy v stat'yu 5 Federal'nogo zakona 'O zashchite detey ot informatsii, prichinyayushchey vred ikh zdorovyu i razvitiyu' i otdel'nyie zakonodatel'nyie akty Rossiyskoy Federatsii v tselyakh zashchity detey ot informatsii, propagandiruyushchey otritsaniye traditsionnykh semeynykh tsennostey" [On Changes to Article 5 of the Federal Law "On Protecting Children from Information Harmful to Their Health and Development" and to Certain Legislative Acts of the Russian Federation for the Purpose of Protecting Children against Information Promoting the Denial of Traditional Family Values].

[85] Federal Law No. 332-FZ of November 5, 2014 "O vnesenii izmeneniy v stat'yu 6 Federal'nogo zakona 'Ob uvekovechenii Pobedy sovetskogo naroda v Velikoy Otechestvennoy voyne 1941–1945 godov' i stat'yu 20.3 Kodeksa Rossiyskoy Federatsii ob administrativnykh pravonarusheniyakh" [On Changes to Article 6 of the Federal Law "On Perpetuating [the Memory of] the Victory of the Soviet People in the Great Patriotic War of 1941–1945" and to Article 20.3 of the Code of Administrative Offences of the Russian Federation].

In recent years, the regime has also made persistent efforts to strengthen its control over history education. In February 2013, Putin ordered the Ministry of Education to create textbooks that would present national history in a "non-contradictory" fashion. The concept of a "unified history textbook" promulgated in October 2013 holds in particular that "the USSR entered the Second World War on June 22, 1941, as a result of the German invasion of its territory,"[86] as if the Molotov-Ribbentrop Pact and the Soviet occupation of the Baltic countries and parts of Poland, Romania, and Finland in 1939 and 1940 had nothing to do with this war. Such was the context in which the Russian authorities had reverted to the idea of a memory law.

The Battle of Two Bills (2013–2014)

Russian ruling circles developed varying notions of how the new law should read. In 2009 and 2010, two United Russia factions had proposed separate drafts of it, neither of which won any government support. This was followed, in 2013 and 2014, by an open competition on the subject between the State Duma and the Federation Council: each house had its own conception of the bill, which the deputies persistently promoted in the teeth of continuing government disapproval. This led to several new drafts being introduced into the parliament.

Some were submitted by a group of Federation Council members led by Boris Spiegel. In response, the authors of the United Russia bill of 2009 came up with the third version of their proposal, which I have earlier called the Yarovaya bill, and will discuss in some detail in the following. Irina Yarovaya, a co-author of the initial United Russia draft, had been the main driving force behind that project since 2010.

Boris Spiegel is a Russian "oligarch" and politician, and an important Russian-Jewish activist. He was a member of the Federation Council in 2003–2013 and for several years worked on its Committee on the Affairs of the Commonwealth of Independent States (CIS). In his capacity of president of the World Congress of Russian Jewry (a position he has held since 2007), Spiegel has worked with both the Ministry of Foreign Affairs and the presidential Commission on the Falsification of History. In June 2010, he created World without Nazism (WWN), an international human rights

---

[86] Kontseptsiya novogo uchebno-metodicheskogo kompleksa po otechestvennoy istorii: Proekt [Concept of a New Set of Instructional Materials on Russian History: Draft], p. 48: www.kommersant.ru/docs/2013/standart.pdf.

movement and NGO, and became its chairman. WWN declared the struggle against Nazi ideology and historical revisionism as its main goal.[87]

However, Spiegel's position differed in one significant respect from that of most other Russian officials involved in the politics of history: he was interested in the memory of the Holocaust, which is even more marginal in Russia than in other Eastern European countries, largely because of the cult of World War II. As we know, for that cult to fulfill its mission, the Soviet/Russian people have to be portrayed as both *the* victim and *the* hero of the war.

In the 1990s, when the war myth temporarily faded in importance, the Holocaust had been recognized in Russia as a major crime against human-ity, but its memory still failed to become an integral part of Russian national memory. Under Putin, the memory of the Holocaust, as well as the notion of human rights, gradually came to be seen as an ideological weapon wielded by the West in its "crusade" against Russia.

The originality of Spiegel's take on historical memory consists in his efforts to integrate the Holocaust into the Soviet/Russian narrative of World War II. During Medvedev's presidency, which was characterized by a rapprochement with the West, attempts to translate the Russian war myth into the language of the European Union's politics of memory were actually well positioned to win the support of the country's leadership. Spiegel's tactic in this was to present Russia as a natural ally of the West against Eastern Europe, where (according to him) the revival of national-ism had led to a "rehabilitation of Nazism."

Spiegel was not alone in using the memory of the Holocaust to render Russian history politics more respectable in the eyes of the international community. For example, in 2008, the Historical Memory Foundation (HMF) was created in Moscow with the support of both Russian nation-alists and the Holocaust Studies Center (HSC).[88] This foundation special-izes in the publication of archival documents (often sourced from the

[87] Alexander Zaitchik, "Anti-Anti-Semitism: World without Nazism Is a Kremlin-Flavored Anti-Defamation League for the Post-Soviet Realm – But Is It Good for Jews?" *Tablet,* September 20, 2010.

[88] In 2008, two books by HMF director Aleksandr Dyukov were published by Modest Kolerov's Regnum News Agency. See Dyukov, *Vtorostepennyi vrag: OUN, UPA i resheniye "yevreyskogo voprosa"* [A Second-Rate Enemy: The OUN, the UPA, and the Solution of the "Jewish Question"] (Moscow: Regnum, 2008); Dyukov, *"The Soviet Story": Mekhanizmy lzhi* ["The Soviet Story": Mechanisms of a Lie] (Moscow: Regnum, 2008). In 2009, the HMF and the Holocaust Foundation co-published a collection of essays *Obshchaya tragediya: Blokada. Kholokost* [A Common Tragedy: The Siege [of Leningrad]. The Holocaust], ed. Dyukov (Moscow, 2009), which included essays by Dyukov and HSC director Ilya Altman. Altman also participated in conferences sponsored by Spiegel, including the 2009 conference in Berlin (www.rosspen.su/ru/

Soviet secret service archives) showing the collaboration of Eastern European governments and nationalists with Nazi Germany in the 1930s and 1940s, with special attention going to Poland, Ukraine, and the Baltic countries.[89] The HMF has endorsed the Kremlin's history politics, including the intention of passing a memory law.

Spiegel's approach has promise insofar as the Nazis did indeed find collaborators in some Eastern European countries – a fact that the politics of memory in those countries tends to obscure. Moscow could therefore hope to build a "coalition of memory" with the West against its Eastern European opponents. However, the traditional "Nuremberg style" anti-fascism would be of little use here, as the negative reception given in the West to the 2009 Russian draft made clear. In contrast, modernizing the concept by integrating the memory of the Holocaust seemed to be a workable solution. Even so, the authorities still preferred to promote the memory of the Holocaust indirectly, by means of an international NGO, and mostly outside the country. Inside Russia, the memory of the Holocaust remained a marginal theme of the state-sponsored propaganda, because it was apt only to mar the purity of the Russian war myth.

Penalizing Holocaust denial was on WWN's agenda from the outset. In November 2011, Spiegel's election as deputy chairman of the Federation Council's Committee on Constitutional Legislation gave him new tools to implement that idea. In May 2012, on Spiegel's initiative, the Interparliamentary Assembly of Member Nations of the CIS approved a model law against the rehabilitation of Nazism and the heroization of Nazi criminals.[90] In Spiegel's view, the adoption of this document would facilitate the passing of similar national laws, in a strategy that had clearly been inspired by the Framework Decision of 2008.

The title of the law resembles that of Zatulin's bill. The twenty-page document is, in fact, quite similar to Zatulin's project in several ways, lifting a number of passages from it in their entirety.[91] This continuity was

---

news/.view/id/345/). Both the HMF and the HSC are members of WWN (http://worldwithoutnazism.org/participants/).

[89] For a list of publications supported by the HMF, see www.historyfoundation.ru/en/publication.php.

[90] Interparliamentary Assembly of Member Nations of the Community of Independent States: Model Law of May 17, 2012 "O nedopustimosti deystviy po reabilitatsii natsizma, geroizatsii natsistskikh prestupnikov i ikh posobnikov" [On the Inadmissibility of Actions Aimed at the Rehabilitation of Nazism, and the Heroization of Nazi Criminals and Their Accomplices]: www.iacis.ru/upload/iblock/397/18_a_2012.pdf.

[91] For example, Article 2 on the principles of the state policies targeted against the rehabilitation of Nazism.

probably due to the fact that Modest Kolerov, Zatulin's collaborator, was involved in WWN's activities and joined its board in 2010.[92] It is important to keep in mind that both projects originated among politicians who were relatively peripheral to the core of the governing circles, although some of them held important positions in the parliament.[93] But for all their similarities, the CIS model law differs from Zatulin's bill in many respects.

The CIS law, which was worded so as to be acceptable to all member nations, appears both less haphazard and less extreme, and is more in line with the equivalent Western legislation. Zatulin's draft focused on what the Russian government had to do to prevent "the rehabilitation of Nazism" in the near-abroad. The model law, by contrast, considers the ways in which member nations should counteract such rehabilitation within their own borders. Similarly to Zatulin's bill, however, the CIS law proposed a complex strategy for promoting the Russian myth of the war and provided definitions of the relevant concepts. Most of those definitions resemble those in the 2009 bill but bring them closer to European standards[94] or to existing Russian legislation.[95] The notion of the rehabilitation of Nazism was considerably expanded in the CIS law and includes a clear reference to Holocaust denial, citing:

> Public approval or denial of crimes against peace, war crimes and crimes against humanity established by the Judgment of the International Military Tribunal as well as the judgments of national, military, or occupation tribunals based on the Judgment of the International Military Tribunal. (Article 1)

---

[92] "Izbrany rukovodyashchiye organy dvizheniya 'Mir bez natsizma'" [The Leadership of the World without Nazism Movement is Elected], June 23, 2010: www.regnum.ru/news/russia/1297189 .html.

[93] As for Zatulin himself, he disappeared from the political scene in April 2011, when, after the disgrace of Luzhkov, his patron, United Russia decided to replace him as deputy chairman of the Duma Committee on CIS Affairs. In the following December, he failed to win reelection to the Duma. Another reason for his fall was arguably linked to his attempt to interfere in the delicate question of "succession." In spring 2011, when it was not yet decided whether Putin or Medvedev would be the United Russia candidate in the presidential elections of 2012, Zatulin openly expressed his support for Putin. See IA REGNUM's Interview of K. Zatulin, April 7, 2011: www.zatulin.ru/index.php?section=news&id=496. He was not the only politician to be punished for sharing his "untimely reflections" with the public. Thus, Gleb Pavlovskiy, one of the architects of the history politics of the 2000s, was also eliminated from "high politics" for having publicly taken position in favor of Medvedev. However, in 2016, Zatulin became an MP again.

[94] Zatulin gives the following typology of Nazi crimes: "War crimes, crimes against humanity, and genocide." In contrast, the model law uses their Nuremberg classification: "Crimes against peace, war crimes, [and] crimes against humanity."

[95] Thus, the CIS law definition (in Article 1) of "Nazi materials" is, for its most part, a verbatim reiteration of the definition of "extremist materials" in the 2002 Russian law on extremism (quoted above).

This wording has replaced the much shorter formulation that was used (parenthetically) in Zatulin's project: "Denial of the Nazi genocide and crimes against humanity." That was a considerable improvement. The reference to "the judgments of national, military, or occupation tribunals based on the Judgment of the International Military Tribunal" was probably borrowed from the United Russia project of 2009. And although the word "Holocaust" is not used in the CIS model law, Holocaust denial obviously falls within its scope. Yet nothing in the language of the law excludes the traditional Soviet notion that unleashing an aggressive war, not perpetrating the Holocaust, was the Nazis' principal crime. Most notably, the quoted passage adopts some of the language of the EU Framework Decision of 2008, which had served as a model for the CIS law.[96]

In contrast to the Framework Decision, however, the CIS law (as well as the United Russia project) refers not to the Charter of the Nuremberg Tribunal, but to its Judgment. Even more importantly, crimes against peace were not mentioned at all in the Framework Decision. Zatulin's project does not mention them either, probably because the phrase "Denial of the Nazi genocide and crimes against humanity," especially given its placement in parentheses, could have been a late addition to the draft, made in haste. By contrast, the omission of crimes against peace from the Framework Decision seems natural: the EU document emphasizes the prevention of crimes of a racist nature and is consequently less interested in the responsibility for the outbreak of war, which is a central concern of history politics in Russia. This obviously reflects the distance between the Western and the Russian interpretations of Nazism.

The CIS model law invites each member nation to create a "body empowered by the state" tasked with coordinating the struggle against the rehabilitation of Nazism (Article 18), which should be made up of state officials and NGO representatives. Providing a detailed procedure for "public anti-Nazi expert examination" is central to the CIS law, and the state agencies are obliged to rely on those examinations in determining whether a given statement displays symptoms of Nazi rehabilitation (Article 13). Obviously, the activists on Spiegel's team were looking for mechanisms that would enable them to control the government's politics of memory. However, the model law left it to national legislative bodies to decide if special criminal provisions were needed to counteract the rehabilitation of Nazism (Article 21).

---

[96] See Chapter 2.

Spiegel's plan had been to use the CIS model law in convincing the Russian parliament to pass a similar bill, and in November 2012, the media announced that the Federation Council had indeed drawn up an "anti-Nazi law."[97] Three weeks later, however, Spiegel fell victim to some serious media mud-slinging. Several nationalist websites published a photocopy (most likely falsified[98]) of a pedophilia conviction he ostensibly received in 1982, which came with a three-year term of imprisonment. Although this highly defamatory accusation resulted in no legal action, Spiegel had in any case to resign from the Federation Council in March 2013 because of a new law that forbade combining seats in the parliament with official positions in international NGOs and involvement in any commercial business. Spiegel chose to keep his business and remain president of WWN. The same law also forced several other Russian politicians out of the parliament.

A few days before his resignation, Spiegel had introduced two bills into the Duma, one long and the other short. The long draft was a verbatim reproduction of the CIS model law,[99] the only difference being that the new project ("Spiegel's long draft") used the term "Holocaust" and explicitly mentioned Holocaust negationism as a form of rehabilitation of Nazism. This highly significant difference distinguishes Spiegel's initiative from all other Russian memory law projects. The word "Holocaust" is, in fact, used in the draft fifty-three times, almost always in the vicinity of the expression "rehabilitation of Nazism." Holocaust negationism was clearly one of Spiegel's main concerns, probably for both tactical and substantial reasons. Nevertheless, the language of the draft offers no clue as to whether Spiegel actually did view Nazi crimes primarily as crimes of a racial nature.

Why did Spiegel not incorporate any mention of the Holocaust in the CIS model law? Probably because he wanted to facilitate the adoption of corresponding national laws by the member states, including the countries of Central Asia that had their own Soviet-style cults of the war and no memories of the Holocaust whatsoever.

Like Zatulin's project, Spiegel's long draft did not provide any criminal penalties for the rehabilitation of Nazism. But he had also prepared

[97] Pyotr Kozlov, "Sovet Federatsii podgotovil zakon protiv natsizma" [The Federation Council Has Drafted a Law against Nazism], *Izvestiya*, November 15, 2012.
[98] Oleg Lurie, "Prigovor, kotorogo ne bylo" [The Verdict That Never Was]: http://oleglurie-new.livejournal.com/75669.html.
[99] Draft Law No. 246071–6 of March 25, 2013 "O nedopustimosti deystviy po reabilitatsii natsizma, geroizatsii natsistskikh prestupnikov i ikh posobnikov, otritsaniyu Kholokosta" [On the Inadmissibility of Actions Aimed at the Rehabilitation of Nazism, the Heroization of Nazi Criminals and Their Accomplices, and Holocaust Denial].

another bill ("Spiegel's short draft") that did. The short draft proposed expanding the list of offenses detailed in Article 282 of the Penal Code, which is titled "Incitement to Hatred or Hostility or the Disparagement of Human Dignity," by including in it the rehabilitation of Nazism and Holocaust denial. Had Spiegel's proposal been accepted, Article 282 would have criminalized

> Actions aimed at inciting hatred or enmity, the rehabilitation of Nazism, the glorification of Nazi criminals and their accomplices, denial of the Holocaust, and also the disparagement of the human dignity of a person or a group of persons on the basis of gender, race, nationality, language, origins, religion, or membership of a social group, whether committed publicly or through the media.[100]

The punishment provided for up to three years' imprisonment (five years if aggravating circumstances were present). This proposal was modeled after European laws that criminalized Holocaust denial and racial discrimination. Spiegel's short draft is quite explicit in categorizing Holocaust denial and the rehabilitation of Nazism as crimes of a racist nature.

After his resignation from the Federation Council, Spiegel remained president of WWN. In 2014, he actively supported, on that organization's behalf, the Russian annexation of Crimea.[101] As for his drafts, each went its own way. The long one, in a modified form, is at the time of writing pending in the parliament, while the short one was rejected by the State Duma on procedural grounds (the absence of official reviews by the government and the Supreme Court). This happened on June 20, 2013, just as United Russia was deciding to revisit its own memory law project in the context of what became known as "the Gozman case."

"Sometimes You're Sorry the Nazis Didn't Make Lampshades out of the Ancestors of Today's Liberals," – that was the subhead the popular Russian daily *Komsomol'skaya Pravda* used for an article by journalist Ulyana Skoybeda that it posted online on May 13. Two days later, following an outcry on social media, the subhead was modified to "Liberals Revise History To Deprive Our Country of Its Roots."[102]

---

[100] Draft Law No. 246065–6 of March 25, 2013 "O vnesenii izmeneniy v stat'yu 282 Ugolovnogo kodeksa Rossiyskoy Federatsii" [On the Introduction of Changes to Article 282 of the Criminal Code of the Russian Federation].

[101] V. Krasnopolskaya, "Boris Spiegel: Ia khochu, chtoby yevreyam Kryma ne nado bylo dumat', kuda ekhat'" [Boris Spiegel: I Wish Crimean Jews Did Not Need to Wonder Where to Go], *Krymskiye Izvestiya* [Crimea News], March 14, 2014: www-ki.rada.crimea.ua/index.php/2011-03-13-12-03–27/13787–2014-03–14-07–42-14.

[102] Skoybeda, "Politik Leonid Gozman zayavil: Krasivaya forma – yedinstvennoye otlichiye SMERSH ot SS" [Politician Leonid Gozman Stated: A Nice Uniform is the Only Difference between SMERSH and the SS], *Komsomol'skaya Pravda*, May 13, 2013. See also Ilia Blinderman,

Vladimir Sungorkin, the *Komsomol'skaya Pravda* editor-in-chief and one of Putin's trusted aides during the 2012 elections, reacted to this scandal in the following way: "Of course it's a monstrous phrase, but she said it because she's a journalist and a pushover for a heated debate. So I don't think that she meant all Russian liberals, only her opposite number... I'll give her a good talking-to.... What's to be done about Gozman, though?"[103]

Leonid Gozman was none other than the "opposite number," one of those whose ancestors, according to Skoybeda, the Nazis should have exterminated. For many years, he had been a leader of the liberal Union of Rightist Forces party. On May 12, Gozman had posted in his blog a highly negative review of a movie that Russian television had broadcast on Victory Day. The movie's title was *SMERSH* (the Russian abbreviation for "Death to Spies," which was the official name of a military secret service during World War II). Can you imagine, asked Gozman, what would happen if a movie called *SS* complete with soldiers in black uniforms fighting valiantly for their country were to be shown in Germany? Then why is this possible in Russia? SMERSH, he continued, "was no less criminal than the SS," and both words should "cause fear and disgust, instead of being used in the titles of patriotic thrillers."[104]

It was not uncommon for the KGB to be compared with the SS during the democratic reforms of the 1990s. In the 2000s, however, the renationalization of Russian politics produced a cult of the state that included the secret services.[105] The latter are seen less as an instrument of political repressions than as the Soviet state's "last resort" in its struggle for the country's survival, especially during the war. Quite a few leading figures of the current regime (Putin among them) are former KGB officers. And this means that questioning the reputation of the secret services is tantamount to challenging the regime.

Most Russian politicians reacted to the scandal as Sungorkin had, holding that the statement about lampshades was indeed politically incorrect, but the real issue was Gozman, who had allegedly insulted veterans

---

"Russian Columnist: 'Sometimes One Regrets that Nazis Didn't Make Lampshades out of the Forefathers of Today's Liberals,'" *Daily News*, May 17, 2013, and Victor Davidoff, "The New Russian Anti-Semitism," *The Moscow Times*, May 27, 2013.

[103] Quoted in "'Komsomol'skaya Pravda' zamenila nekorrektnyi podzagolovok" ['Komsomol'skaya Pravda' Has Fixed an Incorrect Subhead], May 15, 2013: www.bfm.ru/news/216321.

[104] Gozman, "Podvigu soldat SS posvyashchaetsya..." [Dedicated to the Deeds of the Soldiers of the SS...], May 12, 2013: http://leonid-gozman.livejournal.com/150225.html.

[105] See Fedor, *Russia and the Cult of State Security,* pp. 117–183.

and the entire Russian people.[106] In particular, Sergey Zhelezniak, United Russia member and deputy chair of the State Duma, went further, proposing the criminalization of any such "desecration of the memory of the war": "We need to put a stop to unacceptable statements about our victory in World War II," he said.[107]

In June 2013, about thirty Duma deputies representing not only United Russia but also the opposition parties added their names to the Yarovaya bill, which had been stalled in the parliament since 2010. This brought the number of the bill's co-sponsors to almost fifty. However, United Russia decided to modify the draft, because its second version, submitted during the Medvedev détente in April 2010, appeared too moderate now, in the context of Putin's new radical conservative politics.

Irina Yarovaya is a typical figure of the Russian political class. She began her career as the head of a local division of the Yabloko democratic party in Kamchatka region. She failed twice in the legislative elections before changing her political allegiance, joining United Russia in 2007. This time she did become an MP, and moved to Moscow. Shortly after that, she was appointed president of the United Russia Patriotic Club, a job that sat oddly with her formerly democratic persona. Since 2012, she has gained renown as the co-author of several repressive laws.

The news that the Yarovaya bill was going to be reintroduced in the parliament broke on June 24. Four days later, on June 28, Konstantin Dobrynin, Spiegel's former collaborator and his successor as deputy chairman of the Federation Council Committee on Constitutional Legislation, announced that the upper house had also drawn up an anti-Nazi bill. Dobrynin, described by the media as a member of the group of young St. Petersburg lawyers close to Dmitriy Medvedev, is best typified by an article published in February 2014, in which he took exception to the nationalist hysteria in Russia that had resulted from the Ukrainian crisis.[108] After Spiegel's resignation, Dobrynin's task was to promote his predecessor's bills.

[106] Thus, on May 16, the Russian parliament ordered an inquiry into Gozman's comments. See "Duma Orders Probe Into Comparison of Red Army Units and SS," May 16, 2013: http://sputniknews.com/russia/20130516/181186157.html. Soon after that, Gozman was forced to leave Rosnano, a state-owned corporation for innovative technologies where he had served as Director of Humanitarian Projects.

[107] "Yedinoross Zheleznyak nameren nakazat' 'bolotnyi bomond' za somneniya v podvige SSSR v Velikoy Otechestvennoy" [United Russia's Zheleznyak Intends to Punish the "Bolotnaya Square beau monde" for Calling into Question the Deeds of the USSR in the Great Patriotic War], May 14, 2013: www.newsru.com/russia/14may2013/nazlaw.html.

[108] Dobrynin, "Vremya obizhennykh" [A Time of Offended People], February 16, 2014: www.fontanka.ru/2014/02/16/080/.

In June 2013, the two houses of the Russian parliament entered into open competition over the memory law project. By the end of the year, however, it had become clear that neither had succeeded winning the government's support.[109] But in January 2014, a new scandal again redirected public attention toward the question of a memory law. *Dozhd'* ("Rain"), the only relatively independent TV channel in the country, asked its spectators if it had been necessary to defend Leningrad at all costs during the war – should it instead have been surrendered to the Germans in order to avoid an enormous number of civilian casualties and fatalities? But the 1941–1944 siege of Leningrad, which took more than 600,000 lives, is enormously important to the Russian narrative of the war, and the ensuing wave of public indignation against *Dozhd'* was used by the authorities to increase their control over it.[110]

Yarovaya and Dobrynin reacted to this scandal by restating that their projects were on their way to the parliament (although they had both recently been heavily critiqued by the government). In February, the media confirmed that both projects had been disapproved by the Presidential Administration.[111] The government again went on record as supporting of the idea of such a law but not in the form of the Yarovaya bill, which needed "to be significantly improved." The two main arguments for rejecting that bill were its inaccurate language and that it proposed to criminalize offenses that had already been outlawed by the law on extremism and by Articles 280 and 282 of the Penal Code.[112]

A few weeks later, a decisive change occurred. On March 23, Putin signed a law on the annexation of Crimea. On April 4, all the negative reviews notwithstanding, the Duma voted in favor of Yarovaya's project in its first reading. Whatever its drawbacks may have been, the parliament decided that its ideological message was far more important: nobody had

[109] Pyotr Kozlov and Dmitriy Runkevich, "Pravitel'stvo otklonilo zakonoproekt protiv reabilitatsii natsizma" [The Government Has Turned down the Draft Law against the Rehabilitation of Nazism], *Izvestiya*, November 6, 2013. See also Dobrynin's comments (dated as of January 1, 2014): "We failed to convince our respected colleagues from the government that there is a need for such legislation" (http://council.gov.ru/services/discussions/blogs/38237/).

[110] "MPs Urge Nazi Rehabilitation Ban after Nationwide Scandal," January 31, 2014: http://rt.com/politics/russian-nazi-rehabilitation-dozhd-461/.

[111] Dmitriy Runkevich, "Kreml' ne podderzhal zakonoproekt o zaprete reabilitatsii fashizma" [Kremlin Withholds Support from the Draft Law Banning the Rehabilitation of Fascism] *Izvestiya*, February 10, 2014.

[112] Official Response to [the third version of] the Draft Law No. 197582–5. The bill was sent to the government on February 3, and the response was posted on the Duma website on March 13, 2014. Articles 280 and 282 respectively prohibit calls for extremist activity and incitement to hatred.

the right to call "our victory" into question.[113] That decision was supported by 447 of the 449 deputies: the "opposition" parties enthusiastically voted for the bill, showing their solidarity with the Putin regime. The draft as approved in the first reading introduced the following article in the Penal Code:

> The denial of facts established by the Judgment of the International Military Tribunal for the trial and punishment of major war criminals of European countries of the Axis, the approval of crimes established by the above-mentioned Judgment, as well as dissemination of knowingly false information on the activities of the USSR during the Second World War, accompanied by accusations of the commission of crimes established by the above-mentioned Judgment,[114] committed publicly, are punishable by a fine... or by deprivation of liberty for up to three years.[115] (Article 1)

Aggravating circumstances could raise the punishment to up to five years' imprisonment (Article 2). This third version of the law was obviously more radical than its predecessors. First, it no longer protected the reputation of the Western Allies. Second, "false information" is an extremely inclusive formula that allows for the banning of any undesirable vision of history. Third, the Yarovaya bill considers the "artificial fabrication of the prosecutorial evidence" against the USSR an aggravating circumstance (Article 2), and "ill-intentioned" historical research could easily be subsumed under that head.

The Duma's vote was not the end of the battle, though; the Federation Council intended to defend its projects. With the second reading of the Yarovaya bill scheduled for April 23, on April 22, Dobrynin introduced into the Duma new versions of the Spiegel bills that differed from the March 2013 drafts in several respects (to which we will return later). Dobrynin's bills were signed by approximately 30 "senators," or every sixth member of the upper house. Nevertheless, the Yarovaya bill was

---

[113] Ella Shchukina, "Duma protiv posyagatel'stv na pamyat' v otnoshenii sobytiy [sic]" [Duma Is against Infringements on the Memory of Events [of the Second World War]], April 6, 2014: http://scilla.ru/content/view/4613/2/.

[114] Arguably, the authors meant "accusing the USSR of the crimes that the Nuremberg Tribunal viewed as Nazi crimes."

[115] Draft Law No. 197582–5 of February 27, 2014 "O vnesenii izmeneniy v otdel'nyie zakonodatel'nyie akty Rossiyskoy Federatsii (po voprosu ustanovleniya ugolovnoy otvetstvennosti za posyagatel'stvo na istoricheskuyu pamyat' v otnosheniyi sobytiy, imevshikh mesto v period Vtoroy mirovoy voyny" [On Changes to Certain Legislative Acts of the Russian Federation (Regarding the Establishment of Criminal Liability for Infringement on Historical Memory with Respect to Events That Took Place During the Second World War)]. During its long discussion in the parliament, the law's name has been changed several times, but its number has remained the same.

approved by the Duma on April 23, with minor changes, in its second and the third readings. Its discussion in the Federation Council was scheduled for April 29. On April 28, Dobrynin gave interviews predicting that the Council would vote it down.[116] But on the following day, it was almost unanimously approved, with Dobrynin entering the only dissenting vote. These developments could only mean that the favorable decision had not really been taken in the parliament. On May 5, President Putin signed the bill into law.

Let us now compare the Spiegel, Dobrynin, and Yarovaya bills. In its final version, Article 1.1. of what, on May 5, became the Yarovaya Act bans

> The denial of facts established by the Judgment of the International Military Tribunal for the trial and punishment of major war criminals of European countries of the Axis, the approval of crimes established by the above-mentioned judgment, as well as dissemination of knowingly false information on the activities of the USSR during the Second World War, committed publicly....[117]

The law also includes the following provision:

> Public distribution of information expressing manifest disrespect toward society regarding Russia's days of military glory and the commemorative dates associated with the defense of the Fatherland or public insults to the symbols of Russia's military glory are punishable by a fine... or by correctional labor for up to one year. (Article 1.3)

Although the Yarovaya Act uses the language of the Russian war myth, its Article 1.1 looks deceptively similar to various European memory laws. However, its intention was quite different: the Russian statute's aim was to protect the memory of the Stalin regime. And, characteristically, it does so by coopting an infamous formula from the Soviet Penal Code that criminalized "dissemination of knowingly false information denigrating the social and political system of the USSR" (Article 190.1, which was

[116] Irina Tumakova, "Zakon o bor'be s reabilitatsiyey natsisma poyavitsya k 9 maya" [The Law on the Struggle against the Rehabilitation of Nazism Will Appear by May 9], April 21, 2014: www.fontanka.ru/2014/04/21/114/; Mariya Makutina and Zhanna Ulyanova, "V Gosdume zaregistrirovany dva alternativnykh zakona o reabilitatsii natsizma" [Two Alternative Laws on the Rehabilitation of Nazism Are Registered with the State Duma], April 23, 2014: www.rbcdaily.ru/politics/562949991266374.

[117] Federal Law No. 128-FZ of May 5, 2014 "O vnesenii izemeniy v otdel'nyie zakonodatel'nyie akty Rossiyskoy Federatsii" [On Changes to Certain Legislative Acts of the Russian Federation]. The punishment and its enhancement by aggravating circumstances remained the same as in the initial proposal.

typically used against dissidents). Meanwhile, all and every criticism of the war myth could of course be brought under the blanket notion of "false information."

Another important difference between the Yarovaya Act and the European legislation is that the latter normally focuses on crimes against humanity viewed as crimes of a racist nature, which is not the case in the Russian law. The Yarovaya Act actually avoids specifying the crimes whose denial it prohibits. Like the 2010 draft, the adopted bill refers to the crimes *established* by the Judgment of the Nuremberg Tribunal. On the contrary, as we know, most European enactments use the concept of Nazi crimes as *defined* in the Tribunal Charter, without implying that all the facts established by the Judgment are true, a position that is more defensible from the historian's point of view. The Nuremberg Tribunal actually endorsed in large part the Soviet narrative of the war, which is why Putin's ideologists claim to be committed to its "letter and spirit" (even if in some cases they feel free to revise its provisions at will).

Spiegel's short draft is much closer to the Framework Decision of 2008. It specifically ranks the rehabilitation of Nazism alongside Holocaust denial, criminalizing both as crimes of a racist nature. To be sure, the Framework Decision mentions Nazi crimes in general, as defined by the Tribunal Charter, but Spiegel saw no need to refer to any definitions other than those included in his own long draft. A far more important difference between Spiegel's short draft and the Framework Decision, however, consists in the fact that the former penalizes not just Holocaust denial but, more broadly, the rehabilitation of Nazism. In other words, it is far less centered on the memory of the Holocaust. Spiegel's intention was to integrate the memory of the Holocaust into the Russian narrative of the war, not to replace the latter with the former. Unsurprisingly, Spiegel's bill did not penalize denial of genocides other than the Holocaust, because its main target was the rehabilitation of Nazism as a manifestation of racism rather than racism per se.

The difference between the Yarovaya Act and Spiegel's short draft is not limited to the mention of the Holocaust. While Spiegel proposed a modification of Article 282 of the Penal Code, the Yarovaya Act introduced a new article (354.1) into that code. Article 282 is (as the European Commission on Racism and Intolerance describes it) "a major tool in the Russian Federation's fight against extremism."[118] It is also a permanent target of Russian nationalists, who claim that it limits

---

[118] ECRI Report on the Russian Federation (fourth monitoring cycle), June 20, 2013, p. 15.

freedom of expression and call for its abrogation. As for Article 354.1, it appears in Chapter 34 of the code, which deals with "crimes against peace and the security of humankind," and contains articles criminalizing the unleashing of an aggressive war, war crimes, and the like. So, whereas Spiegel viewed the rehabilitation of Nazism and Holocaust denial as crimes of racism, for Yarovaya, the rehabilitation of Nazism is a crime against peace.

These bills reflect two different conceptions of Nazism. In the first instance (Spiegel's), Nazism is seen as a form of racism, and crimes against humanity are presented as its most horrible misdeed. This approach sits well with the form of historical memory that emerged in the West in the 1970s and 1980s. In the second instance (Yarovaya's), Nazism is viewed as a form of militarism, and starting a world war is considered its most serious fault. This approach, which dominated in the West in the 1940s and 1950s, still prevails in present-day Russia. From the first point of view, genocide is "the crime of crimes," and the Jews were the main victims of the war (although Spiegel himself never went so far as to explicitly make that claim). From the second, German aggression against the USSR was Hitler's principal offense and the "peoples of the USSR" (read: Russians), not specifically the Jews, were the war's main victims. The second approach best corresponds to the Putin regime's politics of history. It is therefore no surprise that the Yarovaya draft ultimately won the battle of the bills.

Chapter 34 of the Penal Code also includes Article 357, on the crime of genocide. Memory laws in Europe often materialize in articles criminalizing genocide (or in chapters containing articles on genocide), but the Russian lawmakers chose not to capitalize on this opportunity. That choice was natural for Yarovaya because in her eyes, Holocaust denial was unimportant. But even Spiegel did not dare (and perhaps did not want) to admit that Holocaust denial was central to his bill. The rehabilitation of Nazism, entailing as it does a condemnation of Soviet policies, was more significant to him than Holocaust denial as such.

As we know, Konstantin Dobrynin struggled mightily to pass Spiegel's bills, making his last, hopeless attempt to stop the Yarovaya Act in April 2014. At that point, he decided to modify his own projects. And following the parliament's rejection of Spiegel's short draft in June 2013, this tactical maneuver came as no surprise. Dobrynin's short project of April 2014 offered an amendment not of the Penal Code but of the law on extremism. He proposed to expand the definition of extremism by adding the phrase "the rehabilitation of Nazism and the heroization of Nazi criminals and their accomplices."[119] This was not, however, a merely technical ruse: the Holocaust had actually disappeared from Dobrynin's proposal. Holocaust denial does not figure in his long draft either,[120] which was by then much closer to the CIS model law than to Spiegel's 2013 project. But once Holocaust denial was removed from the list of criminal offenses, Dobrynin's initiative ceased to be a meaningful alternative to the Yarovaya Act.

This last stage of the battle of the bills was, first and foremost, an expression of the institutional competition between the two houses. Dobrynin and his colleagues feared that mention of the Holocaust would undermine their bill's chances. Indeed, criminalizing Holocaust denial had arguably been essentially a matter of tactics for them all along. That said, it may be supposed that the appearance of the Holocaust in Spiegel's 2013 drafts was also largely attributable to tactical considerations, Spiegel's goal having been to make Russian memory laws look as similar to the Western European ones as possible.

The European Commission against Racism and Intolerance noted in its 2013 report on Russia that "the Criminal Code does not penalise the public denial, trivialisation, justification or condoning, with a racist aim, of crimes of genocide, crimes against humanity or war crimes," and recommended that Russia implement those amendments.[121] Russian lawmakers were undoubtedly inspired by the Western example, although not necessarily by this rather importunate urging. However, they misinterpreted – most likely intentionally – the notion of memory law as it had emerged in Western Europe in the 1980s and ultimately engaged an instrument designed to promote a democratic culture of memory in protecting the memory of an oppressive regime.

The Russian bill, which manifestly perpetuates the venerable Soviet tradition of censorship, is almost unique among memory laws, which normally protect the memories of the victims of state policy. The Russian legislators were, rather, seeking to protect the memory of the state against that of its victims. The only legislation by a European Union country comparable to the Russian bill is the French Mekachera Act of 2005, with

[119] Draft Law No. 504840–6 of April 22, 2014 "O vnesenii izmemeniy v stat'yu 1 Federal'nogo zakona 'O protivodeystvii ekstremistskoy deyatel'nosti'" [On Changes to Article 1 of the Federal Law "On Counteracting Extremist Activity"].
[120] Draft Law No. 504872–6 of April 22, 2014 "O protovodeystvii reabilitatsii natsima, geroizatsii natsistskikh prestupnikov i ikh posobnikov" [On Counteracting the Rehabilitation of Nazism, and the Heroization of Nazi Criminals and Their Accomplices].
[121] ECRI Report on the Russian Federation (fourth monitoring cycle), p. 12.

its acknowledgment of "the positive role of the French presence overseas," a provision that was (not coincidentally) removed in response to public outcry. The most obvious parallel to the Russian law, however, is Article 301 of the Turkish Penal Code, which criminalizes insults to the Turkish state and is used to prevent calling the 1915 massacre of the Armenians in the Ottoman Empire genocide.

There were several cases of charges being brought against Russian citizens on the basis of the Yarovaya Act, at least one of which has resulted in a conviction: in June 2016, Vladimir Luzgin was sentenced by a court in Perm to a fine of 200,000 rubles (then about $3,300) for reposting an article claiming that World War II began with the German and Soviet invasion of Poland, which contradicts the interpretation of that event in the Judgment of the Nuremberg Tribunal. The court ignored Luzgin's argument that he had not read the Judgment, stating that he had received a good grade for the modern history course in high school and was therefore knowledgeable enough to understand that the article in question contained "false information" on the actions of the USSR during the war.[122] This case clearly shows that the Yarovaya Act is an instrument of censorship and that the reference to the Judgment of the Nuremberg Tribunal in the law is used to penalize any criticism of the official Soviet/Russian narrative of the war.

Before concluding this chapter, let me mention several recent legislative initiatives regarding historical memory. On April 23, 2014, the very day on which the Duma passed the Yarovaya Act, Mikhail Degtyaryov, a deputy from the far-right Liberal Democratic Party, submitted his own memory bill. This was a purely demagogical gesture, for it was clear that the Duma, including Degtyaryov's own party, would vote for Yarovaya's project. But this is what makes the Degtyaryov draft so interesting: it shows what, from his point of view, his constituency wanted to hear. Those authors who wanted their proposals to succeed normally looked for a more neutral and technical language. But Degtyaryov, with an unusual degree of concreteness, lists in his draft the specific statements that nationalists consider insulting to the Russian memory of the war.

[122] Maksim Strugov, "Ssylka v Nurenberg" [An Allusion to Nuremberg], *Kommersant*, June 30, 2016; Aleksandr Skobov, "Istoriyu rassudyat" [History Will Have a Fair Trial], July 1, 2016: http://graniru.org/Society/Media/Freepress/m.252746.html. On the politics of the past in Perm, see Aryeh Neiser, "How Putin's Russia Is Erasing the Memory of Stalin's Crimes," *Washington Post*, September 9, 2015.

Degtyaryov proposed amending the Penal Code and the 1995 law on the memory of the victory by introducing punishments of up to two years' imprisonment for "discrediting the Victory [capitalized in the document] of the Soviet people in the Great Patriotic War and the military operations of the USSR's armed forces during the Second World War."[123] Degtyaryov also proposed adding to the 1995 law a new Article 6.1 to explain what "discrediting" actually means:

1) Denial of the positive contribution of the Soviet people and the Soviet armies to the victory over the German fascist armies and the armies of the German allies;

2) Equating the liberation by the Soviet armies of the Soviet republics of the USSR and the countries of Europe from the German fascist occupants to the beginning of an occupation [of those countries by Russia];

3) Justification of the actions of the collaborators, they being citizens and residents of the USSR who cooperated with the German fascist occupants;

4) Criticism of the actions of the Soviet armies and the High Command of the Armed forces of the USSR [of which Stalin was the head], accompanied by the justification and propaganda of collaborationism, desertion, and defeatism, i.e., the public dissemination of information aimed at creating among the citizens of the Russian Federation the opinion that in the period of the Second World war the following actions would have been admissible:
     capitulation of the USSR;
     abandonment by the Soviet armies of their military positions.

This text, which is hardly more readable in Russian than in its English translation, invites several reflections. First, it uses traditional Soviet concepts such as "German fascism" and "German fascist occupants." Obviously, Degtyaryov is attempting to use the idiom of the common people. But it also shows that the genealogy of his project differed from that of other recent Russian bills. The rehabilitation of Nazism, including Holocaust denial, is not mentioned in Degtyaryov's project, which does not even attempt to follow any European model and openly protects the

---

[123] Draft Law "O vnesenii izmeneniy v Federal'nyi zakon 'Ob uvekovechenii Pobedy sovetskogo naroda v Velikoy Otechestvennoy voyne 1941–1945 godov' i v Ugolovnyi kodeks Rossiyskoy Federatsii" [On Changes to the Federal Law "On Perpetuating the Victory of the Soviet People in the Great Patriotic War of 1941–1945" and to the Criminal Code of the Russian Federation], Article 2: http://degtyarev.info/document/zakonproekti/139237/.

memory of Stalinism. Second, the law does not forbid questioning the role of the USSR in unleashing the war. Most other projects do that by referring to the Nuremberg Judgment, which established the German responsibility for the war. It may therefore be supposed that for Russian nationalists, starting the war was not necessarily a bad thing. Indeed, the theory according to which Stalin planned to attack Germany in July 1941 but was unable to do so because of the "preemptive" German invasion has its supporters in the nationalist camp, who complain about "Stalin's lost chance" to conquer Europe.[124] As for the rest of it, Degtyaryov's draft offers a good summary of the accusations against the USSR that Russian legislators had long been seeking to penalize.

In 2015 and 2016, the continuing war in Ukraine gave rise to several other initiatives to criminalize insults to patriotic feelings and offenses against the symbols of the Russian state, which were mostly acts of political propaganda with little, if any, practical legislative meaning. The same can be said of certain proposals aimed at putting an end to the re-Stalinization of the country that has been going on in the recent years. Thus, in September 2015, Konstantin Dobrynin introduced in the parliament a bill "On Counteracting the Rehabilitation of Crimes of Stalin's Totalitarian Regime" that clearly had no chance of being adopted. The bill prohibited the denial of those actions "that had been officially condemned by the [Russian] state as crimes of Stalin's totalitarian regime."[125] Dobrynin specifically referred to the 1991 laws on the rehabilitation of victims of political repressions and on the rehabilitation of the repressed peoples. The first of these condemned Stalinism as a "totalitarian state," while the second characterized Stalin's deportations of entire peoples as acts of genocide.[126] But those laws had characterized repressions in a rather general way, without providing a list of concrete, "legally established" historical facts, leaving unclear exactly which denials Dobrynin's bill was seeking to prohibit. The draft forbade "perpetuating the memory of those who were involved in crimes of Stalin's totalitarian regime" (Article 6) as well as creating associations aimed at, and using media with the goal of, rehabilitating Stalinism (Article 8). Certain statements about the past could certainly be subsumed under those prohibitions but punishment was

---

[124] Mikhail Mel'tyukhov, *Upushchennyi shans Stalina: Sovetskiy Soyuz i bor'ba za Yevropu, 1939–1941* [Stalin's Lost Chance: The Soviet Union and the Struggle for Europe, 1939–1941] (Moscow: Veche, 2000).

[125] Draft Law No. 885220–6 of September 21, 2015 "O protivodeystvii reabilitatsii prestupleniy stalinskogo totalitarnogo rezhima (stalinizma)," Article 3.

[126] See Chapter 5.

unlikely to ensue, because the bill did not introduce any new penalties for the acts it had declared illegal.

A month later, Dobrynin's draft was returned to the author on procedural grounds, but he could not continue promoting it, as his parliamentary term was to end in a few days. But his colleague, Dmitriy Gudkov (perhaps the only remaining independent MP), put his signature under Dobrynin's bill and in November reintroduced it in the Duma.[127] The bill was again turned down on procedural grounds and was resubmitted in March 2016. And then, in September, Gudkov predictably failed to win reelection to the Duma.[128] It will come as no surprise to anyone that anti-Stalinist bills have no chance of being passed in Putin's Russia.

---

[127] Draft Law No. 923007–6 of November 6, 2015.
[128] Draft Law No. 1028277–6 of March 26, 2016.

Conclusion

In this book, I have been mostly concerned with memory laws that criminalize certain statements about the past (or memory laws per se), the first of which was passed in Germany in 1985.[1] At the time of writing, twenty-seven European countries (and some non-European states such as Israel and Rwanda) have such laws on their books. Listed in the order in which they passed their first bans on certain statements about the past, they are: Germany, France, Austria, Switzerland, Belgium, Spain, Luxembourg, Poland, Liechtenstein, the Czech Republic, Slovakia, Romania, Slovenia, Macedonia, Andorra, Cyprus, Portugal, Albania, Malta, Latvia, Hungary, Montenegro, Lithuania, Bulgaria, Greece, Russia, and Italy.[2] In addition, several other countries, including Ukraine, Turkey, and the Netherlands, have norms that show some "family resemblance" to those acts and can be considered borderline instances within the same category.[3]

The category of memory laws largely overlaps but does not coincide with Holocaust denial legislation. Struggling against negationism was indeed the initial motivation for adopting such laws, but very soon the scope of that legislation was expanded to include the denial of other

---

[1] Some historians view the 1986 Israeli law criminalizing Holocaust negationism as the first memory law per se and consider the 1985 German law a failed attempt to do so. The latter enactment did indeed criminalize denial somewhat indirectly, but its authors were inspired by the notion of banning the Auschwitz-lie, and the 1985 law was an important step in this direction.

[2] See Chronological Table.

[3] From January 2014 and April 2015, Ukraine had a law criminalizing the denial or justification of fascist crimes against humanity; currently, Ukrainian legislation declares illegal, but does not penalize, the denial of the Holodomor as a genocide of the Ukrainian people (since 2006) and insults to the memory of "fighters for Ukraine's independence" (since April 2015). Turkey has no memory law per se, but Article 301 of its Penal Code, which criminalizes denigration of the Turkish nation, functions de facto as such a law, because assessing the 1915 massacre of the Armenians as a genocide is labeled as exactly that kind of denigration. Finally, the Netherlands, without any law that specifically prohibits Holocaust denial, does have a Supreme Court ruling that negationism, being insulting to Jews, is punishable as a racially motivated defamation of a group of persons (a similar ruling of 1979 was a decisive step in criminalizing denial in Germany).

genocides in order to combat racism and xenophobia in general, not only anti-Semitism. The concept of memory laws emerged in the 2000s in response to that development. And as time passed and more countries began criminalizing statements about the past, other types of memory laws came into being, some of which have little in common with the struggle against racism. Nevertheless, they also ban what their authors view as counter-factual utterances.[4]

Being a historian, I have sought to consider this legislation as a historical phenomenon – in other words, to explore its roots, its main stages of development, and the different forms it has taken in different parts of Europe. While memory laws in a broad sense, or acts that in whatever way regulate collective representations of the past and commemorative practices, are an old phenomenon dating back (at least) to the nineteenth century, laws criminalizing certain statements about the past are a recent invention, and this was my reason for focusing on them.

Of course, making "incorrect" historical claims that would be commonly perceived as heretical in a given society has always been risky, but even the communist regimes, which based their legitimacy on a Marxist conception of history, did not specifically criminalize such claims, persecuting them instead under the rubric of anti-communist propaganda. Ad hoc statutes banning certain statements about the past are a product of Western democracy and Western historical consciousness, an important aspect of what Jürgen Habermas calls the "juridification" of our societies. They came into being at the moment of democracy's triumph: indeed, the French Gayssot Act, the classical memory law, was passed in 1990, only one year after Francis Fukuyama declared that no meaningful alternative to democracy remained after the end of the Cold War.[5]

Paradoxical as it may sound, the "end of history" also gave the past an increasingly central role in political legitimation, but it was now a "new past" that differed substantially from the one constructed by traditional

---

[4] Spain invites a special comment here. Its Penal Code, which banned denial and justification of the crime of genocide between 1995 and 2007 (and again after 2015), prohibited only its justification but not its denial from 2007 to 2015. The Spanish law as it existed from 2007 to 2105 also falls under the concept of memory law viewed as legislation that regulates historical memory but it is not as typical of this category as laws forbidding (counter-)factual historical claims. In fact, the formula "denial and justification," which first appeared in the 1992 Austrian memory law, has since then been used in many national laws and international documents (including the 2008 EU Framework Decision). Following this logic, one can also count as peripheral memory laws – and in any event as their important predecessors – some postwar anti-fascist enactments that criminalize positive assessments of fascist regimes (especially the 1952 Italian Scelba Law and the 1960 East German Penal Code).

[5] Francis Fukuyama, "The End of History?" *National Interest* (Summer 1989), pp. 3–18.

history-based political ideologies. Contrary to how certain historians imagined the "new past" in the 1960s (as a rational construction produced by objective historical research),[6] the past as it is actually being generated and consumed in the age of memory (that is, since the late 1970s) presents as no less politically biased and clearly more fragmented than the "old past" that was structured around master narratives. In a way, its fragmentation has even increased the likelihood of its being used for the purposes of political manipulation. Central to the new past are singular events that are perceived as sacral symbols of particular communities rather than philosophies that offer explanations of global history and legitimize projects of the future. All memory laws per se ban certain statements about concrete events – typically, historical tragedies – that function as such symbols. This makes them a characteristic manifestation of the present-day form of historical consciousness.

There exists a direct interconnection between memory laws penalizing statements about concrete events and their initial goal of banning factually untrue utterances. From this vantage, memory laws prohibit the dissemination of false information, not opinions, which is an important distinction in most legal systems and one of the main arguments in support of those laws. But since those laws have become one of the main instruments of present-day history politics, one can claim that they do not just reflect, but have actually contributed to, the formation of the event-centered historical consciousness.

The genealogy of those laws can be traced to the anti-fascist legislation of the immediate postwar period, which after the collapse of colonialism developed into much broader anti-racist law. Since the 1960s and 1970s, prohibitions of hate speech, which form an essential part of anti-racist legislation, provided the legal framework within which the first bans on certain utterances about the past came into being. Criminalizing Holocaust negationism was a logical outcome of this tendency in the conditions of the late twentieth-century memory boom and the promotion of the memory of the Shoah to the center of Western historical consciousness. I have argued that initially the Holocaust denial laws' main function was to give legal protection to the newly emerging form of Western historical consciousness.

No doubt, origins do matter. It would be misleading, however, to give too much weight to genealogical investigations in assessing the function of prohibitions on certain statements about the past in our societies.

---

[6] See, for example, J.H. Plumb, *The Death of the Past* (London: Macmillan, 1969).

Although those laws are a recent phenomenon, they do have a history, and the two periods in their development are easy to identify. During the initial period, which lasted approximately from 1985 to 1998, those acts were adopted almost exclusively in "old" continental democracies such as Germany, France, Austria, Switzerland, and Belgium, most of which had been directly implicated in the Shoah. Unsurprisingly, the memory of Nazi crimes was their main focus. The passage of those laws contributed to the emergence of the memory of the Shoah as the official memory of the European Union, which gave its full support to the idea of defending that memory by means of criminal law in a series of acts ranging from the 1996 Joint Action to the 2008 Framework Decision. Since the late 1990s and early 2000s, criminalization of denial moved eastward, following the extension of the European Union, whose goal was to create a common vision of the tragic European past that would be endorsed by all member states.

In the Eastern European context, however, that goal was scarcely achievable. The 1998 Polish law set up an alternative model for penalizing statements about the past, banning the denial of both Nazi and communist crimes, which marked the beginning of a new period in the history of memory laws. In the 2000s, most prohibitions of certain historical statements were passed in Eastern Europe, some of those acts reproducing the French/EU model, while others followed the Polish example. This new period was characterized by increasingly manipulative ways of using memory laws as a weapon in the memory wars that were ongoing between and within many European countries, both in the East and in the West (because new initiatives of memory laws also continued to appear in Western Europe, especially in France).

My analysis of legislation criminalizing statements about the past confirms the "polarity" of European memory – in other words, the opposition between Western and Eastern European history cultures. It goes without saying that they share many common features, including the fragmentation and victimization of the past, and a focus on the legacy of World War II (which are also typical of several other regions, such as the United States and the Southeast Asia). However, the difference between the East and the West of the European continent is also quite considerable.

To simplify, the Western European (and North American) model of historical memory is based, on the one hand, on the memory of the Holocaust, which embodies the notion of state repentance for the crimes of the past, the Shoah being commonly viewed as a universal symbol of absolute evil and ultimate suffering; and, on the other hand, on the cult of national heritage (also known as the heritage industry), which allows the creation of a more positive attitude toward the national past while at the same time reducing patriotism to its relatively less dangerous cultural form.

This model is undoubtedly not perfect and can be criticized for stimulating the development of historical mythologies and civil religions, for bureaucratic appropriation and judicialization of the past, and for the political and commercial exploitation of past tragedies and cultural legacy. The Holocaust-and-heritage paradigm emerged in the 1980s and 1990s as a result of a political compromise and the inclusion of the democratic culture of memory, focused on the memory of victims and traditionally promoted by the left, into the post–Cold War political consensus that was being increasingly dominated by neoconservative and neoliberal forces. Despite its liberating and profoundly humanistic aspects, the rise of memory can be considered a corollary of the decay of transformative politics.

Of course, history education and the development of critical thinking would be a far better solution to the problem of dealing with the past in a democratic society than any official history politics. But I am afraid that in the real world this is not yet (and, sadly, may never be) sufficient. Reverting to modern historical consciousness and future-oriented ideologies does not look realistic either; nor it is desirable, for some of those ideologies did indeed produce disastrous effects. This said, the Holocaust-and-heritage model might not be a bad practical solution. It considerably reduces (while not entirely eliminating) the danger of aggressive nationalism in the nineteenth- and early twentieth-century style, with its cult of the nation-state; expresses profoundly humanistic sympathies with victims of the historical processes; and promotes the view of human beings as subjects of culture. Indeed, equating humanity with culture was fundamental to the ideology of the democratic intelligentsia on both sides of the Iron Curtain in the 1960s and 1970s.

The question is, of course, whether criminalizing statements about the past is an appropriate way of disseminating the memory of victims. This book contributes to that discussion by providing history-based evidence in support of the slippery-slope argument – in other words, by showing the tendency toward increasingly manipulative uses of memory laws as they began spreading around Europe and being used outside the political and cultural context in which they had initially come into being. By infringing on freedom of expression to promote humanistic history politics, the old democracies have created a precedent that has allowed some new democracies and authoritarian regimes to use memory laws for nationalist and populist goals.

A crucial point that cannot be overemphasized is that Western European memory laws give legal protection to the memory of victims without victimizing the past to the benefit of nation-states that ban the denial of their own past crimes by adopting those laws. Self-victimization and criminalization of the denial of other nations' misdeeds is far less typical of the old democracies, even if there exists a tendency toward self-victimization in some segments of their populations. In Eastern Europe, by contrast, victimization of the past often (although not always) presents as self-victimization of national communities, the reasons for which are – at least in part – perfectly understandable; nevertheless, this tendency has produced a substantially different form of historical memory and, correspondingly, a different type of memory laws.

Eastern European memory laws came into being partly as a result of pressure from the Council of Europe and partly as a continuation of local legislative traditions, including de-communization laws. Here lies an important distinction between Western and Eastern legislation on the issues of the past: in the West, memory laws have developed on the basis of the postwar anti-fascist legislation and the anti-racist legislation of the 1960s and 1970s, while this tradition, although it was by no means absent in Eastern Europe, has played a marginal role in laying the groundwork for Eastern European memory laws. Indeed, under the communist regimes, anti-fascism and anti-racism were often viewed as parts of the increasingly unpopular communist ideology. This largely explains why the new culture of victimhood, which had been crucial in the emergence of the democratic politics of memory in the West, remained underdeveloped in the former communist countries.

Anti-fascist and anti-racist traditions, although certainly not rejected after 1989, were far less enthusiastically embraced by new democracies that viewed the legacy of communism as a much more serious problem (with Russia as the main, yet partial, exception to this rule, in that anti-fascism, or rather anti-Nazism - largely deprived of its anti-racist content and reduced to an anti-Western ideology - gradually became central to the Russian official national narrative). In addition, since national liberation movements had played a key role in the fall of communism, the latter came to be typically viewed in the region as a pure product of foreign occupation for which local populations had borne no responsibility at all. Correspondingly, past offenses perpetrated by the forerunners of the present-day nationalist movements are often ignored, although some of those forerunners were far-right and openly pro-fascist activists. Despite the undeniable achievements of democratic politicians and intellectuals in promoting the memory of the Holocaust in Eastern Europe, it has not yet become an integral part of national narratives in those countries. Unsurprisingly, many Eastern European memory laws grew out of the logic of de-communization and attempts to recreate national narratives. To be sure, a tendency toward considering communist crimes comparable to the Holocaust also exists in the West, but it has had almost no impact there on free-speech prohibitions.[7]

As mentioned earlier, there are two main types of Eastern European memory laws. Acts that reproduce the French/EU model and forbid the denial of the Holocaust and/or crimes against humanity more generally have been adopted in Albania, Bulgaria, Macedonia, Montenegro, Romania, Slovenia, and Slovakia, while the Czech Republic, Hungary, Latvia, Lithuania, and Poland have penalized the denial of both Nazi and communist crimes.[8] There are obvious differences between those groups of countries, which explain why they have taken different approaches to criminalizing the past. Characteristically, those differences have little to do with their wartime history and involvement with Nazism. Indeed, Bulgaria, Hungary, Romania, and Slovakia, were all Hitler's allies, and quite a few Latvians and Lithuanians served in the SS and/or participated in the extermination of the Jews.

The differences between the two groups of countries are due, rather, to their place within the Soviet system, their historical relationships with Russia, and the success of post-communist transformations (or lack thereof). The countries of the second group are typically more developed economically than those of the first (with the exception of Slovenia), have a more positive experience of market reforms, and are consequently less prone to nostalgia when remembering their communist past. They also have a much stronger record of anti-communist resistance, including the events of 1956, 1968, and 1979, when Hungary, the Czech Republic, and

[7] This tendency manifested itself in the 1985 West German memory law. Bill Niven emphasizes that after the reunification of Germany, the problem of communist crimes there became even more important than it had been in the Federal Republic before 1990, and as a result German memory became closer to that in Eastern European countries, although "the place of Nazism in German memory arguably remains greater." See Niven, "German Victimhood Discourse in Comparative Perspective," in *Dynamics of Memory and Identity in Contemporary Europe*, eds. Eric Langenbacher, Bill Niven, and Ruth Wittlinger (New York: Berghahn Books, 2013), pp. 187–190. On the French debates on Nazi versus communist crimes, see Carolyn J. Dean, *Aversion and Erasure: The Fate of the Victim after the Holocaust* (Ithaca, N.Y.: Cornell University Press, 2010), pp. 58–100. However, by and large, the notion of the uniqueness of Nazi crimes prevails in the West, including in the official EU history politics.
[8] The Ukrainian memory laws of 2015 develop the same approach, by declaring certain statements about the past illegal, although without attaching criminal liability.

Poland respectively became centers of the political unrest in the Soviet Empire; as for Latvia and especially Lithuania, the anti-Soviet guerrilla resistance continued there well beyond the end of World War II. Memories of these movements, and of their suppression by force, have become central to those countries' national narratives. In contrast, Albania, Romania, and especially Yugoslavia (to which Macedonia, Montenegro, and Slovenia belonged) remained more or less independent from Moscow during most of the postwar period, and it was difficult to consider, for example, Yugoslavian communism a consequence of Soviet occupation. As for Bulgaria, memories of its nineteenth-century liberation from Turkish rule by Russia have not been totally erased by the admittedly ambivalent memories of the communist period.

Since the memory of the Holocaust and the Western-style democratic culture of victimhood have not yet become integral parts of the Eastern European historical consciousness, the adoption of Holocaust denial laws presents there as a rather mechanical transplantation of the European Union model, while laws criminalizing the denial of both Nazi and communist crimes seem to more accurately reflect the specificity of the region's historical experience (or at least that of a part of the region). Often, Eastern European liberal democrats and nationalists alike support such laws as well as the notion of communism being just another totalitarian regime, much like Nazism (an idea that the European Union finds hard to fully endorse).

In my opinion, most Eastern European memory laws reflect the manipulative character of those countries' history politics, but this is not because they prohibit the denial of communist crimes. Without entering here into the interminable debate on whether Stalinism and Nazism were two equally criminal regimes,[9] I will argue that the crimes of both were so abominable as to render the quantification of their monstrosity asinine. Victims of both Auschwitz and the Gulag (and of other genocides) are wholly entitled to have their memory reverentially preserved in our societies, and the notion of the duty of memory is fully applicable to all of them. In the same way, crimes against humanity, whether Nazi or communist, must be (and in fact have almost everywhere been) officially condemned by international organizations and national

---

[9] Ian Kershaw and Moshe Lewin, eds., *Stalinism and Nazism: Dictatorships in Comparison* (Cambridge: Cambridge University Press, 1997); Henry Rousso and Richard J. Golsan, eds., *Stalinism and Nazism: History and Memory Compared* (Lincoln: University of Nebraska Press, 2004); Michael Geyer and Sheila Fitzpatrick, eds., *Beyond Totalitarianism: Stalinism and Nazism Compared* (Cambridge: Cambridge University Press, 2009).

governments, and their perpetrators (although not necessarily their deniers) must be prosecuted. The issue with the typical Eastern European memory laws is not that they prohibit the denial of communist crimes but that they do it in such a way as to shift the blame for historical injustices entirely to others and whitewash national romances glorifying their respective nation-states, which entails using the past for the sake of nationalist mobilization rather than for creating a democratic culture of memory. There exists a much stronger tendency in Eastern Europe than in Western Europe to develop state-centered rather than culture-centered historical narratives, and Eastern European memory laws typically protect those narratives.

Russian authorities and, regrettably, some historians tend to misrepresent the Eastern European politics of memory by overemphasizing its nationalist and anti-Russian component and by considering it as the main reason for the memory wars in the region,[10] which allows Putin's history politics to be presented as a legitimate act of Russian self-defense. In fact, the situation is far more complex. On the one hand, not only nationalists but also most democrats in Eastern Europe seem to agree that Nazi crimes and communist crimes have to be treated in the same way. On the other hand, condemning communist crimes in Eastern Europe is important because of the persisting Russian danger; the region's memory wars stemmed from the resurgence of neo-imperialist rhetoric and the cult of the Great Patriotic War in Putin's Russia. The growth of Russian nationalism and neo-imperialism can hardly be considered a mere reaction to the nationalist revival in Eastern Europe: rather, these were parallel and interdependent processes, which were conditioned above all by those countries' internal situations, while developments in Russia were of particular importance to the changing system of international relations and mutual perceptions in the East of the continent. That is why, in my opinion, the lion's share of responsibility for the memory wars in Eastern Europe, as well as for the dangerous deterioration of the international climate over the last years, goes to Putin's Russia. In fact, my analysis of history politics and memory laws in Ukraine confirms this claim.

---

[10] Thus, Alexei Miller, a Russian historian of Eastern Europe, speaks of "the reactive nature of Russian historical politics" and describes the very phenomenon of such politics as an essentially Eastern European (especially Polish and Ukrainian) work product, although he acknowledges the concept's West German roots. See his "The Turns of Russian Historical Politics, from Perestroika to 2011," in *The Convolutions of Historical Politics*, eds. Alexei Miller and Maria Lipman (Budapest: Central European University Press, 2012), p. 256, and "Introduction: Historical Politics: Eastern European Convolutions in the 21st Century," *The Convolutions of Historical Politics*, pp. 1–20.

Typologically, the Russian model of historical memory is similar to its Eastern European counterpart. The short-lived attempts to develop cultural patriotism undertaken by Boris Yeltsin in the 1990s gave place to an aggressive state-centered national narrative under Putin. The victimization of the past tends to be pursued in the region for the nation-state's sake, which is the opposite of how it typically functions in the West. As we have seen, the memory of the Holocaust is either disregarded or used manipulatively in Russia to promote the nationalist mythology, as it is often the case in Eastern Europe too. Russian memory law perfectly reflects Putin's history politics by criminalizing any criticism of Soviet politics during World War II and by giving legal protection to the memory of Stalin's regime. Some Eastern European memory laws also aim to whitewash the national past and downplay the local population's role in the Holocaust, but none explicitly defends the reputation of an oppressive regime, which is why Russian memory law can be seen as an extreme case of the Eastern European model of legislating on the issues of the past. The most obvious parallel to the Russian memory law is Article 301 of the Turkish Penal Code, which prohibits insults to the Turkish nation and aims at preventing the recognition of the extermination of the Armenians in the Ottoman Empire as a genocide.

Was the transformation of memory laws from a means of promoting peace into an instrument of memory wars inevitable or should one view it, rather, as a contingent outcome of local (mostly Eastern European) political constellations? I would cautiously argue that the transition was quite likely to occur in any event, although I certainly do not deny the impact of local circumstances on the ways in which memory laws are used in different parts of Europe.

My reasons for claiming this are not limited to the advance of nationalism and populism in European politics and the formation on the borders of the European Union of authoritarian political regimes (such as Putin's and Erdoğan's), which is too powerful a trend to be considered purely contingent. I am, rather, prompted by my understanding of the rise of memory as an internally contradictory phenomenon. Indeed, the emergence of memory laws was related to other factors, some of which were clearly linked to the triumphant ascent of liberal democracy in the 1960s and 1970s, while others can be seen as signs of its incipient erosion in the decades that followed. The competition of victims was a scarcely avoidable consequence of the formation of the victim culture, especially in the context of the historic turn in late twentieth-century thought, when a relative balance of universalism and particularism, characteristic of nineteenth- and twentieth-century intellectual culture, has shifted toward what I have called the logic of proper names. Laws that penalize the denial of concrete historical events could certainly be, and have indeed been, used to protect essentially universal symbols such as the memory of the Holocaust, but their focus on individual events makes them especially suitable for protecting sacred symbols of particular communities and their national narratives. Those laws largely operate on the level of political symbolism rather than on that of rational discourse (as we know, one of the arguments in favor of memory laws is that truth may not win in open discussion). And nationalism may be more at home in the domain of symbolism, memory, and myth than is democracy. In my view, the cultural meaning of memory laws (their relation to the event-centered form of historical consciousness) largely explains why they could so easily be taken over by national populism.

Index